ASYLUMS, MENTAL HEALTH CARE AND THE...

ASYLUMS, MENTAL HEALTH CARE AND THE IRISH

Historical Studies, 1800–2010

Edited by
Pauline M. Prior

IRISH ACADEMIC PRESS

First published in 2012 by
Irish Academic Press
10 George's Street
Newbridge
Co. Kildare
Ireland
www.iap.ie

ISBN 978-1-911024-62-0 (paper)

British Library Cataloguing in Publication Data
An entry can be found on request

Library of Congress Cataloging-in-Publication Data
An entry can be found on request

Printed in Ireland by SPRINT-print Ltd

DEDICATION

For Bobbie Hanvey, whose happy recollections of his time as a
psychiatric nurse at the Downshire Hospital in the 1960s, are
fictionalised in *The Mental* (Belfast: Wonderland Press, 2002)

Contents

List of Tables

List of Figures

List of Abbreviations

ANZ	Archives New Zealand
Asylums Report	The annual report on the district, criminal and private lunatic asylums in Ireland, with appendices
CSO	Chief Secretary's office (Ireland)
CSORP	Chief Secretary's office registered papers
DH	Department of Health (Republic of Ireland)
DHC	Department of Health and Children (Republic of Ireland)
DHSSPSNI	Department of Health, Social Services and Public Safety (NI)
Dundrum	Central Mental Hospital (formerly Central Criminal Asylum), Ireland
HC	House of Commons
HL	House of Lords
HSE	Health Service Executive, Republic of Ireland
LL	Lord Lieutenant
Irl	Ireland
MPA	Medico-Psychological Association
NAI	National Archives of Ireland
NI	Northern Ireland
NIHA	Northern Ireland Hospitals Authority

PPI	Parliamentary Papers Ireland, Irish University Press Series published by Irish Academic Press, Dublin.
PRONI	Public Record Office of Northern Ireland
PRO (Victoria)	Public Record Office, Victoria, Australia
RMS	Resident Medical Superintendent
ROI	Republic of Ireland
UK	United Kingdom
US	United States of America

Acknowledgements

- We wish to thank the Wellcome Trust, London, for funding the original seminar held at Queen's University Belfast, which formed the basis for this publication.
- We wish to acknowledge the kind permission of the Irish American Cultural Institute to reproduce an article by Pauline Prior and David Griffiths, published in its journal 'Eire-Ireland'. This article appeared as Prior P. M. and D. V. Griffiths (1997) 'The Chaplaincy Question: The Lord Lieutenant of Ireland versus the Belfast Lunatic Asylum', *Eire-Ireland: An Interdisciplinary Journal of Irish Studies*, 33 (2 & 3): 137–53. (Summer/Fall) ISNN 0 013 2683.
- We wish to acknowledge the kind permission of Bill McKnight (author) and Aubrey Playfair (Green Field Productions) to reproduce the following poems written by Bill McKnight, which appeared for the first time on the DVD 'From the Shadows', produced by Green Field Productions. These poems are entitled: *Stillness; Psychiatric admission;* and *Mental illness (a glimpse)*.
- We wish to acknowledge the kind permission of Denise Shine, granddaughter of Thomas Tobin, to use extracts from his diary. He worked as an attendant in Dundrum before emigrating to Australia.
- We would also like to express our gratitude to a number of people who helped in the preparation of this volume: Richard Bennett, custodian of the Richmond Asylum Archives; staff at the National Archives of Ireland, especially Gregory O'Connor; staff at Queen's University, especially library staff Norma Menabney and Donna McCleary; Grace Kelly, researcher at the School of Sociology, Social Policy and Social Work, who organised the Wellcome Trust seminar on which the book is based; Lisa Hyde, the commissioning editor of Irish Academic Press; the anonymous referee, whose valuable comments were highly appreciated. We would also like to thank the many other people who helped

individual contributors research their topics – please see the acknowledgements at the end of each chapter for details of these generous people.

- On a personal level, I would like to thank my partner, Bobbie Hanvey, and my family, who have always encouraged my sometimes eccentric interests.
- We have made every effort to comply with copyright regulations, but if any copyright holders have been inadvertently overlooked, we will be pleased to make the necessary revisions at the first opportunity.

Pauline M. Prior, January 2012

Notes on Contributors

Dr. Damien Brennan, RPN, RNT, G. Dip. Dev S, M. Equal S, M. Ed, PhD. Damien is a Lecturer in Sociology at the School of Nursing and Midwifery, Trinity College, Dublin. Before taking up an academic position over ten years ago, he worked as a psychiatric nurse in Ireland and as a development worker in both Asia and Africa. His research interests include the social trajectory of institutional care; the influence of built environments on care provision and on health and illness; and sociological theory as it relates to health and illness.

Damien's PhD was carried out under the supervision of Professor Holton at the Department of Sociology TCD which was entitled *A Sociology of Institutionalisation of the 'Mentally Ill' in Ireland*. Damien holds a Masters Degree in Education from Trinity College Dublin; a Masters Degree in Equality Studies from University College Dublin; and a Graduate Diploma in Development Studies. He is a Registered Nurse Tutor and Registered Psychiatric Nurse. Damien has contributed articles to many journals, including the *Journal of Psychiatric and Mental Health Nursing* and *The Frontline of Learning*.

Dr. E. Margaret Crawford was a practicing therapeutic dietician for several years before pursuing an academic career in the field of dietary and medical history. Over a period of twenty-five years she has written extensively in this field, specialising in the era of the Great Famine in Ireland. Her major works include *Feast and Famine: Food and Nutrition in Ireland, 1500–1920* (Oxford University Press), written with L.A. Clarkson; and *Counting the People: A Survey of the Irish Censuses, 1813–1911* (Four Courts Press). She has also written numerous journal articles, including work on diet and disease in Ireland in the nineteenth century for *Medical History*; and on scurvy during the Great Famine, for *The Journal of the Society for the Social History of Medicine*.

David V. Griffiths, who grew up in Wales, completed his honours degree in Sociology and Social and Economic History at Queen's University Belfast in 1994. During that time, he carried out the historical research on the Belfast Asylum on which the chapter on 'the chaplaincy issue' is based. He now lives in France.

Dr. Brendan D. Kelly is a consultant psychiatrist at the Mater Misericordiae University Hospital, Dublin and senior lecturer in psychiatry at University College Dublin. He holds a research doctorate in medicine (MD) and is a member of the Royal College of Physicians and Royal College of Psychiatrists. He has published original research work in the fields of medicine, psychiatry, epidemiology, law and medical history. His historical work has focused on Irish asylums during the late nineteenth and early twentieth centuries, with a particular emphasis on archival clinical records from the Central Criminal Lunatic Asylum (Central Mental Hospital), Dundrum, Dublin. His historical articles have appeared in the following journals: *Irish Journal of Medical Science, Irish Journal of Psychological Medicine, Medico-Legal Journal, History of Psychiatry, and Social History of Medicine*. He completed a PhD in History at the University of Northampton in 2011.

Professor Elizabeth Malcolm, MA, PhD, FRHistS, FASSA, is the Gerry Higgins Professor of Irish Studies at the University of Melbourne. She is the author of *Swift's Hospital: a History of St Patrick's Hospital, Dublin, 1746–1989* (Dublin, 1989) and *The Irish Policeman, 1822–1922: A Life* (Dublin, 2006), and the editor, with Professor Greta Jones, of *Medicine, Disease and the State in Ireland, 1650–1940* (Cork, 1999). She is currently President of the Irish Studies Association of Australia and New Zealand (ISAANZ).

Anton McCabe is an Omagh-based journalist, socialist, trade union and community activist. He has researched widely on the history of the labour and trade union movement in the north-west of Ireland. Among his publications are 'The Stormy Petrel of the Transport Workers: Peadar O'Donnell, trade unionist, 1917–20' in *Saothar: Journal of the Irish Labour History Society*, 19 (1994).

Professor Angela McCarthy is Professor of Scottish and Irish History and Associate Director of the Centre for Irish and Scottish Studies at the University of Otago. She has published widely on aspects of Irish and Scottish migration, including *Irish Migrants in*

New Zealand, 1840–1937: 'The Desired Haven' (2005); (as editor), *A Global Clan: Scottish Migrant Networks and Identities Since the Eighteenth Century* (2006); *Personal Narratives of Irish and Scottish Migration, 1921–65: 'For Spirit and Adventure'* (2007); and *Scottishness and Irishness in New Zealand Since 1840* (2011). She has recently combined her interests in migration and ethnicity with mental health and has co-edited with Catharine Coleborne a collection titled *Migration, Ethnicity, and Mental Health: International Perspectives, 1840–2010* (2012). This current research is funded by the Royal Society of New Zealand's Marsden Fund.

Dr. Gillian McClelland graduated from Queen's University Belfast in 1995 with a BA Hons in Social Anthropology and was awarded a PhD in History in 2000. Her PhD research, on Fisherwick Presbyterian Working Women's Association 1870–1914, centred on the social, political, religious and educational contribution of this elite group of Belfast women to the culture of the city. Her recent book *Pioneering Women: A History of Riddel Hall, Belfast 1915–75*, depicts the history of the hall of residence for female students at Queen's University Belfast.

Dr. Ciaran Mulholland, MB, BCh, BAO, DMH, MRCPsych, MD, is a Consultant Psychiatrist at Whiteabbey Hospital and a Senior Lecturer in Psychiatry at Queen's University Belfast. He has published widely in the areas of schizophrenia, first episode psychosis, and on the role of psychological trauma, including political violence in Northern Ireland, in the aetiology of psychosis. He is an active trade unionist and socialist and has long-standing interests in the history of health service trade unionism and the historical development of health services in Ireland and Britain. His work has appeared in many journals including the *Journal of Trauma and Dissociation, Bipolar Disorders, Schizophrenia Research;* and *The Journal of Trauma and Dissociation*

Dr. Pauline M. Prior, BA, MSc (Econ), DPhil, CQSW, is a senior lecturer in Social Policy at Queen's University Belfast. Her first degree, in Sociology and Social Policy, was gained in University College Cork. Before joining academia, she worked as a community development worker in Zambia and Ethiopia, and as a social worker in Northern Ireland. She holds an MSc (Econ) and a social work qualification from the London School of Economics and a DPhil (on mental health policy in Northern Ireland) from York University,

England. Her research covers different aspects of mental health policy, including gender, law, and historical trends in mental health services in Ireland. She has published five books – *Mental Health and Politics in Northern Ireland* (Avebury, 1993); *Gender and Health Care in the UK: Exploring the Stereotypes* (with B. Hayes) (Palgrave-Macmillan, 2003); *Globalisation and European Welfare States: Challenges and Change* (edited with R. Sykes and B. Palier) (Palgrave, 2001); *Gender and Mental Health* (Macmillan Press, 1999) and *Madness and Murder: Gender, Crime and Mental Disorder in Nineteenth-Century Ireland* (Irish Academic Press, 2008).

Dr. Dermot Walsh, consultant psychiatrist, was awarded the 2010 *Outstanding Achievement Award* by the College of Psychiatry of Ireland for his lifetime of work dedicated to all aspects of mental health care in Ireland. Having worked in clinical practice, in research and in teaching in mental health care, he is best known for his role as Inspector of Mental Hospitals in Ireland and as Psychiatric Advisor to the Department of Health, a position that he held from 1987 to 2003. For many years, he was a member of the World Health Organisation (WHO) expert committee for mental health and a consultant with the WHO Regional Office for Europe. Dr. Walsh was also the founder of the *Irish Journal of Psychiatry*. He is currently a member of the Mental Health Commission and continues to carry out research on mental health issues.

Dr. Oonagh Walsh was educated at Trinity College Dublin and the University of Nottingham. A Senior Research Fellow in Medical History at University College Cork, she is the author of *Anglican Women in Dublin: Philanthropy, Politics and Education in the Early Twentieth Century* (Dublin, 2005), and *Ireland's Independence: 1880–1923* (London, 2000). Her book on Irish psychiatry, *Insanity, Power and Politics in Nineteenth-Century Ireland: The Connaught District Lunatic Asylum* will be published by Manchester University Press in 2013. She is a founder member of the Consortium for Medical Humanities, and has published on a variety of social, political and cultural aspects in Irish medical history.

Chronology of Significant Events

in the History of the Provision of Mental Health Services
in Ireland from 1634 to 2010

1634   An Act for 'erecting Houses of Correction and for the punishment of rogues, vagabonds, sturdy beggars and other lewd and idle persons' (10 & 11 Chas. 1. c. 4).

1708   First public provision for pauper lunatics in Ireland – cells erected in the Dublin City Workhouse (established in 1703).

1711   Ten cells erected for insane soldiers at the Royal Hospital, Kilmainham, Dublin.

1729   The Dublin City Workhouse stopped the admission of lunatics in order to concentrate on the care of foundlings.

1757   Dean Jonathan Swift's Hospital for the Insane (St. Patrick's) opened in Dublin for 50 fee-paying patients. Pauper patients were admitted from 1776.

1758   Part of the Dublin City Workhouse was again reserved for lunatics from all over Ireland. The only other public facility was at Newgate gaol in Dublin.

1772   An Act for Badging the Poor (11 & 12 Geo. 111. c. 30). Through this statute, Dublin, Cork, Waterford, Limerick and Clonmel acquired their first House of Industry. By the end of the eighteenth century, small numbers of lunatics and idiots were confined in these houses, some segregated and some mixing with the general pauper population.

1787   An Act for the regulation of gaols (27 Geo. 111. c. 39) empowered Grand Juries to raise funds for maintaining lunatic wards in Houses of Industry. Cork, Waterford, Limerick, Clonmel and Dublin used this legislation to provide separate accommodation for the insane.

1789   A public asylum was opened in Cork – known as the Eglinton Asylum. Dr. William Saunders Halloran, who was the Physician there in the early nineteenth century, wrote widely on treatments for mental disorder. This building later became the Cork District Asylum.

1803   A 'Special Committee to consider provisions for the Aged and Infirm Poor of Ireland, including Vagrants, Lunatics and Idiots' was appointed on the instigation of Sir John Newport, MP for Waterford. It reported in 1804.

1806   Hospitals and Infirmaries (Ireland) Act (46 Geo. 111. c. 95) empowered Grand Juries to present a sum not exceeding £100 for supporting a lunatic asylum. This was used in Dublin, Cork and Tipperary.

1810   The first Retreat in Ireland was opened at Bloomfield, Dublin.

1814   Ireland's first public asylum, the Richmond Lunatic Asylum, Dublin was built with 257 beds. The Parliamentary grant had been approved in 1810. Dr. Alexander Jackson, appointed as manager when it opened in 1815, was the former physician to the Dublin House of Industry.

1817   Report of the Select Committee on the Relief of the Lunatic Poor in Ireland.

1817   Asylums for Lunatic Poor (Ireland) Act (57 Geo. 111. c. 106). This provided the legal basis for the establishment of a network of district asylums throughout Ireland.

1821   The Lunacy (Ireland) Act (1 & 2 Geo. 1V. c. 33): 'An Act to make more effectual provision for the establishment of asylums for the lunatic poor and for the custody of insane persons charged with offences'.

1824   Armagh District Asylum built (160 beds). This was the first district asylum in Ireland. It opened in 1825. Thomas Jackson, former manager of the lunatic department of the Dublin House of Industry and known for his deep commitment to moral methods of treatment, was appointed as superintendent/manager.

1827   The Retreat, Armagh, was opened by the Society of Friends.

1827   District asylums were built in Derry (120 beds) and in Limerick (150 beds).

1829   District asylum opened in Belfast (104 beds). Thomas Cumming appointed as superintendent/manager.

1832   District asylum built in Carlow (100 beds).

1833   District asylums built in Ballinasloe (150 beds) and in Maryborough (170 beds).

1834   District asylum built in Clonmel (60 beds).

1835   District asylum built in Waterford (50 beds).

1835   Dr. Robert Stuart appointed as Resident Medical Officer at Belfast Asylum on the retirement of the manager, Mr.

Cumming. He was the first doctor appointed as manager to a district asylum in Ireland.

1838   The Poor Relief (Ireland) Act (1 & 2 Vic. c. 56). The English Poor Law Commissioners were authorised to form Unions throughout Ireland and to establish a Workhouse in each Union. By 1850, there were 163 Workhouses in Ireland. Most of these Workhouses contained one ward for lunatics.

1838   The Dangerous Lunatics (Ireland) Act (1 & 2 Vic. c. 27) made provision 'for the better prevention of crime being committed by the insane'. This empowered the court to commit a criminal lunatic to gaol. He or she could then be removed to an Asylum by warrant of the Lord Lieutenant.

1841   The Association of Medical Officers of Asylums and Hospitals for the Insane founded in England.   This   was renamed the Medico Psychological Association in 1865 and eventually became the Royal College of Psychiatrists.

1842   The Private Lunatics Asylums (Ireland) Act (5 & 6 Vic. c. 123). By virtue of this Act, the Inspector-General of Prisons was given the added responsibility of inspecting lunatic asylums, and it became unlawful for anyone to keep a house for the reception of two or more insane persons, unless it was licensed.

1843   Report of the Select Committee (House of Lords) on the State of the Lunatic Poor in Ireland.

1843   New Privy Council Rules were introduced by the Lord Lieutenant for all district asylums in Ireland, curtailing the powers of the lay manager and increasing those of the visiting physician. These rules also allowed for the admission of incurables (including people with an intellectual disability and/or epilepsy) to district asylums.

1845   The Central Criminal Lunatic Asylum (Ireland) Act (8 & 9 Vic. c. 107) provided for the establishment of a central asylum at Dundrum, Dublin, for insane persons charged with offences in Ireland. It opened in 1850. This Act also established the Inspectorate of Lunacy and provided for the removal of all lunatics from the Houses of Industry to district asylums.

1852   District asylums built in Kilkenny (152 beds) and Killarney (220 beds).

1852   The Eglinton Asylum in Cork was expanded and renamed the Cork District Asylum (500 beds).

1853   District asylum built in Omagh (300 beds).

1855   District asylums built in Mullingar (563 beds) and in Sligo (470 beds).

1858   Report of the Commissioners of Inquiry into the state of Lunatic Asylums and other institutions for the custody and treatment of the insane in Ireland (appointed in 1857).

1859   Report of the Select Committee (House of Commons) on the Lunatic Poor (Ireland) Bill. The report stressed the need to provide accommodation for those who could pay towards maintenance.

1862   Revision of the Privy Council Rules on asylums. These rules established conclusively the authority of the Resident Medical Superintendent. A qualified physician or surgeon, he was to be responsible for the medical and moral treatment of all patients and for the domestic management of the asylum.

1865   Building started on a district asylum for Downpatrick (300 beds). It did not open until 1869.

1866   District asylums built in Castlebar (260 beds) and Letterkenny (300 beds).

1867   Lunacy (Ireland) Act (30 & 31 Vic. c. 118). The committal of dangerous lunatics to prisons was prohibited under this law.

1868   District asylum built in Ennis (260 beds).

1868   District asylum built in Enniscorthy (330 beds).

1869   District asylum built in Monaghan (250 beds).

1871   The Lunacy Regulation (Ireland) Act (34 & 35 Vic. c. 22). This Act was concerned with the management of the estates and the protection of the property of lunatics.

1875   The Lunatic Asylums (Ireland) Act (38 & 39 Vic. c. 67) permitted patients to leave the asylum on parole for a period not exceeding thirty days.

1875   A capitation grant of 50 per cent of the cost of maintenance of patients, limited to a maximum of four shillings per week, was granted to district asylums from the Exchequer. For the first time, district asylums were partially funded from central government (with no obligation to repay funds).

1877   Report of the Select Committee (House of Commons) on Lunacy law in England. For comparative purposes, evidence was also taken from Scotland and Ireland.

1878   A Lunacy Inquiry Commission was appointed to examine the possibility of additional provision for poor lunatics and idiots in Ireland.

1880   The County Court Jurisdiction in Lunacy (Ireland) Act (43 & 44 Vic. c. 39).

1890   The Lunacy Act (England) (53 & 54 Vic. c. 5). Except for minor details, this did not affect Ireland.

1896   Claremont Street Hospital for Nervous Diseases opened in Belfast.

1898   The Local Government (Ireland) Act (61 & 62 Vic. c. 37) established County and County Borough Councils to take over the functions of the Boards of Guardians and of the Grand Juries. This included administrative and financial responsibility for district asylums.

1899   Antrim District Asylum established, with initial accommodation for approximately 400 patients. This was the last district asylum to be built in Ireland.

1901   The Lunacy (Ireland) Act (1 Edw. VII. c. 17). This was a minor piece of amending legislation.

1906   Report of the Vice Regal Commission on Poor Law Reform in Ireland.

1909   Asylum Officers Superannuation (Ireland) Act (9 Edw. 7. c. 48).

1909   Reports of the Royal Commission on the Poor Laws and Relief of Distress (UK). This included a Report on Ireland.

1917   The Irish Asylum Workers Union was formed when the Irish branch of the British Asylum Workers Association split off from the main union.

1920   The Government of Ireland Act was given Royal Assent on 23 December. Mental health services in Ireland came under two distinct jurisdictions from this date onwards – Northern Ireland (part of the United Kingdom) and the Republic of Ireland.

1923   The Local Government Act (NI) (13 & 14 Geo. 5. c. 31) authorised the payment, to district asylums in Northern Ireland, of a fixed grant based on the average payments in 1918, 1919 and 1920. This grant of £37,079 remained static until 1940, in spite of efforts by local councils to persuade the government to return to a per capita payment based on patient population.

1927   Report of the Commission on the Relief of the Sick and Destitute Poor (including the Insane Poor) in the Irish Free State/Republic of Ireland.

1929   Criminal Lunatics Act (NI) (20 Geo. 5. c. 19). This established a Criminal Lunatic Asylum in Northern Ireland in part of Derry Prison, to take patients formerly sent to Dundrum.

	This was a temporary measure, which lasted for just a few years.

1932   Mental Treatment Act (NI) (22 & 23 Geo. 5. c. 15). The most important elements of the Act were the replacement of the language of lunacy and vagrancy by the language of mental illness and disorder; the introduction of new procedures (as Voluntary or Temporary patients) for admission to treatment; and the extension of treatment for mental disorder outside of the mental hospital.

1938   Criminal Lunatics Act (NI).

1933   The last district mental hospital to be built in the Republic of Ireland opened in Ardee, Co Louth.

1940   Local Government (Finance) Act (NI). This increased the block grant to mental hospitals to a sum not exceeding £60,000 – an unsatisfactory state of affairs for service planners, who favoured a return to a per-capita grant.

1942   First Child Guidance Clinic opened in Northern Ireland at the Royal Belfast Hospital for Sick Children under the Child Guidance Council for Northern Ireland.

1943   Mental Hospitals Association (NI) formed.

1945   The Local Government (Finance) Act (NI) increased the block grant to mental hospitals in Northern Ireland to a sum not exceeding £90,000.

1945   The first psychiatric social worker was employed in Northern Ireland. This was a direct appointment by the Ministry of Health and Local Government (NI) for the aftercare of members of the armed forces discharged on psychiatric grounds.

1945   The Mental Treatment Act in the Republic of Ireland. The old discourse of 'lunacy' and 'pauperism' was replaced by medical terminology – the word 'asylum' was replaced by 'hospital' (in fact, asylums had been redesignated as mental hospitals in 1927), 'attendant' by 'nurse' and 'inmate' by 'patient'. Recourse to a judicial authority for admissions was abolished completely and outpatient clinics were introduced.

1947   Health Services (Financial Provisions) Act (in the Republic of Ireland). Up to then, costs of all mental health services were borne by local rates (county and county borough). By virtue of this Act, 50 per cent of revenue expenditure was refunded to each authority from central government funds. The Central Mental Hospital, Dundrum (formerly the Central Criminal Lunatic Asylum for Ireland) was funded by the Department of Justice.

1948   The Health Services Act (NI). All hospitals, including mental hospitals (which had been administered by local councils), were transferred to the control of the Northern Ireland Hospitals Authority (NIHA). This brought to an end the financial burden of mental hospitals on local rates.

1948   The Mental Health Act (NI) (11 & 12 Geo 6. c. 17). The most important elements of the new Act included the total removal of judicial procedures (certification) from methods of admission to mental hospital; the inclusion of mental illness and mental handicap/ intellectual disability in the same piece of legislation; a new emphasis on the promotion of mental health rather than the treatment of mental illness; and the establishment of a separate Special Care Service for people with 'incomplete or arrested development of mind'.

1948   The Retreat at Armagh closed. This was the last private asylum/mental hospital in Northern Ireland. For the remainder of the century, psychiatric hospitals were all public facilities.

1949   The Welfare Services Act (NI) (13 & 14 Geo. 6. c. 30). This Act abolished the existing Poor Law structures relating to Workhouses and gave permissive powers to local authorities to provide accommodation for persons in need. This formed the legislative basis for welfare services for people with mental illnesses.

1949   Mental Patients Affairs Order (NI).

1951   The NIHA published a special report on the medical and social problems of old age (by Adams and Cheeseman). This highlighted the problem of geriatric patients in mental hospitals in Northern Ireland.

1952   Dr. John Dunne was appointed as the first Professor of Psychiatry in University College Dublin (UCD).

1957   Mental Health Exhibition staged at several centres in Northern Ireland.

1957   The first Professor of Mental Health in Northern Ireland, Dr. John Gibson, was appointed at Queen's University, Belfast.

1958   The long awaited Special Care 'colony' (for people with an intellectual disability) opened at Muckamore Abbey, Antrim – for 200 patients (there had been 17 patients there since 1949). During the following year 300 beds were added. The planned capacity was for 1,000 beds. This provision brought to an end the controversy surrounding the presence of children in mental hospitals in Northern Ireland. However, the idea of a 'colony' was already out of date by the 1960s and the presence of such a large number of patients in one facility became increasingly problematic. At the end of the twentieth century, efforts were made to re-settle most of the residents to community-based residential facilities.

1958   Numbers of patients in public mental hospitals in the Republic of Ireland reached a peak of 20,046.

1959   The Northern Ireland Association for Mental Health (NIAMH) formed. The first committee represented influential legal, political and medical opinion.

1959   Numbers of patients in public mental hospitals in the Republic of Ireland fell slightly to 19,590. These patients were in 18 district and three auxiliary hospitals. Four of the district hospitals had almost 2,000 patients, Cork, Grangegorman, Portrane and Ballinasloe. Another 1,019 were in private mental hospitals, a slight decrease on the previous year (see chapter by Dermot Walsh for further detail).

1960   Numbers of patients in public mental hospitals in Northern Ireland reached a peak of 6,452.

1961   The Mental Health Act (NI) (10 Eliz. 2 c. 15). The main elements of the Act included the complete removal of judicial procedures from treatment of patients in mental hospitals; the establishment of a Mental Health Review Tribunal for Northern Ireland; and a commitment to funding organisations engaged in the promotion of mental health.

1961   The first mental health Day Hospital in Northern Ireland opened at Clifton Street Belfast.

1961   A Commission of Enquiry on Mental Illness was established in the Republic of Ireland. It reported in 1966. (See below.)

1962   The Mental Health Review Tribunal for Northern Ireland, appointed under the Mental Health Act (NI) 1961, began its work.

1963   The Industrial Therapy Organisation (ITO) was set up in association with the Downshire Hospital, Downpatrick, to provide rehabilitative work for patients with mental illnesses.

1964   As no facility existed in Northern Ireland, arrangements were made with Health Departments in England and Scotland for the provision of special accommodation for persons from Northern Ireland requiring treatment and detention on account of dangerous, violent or criminal 'propensities'. Carstairs Hospital, Scotland was used from then until the early twenty-first century (for mentally disordered offenders).

1965   Shaftsbury Square Hospital for alcoholism and drug addiction opened in premises previously occupied by Belfast Ophthalmic Hospital.

1966   The Report of the Commission of Inquiry on Mental Illness in the Republic of Ireland was published. It made many important recommendations, including a move to a model of care which would incorporate community and short-term care in addition to long-term hospital care; collaboration between psychiatry and other health professionals in the provision of mental health services, special services for children and adolescents and public education programmes on mental health and illness.

1968   A decision was taken to discontinue farming at mental hospitals in Northern Ireland.

1975   The first Strategic Plan for Health and Personal Social Services in Northern Ireland was published. One of its eight objectives was 'the development of community health and social care for the mentally ill' and the 'relief of overcrowding in psychiatric hospitals'.

1978   The Chronically Sick and Disabled Persons (NI) Act (1978 c. 53) included people suffering from a mental disorder within its terms of reference.

1979   Workshops with designated places for people with mental illness began to open in Belfast, for example, Beech Hall and Tamar Street (1979) and Ravenhill Workshop (1981).

1981   The Health (Mental Services) Act was passed in the Republic of Ireland. It was never implemented.

1981   A Study Group on the Development of Psychiatric Services was set up by the Minister for Health in the Republic of Ireland. It reported in 1984 (see below).

1981   Report of the Northern Ireland Review Committee on mental health legislation (appointed in 1978) published. (Chairperson: MacDermott).

1984   Report of the Review Committee on Services for Mentally Ill people in Northern Ireland published: *Mental Health – the Way Forward.*

1984   Report of the Study Group on the Development of Psychiatric Services in the Republic of Ireland published – *The Psychiatric Services, Planning for the Future.* It recommended that services should be comprehensive and wide ranging, including community based and hospital services, with acute services based in psychiatric units in general hospitals, with plans to discharge current long-stay patients into community-based housing.

1986   Mental Health (NI) Order [SI No. 595 (NI. 4)]. This differed from earlier legislation in a number of ways, for example, in its definition of mental disorder – excluding certain 'disorders' from the remit of the Order; the Approved Social Worker was introduced into compulsory admission procedures; and the concept of admission for 'assessment' rather than 'treatment' appeared for the first time; patients' rights were further protected by the enhanced authority of the Mental Health Review Tribunal and by the establishment of the new Mental Health Commission.

1986   Establishment of a Mental Health Commission for Northern Ireland.

1986   Publication of the *Regional Strategy for Health and Personal Social Services 1987–92*. One of the three objectives of the *Strategy* was to bring about a shift in the balance of care from institutional care to care in the community, with a planned reduction of 20 per cent in the numbers of people in psychiatric hospitals.

1987   Efforts by the Minister for Health in the Republic of Ireland to close two large psychiatric hospitals in Carlow and Castlerea failed due to opposition from the public.

1989   Disabled Persons (NI) Act (1989 c.10). This Act referred specifically to people suffering from a mental disorder and included a requirement on the DHSS to produce a report on service developments (S. 10).

1990   Publication of *People First – Community Care in Northern Ireland for the 1990s*.

1991   *Regional Strategy for Health and Personal Social Services for 1992–97* published. It had mental health as one of its 'target areas of concern' and stressed the need to continue the trend towards a community-based service and a further reduction of psychiatric beds by 20 per cent. The aim was that by the year 1997, the number of people in psychiatric hospitals in Northern Ireland would be 1,500.

1991   The inpatient population in publicly funded psychiatric beds had fallen to 8,207 in the Republic of Ireland (from a high of 20,046 in 1958).

1992   The publication of a *Green Paper on Mental Health* in the Republic of Ireland, which formed the basis for discussions on all aspects of the services, including the law.

1995   The publication of a White Paper *A New Mental Health Act* in the Republic of Ireland. It contained new procedures for admissions and discharges for voluntary and involuntary patients, a review of detention orders, and discussions on consent to treatment and on mentally disordered offenders.

1996   Professor Michael Fitzgerald was appointed as the first Professor of Child Psychiatry in Ireland (at TCD).

2001   Mental Health Act – in the Republic of Ireland, based on the 1995 White Paper. It provided the basis for the setting up of Mental Health Tribunals and a Mental Health Commission, in addition to many changes in procedures aimed at improving services.

2002   Our Lady's Psychiatric Hospital Cork closed. Opened in 1789 as the Eglinton Asylum, it became the Cork District Asylum in 1852, remaining one of the largest psychiatric hospitals in Ireland throughout the nineteenth and twentieth centuries. The building has now been converted into residential apartments.

2002   The Bamford Review of Mental Health and Learning Disability in Northern Ireland began its work to review the law and services for people with mental disorders or intellectual disabilities. The Review published a number of reports from 2002–07, one of the most influential of which will form the basis for new legislation – both mental health legislation and capacity legislation.

2003   The newly formed Mental Health Commission began its work in the Republic of Ireland.

2004   A new Inspectorate of Mental Health Services replaced the Inspector of Mental Hospitals in the Republic of Ireland.

2004   Health Act – for the Republic of Ireland – the abolition of health boards and the establishment of the Health Service Executive (HSE). Regional programmes for mental health were replaced by a centralised directorate for mental health services.

2006   Criminal Law (Insanity) Act – in the Republic of Ireland, based on the 1995 White Paper.

2006   Publication of the report from the expert group on Mental Health Policy. It had been appointed by the Minister of State at the Department of Health and Children in 2003 – *A Vision for Change*. The recommendations in the report reflected the fact that the group had sought and listened to the views of service users and other stakeholders. For example, the importance of working towards recovery and re-integration through the provision of accessible community-based services was emphasised. (See chapter by Dermot Walsh for further discussion).

2010   The Minister of State at the Department of Health and Children announced the sale of former psychiatric hospital and land, with a view to funding new community-based facilities to allow for the closure of all old hospitals.

2010   On 31 March 2010, there were 2,812 persons resident in psychiatric units and hospitals in the Republic of Ireland, a reduction of almost 500 since 2006, and of 83 per cent since the first Medico-social Research Board (MSRB) census of 1963. Of these, 715 were in general hospital units, 1,309 in old psychiatric hospitals, 551 in private hospitals and 99 in the Central Mental Hospital.

2010   In Northern Ireland, the average number of available psychiatric beds decreased by 10.3 per cent between 2005/6 and 2009/10 – from 1,110 beds in 2005/6 to 996 beds in 2009/10. The average number of admissions per bed was six, while the average length of stay was 54.4 days (an increase of seven days since 2005/6).

1

Introduction

Pauline M. Prior

When Thomas Spring Rice, Whig politician and life governor of
Limerick House of Industry, appeared before the Select Committee
on the Lunatic Poor in Ireland in 1817, he described the accommodation for people with mental disorders as unfit for dogs.

> I hold in my hand a plan of the Lunatic Asylum of Limerick, in
> which the accommodation afforded to the insane will appear to
> be such as we should not appropriate for our dog-kennels; it
> consists of one arcade, an open arcade, behind which cells have
> been constructed with stone floors, without any mode of heating
> or of ventilating and exposed during the whole of the winter to
> the extremities of the weather.[1]

Spring Rice also told the committee that because of the overcrowding, disturbed patients were physically restrained in a way that led
to them losing the power of their limbs.

> The usual mode of restraint was by passing their hands under
> their knees, fastening them with manacles, fastening both
> about their ankles, and passing a chain over all, and then fas-
> tening them to a bed.[2]

The appalling conditions in this and other establishments led to
situations in which corpses lay for days without being removed, and
female inmates were sexually exploited by those responsible for
their care.[3] The report of the Select Committee added to the growing
evidence of the terrible conditions under which most people with a
mental disorder were cared for within the public system in Ireland.
At this time, the facilities for this vulnerable section of the population consisted of the privately funded St. Patrick's Hospital, Dublin,
and the publicly funded Richmond Asylum (opened 1815), two
small asylums at Cork and Wexford, and some beds attached to
Houses of Industry and to gaols in other large towns.[4]

Alongside the evidence of neglect and abuse, was a growing optimism about care and treatment. Another witness to the 1817 Select Committee, John Leslie Foster, Governor of the Richmond Asylum, Dublin, spoke of a 'new and an improved system of treatment' at his asylum.[5] He told the committee of the advances made by Dr. Philippe Pinel in France. He had replaced coercion with a 'more gentle mode of treatment'. Foster also spoke of Mr. William Tuke and the Quaker approach at the York Retreat in England. This new system was being tried out at the Richmond and was, according to Foster, very successful.

> I beg to add as proof of this, that there is not in the Richmond Lunatic Asylum, to the best of my belief, a chain, a fetter, or a hand cuff.

And

> I do not think, that out of the two hundred patients, there were above three or four to whom even the application of the strait jacket was found necessary: the disorder is treated not so much as a subject of medical care, as of the superintendence of the person, who is termed the moral governor, and whose particular business it is to attend to the comfort for the patients, to remove from them the causes of irritation, to regulate the degrees of restraint, and to provide occupation for the convalescent.[6]

It is highly likely that there was some exaggeration in Foster's positive view of treatment at the Richmond, given the constraints of a high level of demand for places and a low level of funding. However, what this submission to the Select Committee showed was a new optimism about the possibility of caring for people who had been regarded up to then as incurable and dangerous.

As a result of the work of this Select Committee, and of the political will of Sir Robert Peel, appointed Chief Secretary for Ireland in 1812, district asylums were set up throughout the country. By the mid-century, there were ten district asylums providing over 3,000 beds in total.[7] By then, the management of asylums had passed out of the hands of lay managers. By the 1860s, all of the asylums had medically trained managers (known as the Resident Medical Superintendent), who were assisted in relation to the physical health of patients by an independent doctor (known as the Visiting Physician).

However, there were still problems in meeting the growing

demand for places for people suffering from mental disorders. These problems were articulated in the evidence presented to the Commissioners of Inquiry into the state of Lunatic Asylums in Ireland in 1857. According to the report from this inquiry, there were 9,286 insane poor in Ireland in January 1857.[8] This number was made up of 5,934 'maintained at the public charge' and 3,352 'at large'. Of those in public institutions, 3,824 were in district asylums and the remainder were in workhouses (1,815) or in prisons (295).[9] The commissioners deliberately omitted those from 'the wealthier class' from this number, as this would confuse the estimate for public provision. However, they did note that there were 459 patients in 'Licensed Houses and Benevolent Institutions' at this time.[10]

As the purpose of this inquiry was to examine the state of asylums, we get a very detailed picture of the improvements that had taken place since the beginning of the century. District asylums built in the early years were, understandably, less well appointed than those built in the 1850s. Many of the early asylums had no water, no place of worship, no ventilation and no water closets.

> The patients, as in Carlow, being left to wash in the open courts under shelter of a shed: and, at most, one bad and imperfectly constructed bath being provided, for each side of the building.[11]

Some of these faults were rectified in asylums built in the 1850s:

> Improvements are perceptible in the provision of lavatories and bath rooms, with a proper supply of water, of recreations halls, chapels, and vastly superior kitchens and offices, as well as infirmaries and arrangements for ventilation.[12]

However, all was not well. Airing courts and day rooms were usually on the northern side of the building and were 'cold and cheerless', the sewerage system and water supply was often 'imperfect or ill-planned', and the quality of water often questionable. Even where there were water closets, they were often kept locked so that the patients could not use them. The same held for fire-places – some were never used, serving only as ornaments, while others were so badly situated that they were 'of little effect'. The list went on – ventilation systems did not work, recreation halls were not used, and walls were bare and cheerless.

> In corridor or day-room, the lunatic sees nothing but the one undiversified white wall – giving to these hospitals, intended for the restoration of the alienated mind, an air of blankness

and desolation more calculated to fix than to remove the awful disease under which it labours.[13]

The cumulative effect of poor physical conditions, inadequate clothing, relatively little care of the sick and instances of neglect and restraint, was a situation of detention rather than of care. In spite of the existence of Privy Council Rules, requiring strict regulation and reporting of all instances of restraint, there was evidence of whole-sale use of mechanical restraint without authorisation of the asylum manager or of the Visiting Physician.

> In Armagh Asylum … a patient on the female side, was strapped down in bed, with body straps of hard leather, three inches wide, and twisted under the body with wrist locks strapped and locked, and with wrists frayed from want of lining to straps: this patient was seriously ill.[14]

And

> In the Carlow Asylum, we found that a man suffering from dropsy was tied down to bed, and locked up in his cell, without the knowledge of the Resident or Visiting Physician.[15]

The commissioners made a number of recommendations based on the evidence gathered from witnesses and from their own visits to a range of institutions that housed people with mental disorders. Among these were proposals to build additional asylums and to improve the standard of care throughout the asylum system, by linking up with medical schools and by monitoring the implementation of existing Privy Council Rules through proper inspection.

Spurred on by this report and the work of the newly established Inspectorate of Lunacy (set up in 1845), money was made available by the government for the expansion of the asylum system, both in terms of numbers of asylums and size of patient population. By the beginning of the twentieth century, there were twenty-two asylums in Ireland, providing over 16,000 beds funded from the public purse.[16] In addition there were privately run establishments, which included 'benevolent institutions' and 'licensed houses'.[17] The largest and most famous benevolent institution was St. Patrick's Hospital, Dublin, but there were also two small Quaker Retreats in Ireland, at Bloomfield, Dublin and at Armagh.[18] Though Ireland did not experience the expansion in private 'madhouses' characteristic of England at the time, there were twelve licensed houses which provided care for small numbers of patients.[19]

Alongside the growth in asylum size and number was the development of a new specialty within medicine.[20] Irish psychiatry emerged and flourished in the second half of the nineteenth century, helped in no small measure by the powerful influence at Dublin Castle of Dr. Francis White, appointed as the first Inspector in Lunacy for Ireland. From 1841, White had special responsibility for asylums within the Inspectorate of Prisons. From the beginning, he was a strong advocate of a medical approach to the care and treatment of mental disorder. He worked tirelessly to establish a highly professional inspectorate which oversaw standards of care throughout the asylum system. As jobs in the asylum system increased, so too did the number of Irish doctors interested in this area of medical care. Some, like Dr. Oscar Woods, Dr. M. J. Nolan and Dr. Conolly Norman, became active members of the Medico Psychological Association of Great Britain and Ireland and published their case histories in the *Journal of Mental Science* (later to become the *British Journal of Psychiatry*). It was not all plain sailing, however, as evidenced in the many disputes between medical superintendents and visiting physicians, and in the enquiries into the management of some local asylums by the Inspectorate of Lunacy.[21]

By the time Ireland became a state in its own right in 1921, the asylum system was in trouble. It was overcrowded, under-funded and marginalised. Mental health care was not a popular medical specialty in the early twentieth century. Since 1921, two different systems of health care and of legislation have been in operation in Ireland. The Republic of Ireland developed a dual system of public and private provision, while Northern Ireland moved towards a heavy reliance on the public sector, reflecting patterns of health service delivery in other parts of the United Kingdom. However, mental health services in both parts of Ireland have been influenced by the highly institutionalised system of care inherited from the nineteenth century.

By the mid-twentieth century, it became clear throughout the western world, that the institutional approach to mental health care was neither financially viable nor medically necessary. New drugs and technical advances in medical science, plus a greater understanding of mental health and illness, made care in the community a possibility. However, it took another half century for the structures of the highly centralised, highly institutionalised care system set up in nineteenth-century Ireland to change. This was due largely to the economic and political interests surrounding the downgrading or closure of mental hospital services. Some of the special reports on mental health services in the Republic of Ireland highlighted the slow rate of progress. In 1984, the authors of *Planning for the Future* found psychiatric services to be below an acceptable standard.

> At present, the psychiatric hospital is the focal point of the psychiatric service in most of the country. Large numbers of patients reside permanently in these hospitals. Many of them have lived there for years in conditions which in many cases are less than adequate because of overcrowding and capital underfunding ... The hospitals were designed to isolate the mentally ill from society and this isolation still persists.[22]

The report went on to recommend a total reorganisation of the services, with a view to moving to a new model of mental health care. As outlined in *A Vision for Change*, a report published in 2006, this new model of care would involve a radical shift in service delivery, from hospital to home.

> It was to be comprehensive, with a multidisciplinary approach, provide continuity of care, and be effectively coordinated. This new service was to be community-oriented to the extent that care should be provided in an individual's home, with a variety of community-based services, and was to provide support to families.[23]

By 2006, when *Vision for Change* was published, there had been considerable progress. Psychiatric units in general hospitals had increased, as had community-based residences and day-care centres. Some of the large mental hospitals, originally built as asylums, continued to function as psychiatric hospitals but the total number of psychiatric beds had decreased by approximately 67 per cent (from 12,484 in 1984 to 4,121 in 2004) as had the rate of psychiatric admissions.[24] However, the community care model as envisaged in *Planning for the Future* in 1984 had not materialised. Multi-disciplinary community-based mental health teams responding flexibly to the needs of people seeking help from the psychiatric service remains a dream for the twenty-first century.

THE STUDIES IN THIS COLLECTION

In spite of the radical changes in mental health care in Ireland in the past two centuries, many aspects of the service have not been fully explored by historians. This book presents a collection of essays from scholars working on a range of topics surrounding the care of Irish people with mental illnesses, as well as some poetry and prose from service users. Most of the studies are based in Ireland, but two explore the problems faced by Irish people who emigrated to Australia and New Zealand in the nineteenth century. The data for the studies comes from a variety of sources. In the twentieth century, these include newspaper reports, hospital newsletters, government reports and personal experiences of staff and patients. In the nineteenth century, they include asylum records, annual reports of the Lunacy Inspectorate, reports of select committees, and articles in medical publications such as the *Journal of Mental Science* and the *Dublin Quarterly Journal*. All of the research presented in this collection builds on the early work of Finnane, Malcolm, Robins and Williamson and the more recent work of Kelly, and Prior.[25] The book is far from being a comprehensive account of the history of Irish mental health services. Rather, it is an introduction to this under-researched area of Irish history.

In Part One of the book, which covers the twentieth century, we get a flavour of what was happening in two large mental hospitals (former asylums), one in the Republic of Ireland and one in Northern Ireland. These are two quite different stories; the first based on newspaper coverage of a single event and the second on accounts of everyday life published in a hospital magazine. In Chapter 2, Anton McCabe and Ciaran Mulholland tell the story of a nursing strike in 1919 that captured the imagination of the public and led to the great improvements in salaries and working conditions for psychiatric nurses throughout Ireland. At the time of the strike, Irish asylum attendants/nurses experienced low wages and poor conditions, were mostly untrained, and were regarded with disdain by physicians and asylum management committees. Early attempts to organise trade unions for asylum attendants met with official hostility and summary dismissals. The unions had only a precarious toe-hold, and had achieved little by the time of the first all-out strikes in Monaghan and Letterkenny in March 1918. A few months later, the Monaghan attendants seized their asylum and ran it as a Soviet, an event which shook the asylum system. Not only were improved wages and conditions achieved locally, but the Monaghan events led directly to the establishment, for the first time, of national terms and conditions for all attendants/nurses in asylums in Ireland. The 'Monaghan Asylum Soviet' served notice that the attendant/nurse could no longer be treated with contempt. The action of this brave group of staff had a profound impact on the future of the mental health nursing profession and on the mental hospital system as a whole.

In Chapter 3, Gillian McClelland takes us to a different place, both in time and perspective. Here, we get a glimpse of patient life in the 1960s, a time of great hope and renewal in the mental health services in Northern Ireland. Hospital magazines were a feature of hospital life during this period. The magazine in Holywell Hospital, Antrim (formerly Antrim Asylum), called *Speedwell*, was published from 1959 to 1972. It became the voice of patients and staff during this time of great change in Holywell Hospital and in all six large psychiatric hospitals in Northern Ireland. Anti-psychotic drugs were introduced in the late 1950s, making care in the community a possibility; the idea of the 'therapeutic community' was just emerging; and new mental health laws gave patients more protection and enhanced rights. As ward doors were unlocked and high walls dismantled, public attitudes towards mental illness began to change. As a result of this, large mental hospitals became less isolated from society. The realities of everyday life in Holywell Hospital, which had almost 800 beds at the time, are described in poetry and prose by staff and patients. The hospital was changing from what Erving Goffman describes as a 'closed' community to one which was more open to outside influences. However, it continued to be a 'community' for a large number of people, many of whom had been patients for a long time.[26] During the 1950s and 1960s, this community had employment opportunities within its walls – on the hospital farm, in the gardens and in the laundry. It also had a wide range of leisure activities, including regular outings to the beach and to concerts, competitive sporting events involving staff and patients, and regular performances from the resident hospital dance band and amateur theatre group. At this time, Holywell also boasted a beauty salon and a branch of the Women's Institute. In *Speedwell*, patients expressed their feelings about their lives in this community through prose and poetry. These were lives that included medical treatment but were not defined by it. Gillian McClelland explores some of this material, providing the reader with a unique insight into everyday life in a mental hospital at this time of major change.

Chapter 4 is written by one of the best known mental health professionals in Ireland, Dr. Dermot Walsh. From his position as Inspector of Mental Hospitals for many years, he had a bird's-eye view of developments in mental health services in the Republic of Ireland. In this chapter, he shares with us some of his thoughts on the changes that occurred in policies and services between 1959 and 2010. It describes these in some detail and identifies some of the forces – social, political and professional that underpinned them. He also highlights the interplay of public concern and legislative change which shaped a vision for Irish mental health services in the future.

In 1959, there were almost 20,000 inpatients in Irish psychiatric hospitals. All but one of these hospitals had been built in the preceding century and the mores and traditions of that era still governed their daily operation and culture. Physically isolated from their communities by high walls and 'sentried' entrance gates, they represented a socio-economic reality of considerable local importance, providing employment and supporting local trade. However, the aloofness of their complacency was being threatened elsewhere, notably in the neighbouring island of England, where their replacement by general hospital psychiatry and care in the community was not only being mooted, but being operationalised. Furthermore, it was becoming apparent even to the only moderately critical eye that living conditions behind the walls were less than acceptable in a modern state. From this situation emerged the Commission of Enquiry on Mental Health. Established in 1961, it called it as it saw it and it was not a pretty picture. Institutionalisation was the norm to which there was little alternative, and professionalism in care was poor and limited to doctors and nurses. Child psychiatric services did not exist and almost one fifth of residents were hospitalised, not because they were mentally ill, but rather because they were 'mentally handicapped'.

Further government bodies reported in 1984 and 2006 and White and Green Papers on services and mental health legislation appeared in 1992 and 1995. Meantime, the Medico-social Research Board, later to become the Health Research Board published annual reports of the activities of inpatient services and carried out censuses of residents periodically. The Inspectorate of Mental Hospitals and later the Mental Health Commission reported annually on conditions, and the latter body used statutory powers to remove approval for the reception of patients from at least one service. Legislation, too, underwent change, with the full implementation of the Mental Health Act 2001 in November 2006, allowing the setting up of tribunals to review involuntary admission and detention. The Criminal Law (Insanity) 2006 was commenced in that year also.

The impact of these initiatives, together with greatly improved staffing, training and professionalism of those in the service, led, inter alia, to a service that now had moved towards community care, so that residents had dropped below 3,000 by 2010 and several of the nineteenth-century hospitals had closed. Nonetheless, as argued by Walsh, there was little room for complacency as many services still lacked multi-disciplinary teams and community physical provision, such as day hospitals and rehabilitation units were still lacking in many locations. In addition, some of the general hospital units of an earlier generation were becoming obsolete for their purpose. Budgetary constraints on professional recruitment and the acquisition of community structures determined by the looming recession were casting a considerable shadow which only increased commitment and sustained endeavour could counter.

We end this section with some poetry written by former service users/survivors of the psychiatric system, and some articles by patients and staff which appeared in hospital magazines, giving us another perspective on mental health services during the second half of the twentieth century.

In Part Two, we move back to the nineteenth century, with research covering various aspects of mental health policy and service delivery. As the contributors to this volume come from different disciplines (history, medicine and social policy), the chapters reflect a miscellany of interests and of approaches.

In Chapter 6, Elizabeth Malcolm, using Australian archives, examines the cases of Irish people committed to several large asylums in the colony of Victoria, Australia, during the late nineteenth century. The asylums studied include Yarra Bend (opened in 1848) and Kew (opened in 1871), both in Melbourne, and Ararat (opened in 1867) and Beechworth (opened in 1867) in rural Victoria. The English asylum expert, Henry Burdett, claimed in 1891 that 'lunacy is more general in Victoria than in the other Australian colonies', and he provided statistics on asylum populations to support this assertion. During the 1870s, it was estimated that 70-80 per cent of those in Victoria's asylums were immigrants, many having been lured to the colony by the 'gold mania' of the 1850s and 1860s. A significant number of these new arrivals were Irish immigrants, with the Irish forming nearly one-quarter of the colony's population by 1871. Critics of Irish migration suggested that they were heavily over-represented in the asylums. However, this claim has not been systematically investigated.

In this chapter, Malcolm explores the records of Irish people committed to Victoria's asylums during and after the gold rushes, in order to understand who they were, why they were committed and in what ways they differed from their fellow inmates. In common with asylum committals in Ireland and elsewhere, post-natal depression, grief at the deaths of children, alcoholism, head injuries and poor physical health, are all evident as precipitating factors in Yarra Bend Asylum's patient records. In addition, the records of Yarra Bend do offer some evidence that 'gold fever' did play a role in the high committal rates evident in colonial Victoria. The rushes certainly left many 'disappointed' as very few achieved the wealth that they had dreamt of. Most overcame their disappointment, married, and moved on to other jobs or to other places – even, in the case of the perennially optimistic, to other rushes. But for a number, the disappointment was too devastating for them to be able to transcend it. Perhaps this was especially true of those Irish men who had no family in the colony, but parents and siblings back 'home' with high expectations of a regular flow of remittances.

In Chapter 7, Angela McCarthy brings the reader to New Zealand, where Irish migrants also featured in asylum records. McCarthy explores the records of two asylums, Dunedin and Seacliff, during the period 1863–1909, with a particular focus on the family. She suggests that though the interaction between family issues and madness has received considerable attention in studies of the asylum, there are two significant omissions in the research. First, the actual constitution of the family is rarely discussed explicitly, at least not in detail or quantitatively. For example, we are rarely told if the term 'family' includes or excludes spouses, siblings, parents, children, or other extended family members. Such an omission is surprising in the light of David Wright's reflections on this very issue more than a decade ago, querying whether nuclear or extended family members undertook the committal of an individual to an asylum.[27] McCarthy suggests that a deeper investigation of the family involved in this process is also critical in light of the influential 'atomisation' thesis put forward by historian Miles Fairburn – that 'most colonists … had already severed their links with place, family, friends and community in the great uprooting that led them to New Zealand'.[28] A second area of under-reporting in current research, according to McCarthy, is the link between the patient and family members who live in a different country. Family connections explored in studies of the asylum are predominantly confined to the country in which the asylums are located. The operation of transnational communications between home and abroad is strikingly absent.

In this chapter, McCarthy seeks to redress the balance in current research by examining family networks that existed for Irish patients in New Zealand asylums, and by exploring efforts made by patients to maintain and/or restore their family networks, including their connections to Ireland. Her study shows that many Irish migrants confined to the public asylums in New Zealand, moved within networks of family and friends and did not operate as 'atomised' beings. While Irish people who came to the colony as young adults lost their parental connections, they were often able to link up with siblings and become part of an extended network, comprising aunts, uncles and cousins. Though most relationships cited in asylum records were those of spouse or offspring, this does not mean that Irish patients were without other wider networks in the colony. It may merely reflect the fact that this was the prime relationship noted in the documentation.

In the next six chapters, we return to Ireland, to look at what was happening in the inspectorate and in four district asylums – Belfast Asylum, the Richmond Asylum, the Central Criminal Lunatic Asylum, and Ballinasloe Asylum. In Chapter 8, Pauline M. Prior and David Griffiths, examine official reports, minutes of asylum meetings and newspaper articles, to uncover the unholy war waged by the governors of the Belfast Asylum against the Lord Lieutenant of Ireland in an effort to avoid appointing chaplains. All asylums were required to employ and pay chaplains to look after the spiritual wellbeing of patients. In most asylums, this meant the appointment of two chaplains – one Catholic and one Protestant. However, in Belfast, matters were not so simple, due to the presence of more than two religious denominations and to the fact that the resident medical superintendent at the time, Dr. Robert Stuart, had always regarded it as his responsibility to look after the spiritual health of his patients. In order to prove that their stance was legally correct, the governors entered into litigation against the Lord Lieutenant of Ireland, a case that was heard in the Dublin courts. This chapter investigates the motives that inspired the board to defy such a powerful opponent. Documents of the period reveal a solid network of social support for the Belfast governors, based on a deep-seated resentment of colonial administration; opposing views on the role of religion in the treatment of the insane; and professional rivalry between Dr. Francis White, inspector in lunacy, and Dr. Robert Stuart, resident medical superintendent of the Belfast asylum. It is a fascinating story of the power struggle between local and central government over an issue (religion) that continued to dominate political life in Belfast for another century.

A completely different problem is the focus of the study presented in Chapter 9, by E. Margaret Crawford, whose expertise in dietary matters during and after the Famine in Ireland is well recognised.[29] This was an outbreak of a 'mysterious malady' in the Richmond Asylum in Dublin during the period 1894 to 1898, a malady which brought many experts from other countries to explore the possibility of an occurrence of beriberi among patients and staff. According to Crawford, institutions in nineteenth-century Ireland – prisons, workhouses, and hospitals – were often faced with episodes of epidemic diseases, normally listed under the umbrella term of 'fevers'. However, an unfamiliar disease affecting more than 500 patients and a few staff in the Richmond asylum was diagnosed, rather bizarrely, as beriberi. Beriberi is caused by a deficiency of the B vitamin, thiamine, and is most commonly found among rice-eating populations in Asia. The link between rice consumption and beriberi was known in the 1890s, but not the association with thiamine.

In this chapter, Crawford poses the question: How did it happen that the symptoms suffered by patients in Richmond were thought to be connected to an exotic Asian disease? To answer this question, she explores the debates about the outbreak found in the records of the Lunacy Inspectorate, in medical journal articles and in parliamentary papers, as the unusual nature of this illness attracted the attention of the inspectors, of politicians and of newspaper editors. The resident medical superintendent of the Richmond asylum, Dr. Conolly Norman, was so concerned by the outbreak that he sought the advice of several eminent medical specialists from Dublin, London and the Netherlands, some of whom had experience of treating beriberi in the Far East. The question was whether or not the symptoms exhibited by the sick in Richmond were characteristic of beriberi. Having studied the debates in parliament and in the medical literature of the time, and having reflected on the evidence, including information pertaining to the diets of those at the Richmond during the period of the outbreak, Crawford proposes a new explanation for this extremely unusual medical episode.

Another medical diagnosis behind mortality statistics is examined in Chapter 10, by Brendan Kelly, who brings his medical expertise to bear on his re-examination of records on specific aspects of the phenomenon of tuberculosis in one asylum (the Central Criminal Lunatic Asylum, Dundrum, Dublin). His study is based on an original analysis of the archival clinical records of three patients who died in the asylum and whose deaths were attributed to tuberculosis. The mid- to late nineteenth century saw a dramatic increase in the number of asylum beds in many countries, including Ireland. Notwithstanding these increases in capacity, Irish asylums were quickly overcrowded, owing chiefly to the rapid increase in the numbers of individuals who presented to the asylums in search of treatment. Tuberculosis, which was a substantial problem in the Irish general population around the end of the nineteenth century, quickly became a problem in these increasingly overcrowded, unsanitary institutions. The cases examined by Kelly demonstrate many of the diagnostic challenges in relation to medical illness (in this case, tuberculosis) amongst asylum inpatients; some of the key therapeutic challenges in relation to both medical and psychiatric illness; and the possible role of the asylum environment in alleviating and/or contributing to the tuberculosis problem at the end of the nineteenth and start of the twentieth century.

In Chapter 11, Pauline M. Prior explores some of the issues that were of concern to the Lunacy Inspectorate in the second half of the nineteenth century and in the early years of the twentieth. Between the time of its establishment in 1845 and its transformation into a new organisation in 1921, seven doctors held the position of inspector. These were Dr. Francis White, Dr. John Nugent, Dr. George William Hatchell, Dr. George Plunkett O'Farrell, Dr. E. Maziere Courtenay, Dr. Thomas I. Considine, and Dr. William R. Dawson. The inspectors visited each asylum at least once per year, and their annual reports are full of information on patients, on staff and on problems raised by managers or inspectors. In the mid century, the main issue dominating annual reports was that of overcrowding in asylums and the growing demand for more beds. A period of expansion began in the 1860s, leading to an increase in the size and the number of asylums. However, in spite of this expansion, the demand continued to exceed supply. Reports on the 'alleged increase in insanity' failed to come to any conclusion on what was causing the problem. In addition, by the end of the century, not only were the asylums overcrowded, but they were also underfunded, as Grand Juries struggled to keep up with the cost of a system that had far exceeded all earlier cost projections. These costs were discussed frequently in the reports of the inspectorate, but in spite of the building of some auxiliary asylums (which were cheaper to run) for chronic patients, the problem was not solved.

The final issue explored by Prior in this chapter is not new to those who monitor mental health services today – the possibility of abuse or neglect of patients. Although this was not an issue that was publicly debated in the nineteenth century, it featured frequently in the annual reports of the inspectors. Each asylum had to report all suicides and any cases in which patients were injured (either accidentally or maliciously), especially if this injury led to the death of a patient. The kind of problems discussed by the inspectors covered a range of situations, including the injury of a patient by an attendant; the death of a patient due to the neglect or during the absence of an attendant or servant; the abuse or injury of one patient by another in the absence of proper supervision by staff; the involvement of staff in the escape of one or more patients and, finally, evidence of a lax approach by a resident medical superintendent towards staff who transgressed. In the most extreme cases of abuse or neglect, the staff member was charged with a criminal offence and appeared in court. In less extreme cases, the courts were not involved, but the staff member was often dismissed or given a disciplinary warning. Overall, it appears that during the second half of the nineteenth century, the issue of physical abuse or neglect of patients was taken seriously by the authorities – the governors of the asylum and the Lunacy Inspectorate.

In Chapter 12, we return to a district asylum, this time in Ballinasloe, Co Galway, a dominant institution in the west of Ireland. As earlier chapters have indicated, the development of the District Asylum system involved complex negotiations of power and authority, with staff, patients and the wider community seeking particular advantages from the institutions. From its origins as a regime predicated on moral therapeutic principles, the asylums gradually moved towards a more medicalised model, with the resident medical superintendent assuming a dominant role by the century's end. This chapter examines that process at the Connaught District Lunatic Asylum at Ballinasloe and focuses in particular on the experiences of two of that institution's physicians – Dr. William Heise, the first such appointment (as the visiting physician) and Dr. Robert Vicars Fletcher, who as the second resident medical superintendent at Ballinasloe had a highly developed sense of the primacy of professional medical care. Their experiences are reflective of many others in the system throughout Ireland and illustrate the manner in which the asylums moved from a paternalistic, philanthropic model of care and containment, directed by the lay Boards of Governors, to scientific, medical institutions that depended on the acquisition of empirically based university training and which relegated non-specialists to predominantly administrative roles.

We end this section of the book with some extracts from official documents, such as asylum reports and Privy Council Rules, which reflect official thinking about the care and containment of people with mental disorders in nineteenth-century Ireland, and some extracts from articles written by Irish psychiatrists in the *Journal of Mental Science*. These articles reflect some of the medical thinking of the time on issues such as the causes of mental illness (discussed in relation to general paralysis) and on the reasons for the ever grow-ing demand for more asylum places. The question asked in this last article continued to be asked right up to the late twentieth century – do the Irish have a higher incidence of mental illness than other ethnic groups?

Part Three of the book focuses on some general trends in mental health services in the past two centuries. In Chapter 14, Damien Brennan applies a sociological analysis to a study of the rise and fall in patient numbers in asylums/psychiatric hospitals in Ireland over the past two hundred years. While inpatient numbers may reflect an increase or decrease in mental disorders in the Irish population, Brennan asks us to look for other explanations for this pattern of service use. Building on evidence drawn from an original data-set, mapping the psychiatric inpatient population in Ireland from 1817 to 2000, he demonstrates that the Irish data reveals an overall trajec-tory of institutional residency that began at a low level in the early nineteenth century, increased rapidly between 1830 and 1890, continued to increase at a steady pace until 1956, and then began a steady decline that has continued until the present time.

While this is not an unusual pattern of asylum occupancy, the Irish case does not conform to established sociological theories or 'grand narratives' that seek to explain these patterns. These theories link asylum expansion and decline to classic trends in industrialisation. They also link asylum expansion to the involvement of private/commercial enterprise or of religious organisations in institutional ownership or management. However, the evidence presented here in relation to the Irish situation does not support any of these theories. In the light of this, Brennan suggests a new theoretical explanation, one that points to specific points of 'social conjuncture' at times of change in patterns of psychiatric bed occupancy. He identifies a number of core features that impacted on each point of social conjuncture – the political context; the relationship between church and state; the changing economic structures and social deprivation; the growth of professionalism; the impact of legal changes on systems of admission and discharge; changes in categorisation and diagnostic criteria; international developments in mental health care; and, finally, family dynamics. He argues that these points of 'social conjuncture' are seminal in understanding the shaping and reshaping of a social tendency to institutionalise people with mental illnesses in Ireland. Whether or not you agree with this new theoretical approach to understanding psychiatric institutionalisation in Ireland, the discussion will give you food for thought.

In the final chapter of the book, Pauline Prior gives a brief overview of legal changes which have formed the basis for the delivery of mental health services on the island of Ireland from 1800 to 2010. Having come from the same position in the nineteenth century, mental health services and the legal basis for these services diverged in 1921, as Northern Ireland became part of the United Kingdom, with similar but not identical health policies, while the Republic of Ireland followed its own path. The legal basis for the provision of the first publicly funded mental health service in Ireland was laid in the early nineteenth century, with Lunacy Acts in 1817 (57 Geo. 3 c. 106), in 1821 (1 & 2 Geo. 4 c. 33) and in 1826 (7 Geo. 4 c. 14). These Acts gave power to Grand Juries to build and maintain a network of district asylums throughout the country. They also outlined the procedures for admission and discharge from these asylums of people who were 'of unsound mind'. These laws also aimed to protect people from unlawful confinement and from financial exploitation by unscrupulous relatives. Within a few years, there were not enough asylum places for those seeking admission, leading to the introduction of legislation for 'dangerous lunatics' in 1838 (1 Vic. c. 27) and 1867 (30 & 31 Vic. c. 118), which allowed for the direct admission of those deemed to be 'dangerous lunatics' to prison, while waiting for places in an asylum. As discussed earlier, this served to increase the number of admissions and to link dangerous behaviour with mental disorder.

In the twentieth century, the focus of the law changed, from confinement to treatment, with the Mental Treatment Acts/Orders in

Council of 1932, 1948, 1961, and 1986 in Northern Ireland, and the Mental Treatment Act of 1945 in the Republic of Ireland. These laws emphasised the need to facilitate access to treatment for someone with a mental illness. In order to do this, some of the legalistic restrictions contained in the laws of the previous century disappeared. Voluntary rather than compulsory admission to psychiatric hospital became the norm, as mental health services became more integrated into general health systems in both parts of Ireland. With developments in medical science, outpatient and community-based treatment became real possibilities in the mid century. These developments were reflected in the debates that took place every time the laws were reviewed. Though many efforts were made to initiate change in the law in the Republic of Ireland, the rate of progress was much slower than in Northern Ireland. As the end of the century approached, new problems were emerging that were not adequately covered by the existing legislation in either part of Ireland – the Mental Health (NI) Order 1986 and the Mental Treatment Act 1945 in the Republic of Ireland. For example, the human rights lobby argued that patients and potential patients were not well protected; psychiatrists proposed the introduction of community service orders (i.e. powers to compel an individual to take medication at home); and the dementia lobby highlighted the need for protection for people who had lost capacity, but who were not covered by mental health laws. In the Republic of Ireland, the Mental Health Act 2001 and the Mental Capacity Bill 2009, provided legal guidance on some but not all of these issues. In Northern Ireland, the recommendations of the Bamford Review of mental health and learning disability services, which worked from 2002 to 2007, have not yet been translated into law. However, it is hoped that the next round of legislation in Northern Ireland will incorporate their recommendations, ensuring a much higher level of legal protection for people who are mentally ill or who have lost capacity, while not hindering access to services.

NOTES

1. *Report of the Select Committee on the Lunatic Poor in Ireland*, with Evidence. Evidence, p.14, given on 7/6/1817. HC 1817 (430) viii, 33. (Hereafter, Select Committee 1817).
2. Ibid.
3. Ibid.
4. *Select Committee* 1817. Appendix to Evidence, p.33.
5. *Select Committee* 1817, Evidence, p.10, given on 25/3/1817.
6. Ibid.

7. M. Finnane, *Insanity and the Insane in Post-Famine Ireland* (London: Croom Helm, 1981), Table A, p.227; Williamson, 'The beginnings of state care for the mentally ill in Ireland', *Economic and Social Review*, 10.1 (January 1970): pp.281–90.

8. *Report of the Commissioners of Inquiry into the state of Lunatic Asylums and other institutions for the custody and treatment of the insane in Ireland. Part 1: Report; Part 2: Evidence and documents.* HC 1857–8 [2436] xxvii.1. (Hereafter, *Inquiry on Lunatic Asylums* 1857).

9. *Inquiry on Lunatic Asylums* 1857, Part 1, Report, p.2.

10. Ibid.

11. *Inquiry on Lunatic Asylums* 1857, Part 1, Report, p.13.

12. Ibid.

13. *Inquiry on Lunatic Asylums* 1857, Part 1, Report, p.14.

14. Ibid., p.16.

15. Ibid., p.17.

16. Finnane, *Insanity and the Insane*, Table A, p.227.

17. *Inquiry on Lunatic Asylums* 1857, Part 1, Report, pp.33–9 and Appendix 1, p.126.

18. For a history of St. Patrick's Hospital, see Elizabeth Malcolm, *Swift's Hospital* (Dublin: Gill and Macmillan, 1989).

19. See William Parry-Jones, *The Trade in Lunacy* (London: Routledge and Kegan Paul, 1972); Inquiry on Lunatic Asylums 1857, Part 1, Appendix 1, p.12.

20. M. Finnane, 'Irish psychiatry, Part 1: The formation of a profession', pp.306–13, in G.E. Berrios and H. Freeman (eds), *150 Years of British Psychiatry 1841–1991* (London: Gaskell, 1991); David Healy, 'Irish psychiatry, part 2: Use of the Medico-Psychological Association by its Irish members – plus ca change!', pp.314–20, in Berrios and Freeman, *150 Years of British Psychiatry*.

21. See one example at the Central Criminal Asylum, Dundrum, in Pauline M. Prior, *Madness and Murder: Gender, Crime and Mental Disorder in Nineteenth-Century Ireland* (Dublin: Irish Academic Press, 2008), pp.69–75.

22. Department of Health, *The Psychiatric Services – Planning for the Future* (Dublin: Stationery Office, 1984), p.xi.

23. Department of Health and Children, *A Vision for Change – Report of the Expert Group on Mental Health Policy* (Dublin: Stationery Office, 2006), p.54.

24. Department of Health and Children, *A Vision for Change*, Table 6.1, p.55.

25. Finnane, *Insanity and the Insane*; Malcolm, *Swift's Hospital*; Kelly, B.D. 'Structural Violence and Schizophrenia', *Social Science and Medicine*, 61 (2005), pp.721–30. Kelly, B.D. 'The Power Gap: Freedom, Power and Mental Illness', *Social Science and Medicine*, 63 (2006), pp.2118–28: Prior, *Madness and Murder*; Joseph Robins, *Fools and Mad: A History of the Insane in Ireland* (Dublin: Institute of Public Administration, 1986): Williamson, 'The beginnings of state care'.

26. E. Goffman, *Asylums: Essays on the Social Situation of Mental Patients and other Inmates* (Chicago: Doubleday, 1961).

27. D. Wright, 'Getting out of the Asylum: Understanding the Confinement of the Insane in the Nineteenth Century', *Social History of Medicine*, 10:1 (1997), p.150.

28. Miles Fairburn, *The Ideal Society and its Enemies: The Foundations of Modern New Zealand Society, 1850–1900* (Auckland: Auckland University Press, 1989), p.94.

29. L.A. Clarkson and E. Margaret Crawford, *Feast and Famine: A History of Food and Nutrition in Ireland 1500–1920* (Oxford: Oxford University Press, 2001).

PART ONE
TWENTIETH CENTURY

2

The Red Flag Over the Asylum: The Monaghan Asylum Soviet of 1919

Anton McCabe and Ciaran Mulholland

They are dismissed from service in the asylum unless they at once withdraw from the Society.
(Resolution passed by meeting of the Irish Division of the Medico-Psychological Association, on newly formed Asylum Attendants of Ireland Trades Union, 7 May 1896. Reported in *Journal of Mental Science*, July 1896, pp.600–601).

We did set up a Soviet Committee there, we hoisted the Red Flag, we controlled the service and no community interest suffered.
(Peadar O'Donnell, on the Monaghan Asylum Strike, *Derry Journal*, 28 February 1919).

INTRODUCTION

In the late nineteenth century, medical superintendents exercised almost total control over the day-to-day lives of both patients and staff.[1] The prevalent attitudes of the physicians of the time are well illustrated in the pages of the *Journal of Mental Science* (now the *British Journal of Psychiatry*), the periodical of the Medico-Psychological Association (MPA). In November 1890, the Scottish meeting of the MPA discussed the question of discipline amongst asylum employees. The President, Dr. Yellowlees, argued that 'as a matter of asylum discipline, one ought often to dismiss instantly'.[2] Dr. Yellowlees successfully inserted a new clause into the 'Declaration', signed by new employees at the time, allowing super-intendents to dismiss staff 'upon such evidence or information as may seem to the Medical Superintendent to be sufficient'. In order to obtain employment, potential attendants had to

...promise to obey the Rules of the Institution, to faithfully execute the orders that may be given by my Superior Officers and to perform any duty assigned to me, although not of the kind for which I am chiefly engaged (and to) acknowledge the right of the Medical Superintendent to discharge me without warning for acts of harshness or violence to Patients, intemperance, immoral conduct, or disobedience to orders.[3]

There was no question of employee rights and trade union membership was anathema. It would take thirty years of struggle to establish effective trade unionism in the asylums. The 'Declaration' illustrates the lowly position of attendants in 1890, but also gives some clues as to why the attendants revolted again and again until successful, often displaying great bitterness towards the medical men who sought to control their lives.

MANAGEMENT OF THE IRISH ASYLUMS

By the early part of the twentieth century, asylums in Ireland were managed by local management committees appointed by county councils under the 1898 Local Government (Ireland) Act.[4] The committees were dominated by the clergy, farmers, shop-keepers and publicans. Also, in 1898, the financing of the asylums was altered, so that an upper limit was set on the funds available from central government. The effect of this change was increasing financial stringency over the following years. At one Irish asylum, the Richmond, for example, the annual cost per patient increased from £25 16s 5d in 1913–1914 to £58 13s 2d in 1919–1920. The capitation grant paid by central government came to only £10 per year. The increased costs were thus borne by the rate payers. The rules meant that even this low level central grant was not paid in full if local taxation fell short. At the Richmond the full grant was not paid from 1910–1911 onwards for this reason.[5]

Management committees responded to these financial pressures by adopting a parsimonious attitude towards their employees. In 1911, a meeting of the Donegal Asylum Committee unanimously opposed a Bill before parliament which sought to restrict the hours of duties of attendants to sixty per week, to pay overtime after sixty hours, and to award a pension after twenty-five years' service.[6] One member, Monsignor McGlynn, argued that the proposals 'would be grievously oppressive of the ratepayers and they would, moreover, endanger the proper discipline among asylum attendants. This poor country has suffered quite enough already through being needlessly compelled to keep house up to the standard or fancy of its rich neighbour.'

Agreeing, Father Cannon, parish priest for Carrick, said, 'this would place another very heavy strain on the already overburdened ratepayers of Ireland ... the public bodies of Donegal should be up and doing in opposition to the Bill. The provision about pensions was equally dangerous and should be opposed with equal vehemence.'

THE ASYLUM ATTENDANTS

By the late nineteenth century, considerable numbers were employed in the asylums. There were '20,000' or more in Britain[7] and over 700 in Ireland.[8] The heavy, dangerous work and the poor pay meant that there were always problems with recruitment. Height and strength were for many years the only essential requirements for the selection of new staff. In the 1890s, wages in Irish asylums varied between one third and one half of those in British asylums. In Derry in 1910, the annual wages of male attendants was £20 to £25 and females received £12 a year, though food, accommodation and uniforms were also provided. Staffing levels were very low – Sligo was typical, with a ratio of one male attendant to seventeen patients and one female attendant to fifteen patients. The hours were long, with little time off – the average weekly hours were 82.5 for day attendants and 75 for night attendants. In the Central Criminal Lunatic Asylum in Dundrum, staff never had a clear day off except when on leave.[9]

Committees were very reluctant to pay pensions, seeing them as an 'unwarranted imposition' on the tax payer and 'encouraging improvidence'.[10] Staff turnover was high, though unemployment, particularly in rural areas, meant that employees tended to stay in post for longer than was typical in England. However, many staff only stayed long enough to earn the sum necessary for emigration. The majority of attendants were untrained, though in 1894 the Richmond Asylum instituted training, leading towards the examination for the certificate in mental nursing of the Medico-Psychological Association (MPA).[11] In 1896, the asylum inspectors succeeded in gaining government approval for a scheme which awarded staff an extra £2 a year if they passed the MPA examination. The Richmond Board of Governors agreed to a rise of £1 only.[12]

Some medical superintendents recognised that times were changing. In his Presidential Address to the MPA in 1893, J. Murray

Lindsay referred to 'the eight hours' labour wave, which is rolling along' and which would 'surround asylum attendants, where long hours on duty, fourteen hours, from 6.00 am to 8.00 pm, have often been the subject of remarks and pity by asylum medical officers'.[13] He doubted, however, whether the ratepayer would be prepared to shoulder the extra costs that a reduction in hours would necessitate. Whereas Dr. P. W. MacDonald did not believe 'that the nurses and attendants in the asylums of this country wish for an "eight hour day", nor do I believe that there is any general dissatisfaction with the present rate of wages and leave of absence'.[14] He did accept that there was restlessness amongst staff concerning pensions and that 'the spirit of discontent and restlessness is on the increase.'[15]

THE NATIONAL UNION OF ASYLUM ATTENDANTS IN IRELAND

In April 1896, the first attempt at forming a union for Irish asylum attendants occurred, when the National Union of Asylum Attendants in Ireland was formed by staff at the Richmond Asylum.[16] The Board of Governors and the Medical Superintendent, Dr. Conolly Norman, dealt swiftly with what they saw as a threat to their primacy. The *Journal of Mental Science* dealt with the issue at some length in a report of a meeting of the Irish Division of the MPA.

> Dr. Norman said he thought he was justified in quoting to the Association the published rules of the Society or Trades Union referred to. He quoted from a printed copy such as were on sale. The persons who had framed this curious document seemed to think a combination of attendants had the power of taking from the Governors of Asylums the right of managing the institutions which was committed to them by Act of Parliament. Continuing, Dr. Norman said these rules which he had laid before them simply expressed a determination to endeavour to specially create, in this particular case of atten-dants, a Trades Union, the principal end of which, as of all such organisations, was the perfecting of the ordinary Trades Union weapon – the weapon of strike. He did not anticipate any danger so far as his own asylum was concerned. In the Richmond Asylum the decisive and prompt action of the Board had, as they would gather from the newspaper report, put a stop to this business, but it might possibly break out in other asylums, and may under other circumstances, and in the hands of a Board less firm and determined, give a good deal of trouble.

It occurred to him that this was a matter which, considering the fact that the attendants of Irish Asylums are virtually civil servants, are persons appointed and dismissed under the regulations of an Act of Parliament, and eligible for pension after service for a comparatively brief time, should be taken into serious consideration by the Executive when it is proposed to make rules and regulations for the various District Asylums in Ireland.[17]

An editorial in the *Journal of Mental Science* backed the Irish Division of the MPA.

The attempt to form a trades union of attendants in Ireland has been quashed with the firmness and promptitude that the occasions demanded. A trades union is as impossible in an asylum as in the army or navy. Discipline would be impossible, and no confidence could be placed on a staff which would at any moment be paralysed by the action of an irresponsible and often tyrannously autocratic trades union committee. The Report of the last meeting of the Irish Division in "Notes and News" forms a permanent record (if any were needed) of the right method of dealing with such attempts at insubordination.[18]

The Honorary Secretary of the union protested at Dr. Norman's attitude in a letter in the Daily Independent[19] and stated that 'the very Head of the asylum, and their medical superintendent, is a member of one of the closest trade unions that could be found in the country'. The sacking of two attendants who refused to leave the union was raised in the House of Commons by a Mr. Field. He asked the Chief Secretary whether he was aware that James Duffy and Frederick Brunton had been dismissed by the Richmond Asylum on 6 May and asked for an enquiry. The Chief Secretary refused the request, stating that 'The appointment and dismissal of asylum attendants devolve by law upon the Board of Governors alone.'[20] In August 1900, two attendants at the Portrane auxillary asylum (built to relieve overcrowding at the Richmond) led another revolt.[21] James Brennan called a meeting to complain about the poor standard of food provided for the attendants and eighteen attendants signed a letter of complaint to Dr. Norman. Once again Norman took strong action. Brennan backed down in the face of intimidation but Denis O'Donoghue, a charge attendant, stood firm. Both men were sacked, a third attendant was reduced from second to third class and all the signatories were forced to apologise for their 'gross and utterly uncalled for statements'.

THE ASYLUM WORKERS' ASSOCIATION

In 1895, the Asylum Workers' Association (AWA) was formed in Britain by the MPA. In Adam's words it 'clearly came into being at the drop of a hat', and its inception coincided with the decision of the Royal British Nurses Association (RBNA) not to recruit in the asylums.[22] The AWA began recruiting in Ireland in 1898 and by 1909, it had nearly 300 members drawn from eleven asylums.[23] The establishment of the AWA was a conscious attempt to prevent the development of genuine trade unions. In 1911, its Honorary Secretary went out of his way to deny that it was a trade union, stating in a letter to the Irish Times that there was 'no taint of trade unionism' in the constitution of the Association.[24]

The AWA outlined its objectives, which owed much to the RBNA, in the first issue of its journal, *Asylum News*:

1. To improve generally the status of asylum nurses and attendants.
2. To secure the sympathy and co-operation of all those interested in institutional work and efforts.
3. To provide a home of rest and nursing for those engaged in asylum work.[25]

The historian of the AWA states that 'its contributions and government were entirely paternal' and that its annual meetings 'consisted largely of uplifting speeches by distinguished Honorary Vice-Presidents; no mental nurse ever seems to have spoken and it is doubtful if any attended'.[26] According to Adams, the AWA had 5680 members by 1904.[27] Walk does credit the AWA with a genuine desire to 'improve the professional status of the mental nurse' and remarked on its campaigns to improve pensions and to ensure that attendants were covered by the proposed state registration scheme for nurses.[28] In 1909, the Asylum Officer's Superannuation Act guaranteed pensions to certain long-standing staff. However, as many attendants already had a non-contributory pension and, thus, were actually worst off, a wave of resignations from the AWA followed as a result of the change.[29]

The AWA was always open to 'the charge that the Association did not represent the interests of the class of employees it pretended to serve'.[30] The AWA folded at an extraordinary general meeting on 15 October 1919. With the growth of genuine trade unionism the reason for its existence had disappeared. According to Adams

It was clearly the asylum attendants who had finally decided that the fiction of a common basis of interest between Doctors and Attendants in the hospital service was no longer tenable as a basis for an organization. But they were forced to this conclusion by wider social and political events in which the irreconcilable nature of class interests was manifesting itself.[31]

THE NATIONAL ASYLUM WORKERS' UNION OF GREAT BRITAIN AND IRELAND

The National Asylum Workers' Union of Great Britain and Ireland (NAWU) was founded at a meeting in the Mason's Arms Hotel in Manchester on 9 July 1910.[32] The Asylum Officer's Superannuation Act, which took compulsory deductions from already small pay packets, acted as a final spur to already dissatisfied staff. The drive towards 'education' when all other issues were neglected was a cause of resentment. The NAWU founding manifesto stated 'Our minds are not improved, because the conditions of our labour are such that they shut us off from the wider range of Humanity and of books ... apart from any true education, we cannot attain to any real moral greatness.'[33] Its founding objectives were

1. To improve generally the conditions of asylum workers.
2. To reduce the hours of labour by Act of Parliament.
3. To abolish the age limit of the Pensions Act.
4. To provide allowance for the protection of victimised members of the union.
5. Generally to regulate relations between employers and employees.[34]

For thousands of nurses and attendants, the AWA had had its day and genuine trade unionism was required. A manifesto, written by the socialist Reverend Samuel Proudfoot, was circulated to 30,000 workers seeking recruits for the NAWU. Within months, the new union had 2000 members.[35] It was much easier to recruit than it was to achieve recognition from asylum boards. In most places this did not happen until 1919. In the meantime, victimisation of union activists was common, and medical superintendents were the object of much bitterness. A letter in the NAWU magazine in December 1912 declared: 'You have imposed on the staff a fear and subservience to which you have no earthly right, and conditions of life which no employer of labour would dare to impose upon those whom he paid.' The bitter writer continued 'asylum psychiatrists are anyway not among the highest of the calling, indeed, they could not hold down a proper position as a family doctor does'.[36]

Eventually accumulated tension exploded to the surface in a series of strikes. The first strike in an English asylum occurred on 14 May 1913, when 35 men at Rainhill Asylum refused to work when porridge was substituted for meat at breakfast.[37] The strikers were forced to apologise to keep their jobs. A more extensive and organised strike took place on 4/5 September 1918, when 429 staff went on strike at Winnington, 200 at Prestwick and a smaller number at Winwick.[38] The aims of the strike were not achieved, but the union grew in strength as a consequence of its action, gaining 2000 new members over the next few months.[39]

The NAWU recruited well in Ireland and by 1912 it had branches in Cork, Dublin, Kilkenny, Killarney, Limerick, Portrane and Waterford. Despite this, the position of attendants did not improve significantly. During the 1914–1918 War, there was no increase in pay despite huge increases in living costs. According to the Voice of Labour in December 1917, the cost of living had risen 106 per cent since the start of the war. It stated that 'sugar, tea, butter, margarine and milk are now practically unprocurable at any price. Bread, potatoes and meat are so high in price as to be almost beyond the reach of the average worker.'[40] War-time conditions radicalised working people. Relatively full employment and the war-time boom in production put workers in a strong bargaining position. Trade Union membership mushroomed, increasing by 2.5 times in the years 1916 to 1918.[41] The most militant union, the Irish Transport and General Workers' Union (ITGWU), had the biggest growth. In the five years from 1915 to 1920, its membership increased from 5,000 to 120,000. The Irish Labour Party and Trade Union Congress supported the Bolshevik Revolution and stood on the left of the European Socialist Parties. In November 1918, the Voice of Labour declared: 'Thanks be to God that we have lived to see this day. The Red Flag of the Worker's Republic is flying over three-quarters of the continent of Europe.'[42] Against this background of discontent, increasing working-class militancy and a certain momentum in favour of the establishment of Irish based unions, representatives from the majority of Irish asylums convened in the Trades Hall in Dublin and formed the Irish Asylum Workers Union (IAWU) in October 1917.[43] The new union soon became involved in a series of disputes. The most significant of these occurred in Monaghan. This dispute is the focus of this chapter. As a result of the impact of these actions, the NAWU was quickly eclipsed by the IAWU.

THE FIRST MONAGHAN STRIKE

The Monaghan Asylum was built in 1869. Originally, it had 340 beds but by 1904 this number had increased to 673.[44] Despite this increase, it remained dangerously over-crowded. Between 1871 and 1911 there was a 202 per cent increase in the first admission rates to the asylum.[45] One result of the overcrowding was that in 1911, 93.4 per cent of male admissions and 97.5 per cent of female admissions were 'dangerous lunatic' committals. The male figure is only surpassed by two other Irish asylums and the female figure is higher than in any other Irish asylum at the time.[46]

In March 1918, 96 attendants at the Monaghan Asylum went on strike, demanding higher pay and union recognition. They picketed the asylum and chased a retired nurse and a woman from Belfast who arrived with the resident medical superintendent and who tried to cross the picket line. Dr. McKenna, Bishop of Clogher and Chairman of the Asylum Committee, stated bluntly before the strike, that under no circumstances would it be just or lawful for the attendants to go on strike and that the Committee could not approve of the union. During the strike the Asylum Committee passed a resolution sacking all the attendants and ordering them to leave the asylum. Despite these threats, only one union member went into work. The strike lasted for one week and ended when the Asylum Committee conceded a war bonus of four shillings and, significantly, union recognition. The strikers accepted these concessions somewhat reluctantly, as all of their demands had not been met. Nevertheless, the new union had made its mark.[47]

In September 1918, the attendants threatened to strike again unless they were paid £1.00 over the pre-war rate and granted a 56-hour week.[48] A few weeks later, a temporary attendant was dismissed for taking part in the March strike.[49] In November, the Asylum Committee met and rejected the attendants' application.[50] Instead, the Committee recommended that

> ... the attendants and nurses get off duty and be allowed out on a one hour pass one day every alternate week, provided the resident medical superintendent finds this can be done without interfering with the proper and effective running of the asylum.[51]

It went on, however, to 'warn the staff that, if another strike takes place and the lives of patients are imperiled … they will be liable to have their services dispensed with'. The committee also refused to pay attendants and nurses for the week of the March strike.[52]

PEADAR O'DONNELL ARRIVES

In December 1918, the Asylum Workers' Union in Monaghan invited Peadar O'Donnell to come down from Derry to negotiate on their behalf, as they had no full-time officials of their own.[53] O'Donnell was one of the most significant figures on the Irish left in the twentieth century. He was born on 22 February 1893, in the townland of Meenmore, about two miles outside Dungloe in Donegal.[54] He was an organiser for the Irish Transport and General Workers' Union from September 1918 to December 1920. Prior to that, he had been a prominent activist in the Irish National Teachers' Organisation (INTO) and had been teaching on Arranmore Island off Donegal. O'Donnell started with the ITGWU on 13 September.[55] He started in style. He spoke in the City Hall, Armagh, on 2 October and in Roscommon on 4 October.[56] He received some training in Liberty Hall, the ITGWU's headquarters in Dublin, and spent a short time in the west of Ireland after John Lynch, the main organiser based in Sligo, was jailed.

Before Christmas 1918, O'Donnell began organising in Ulster, living his life on the road. Where exactly he was based initially is uncertain, though his main activity was in Counties Monaghan and Cavan. He lived with the Emerson family at North Road, Monaghan town, between January 1919 and February 1920.[57] The *Voice of Labour* some-times referred to him as 'Monaghan Peter'.[58] The branch secretary of the union in Monaghan Asylum was John Lawless, the asylum engineer, and he and O'Donnell appeared at a meeting of the Asylum Committee held in Cavan on 21 December 1918. Their appeal on behalf of the workers for an increase in wages was refused. On 18 January 1919, a further IAWU deputation, including O'Donnell, again applied to the Committee.[59] In attendance for the Committee were Dr. McKenna, Thomas Toal JP, Owen Hughes JP and Dr. Conlon, the resident medical superintendent. The Committee members were far from sympathetic and their tone was somewhat patronising. McKenna, when addressing the workers' grievances, stated 'we have been considering them so long that I am tired of the whole thing.' Dr. Conlon argued that the staff had little cause for complaint. He went on 'they work twelve hours a day for seven days, but they get off every 13th day and every 4th Sunday from 10 o'clock.' Thomas Toal demanded of O'Donnell 'are you giving credit for that?' Toal went on to state that the annual wage of the attendants was sufficient at £60–£70 per year. O'Donnell referred to 'the likelihood of a strike' and the Committee was warned that 'a series of public meetings had been organized by the Workers Union to be held in Monaghan and Cavan to bring before the public the position of the attendants … A petition has been signed throughout the two counties.'[60]

THE OCCUPATION BEGINS

According to the *Anglo-Celt*, a large meeting of attendants was held on 24 January and a decision was made to take action.

> On Thursday evening a hurriedly convened meeting of the attendants and nurses was held and they decided to go on strike to enforce their full demands. They finished their work, saw the patients to bed and then went off duty. A number of attendants and nurses remained in the wards under the direction of the strike committee in order to see that the patients did no harm … Relief parties were sent in with similar duties.[61]

The occupation was to last twelve days in total and 200 attendants were involved. By one account, 'The women were even more determined that the men…'[62] The *Northern Standard* reported:

> Most of the attendants were on strike yesterday morning … to try and enforce the demand for a further increase in wages and equal terms for male and female worker a… Mr. O'Donnell, the representative of the Asylum Workers' Union, remains in town and we understand Mr. McKeag, representing the General Workers' Union, is also in town. The question of a general strike of the workers, in sympathy with the asylum attendants, had been mooted but so far there is no indication of such a development taking place.[63]

On the 25 January, the day after the occupation began, the Asylum Committee (Thomas Toal in the Chair, with Owen Hughes JP and John Smith JP) again met and again received a deputation, this time consisting of O'Donnell, Lawless, four male and four female attendants.[64] The names of the attendants who participated in the

Monaghan events are mostly lost to history, but we know from the son of one of those involved that two other prominent activists were Mark Maxwell and Willie Haire.[65] The deputation put forward five basic demands: a 56-hour week with time and a half for overtime, liberty for the married attendants to leave the asylum after work, an all-round increase of £1 on pre-war rates, skilled workers to get the going rate for their particular craft, and equality of treatment for female staff.[66] The deputation stated that the working hours in ten asylums were less than in Monaghan (including in the geographically closest asylums, Omagh, Letterkenny, Derry and Armagh). O'Donnell argued in support of equal pay for women, a very radical demand for 1919. As he stated, 'woman attendants could spend money as easily as the men; certainly their work was the same.' The Committee offered a number of concessions. A 56-hour week was granted, but only by including the annual holidays into the accounting. Married attendants were to be allowed to leave the asylum after their day's work. Skilled men would receive the rate for their craft. Compulsory over-time would be abolished after 7 February 1919. The War Bonus was refused, however, and a lower increase was offered to female attendants than male. Negotiations broke down on this point. O'Donnell insisted that the female attendants' increase be the same as that of the married men. He went on to say that 'as the question of the female workers had not been settled, nothing was settled.' He stated bluntly 'I have sufficient power to enforce anything I want to enforce … The time is coming when we will not have to spend all this time in getting our demands.'[67]

With no agreement, the occupation continued. The headline of the *Anglo-Celt* on 1 February 1919 read 'Strike at Monaghan Asylum – Red Flag over the Building'.[68] The paper went on to inform its readers that 'The red flag is over Monaghan Asylum where the officials on strike have barricaded themselves in. A large force of police has been on the scene.' The *Voice of Labour* welcomed the strike with the headline: 'The Stay-in Strike – New Laurels for Transport Union'. It continued

> The development of a new tactic in labour struggle is to be credited to the Monaghan Asylum Workers' Union … failing to bring the Monaghan Asylum Committee to reason, the men decided that public safety would be endangered if they went on strike by leaving the building. They inaugurated the stay-in strike instead. The Red Flag was hoisted on the asylum and the staff discharged its ordinary duties, reorganising them to give more leisure to themselves. Efficiency was increased.[69]

O'Donnell ensured the patients were well looked after and that staff discipline was maintained. He suspended the matron for 'insubordination' and made a new appointment. He also 'fined' two of the staff – one for not being on duty at the proper time and the other for extravagance in the use of gas. A man who was spreading defeatism was locked in a padded cell.[70] During the dispute there were no deaths in the institution and no report of any patients coming to harm.[71] O'Donnell announced that a 48-hour week was being introduced in the Asylum, that extra staff were thus required, and that applicants should apply to him. On the Sunday of the strike, all patients who could attend Divine Service were taken to the church in the grounds by the strikers. Reporters were allowed into the building after questioning. O'Donnell told the reporters 'I look to it that we are fighting the last fight insofar as strikes in lunatic asylums are concerned.'[72]

UNDER POLICE SIEGE

From the outset, the authorities were determined to take a tough line. One hundred and twenty-five police were brought in by train to besiege the building, though there was a remarkable absence of hostile feeling between the police and the strikers. Dances were held and games of football were played involving police and strikers.[73] It was also rumoured that strikers swapped uniforms with members of the Royal Irish Constabulary (RIC) so that they could leave the asylum during the strike.[74] The power of O'Donnell was reflected in the fact that the password to gain entry to the asylum was 'O'Donnell Abu' – a mark of respect for the strike leader.[75] It would be untrue to say that the RIC were happy with their lot. According to one report, they 'complained bitterly about their beds of straw and the general lack of accommodation'.[76]

On Tuesday, 28 January, a rumour went around that the military police were going to enter the building. The strikers appeared to have advance warning of a possible assault on the building, perhaps from the police themselves. Strikers swapped clothes with patients, according to one newspaper report: 'the attendants were very active and ready for attack. Many of them were dressed up in patients' uniforms and it was quite impossible to distinguish them from patients.'[77] The *Anglo-Celt* also reported

> On Wednesday evening it was discovered that the attendants and nurses had profited by the warning and had taken possession of

the main block of buildings, cutting off outlying portions of the institution and all the doors and passages had been blocked and barricaded, windows had been sealed up and a guard had been placed at each main door. Dr. Kevin P. Neary, Assistant Medical Officer, and Miss Shaw, Matron, were made prisoners in order that the inmates, who were closed in with the strikers, might be attended to. The Red Flag was hoisted over the building.[78]

The store-keeper, believing that the strikers were going to rush the stores, gave the keys to the police. The *Northern Standard* stated that 'Conlon went personally and opened the store, no attempt being made by the strikers to interfere with him or carry out the threat to steal the store provisions.'[79] The strikers did attempt to arm themselves. 'One of the carts delivering goods at the stores was commandeered and brought a load of shovels, spades and pitchforks from the farmyard.'[80] Many of the strikers feared death or serious injury and consequently sought the help of their clergy. 'On Wednesday morning, a priest heard the confessions of the Catholic strikers', and the clergy of other dominations were also present.'[81] It was noticeable during the strike that differences between the Catholic and Protestant staff were of no importance. On Friday 30 January, Dr. Conlon, the medical superintendent, sacked all the strikers (in consultation with two members of the Asylum Committee and H. Murphy, the solicitor to the county council) and demanded that they leave the premises. The following day, he 'went to the main buildings and delivered the letters addressed to each striker through a small pane of glass, but the bundle was promptly picked up and thrown out in the doctor's presence'.[82]

'COMPLETE VICTORY'

Violence was avoided and negotiations commenced, with the help of a Father McNamee, later Bishop of Ardagh, as an intermediary. McNamee later related what happened when he entered the asylum. An old woman came hobbling up to him, with a red handkerchief on her head, stood beside him, pulled up her skirt, showed him a pair of trousers and said 'Excuse me Father. It was Peadar O'Donnell.'[83]

The strike ended in victory for the IAWU. There was a promise of no victimisation. A 56-hour week was agreed and permission for married attendants to leave the premises after work was granted. Women achieved the same pay rise as men. The Asylum Committee also agreed to press for a national meeting of asylum committees to establish a General Committee of Asylums and to set a national scale of pay, hours and conditions. If these terms were not met within twelve months, all matters were to be settled by a binding Court of Arbitration, consisting of one person appointed by the workers, one by the committee and one umpire. According to the *Voice of Labour* 'Complete victory has been won.'[84] The strikers returned to work on Tuesday 4 February. On the previous night a Victory Dance was held in one of the large dining halls.

> A large crowd was present from the town. Police, strikers, some inmates and outsiders including Sinn Feiners, Nationalists and Unionists, all were gathered together and enjoyed a good night's dancing.[85]

The Asylum Committee members did not take their defeat well. At a meeting on 15 February, a Mr. Harmon stated that he 'would have voted for the dismissal of the staff. If they ever made a demand for a further increase, get rid of them all together.' A Mr. Reilly backed his hard line, saying: 'Call in the special staff; get in police and soldiers and keep them there until the new staff are installed.' Harman continued, 'they will put the farmers of the county out of their homes.'[86]

The strike had repercussions throughout Ireland and Britain. It shook the asylum establishment and the ruling class in general. Representatives of the local 'respectable' society rallied against the strikers. The *Northern Standard* attacked the asylum workers in an editorial after the strike stating 'It was not a strike in the ordinary sense of the term – it was a revolt against the authority of the Joint Committee and the Resident Medical Superintendent.'[87] O'Donnell '… seems to have taken the higher staff by surprise. He entered the building without any authority, arrogated himself to the position of "boss of the show" and directed affairs as if he had been clothed with full powers…'[88] The Monaghan Branch of the Ulster Farmers' Union called for the dismissal of the strikers.[89] The local rural district council, dominated by Nationalists, passed a motion rejecting the demands of the strikers.[90] A number of local prominent citizens discussed holding a public meeting to back the Asylum Committee.[91] At the same time as the strike, Belfast was paralysed by a strike of engineering workers and controlled by a strike committee, and Europe was convulsed by revolutionary upheavals.[92] The authorities were fearful of strikes spreading throughout the country. When the red flag was raised over the building, the *Dundalk Democrat* informed its readers 'We know what it has stood for – in Paris, in Russia, in Berlin two weeks ago.'[93] It was not just locally that the strike made news. It was raised in the House of Commons, by Major Newman, the Unionist MP for Enfield. He stated that the workers had 'established a local Soviet or Committee' and alleged that they had help from the patients to do so.[94] The MPA complained grumpily about the advent of successful trade unionism. One speaker at a special meeting called to discuss events, drew laughter when he joked that 'the less wages you pay, the better nurse you get'.[95]

The Monaghan events established a new method of struggle for the Irish labour movement. Prior to the Monaghan Soviet, there had been only one other workplace seizure, this being the fairly small scale occupation of a tailor's workshop at York Street, Dublin in November 1918.[96] After Monaghan there were at least a further hundred occupations in the years to 1923, with eighty in 1922 alone.[97] Occupying and running a mill, creamery or factory, or even an entire city, under workers control, became a commonplace weapon for militant trade unionists. Peadar O'Donnell and the Monaghan Asylum staff were instrumental in establishing this new method of struggle. In April 1919, the whole city of Limerick was run as a Soviet. A workers' government regulated prices, distributed food and even printed its own money. Sections of the Belfast press dubbed the 1919 Belfast engineering strike 'The Belfast Soviet'. Labour leader, Cathal O'Shannon, stated that 'the soviet was the only one that would confer freedom in Ireland' and called on the English working class to set up an 'English Soviet Republic'.[98]

The strike broke through a number of previous barriers. In particular, the fact that woman achieved the same rise in pay as men was highly significant as equal pay was not achieved in many industries until the 1970s. It was also a major breakthrough that married men were allowed to leave the asylum after work. The strike was watched keenly by staff all over Ireland. The *Dundalk Democrat* reported that message of support had been sent from Letterkenny and Clare Asylums.[99] The IAWU grew rapidly on the back of its militant and successful actions. The new union affiliated to the Irish Labour Party and Trade Union Congress in 1918 and registered as a union in 1920. It had 2122 members by that year.[100] The first Monaghan strike in 1918 was followed by strikes in Letterkenny[101] and Armagh[102] in March 1918, Limerick[103] in August 1918, Clare[104] in September 1918 and Portlaoise[105] in November 1918 and strikes spread through other asylums after the Monaghan seizure. In the most significant, in June 1919, attendants in Clonmel Asylum went on strike for thirteen weeks, though other strikes were settled more quickly.[106] A one-week strike in Limerick in 1919 was 'amicably settled' by the concession of higher wages and the introduction of a 56-hour week.[107]

According to Robins, 'there is no doubt that the asylum staff in general benefited considerably during these years from the pressures of their union.'[108] The negotiators in Monaghan were aware of the importance of a significant victory in one asylum for all attendants, and were keen to see national rates and conditions established. Their intent was that what they had won in Monaghan could be achieved for all asylum staff. A conference of Irish asylums was finally held on 5 May 1921 at the Richmond Asylum, Dublin, at which the issues of national rates of pay and national conditions were discussed.[109] Representatives from Ballinasloe, Clonmel, Ennis, Enniscorthy, Kilkenny, Limerick, Maryborough, Richmond and Sligo attended. Pay was tied to training in the discussions. It was suggested that a national pay rate be adopted and that all staff should obtain the MPA certificate of proficiency as a condition of permanent employment.

Another effect of the Monaghan events was to give a huge impetus to trade union recruitment all over south Ulster. In Monaghan itself during the strike, a large crowd had gathered at the asylum gates shouting 'Up the Strikers'.[110] The Workers' Union in the town met to discuss organising strike action throughout the town if the strike was not settled.[111] The Irish Transport and General Workers' Union recruited workers of all political and religious persuasions in the area.[112] Nurses and white-collar groups, like the officials of the Clones Poor Law Union (or workhouse) in County Monaghan, previously unorganised, began to join unions.[113] The Poor Law Guardians reacted by banning O'Donnell from the workhouse.[114] The Chair, Hugh Gordon, stated 'Mr. O'Donnell, as you are aware, is out for dirty work and is out for trouble...'[115] O'Donnell was able to tell a meeting in Clones, that in the four months since he had become an organiser, he had been involved in forty-eight wage movements and three strikes.[116] According to the *Voice of Labour*, he had 'blazed a trail of glory clean across Ulster'.[117] Soon after the seizure of Monaghan Asylum O'Donnell led an equally historic strike at Caledon Mill.[118] The increase in trade union militancy had an impact on the January 1920 local elections. In nearby Cavan, seven Labour councilors were elected, making Labour the largest single party. Importantly, in a time much more chauvinist than now, two of the Cavan candidates were women and Mary Brady became the first woman Labour councilor elected in Ireland.[119] Labour in Monaghan also made a breakthrough, winning three seats[120] and one Labour councillor was elected to the Clones Urban District Council.[121] The *Northern Standard* speculated that 'the memorable strike of the Asylum Workers' was an important factor in Labour's success.[122]

'THERE WILL BE ANOTHER DAY'

What was the role of Peadar O'Donnell in these events and in the history of Irish asylums? O'Donnell never worked in an asylum. Yet, in leading and inspiring the Monaghan attendants he impacted on life in the asylum system like few others. He, and the ordinary attendants, who dared to stand up, struck the shackles from the attendants just as Pinel had done for his patients a century earlier. O'Donnell was to remain an important figure on the Irish left for half a century.[123] The Monaghan Soviet and the strike wave of 1918–19 changed the face of the asylum system forever. The attendants won not just improved pay and conditions but also wrested respect and the right to be listened to from very reluctant management committees. These gains were not all sustained in the years of economic down-turn from 1922 onwards. The defeat of the union after a bitter and violent strike in Letterkenny in 1924 was the most important turning point.[124] The membership of the IAWU (known as the Irish Mental Hospital Workers Union from 1922) fell to 1235 in 1925 and to 909 in 1926 as the labour movement generally went on the retreat. In 1926 the union was mostly taken into amalgamation by the Irish Transport and General Workers' Union.[125]

Despite the setbacks, a marker had been laid down. The title of O'Donnell's account of these times proclaims *'There Will Be Another Day'*. Toeholds were maintained and re-organising began in the 1930s, but it would be the 1950s before trade unionism became firmly implanted in Irish asylums. It was not until 1955, when most mental hospital staff joined the ITGWU, that parity of conditions between different hospitals was finally achieved.[126] It was not easy to organise trade unions, in asylums or elsewhere, in those early days. In O'Donnell's own words 'It was very slow and plodding work.'[127]

> This I learned the hard way, from mistakes made organising new trade union branches in small towns. You held a good

meeting, enrolled members and went on your way. You came back to find the branch had fallen apart. Eventually you met one man at lunch hour, called on another man at his home, sat with a group of two or three. You rested your branch on firm men. That branch grew.[128]

NOTES

1. The authors would like to acknowledge the assistance of Michael Walker, Greater London UNISON, Theresa Moriarty of the Irish Labour History Museum in Dublin and Ciaran Crossey of the Linenhall Library, Belfast.
2. *Journal of Mental Science*, January 1891, pp.196–9.
3. Ibid.
4. See J.C. Beckett, *The Making of Modern Ireland, 1603–1923* (London: Faber & Faber, 2008).
5. J. Reynolds, *Grangegorman: Psychiatric Care in Dublin since 1815* (Dublin: Institute of Public Adminstration, 1992), p.219.
6. *Derry People*, 15 July 1911.
7. *Journal of Mental Science*, April 1896, p.467.
8. *Journal of Mental Science*, October 1896, p.908.
9. M. Finnane, *Insanity and the Insane in Post-Famine Ireland* (London: Croom Helm, 1981), p.181.
10. Ibid.
11. Reynolds, *Grangegorman*, p.189.
12. Ibid.
13. *Journal of Mental Science*, October 1893, p.478.
14. *Journal of Mental Science*, July 1896, p.633.
15. Ibid.
16. *Journal of Mental Science*, August 1896, pp.656–8.
17. Ibid.
18. *Journal of Mental Science*, July 1896, pp.600–1.
19. *Daily Independent*, 15 May 1896.
20. *Hansard*, HC Debates, 11 June 1896, vol. 41 pp.832–3.
21. Reynolds, *Grangegorman*, p.194.
22. Adams, 'From Association to Union'.
23. *Irish Times*, 25 September 1911.
24. Ibid.
25. *Asylum News*, May 1897.
26. A. Walk, 'The History of Mental Nursing', *Journal of Mental Science* 107 (1961): 1–17.
27. Adams, 'From Association to Union'.
28. Walk, 'The History of Mental Nursing'.
29. Ibid.
30. Adams, 'From Association to Union'.
31. Ibid.
32. P. Nolan, *A History of Mental Health Nursing* (London: Chapman and Hall, 1993), p.76.
33 Walk, 'The History of Mental Nursing'.
34. Ibid.
35. Ibid.
36. *NAWU Magazine*, December 1912.
37. Nolan, *A History of Mental Health Nursing*, p.77.
38. Ibid.
39. Adams, 'From Association to Union'.
40. *Voice of Labour* (Paper of the Irish Transport and General Workers' Union), December 1917.
41. D. Nevin (ed.), *Trade Union Century* (Cork: Mercier Press, 1994), p.55.
42. *Voice of Labour*, November 1918.
43 NAWU Magazine, November 1917 and August 1924.

44. Finnane, p.227.
45. Ibid.
46. Finnane, *Insanity and the Insane*, p.231.
47. Anglo-Celt, 6 April 1918.
48. Ibid., 21 September 1918.
49. Ibid., 12 October 1918.
50. Ibid., 27 November 1918.
51. Ibid.
52. Ibid.
53. A. McCabe, 'The Stormy Petrel of the Transport Workers', *Saothar*, 19 (1994): 41–52.
54. Ibid.
55. Letter from Padraig O'Cnaimhsi, Meenmore, Arran Island, Ireland, 19 October 1993.
56. *Voice of Labour*, 5 October 1918.
57. Interview with Lucius Emerson, 12 December 1993.
58   *Voice of Labour*, 15 March 1919.
59. *Northern Standard*, 18 January 1919.
60. Ibid.
61. *Anglo-Celt*, 1 February 1919.
62. *Dundalk Democrat*, 1 February 1919.
63. *Northern Standard*, 25 January 1919.
64. Ibid.
65. Maxwell was also to the fore when unions were reintroduced in Monaghan in the late
     1920s and was still involved in union delegations in the 1940s. Source: Interview with
     Noel, the son of Mark Maxwell, 1998.
66. *Northern Standard*, 25 January 1919.
67. Interview with John, the son of Mark Maxwell, 1998.
68. *Anglo-Celt*, 1 February 1919.
69. *Voice of Labour*, 8 February 1919.
70. P. O'Donnell, *There Will Be Another Day* (Dublin: Dolmen Press, 1963).
71. *Anglo-Celt*, 8 February 1919.
72. Ibid.
73. *Northern Standard*, 8 February 1919.
74. Interview with Mark Maxwell's son, John, 1998.
75. *Northern Standard*, 8 February 1919.
76. *Anglo-Celt*, 8 February 1919.
77. Ibid.
78. *Anglo-Celt*, 1 February 1919.
79. *Northern Standard*, 8 February 1919.
80. *Dundalk Democrat*, 1 February 1919.
81. *Anglo-Celt*, 1 February 1919.
82. *Anglo-Celt*, 8 February 1919.
83. Interview with Pat Murray, Monaghan County Museum, 1993.
84. *Voice of Labour*, 8 February 1919.
85. *Anglo-Celt*, 8 February 1919
86. *Anglo-Celt*, 15 February 1919.
87. *Northern Standard*, 18 January 1919.
88. Ibid.
89. *Northern Standard*, 1 February 1919.
90. *Northern Standard*, 25 January 1919
91. *Northern Standard*, 1 February 1919.
92. P. Berresford-Ellis, *A History of the Irish Working Class* (London: Pluto Press, 1985).
93   *Dundalk Democrat*, 1 February 1919.
94. *Hansard*, HC Deb 20 February 1919, vol. 112 cc. 1116-7
95. *Journal of Mental Science*, 20 February 1919, p.127.
96. E. O'Connor, *Syndicalism in Ireland 1917–1923* (Cork: Cork University Press, 1988).
97. Ibid.
98. Ibid.
99. *Dundalk Democrat*, 9 February 1919.
100. S. Ward-Perkins (ed.), *Select Guide to Trade Union Records in Dublin* (Dublin: Irish Labour
     History Society, Irish Manuscripts Commission, 1995), p.10.

101. *NAWU Magazine*, April 1918.
102. Ibid.
103. *NAWU Magazine*, September 1918.
104. Ibid.
105. D.A. Murphy (ed.), *Tumbling Walls. The evolution of a community institution. St. Fintan's Hospital Portlaoise, 1833–1983* (Midland Health Board, 1983), p.40 and p.51.
106. J. Robins, *Fools and Mad: A History of the Insane in Ireland* (Institute of Public Administration, 1986), p.41.
107. *Journal of Mental Science*, January 1921, pp.95–6.
108. Murphy, *Tumbling Walls*.
109. Reynolds, *Grangegorman*.
110. *Dundalk Democrat*, 1 February 1919.
111. *Dundalk Democrat*, 8 February 1919.
112. *Voice of Labour*, 10 May 1919.
113. *Anglo-Celt*, 12 July 1919.
114. *Anglo-Celt*, 16 August 1919.
115. *Northern Standard*, 16 August 1919.
116. *Anglo-Celt*, 15 February 1919.
117. *Voice of Labour*, 2 January 1920.
118. *Northern Standard*, 1 March 1919.
119. *Anglo-Celt*, 17 January 1920; *Anglo-Celt*, 24 January 1920.
120. *Northern Standard*, 17 January 1920.
121. *Anglo-Celt*, 24 January 1920.
122. *Northern Standard*, 11 October 1919.
123. For more on Peadar O'Donnell, see McCabe, 'The Stormy Petrel of the Transport Workers' and O'Donnell's own accounts of his life in P. O'Donnell, *Monkeys in the Superstructure* (Galway: Salmon Publishing Ltd., 1986) and O'Donnell, *There Will Be Another Day*.
124. *NAWU Magazine*, April 1924.
125. Ward-Perkins, *Select Guide to Trade Union Records in Dublin*, p.10.
126. D.A. Murphy, *Unpublished manuscript on union organisation in Cork Asylum, 1906–1960s*. (Our Lady's Hospital Cork Historical Society, 1973), pp.43–7; Robins, *Fools and Mad*, p.184.
127. O'Donnell, *Monkeys in the Superstructure*, p.10.
128. O'Donnell, *There Will Be Another Day*.

3

Speedwell Magazine: An Insider View of Holywell Psychiatric Hospital, Antrim, 1959–1973

Gillian McClelland

This chapter aims to explore the culture of Holywell Psychiatric Hospital, Antrim, Northern Ireland during the period 1959–1973, with the help of *Speedwell*, the hospital magazine. Through the pages of this magazine, we can build up a picture of the daily life of the hospital, developing an understanding of staff–patient relationships, discovering an impressive array of leisure, sporting, ceremonial and recreational activities, and gaining some insights into the changing nature of mental health care at a time of radical change. The discussion is based on a complete run of the magazine, from 1959 to 1973, with every issue full of poems, essays, jokes, cartoons and hospital information, written by staff and patients.

CHANGES IN MENTAL HEALTH CARE

Psychiatric hospitals in the United Kingdom (UK) and Ireland during the early decades of the twentieth century were places of confinement rather than of treatment and care,[1] but conditions throughout the UK had been improving since the 1920s and, following the Mental Treatment Acts of 1930 (England and Wales) and 1932 (Northern Ireland), patients were allowed to wear their own clothes, entertainment was provided, and occupational therapy, based on a model developed in the Netherlands, was introduced.[2]

In 1948, when the NHS came into existence in the UK, the contribution of Northern Ireland to the British war effort during World War II was rewarded by a financial commitment to the building of a comprehensive health service in Northern Ireland in the post-war era. This led to a massive expansion in mental health services which had been severely underfunded since the late nineteenth century.[3] New ideas began to emerge from the Tavistock Clinic, London, including that of a 'therapeutic community', as developed by Maxwell Jones in the mid-1940s.[4]

> Based on ideas of collective responsibility, citizenship and empowerment, therapeutic communities are deliberately structured, in a way that encourages personal responsibility and avoids unhelpful dependency on professionals. Patients are seen as bringing strengths and creative energy into the therapeutic setting and the peer group is seen as all-important in establishing a strong therapeutic alliance.[5]

Some of these ideas had already influenced psychiatry in Northern Ireland, as evidenced in the discussions that led to the passing of a new piece of legislation – the Mental Health (NI) Act 1948, which had no counterpart in other parts of the UK, but paralleled similar legislation in the Republic of Ireland (Mental Health Act 1945).[6] The model of a therapeutic community was endorsed in the report of the World Health Organisation (WHO) expert committee on mental health of 1953.[7] Priorities included the preservation of the patient's individuality and the promotion of activities that mimicked a working day for all patients.[8]

During the 1950s and 1960s, the patient experience began to change due not only to the influence of radical ideas, such as those of Maxwell Jones and of the anti-psychiatry movement, but also to the impact of scientific developments and economic pressures on the public purse. Following what Kathleen Jones terms the 'pharmacological revolution' of the 1950s, there were dramatic changes in the experiences of mentally ill people. 'Once the more bizarre symptoms of mental illness could be controlled, mental illness itself seemed to disappear.'[9] The role of the mental hospital as a place of confinement for untreatable conditions was now open to question, and Enoch Powell, the UK Minister of Health 1960–63, seized the opportunity to oppose the abolition of the mental hospital system.[10] In 1961, he argued for a reduction in mental health beds in England and Wales by more than 50 per cent, or by 75,000 beds, over the next fifteen years.[11] From then on, a fundamental change in mental health policy was inevitable. The principles underpinning this policy were enunciated in the recommendations of the 1957 Royal Commission on mental illness and mental deficiency: 'There should be a general re-orientation away from institutional care in its present form and towards community care.'[12] This principle was enshrined in the Mental Health Acts in 1959 (England and Wales) and in 1961 (Northern Ireland).[13]

As the anti-psychiatry movement gained pace in the US and in the UK, clinicians began to recognise the negative effects of long term institutional care. The American sociologist, Erving Goffman studied the impact of institutional life on individuals during the 1950s and found that some of the symptoms being displayed were a normal reaction to the kind of life imposed on these patients and had little to do with their mental illness.[14] His work confirmed the theory of British psychiatrist, Russell Barton, who claimed that psychiatric patients suffered from two 'illnesses'; the mental health problem which led to their admission to hospital and the sickness that resulted from institutional practices.[15] The French philosopher and historian, Michel Foucault, labelled doctors as agents of social control in institutions that were there not to cure patients, but to show the grim consequences of abnormal behaviour.[16] Other theorists, such as the psychiatrists R. D. Laing, and Thomas Szasz, and the sociologist Andrew Scull, had slightly different theories about the role of the psychiatric institution in society, but all pointed to the fact that mental health care as it was being practiced was not 'curing' patients but was adding to their problems.[17] The period covered by *Speedwell*, the Holywell Hospital magazine, was one in which all of these ideas were floating around. Some of them permeated the walls of mental hospitals in Northern Ireland.

HOLYWELL HOSPITAL

Holywell Hospital opened in 1899 with 400 beds. It was the last district asylum to be built in Ireland. Patient numbers increased following the introduction of the NHS in 1948, reaching a high point of 827 in 1958.[18] When the hospital magazine ceased production in 1973, the number of inpatients had fallen to 611.[19] During the early 1960s, the medical and nursing staff consisted of three consultant psychiatrists, three registrar grade psychiatrists and 243 nurses.[20]

In his history of Holywell Hospital, Marc Mulholland argues that the hospital was 'well integrated into the Antrim community' and local people accepted the 'presence of an asylum' close to the town, possibly because it was also a major source of employment for both men and women. In addition, throughout the 1950s and 1960s, Holywell was a social venue. The monthly dances attracted crowds of over 500 people and all the popular 'showbands' of the era played there. Dinner dances, though less frequent, were attended by prominent locals. However, Mulholland also notes that while the aim of having patients act as cloakroom attendants and ticket collectors was to encourage interaction between patients and the public, 'lurid tales of lunatics in cells off the corridors leading to the dance hall (they were actually only offices) continued to send a frisson through impressionable youth'.[21] The admission in 1953 of Iain Hay Gordon to Holywell, as a 'criminal lunatic', aroused a great deal of disquiet in the area. Hay, who was convicted of the murder of the daughter of a high court judge, spent seven years in Holywell, before being released to his native Glasgow.[22] In fact, he presented no danger to anyone and his murder conviction was overturned in 2000.[23]

Patient numbers began to decrease in the early 1960s, due to the introduction of psychotropic drugs, new policies on community care and changes in medical treatment such as the opening of a Day Hospital. The principles of the 'therapeutic community' were reflected in the organisation of sporting and leisure activities on the wards. The ideal was taken further in the newly established Day Hospital, where a decision was made not to employ an occupational therapist, but rather to allow patients to organise their own activities. According to the consultant, Dr. Roger Whiteley:

> For a trial period of one year (1962) the Day Hospital has not asked for an Occupational Therapist and instead has dealt with occupational, recreational and social activities on a therapeutic-community basis, that is to say the patients themselves have been responsible for programming their own activities, usually through a Committee. This venture has been highly successful and I feel that, in general, the patients have been happier and more responsible individuals. A fully qualified Occupational Therapist, or even an Assistant with long experience, would not easily fit into our present therapeutic-community atmosphere.[24]

What was happening at Holywell Hospital was representative of wider efforts to move away from the stigma of asylum containment to a modern professional service. This newer form of care was associated with the milder forms of mental disorder which could be treated in psychiatric units in general hospitals and in day hospitals, allowing as many patients as possible to remain in the community while receiving drug therapy.[25] The aim of this new approach was to emphasise the fact that a person with a mental illness could live a normal life. Consequently, staff members should no longer be seen simply as custodians of chronic patients but rather as medical professionals with a valuable curative role to play.

However, Holywell had a problem attracting suitably qualified nursing staff during this period. In the mid-1950s, 60 per cent of female nurses and 36 per cent of their male counterparts were unqualified.[26] This was not an unusual situation within the UK, as mental health nursing was a low status occupation. In an effort to raise the level of qualification among the nursing staff, the Northern Ireland Hospitals Authority (NIHA) established a preliminary training unit for nurses at Holywell in the early 1950s. However, standards continued to be low due to the fact that it was staffed by one male and one female tutor – both of whom were unqualified. Efforts to attract qualified staff included the establishment of a Staff Recreation Club in 1951. Activities included dancing, the formation of the hospital band, badminton, tennis, football, billiards, table tennis, whist drives and staff parties. The community feeling which developed had a positive impact on staff recruitment and retention and was appreciated by the management committee.[27] Many pages of *Speedwell* were devoted to the various social activities of both staff and patients. Further efforts to attract new staff led to the reduction of restrictions on the social life of nurses. For example, it was no longer compulsory for nurses to live-in and by the late 1960s residence on site was provided only for trainee female nursing staff. However, some of the old ethos continued and discipline on the wards continued to be strict until 1967, with nurses having to 'stand to attention as doctors passed through wards' symbolising the hierarchical structure of the hospital.[28] However, change was on the way. By the time of the last issue of *Speedwell*, Northern Ireland was under Direct Rule from Westminster. As a consequence of the civil rights movement, which highlighted sectarian policy decisions within local councils, the NIHA was abolished and all health and social care services moved to the new structures as recommended by the Macrory Report. Holywell Hospital was now part of the mental health service of the Northern Health and Social Services Board (NHSSB), and led to what some viewed as 'the end of Holywell's autonomy'.[29]

HOSPITAL MAGAZINES

Goffman's study in the 1950s of 'total institutions' in the United States found that practices developed to bond staff and patients together in mutual support and understanding.[30] One of the most common of these practices was the publication of a hospital magazine.

> The printed content is such as to draw a circle around the institu-
> tion and to give the accent of public reality to the world within ...
> The writing is done by inmates but expresses the official view
> of the functions of the institution, the staff's theory of human
> nature, an idealised version of inmate-staff relationships, and
> the stance an ideal convert ought to take – in short, it presents
> the institutional line.[31]

Hospital magazines developed in the early decades of the twentieth
century in the UK, America and Canada. However, until recently the
genre has not attracted much academic interest, with the exception
of Jeffrey Reznick's study of hospital magazines during the Great
War. These publications developed from 'Trench Journals'. By 1915,
nearly every military hospital produced a 'Trench Journal' under the
heading of 'literary projects'. The format included an editorial by the
commanding officer or matron, pen and ink sketches of hospital life,
institutional recreation news, concert announcements 'censored
humour about staff, patients and ward life' as well as local businesses
advertisements.[32] According to Annmarie Adams, some of these
early hospital magazines were used by architects to promote their
designs and planning agenda amongst hospital staff.[33] Other views
on hospital magazines include those of Lester D. Freidman, who
argued that professional hospital magazines in the 1950s served 'as
a professional version of popular home design magazines'. They presented the hospital through 'the lens of domesticity' (with explicitly
gendered labour categories).[34] For hospital managers, the magazine
could be viewed as a public relations exercise. For example, in 1965,
Alden Brewster Mills wrote that a 'hospital can build a reputation
for intelligent leadership most quickly by contributing thoughtful
and significant articles to the hospital magazines'.[35] All of these
themes can easily be detected in the pages of *Speedwell*. However,
though we get some insider views, there is little doubt that, as
observed by Goffman, in the hospital magazine patients can only
'introduce whatever open criticism of the institution the censors will
permit; they add to this by ways of oblique or veiled writing, or
pointed cartoons'.[36]

SPEEDWELL

Speedwell magazine was first published in 1959, to support the policy of
the resident medical superintendent (RMS), Dr. G. M. Smith, to
establish a 'therapeutic community'. It aimed to appeal to 'patients,

staff, their friends, and any other persons interested in the life of the Hospital'. Dr. Smith wrote in the first issue

> Here patients and staff work together; their work, recreation and social activities are all centred around the idea of treatment, this means the solving of personal problems, the easing of emotional distress, the arousing of new interests.[37]

Each issue of *Speedwell* included news about Holywell events and personalities, a parson's page, notes on health and beauty, sport and various homilies and competitions. It was, therefore, typical of its genre and time, as shown by Gavigan in his study of hospital magazines in the early 1960s.

> In an attempt to determine what material a hospital magazine should contain, a questionnaire was prepared and submitted to the patients and employees of a state hospital. The similarity of the preferences of the patients and employees was marked. Preference was shown for material dealing with the calendar of events and report of activities and events occurring at the hospital, fiction, humour, editorials, sports, cartoons and articles dealing with mental hygiene. A dislike was shown for articles of a historical, instructional and biographical character, and those whose nature would appeal to children and adolescents. There was a marked desire for photographs to be included in the magazine. As to the length of article, the majority preferred those of one page or less.[38]

Speedwell differed from some of the more prestigious hospital magazines in that patients as well as staff and 'friends' could contribute. There were twenty-three members of staff on the editorial committee and the name 'Speedwell' came from a competition won by a 'female patient who has now recovered and returned to her home'. According to the first issue, published in the summer of 1959, the magazine aimed to 'provide a means of self-expression to the literary minded amongst us'.[39] The cartoons from this issue, reflected the organised chaos in the magazine's office.[40]

"Oh yes, now I remember.   We received your letter
this morning"

The general tone is generally one of light-heartedness and polite humour. It is full of devotional verse and self-congratulatory accounts of outings and events. Critics of the hospital or the staff are virtually absent – a feature found in similar magazines.

> As a work of reference it is unsurpassed, as a hospital magazine its banality and lack of imagination beggar description … reviews, hospital notes – but these are the most lifeless part. Otherwise there is nothing. Not an opinion, not an idea: not a good piece of writing, not an original thought: nothing but clumsily written records which make history a duller business than it need be.[41]

Nevertheless, *Speedwell* gives us an opportunity to view Holywell Hospital from the perspective of some of the staff and patients over the course of a thirteen-year period of radical change in mental health services.

Although the idea of the therapeutic community was said to be at the core of the hospital magazine project, some of the contributors to *Speedwell* did not always present a picture of a fully functioning therapeutic community as envisaged by Maxwell Jones. There is an initial emphasis on the community feeling between staff and patients, a downplaying of the divisions between the two groups. For example, in the first issue of *Speedwell* a light-hearted poem was printed anonymously

Dilemma

Patient:
> Every morning when I rise
> I get dark spots before my eyes;
> Every night when I go to bed
> I feel a pain across my head;
> Every day about eleven
> I wish that I were safe in heaven;
> Every evening after tea;
> I think that I am all at sea;
> Every time I try to mend
> I have a horrible week-end.

Doctor:
> And do you very often find
> That you are half out of your mind?
> And when you try to work or play

Your thoughts are twined the other way?
And if you try to concentrate
the effort keeps you up quite late?
And do you think when day is done
You are not having any fun?
Is this how you feel?
Well isn't it odd
I feel the same myself, by dod![42]

Some of the cartoons in the magazine indicated that doctors are not always efficient in everyday life, nor can they be relied upon to be on time to see their patients.[43]

One contributor, who called himself the 'observer', portrayed the medical staff as remote figures who did not visit the wards frequently and when they did so it was in a very formal capacity. In the Autumn 1961 issue, we read:

> (T)heir visits have much of the perfunctory character of inspections by Government officials for whom special preparation is made – with the result that they do not see the normal working of the hospital as it proceeds from day to day.[44]

Another critical article by a patient, signing himself *'Rara Avis'* (a rare bird) who had been 'coming to and from Holywell Hospital for a dozen years' managed to get through the censors. This patient did not see much evidence of the democratic therapeutic community envisioned by the resident medical officer. On the contrary, he claimed that all too often the institution forgot that

> … the patient is the most important person in any hospital …the true role of the patient has been conveniently sacrificed on the altar of something approaching hero worship for the staff, and of the medical staff in particular.[45]

Rara Avis had five full pages of 'constructive criticism' to deliver despite recognising that his 'miscellaneous thought' would not be the only thing to 'strike' him when 'some other people read this article'.[46] He was unrepentant, claiming that his views 'may well represent the consensus of opinion – on the part of the patients at any rate'.[47] He pointed out that 'if any man thinks this article has been too vitriolic, then it may be that the truth is biting sore.' However, in his introductory paragraph, *Rara Avis* acknowledged that 'there is a great deal more to commend at Holywell than there is to criticise or condemn.'[48] The staff member who became a patient himself explained away criticism of nurses by patients in his article entitled 'Appreciation'.

> They don't appreciate what the nurses are doing for them. With some this could be related to their illness, but to others it is just lack of knowledge on their part and the non-acceptance that the doctors and nurses do know best.[49]

He argued that simple kindnesses by staff members meant a great deal to patients and that 'no words however superlative could express my feelings for them'. He trusted that when the 'critical patients' are cured, or as he expressed it, 'when they are again essential members of the community', they will come to the same conclusion.[50]

However, there were some patients who showed their appreciation of the staff in poetry. A female patient identified only by her initials (M.E.) dedicated the following to 'all nurses'.

Hands

> Blessed are the hands that heal,
> Hands beneath whose touch we feel
> Pain relieved and strength renewed;
> I think with constant gratitude
> Of hands that serve humanity;
> Hands that soothe and serve and mend.
> Helping, easing, comforting,
> Dressing, feeding, bandaging.
> I'll remember gratefully
> The hands that have bestowed on me
> Life's best gift, its greatest wealth-
> The gift of healing and of health.[51]

The same patient eulogised the night nurse.

The night nurse

With her little light burning,

I see her sitting there; She is a bit of comfort
To the patients in her care.

She is our Guardian Angel,
Who always lingers near,
Whenever there's an urgent call
She's always there to hear.

We could not do without her,
She is our only light,
She is our only comfort
In the darkness of the night.[52]

COMBATING STIGMA

Goffman observed that people who are stigmatised often organise themselves into groups and networks and that they often represent themselves through newsletters, magazines and books.[53] Some of the contributions to *Speedwell*, confirm the importance of the written word in making stigma visible. The following article in April 1968, by an 'Ex-patient' who had been both a nurse and a patient, explores the reality of stigma.

> To many temporary patients …. it was a turmoil before they entered Holywell Hospital and from the first day began their recovery, step by step…..until the giant step of facing the public and their friends, who knew they had been patients. I, myself have worked as a mental nurse and used to be amazed at the things people said to me when they learnt of my occupation. 'You must need great patience to deal with those…'[54]

The writer went on to express a longing that:

> If only the discharged mental patient could be treated like the discharged general hospital patient, just accepting that they had an illness which was cured and they are probably needing their friends more to help them find their place in society again.[55]

Since 1955, a group of thirty patients, accompanied by three members of staff had taken an annual week's holiday in the north Antrim coastal town of Carnlough. The RMS was so impressed by the 'improvement in their conditions and appearance generally, brought about by this temporary change of environment', that he suggested in 1956, that a permanent holiday home be purchased. It was hoped that it would be of benefit to long-stay patients for an annual holiday and for those 'progressing towards recovery' it would act as convalescent and rehabilitation centre where patients could become 'better conditioned to normal civilian life' away from institutional life 'in an informal carefree atmosphere'.[56] This was a more difficult project than was anticipated and the purchase did not go ahead. In the first issue of *Speedwell* in 1959, a contributor wrote that 'the Portrush people would not agree to our taking a house in the town to use as a holiday home and convalescent unit.' The stigma attached to psychiatric patients led to the rejection of Holywell Hospital's plans for a holiday home in this busy seaside resort. The writer expressed regret at this outcome and told the readers that the authorities were still looking for a 'suitable place' . He added his own plea 'Any offers?'[57]

The process of gradual modernisation at Holywell Hospital included a public relations exercise to 'lessen public prejudice against mental illness and mental hospitals'.[58] In 1960, a Belfast cine film group produced a twenty-minute film in colour about Holywell Hospital, and contacts with outside organisations such as churches and professional bodies were used to encourage organised visits to the hospital. In that year alone, 1,400 people viewed Holywell Hospital.[59] The launch of *Speedwell* may well have been part of this exercise. The heightened profile of the hospital was not an unmixed blessing. In 1961, an article by an unnamed 'observer' wrote of this public relations exercise as an 'ever-growing tendency to over-run the hospital with groups of visitors of all kinds'. While accepting the benefits of outside scrutiny the writer argued that there was a danger 'of making show-places of such institutions. Many members of the public are inclined to regard their visits in the nature of visits to the zoo– on the look-out for the macabre– casting furtive glances at the "inmates"– especially while being led through the dining-rooms at meal hours.'[60] The 'observer' argued that the feelings of patients, especially 'the more sensitive' were upset by the 'intrusion of strangers'. As he saw it, the primary role of the hospital and medical staff was to provide a therapeutic environment for patients.

> All those who are in charge of the sick should cultivate, above all things, the grace of sympathy – seeking to 'feel with' and 'for' those whom they endeavour to help and restore to health.[61]

POETRY AND WRITING AS THERAPY AND PROTEST

The authors of most articles in *Speedwell* were members of staff, as were the editorial committee members. Articles, poems etc contributed by patients were often labelled as being 'from the pen of a patient', 'ex-patient', or 'observer'. While these patient entries did not dominate the magazine, they made a valuable contribution to its overall importance. The value of writing poetry is now widely recognised as therapeutic.[62]

Speedwell often included religiously focused articles such as the 'Parson's Page' and many of the patients' poems were of a devotional nature. Some also expressed their sorrow and regret about the way they lived their lives. In the following poem, three patients in Tobernaveen Unit, the admissions unit for patients with alcohol problems (JERL, KK and ST), combined their thoughts.[63]

A Prayer

Now I kneel in deep despair,
Confessing my sins to you:
I ask you Lord to comfort me
And let me start anew.

Others expressed their reliance on God for psychological support.

There's an arm around your shoulder

There's an arm around your shoulder
Every minute of the day,
Guiding you, protecting you,
As you go your way.

Altho' you may not see it;
It is there just the same,
For it's the arm of Jesus
Who is with you night and day.

If ever you're in trouble,
If in sickness or in health,
Jesus will always help you
If you have faith in Him yourself.

So, if you believe, as I believe,
And have faith the way I do,
Jesus will always help you
And he will see you through.[64]

This type of poem, expressing a deep religious faith, with an added note of proselytising fervour, was a frequent feature in patients' pages. Another female patient (identified as F.T.S.) found solace in the fact that she believed her late mother was watching over her.

My mother

She will walk with me down through the valley;
She will walk with me over the plain,
When in the shadow or in the sunshine,
If she goes with me I'll not complain.
She will walk with me through life's fair morning,
And when the shadows of evening must come;
Living and dying she will not forsake me-
She will walk with me to heaven, my home.[65]

A long-term patient, Robairt Clough, frequently contributed poems on various subjects. This poem looked at ward-life from a positive perspective.

Holywell rhymes

Little drops of medicine,
Little coloured pills,
Cure us of all ailments,
Cure us of all ills.

Doctors with a stethoscope,
Doctors with a bag,
Make us fit and healthy,
Cheer us when we flag.

Pretty little nurses
Nurses bold and strong,
Nurses with a banjo,
Nurses sing a song.

Wardsmaids with the dinner,
Wardsmaids with the tea,
Keep our tummies happy,
Until the day we're free.

Little drops of medicine,
Little coloured pills,
Settled all our ailments,
Cured us of our ills.[66]

This poem tells us something of the various roles of the hospital staff – the differences between doctors, female and male nurses and the 'maids'. These ranged from the provision of food, physical and medical care, to various ways of cheering patients up when they are depressed. They included reassurance, music and song. In contrast, a comment by the patient who identified himself as *Rara Avis* on the morale of some Holywell staff, pointed out the irony of the situation when at times patients were happier than those who cared for them.

> How Irish it is to find certain doctors and nurses with faces like tin-openers, brow beaten by anxiety and seriousness of mind, coming along to try making us happy. Hie, ye Gods![67]

A less positive comment on meals than that of Robairt Clough is given by another patient who had 'many years' of experience of these culinary delights. His 'tummy' was not so happy.

> To blazes with powdered egg, rissoles, and the usual breakfast helping of plywood (so sorry, I mean hard, brittle, over-salted streaks of an excuse for bacon). Then there come the eternal beans!![68]

ON CURES AND FREEDOM

Clough's poem also looks forward to being cured of his 'ill' and being 'free'. However, the cycle of acute admission, discharge and readmission to psychiatric hospitals (often known as the 'revolving door syndrome') continued to happen in spite of advances in medical care. There is no mention in Clough's poem of the very real prospect of readmission to hospital, although this was the reality of his experience as shown by the fact that he was a regular contributor to *Speedwell* throughout the 1960s and early 1970s. In 1960, 25.3 per cent of admissions were people who had been readmitted within six months of discharge and despite changing mental health policies, this pattern remained unchanged for the next forty years.[69]

The light-hearted mention of 'little drops of medicine' and 'little coloured pills' trivialised the real problems associated with psychiatric treatments which included insulin coma therapy (ICT) for schizophrenia and electro-convulsive therapy (ECT) for mood disorders, both of which were used at Holywell at the time.[70] ICT was used from the 1930s until the 1960s, though its effectiveness was frequently questioned.[71] ECT was widely used 'enthusiastically', even 'indiscriminately' until the 1970s, by which time it had aroused public mistrust.[72] Liberal commentators, powerful patients' lobbies, especially in America, and the 1975 film *One Flew over the Cuckoo's Nest* added to the questioning of invasive therapies such as ECT.

There are instances in *Speedwell* when the lack of discussion speaks volumes – medication was accepted by the patients as were its side effects. *Rara Avis* described the bed-time routine

> Ah! What is that I hear? – 'tis the final blast of the ref's whistle, and behold! a bespectacled gent on the touchline yelling – 'Paraldehyde all round – free drinks on the house!'.[73]

Maybe this 'two drachms' of medication explains why the laughter amongst patients became 'uproarious as a rule just before bedtime'.[74] Paraldehyde was used as a hypnotic and a sedative from the 1880s, and even in the middle of the twentieth century 'the smell of paraldehyde permeated hospitals'.[75]

BOREDOM

Speedwell describes the way in which life in Holywell Hospital dealt with what Goffman called 'the social disconnections' experienced by inpatients and the consequent failure (in most cases) to 'acquire within the institution gains that can be transmitted to outside life' such as money earned, a career established and marriages or partnerships formed.[76] The resulting perception of 'dead and heavy-hanging time' probably explains the premium placed on what might be called 'removal activities'.[77] Goffman argues that these voluntary and light-hearted activities lift the patient's spirits and take 'the participant out of himself'. They 'mercifully' kill time. The 'removal activities' in Holywell were usually collective – field games, dances, playing in an orchestra or band, singing, amateur dramatics, lectures, debating societies, occupational therapy. Writing for the hospital magazine was one example of officially sponsored activities, which was both collective (contributing to reports of the various societies) and individual (composing poetry and devotional verse as result of 'reverie-plus').[78] These activities can all be described as 'occupational therapy' as described in 1979:

> For the occupational therapist the word occupation should imply a whole range of activities, from those which have in them some element of fantasy and creativity, however unrealistic, to those which are realistic and socially contributory.[79]

Initially associated with basket weaving, occupational therapists acquired professional status from the 1940s onwards.[80] Holywell's Annual Report for 1960 provides us with a description of other activities that were included as occupational therapy. These were two schemes for the manufacture of boxes and crates for use by 'outside concerns' with an emphasis on the work being therapeutic.[81] The RMS, Dr. Smith, was enthusiastic about developing occupational therapy, aiming to extend and reorganise this form of treatment for patients in all departments, arguing that work could be carried out by patients under the supervision of a small number of staff.[82] Smith had faced considerable opposition to his ideas, as they were seen by some as a ruse to secure cheap labour by both patients and staff. A contemporary report by the King's Fund was also critical of the work carried out in most psychiatric hospitals in the UK.

> The type of work is monotonous and repetitive. At present the work in units is surprisingly lacking in variety and few attempts appear to have been made to encourage and inculcate new skills or to relate work done to the opportunities available in the locality. However, the desirability of doing this depends on whether an ITU is intended primarily to engender and improve working habits in patients who have lost them, or to prepare patients for jobs appropriate to their skills and aptitudes.[83]

Opposing views on work can be seen clearly in different articles appearing in patients' pages. Some of these were very positive such as that from 'R' (probably Robairt Clough).

Holywell House 1967

Occupational therapy reigns there –
A thing of rugs and many ploys
And joy to find one can use one's hands,
And incidentally lifts the mind
From such-like things as headaches
And trivial worries.
And over all Sister Potter presides,
And often has to guide
Our inexperienced and clumsy hands-
It is a happy ship…

From painting empty tins to
Covering chairs.
Below in kitchen Mrs. Alexander taught

The cooking of domestic arts,
And last but not least
As a solace to the mind,
We repaired to the wooden hut
For painting classes.[84]

However, some contributions to the debate were more ambivalent:

The Laundry

We go to the laundry each morning
With never a frown on our face.
We all tackle work without warning,
Doing things with precision and grace.
We shake and we fold from morning to night
From Monday till Friday at four;
When we think we have our work done,
The porter brings round a truck more.

To the canteen at ten and the canteen at three,
Fifteen of us trip in a row.
It's nice to know you have ten minutes break
Till the machines are again on the go.
The pressing-machine stands in a spot by itself
Where they press coats and frocks by the score,
Then they're all neatly folded and put on a shelf
To await the arrival of more.

But when we all get well
To our homes we will go,
To our dear ones our story we'll tell
Of the good old times we used to spend
In the laundry at Holywell.[85]

While this contributor appears to accept the value of this repetitious work, she hoped to look back on it with nostalgia rather than enjoying it for its own sake. *Rara Avis* was characteristically scathing on the issue.

At Holywell and elsewhere, every whim and fancy of the staff is usually vented upon the patients, and particularly those inclined to servility. One is certainly not reminded of behaviour becoming a hospital ward when a 'crabbit' dictatorial and domineering nurse of whatever calibre literally 'gulders' a patient's surname, and does not request, but commands him to undertake some menial task, such as washing out lavatories, sweeping and polishing floors, hauling and pulling furniture from one end of the hospital to the other, - and not forgetting the doctor or nurse who likes to take advantage of the fact that he can have his car washed and polished for nothing. *Quid nunc*? (What now?).[86]

These nurses are, he points out, the 'exception rather than the rule', nevertheless the forms of work to which patients are 'driven' seldom varied from what in essence constituted 'free and forced labour'. There was some justification in this accusation, as patient labour was not replaced by that of paid domestic and other staff until the early 1970s. For *Rara Avis*, writing in 1964, the occupational therapy units were 'most successful'. *Bird's Nest Soup*, a survivor's account of twenty years as a patient in a mental hospital (first published in 1971) describes work in the sewing room in a similar establishment to Holywell Hospital.

Talking was not encouraged. Nurse Best was in charge there, and she was a kind, tolerant person … but she insisted on the patients' attention to work primarily. It was soulless utilitarian work. The clothes each patient wore were made here by other patients … I made four chemises, sometimes five, per day, when I worked there, for almost four years.[87]

Rara Avis's comment that work should be carried out in 'bright and congenial surroundings' suggested that conditions were less than ideal in Holywell. He also suggested that it was 'essential' that there was an 'adequate variety of pursuits to cater for as many tastes as possible'. The plea was that the authorities should recognise that all patients were not the same and could not be treated as if they were. 'A man or woman ought never to be asked to do something which is neither interesting nor significant to him or her.' He suggested that 'occupational therapy should, in so far as is possible, be a labour of love, and something which the patient daily looks forward to with enthusiasm.'[88]

In the mid-1960s, the Northern Ireland Hospitals Authority (NIHA) set up a working party to advise the authority 'generally on all aspects of the therapeutic occupation of mental hospital patients'.[89] The King's Fund report had found that, in general, there was a lack of 'male jobs where strength and energy are required'. However, in Holywell Hospital the on-site farm served this function. From its opening in 1899, Holywell had its own working farm

(Springfarm) which had a dairy, cattle byres and a horticultural club which was run voluntarily by a male nurse.[90] Farm work was viewed by the first RMS as 'a curative agent in the treatment of insanity'.[91] By the late 1960s, Springfarm employed forty male patients as well as four staff.[92] In 1970, the assistant secretary argued that it was 'an economically sound unit' playing a 'very prominent part in the therapeutic occupation of patients within a rural and stable environment'.[93] However, the sale of hospital farms was already on the cards by then.

THE SOCIAL SCENE

Life in Holywell Hospital was not dominated by work and it appears from *Speedwell* and from other hospital magazines that the staff and patients had a very busy social schedule.[94] In 1960, an entertainments officer was appointed to develop physical education, recreation and entertainment. An art therapy class was started with both therapeutic and diagnostic purposes.[95] Even *Rara Avis* praised the efforts of management: 'no praise of mine would be too high for the entertainments and recreational facilities available for patients and staff.' In the mid-1960s, the weekly programme included dances on Mondays, concert rehearsals on Tuesdays, films on Wednesdays, and a camera club or debating society (which had more than 120 members in 1959) on Thursdays. On one club night, the principal of Antrim Technical College brought his slides of Ireland to the recreation hall to show to the audience who were then invited to show any coloured slides of their holidays as these were 'always of interest to the patients' at future sessions.[96] For a period, the debating club's programme centred round 'Tall stories, true or false', which were received with great enthusiasm.[97] On weekend evenings, there was a choice on Friday between bingo (for both men and women) or a whist drive, and on Saturday the patients' social club had its meeting. Winter meetings were 'spent in a sing-song and games' under the management of a long-stay patient who had given many years service.[98] During the summer months, members were taken to seaside resorts such as Newcastle, Bangor and Donaghadee.[99] Patients had to apply to the hospital secretaries to join the club, a committee decided whether the applicant was 'suitable' and names were subsequently forwarded to the matron or chief male nurse for approval for membership.[100]

Religious observance was also an important event. Both Protestant and Catholic clergymen were involved in religious ceremonies and

Christmas and Easter plays. A weekly Sunday service was relayed from the recreation hall to the wards. However, attendance at services varied and in 1968 a combined harvest service with the assistance of Dunamuggy church (of Ireland) choir was 'unfortunately poorly attended by both staff and patients' with the exception of the 'ever faithfuls'.[101]

There were also events based on radio and television programmes, such as the panel game 'Twenty Questions' and musical evenings based on 'Juke Box Jury' and 'Top of the Pops'.[102] Staff and patients competed in all of these events. A talent competition catering for all tastes, held in November 1962, included 'instruments, folk songs, pop songs, story-telling, recitation and even the Twist!'. The judges were so impressed that they could not pick a 'top winner' and the new matron presented prizes to all the participants.[103]

Sport also had its place in the social calendar, with annual sports days a feature of the 1950s and 1960s. Tennis was played in the summer and there were two badminton courts in the grounds. Bowling, table tennis and other indoor games were enjoyed on Saturday evenings in the recreation hall during the social club meetings.[104] Swimming sessions were also an important part of the programme of activities. Male and female patients were taken to the local 'Baths' on separate weekly sessions. *Rara Avis* gives his views in the following extract:

Value of Swimming

The practice of swimming stimulates and strengthens the general muscular and mental conditions. It has a tremendously important advantage in the complete mastery of fears and the development of confidence and it helps to break down inferiority complexes and is considered to be of tremendous therapeutic value.[105]

From the 1950s, Holywell teams were involved in competitive sporting activities with other psychiatric hospitals. In 1968, twenty members of the patient indoor bowling team played against Londonderry and Gransha Hospital and the Tyrone and Fermanagh Hospital. According to *Speedwell*, the excitement among the participants was 'difficult to stifle'.[106] Badminton, football, floor-golf and peg quoits (for patients aged 50 to 70 years) were all played competitively amongst the eight Northern Ireland psychiatric hospitals.[107]

During the summer, there were also trips to County Antrim beauty spots on Thursday afternoons. Until 1965, the 'Special Care patients' and the older male and female mentally ill patients travelled with the recreation staff for picnics. The Ballycastle Lammas Fair was also an annual event enjoyed by the male patients (no explanation for the exclusion of women was given) who 'returned late and tired but happy'.[108] However, the outings were somewhat spoiled by the fact that the only available transport was the hospital van. This was a closed vehicle without windows and the patient experience was 'marred by the fact of not being able to see where' they were going.[109] A voluntary effort by staff led to a 'concert party', a 'Guest Tea' and other fundraising efforts, which resulted in the purchase of a patient mini-bus.

Contemporaneous accounts of life in long-stay psychiatric hospitals in Northern Ireland and elsewhere in the UK suggested that similar activities happened in other large psychiatric hospitals. Goffman suggested that:

> Every total institution can be seen as a kind of dead sea in which little islands of vivid, encapturing activity appear. Such activity can help the individual withstand the psychological stress usually engendered by assaults upon the self.[110]

At this time when inpatient numbers were high in Holywell, such 'removal activities' were essential in the maintenance of patient morale. Throughout the 1950s and 1960s, staff and patients collaborated in making the most of holiday periods. At Christmas, groups of patients were taken to Belfast to see the lights and decorations in Belfast city centre, there were patient concerts and nativity plays. Rehearsals began in early November, a carol service was held in the third week of December and a group of carol singers did a tour or the wards on Christmas Eve.[111] Every Christmas Day, the Holywell (staff) Dance Band played and children of staff were given presents by Santa Claus. At Easter, the celebrations included a Good Friday Passion play, a concert and, on Easter Monday, parades with prizes awarded for the best bonnets for both men and women. All of these events included staff and patients, with support from local musicians. As Goffman argues, these activities brought staff and patients together, promoting good relations in what was a 'total institution'. 'These practices express unity, solidarity, and joint commitment to the institution rather than differences between the two levels.'[112] In this way, individuals became part of the life of the institution. Whether they knew it or not, patients allowed their personalities to be moulded into this new reality, making it difficult for most of them to adjust to life outside the institution.[113]

THE END OF AN ERA

From the 1972 spring edition of *Speedwell* onward, we can see that the idea of a large psychiatric hospital as a 'therapeutic community' was being questioned from all angles. Dr. Smith, its champion, had retired as RMS in 1967 and was replaced by Dr. Enda Casement who faced a different type of management from the newly formed Northern Health and Social Services Board (NHSSB). The general policy was to 'reduce the old asylums to core services and integrate psychiatric care into general health care ... the funds for this revolution, however, were inordinately slow in materialising.'[114] The Hospital Plan for Northern Ireland 1968–78 recommended the integration of hospital, general practitioner and local authority medical services. However, it did not promise to provide any psychiatric 'treatment beds' in association with any proposed general hospital. Reform was further delayed due to the restructuring of local government and the loss of power by the Stormont government. From October 1973, Holywell lost its management committee and a new regime of hospital management from the NHSSB began. The new emphasis was on community care. The hospital's facilities went into decline over the succeeding two decades and by the 1980s, it reached a point where 'provision on the site [was] unacceptable by present day standards'.[115] A programme to reduce bed numbers was begun in Holywell as in other large psychiatric hospitals in Northern Ireland.

In parallel to changes in mental health policy, the 'troubles' were at their height in 1972.[116] Concerts and sporting matches as well as inter-hospital events, such as prize givings and 'get-togethers', were cancelled due to the civil unrest. Patients and staff were 'bitterly' disappointed. While a few tournaments were played amongst Holywell patients, there was 'not quite the same interest'. A contributor to *Speedwell* lamented: 'still, one keeps on hoping times will return to normal soon, and we will be able to travel and take part in the usual competitive games.'[117] The following year, the ban was lifted and life at Holywell went back to normal.[118] However, the conflict in Northern Ireland permeated every aspect of life.[119] Two poems by Robairt Clough give us some idea of how the political situation affected one patient.

> For there's shooting and there's murder there,
> And dark deeds in the night:
> Why in our land of beauty

Must we Irish always fight?
… I hope I'll live to see the day
When all the hatred's gone.[120]

His second poem expresses his distress at the conflict.

Slemish

I saw the sun float mistily
O'er Slemish's eastern edge,
And saw the blood-red berries shine
In every quick-thorn hedge
As red and warm and scarred with thorn
As Jesus' drooping head.
I wept a while for the young
Our blessed Irish dead.

We've fought and bled a thousand years,
Nor won since brave Boru
And just as Bruce's spider strove
We fall to rise anew.
No comfort from a widow's tears
Or grandpa's wrinkled brow,
Our heads, though bloodied,
Still held high
And proud,
Unbowed

What have we won?
That this day's sun
Can reap those wasted years?
I mind we once united were,
United Irishmen!
Shoulder to shoulder, side by side,
The paths of death we trod,
And cared no fig with which foot
We dug the peaty sod.[121]

Inside the hospital, the winds of change were also blowing among the patients as reflected in the lack of interest among patients in some of the social events. In 1972, we hear that there was a 'very poor attendance' at the weekly film show. Enquiries by the recreation hall staff revealed that 'TV was the enemy and that the nursing staff found it difficult to get patients to attend'. The once-popular dances experienced a lack of enthusiasm and it was reported that despite the resident hospital (staff) dance band 'numbers had also fallen away'.[122]

The last issue of *Speedwell* was published at Christmas 1973. It was a much smaller version of the magazine – not only had the number of pages shrunk from fifty-two to twenty-three pages, but the production team had fallen from twenty-three to nine. There were difficulties in obtaining contributions, as many of those responsible for the magazine had been transferred to new positions in the restructured health services. The long-serving editor, who had held the position since 1959, resigned in order to encourage 'an infusion of new blood'. Inpatient numbers were reducing as were the sporting and leisure activities. The only 'sport' mentioned in this issue was draughts and the Northern Ireland Mental Health Association (Antrim Branch) appears to have been the only provider of evening activities. It met only once a week and organised a monthly speaker. Other articles included recipes, fashion and beauty, notices contributed by the Nurses' Christian Fellowship and Domestic Staff Notes.[123] The only original poem was by Robairt Clough, who had been a regular contributor for many years. The poem had been written in 1971, when he was 'in hospital'. He was now referred to as a former patient.

Mo(u)rning '71

No pulsing life is ours to know,
The world is but a picture show,
The 'box', the press, the subtle rumour
Spreading like an ugly tumour
Hear the country's going to ruin
Instead of being up and doing.

Soldiers shot and houses burning,
Bricks are flying, children crying
That's the way my thoughts are turning,
Although at heart for home I'm yearning
Fireside glow and children's laughter.
These are what I'm longing after.

Yet here am I in dull confinement,
Tho' modern methods, all refinements,
A patient still, impatient yet
To see the wider fields beyond

Slieve Donard, where the heather blows;
E'en last night I dreamed of snows,
Of sea and mountain, bog and heather,
But woke to find a shapeless shadow.

Let me roam and let me wander
Through the sunny world out yonder-
Mournes I long for,
I'm not done for
Morning's here but I'm in mourning.
But perhaps this lane will have a turning
Travel along- sing a song
Don't fence me in.[124]

This poem, by a patient who had been so positive about life in Holywell, with its occupational therapy and recreational activities, now saw it as 'dull confinement'. In Holywell Hospital by 1973, facilities 'were generally cramped', occupational therapy was 'substandard',[125] and the hospital farm (Springfarm) was in the process of being sold.[126] By the time *Speedwell* had printed its last issue, the centrally organised Industrial Training Unit, which prepared patients to enter the workforce by employing them in the fulfilment of real contracts, was training 150 patients from Holywell.[127] The final annual report of the NIHA reported that 'work-therapy' still played an important role in the rehabilitation of patients and would be 'developed' further.[128]

Research commissioned in 1998, by the NHSSB, on the experiences of inpatients in Holywell, suggests that the period covered by *Speedwell* was a time when Holywell was at its most active.[129] For patients in the 1990s, some of whom had many admissions (up to sixteen) for periods of a few days to seven months, the experience was one of boredom: 'Several interviewees cited the evenings as being difficult to fill.'[130] Comments included 'Evenings are a long time, there's an awful shut-in feeling'; 'Actually there's nothing to do but sit and wait, you could be waiting for the next meal, television's difficult because concentration isn't the best'.[131] The only activities seem to be limited occupational therapy, relaxation classes and a 'multi-gym'. Patients said: 'we sort of sat and chatted most of the day' amongst themselves. Several respondents agreed with the patient who said 'I'd like them to have more discussion groups where we all meet in a room and talk.'[132]

It seems that changes in psychiatric care have not led to a better inpatient experience in Holywell.[133] Although many improvements have been made in hospital-based care, evidence from the early twenty-first century indicates that there is 'incontrovertible and compelling evidence' that service users find hospital care 'neither safe nor therapeutic'.[134] In contrast, as *Speedwell* shows, the therapeutic community was central to the life of Holywell Hospital in the 1960s.

In conclusion, it can be said that an analysis of *Speedwell* between 1959 and 1973 provides us with an insight into the life of a psychiatric hospital at a time of transition from the old-style asylum with poorly qualified staff, where both staff and patients suffered from the stigma associated with mental illness, to a modern professionally delivered mental health service where the majority of patients are treated in the community and hospital treatment is used only in times of crisis. The period covered by the magazine was one when there was a great deal of criticism of psychiatric services. However, the pages of *Speedwell* suggest that it was a unique time in Holywell, where there was indeed a 'therapeutic community' of staff and patients (perhaps not all) who worked and socialised together. Activities served all tastes, from competitive sport to music, light entertainment, drama, cinema, dance, photography and art.

For some patients, the magazine provided a unique and valuable forum for their literary talents. It also allowed patients to air their grievances and offer 'constructive' criticism. As it was aimed at both staff and patients, it also reduced barriers between them and added to the sense of community. However, the hospital was not a substitute for home, and institutions like Holywell had a negative impact on patients who were confined there for long periods. What *Speedwell* has shown us it that this was a world within a world, inhabited by ordinary people who had a variety of talents, interests and emotions. Holywell Hospital was a 'total institution' and *Speedwell* was an instrument of cohesion within this very confined environment. As such it gives us a valuable insight into this period in the history of mental health services.

NOTES

1. Kelly, B.D., 'The Mental Treatment Act 1945 in Ireland: An historical enquiry', *History of Psychiatry*, 19: 1(2008): 47–67, p.61.
2. Jones, K., *Asylums and After: A Revised History of the Mental Health Services: From the Early 18th Century to the 1990s* (London: Athlone Press, 1993), p.174.
3. Prior, P.M., 'Mental Health Policy in Northern Ireland' in *Social Policy and Administration*, 27: 4 (1993): 323–34, p.323.
4. Manning, N., *The Therapeutic Community Movement: Charisma and Routinisation* (London: Routledge, 1989).
5. Campling, P., 'Therapeutic Communities,' *Advances in Psychiatric Treatment*, 7 (2001):

365–72, p.365. The 1980s and 1990s saw many of these units close.
6. Prior, P.M., *Mental Health and Politics in Northern Ireland: A History of Service Development* (Aldershot: Avebury Press, 1993).
7. WHO, *Expert Committee on Mental Health: 3rd Report* (Geneva: WHO, 1953).
8. Haigh, R., 'Acute wards: problems and solutions modern milieux: therapeutic community solutions to acute ward problems,' *Psychiatric Bulletin*, 26 (2002): 380–2.
9. Jones, *Asylums and After*, p.179
10. Beckett, C., *Thatcher* (London: Haus Publishing, 2006).
11. Enoch Powell, speech given at annual conference of the NAMH (London) in 1961. Available at http://www.nhshistory.net/watertower.html [accessed 28 November 2011].
12. *Report of the Royal Commission on mental illness and mental deficiency* (London: HMSO, 1957).
13. Webb, M., Roy McClelland, Glenda Mock, 'Psychiatric services in Ireland: North and South', *Irish Journal of Psychiatric Medicine*, 19:1(2002): 21–6.
14. Goffman, E., *Asylums: Essays on the Social Situation of Mental Patients and Other Inmates* (Chicago: Doubleday, 1961), p.4.
15. Barton, R., *Institutional Neurosis* (Bristol: John Wright, 1959).
16. Foucault, M., *Discipline & Punish: The Birth of the Prison*, (NY: Vintage Books, 1995). First published in 1975.
17. Szasz, T.S., *The Myth of Mental Illness: Foundations of a Theory of Personal Conduct* (New York: Dell, 1961), p.174.
18. Mulholland, M., *To Care Always: 100 Years of Holywell Hospital, Antrim, 1898–1998* (Antrim: Holywell Hospital, 1999), p.67.
19. Ibid.
20. Northern Ireland Hospital Authority (NIHA) *Annual Reports* for 1960 (p.43) and 1964 (p.131) (Belfast: NIHA, 1961 and 1965).
21. Mulholland, *To Care Always*, p.25.
22. Ibid., pp.59–60.
23. Cowan, R., *Guardian*, 21 December 2000.
24. Mulholland, *To Care Always*, p.66.
25. Ibid.
26. Ibid., p.69.
27. Ibid., p.73.
28. Ibid., p.88.
29. Ibid., p.83.
30. Goffman, *Asylums*, p.95.
31. Ibid., p.96.
32. Reznick, J., *Healing the Nation: Soldiers and the Culture of Care-giving in Britain During the Great War, 1914–1918* (Manchester: Manchester University Press, 2004), p.68.
33. Adams, A., *Medicine by Design: The Architect And The Modern Hospital, 1893–1943* (Minneapolis: University of Minnesota Press, 2008), p.96.
34. Friedman, L.D. (ed.), *Cultural Sutures: Medicine and Media* (Durham, US: Duke University Press, 2004), p. 6.
35. Brewster Mills, A., *Hospital Public Relations Today* (Chicago: Physicians Record Co., 1965), p.237.
36. Goffman, *Asylums*, p.96.
37. *Speedwell*, Holywell Hospital, Antrim, Issue 1 (Summer 1959), p.2.
38. Gavigan, A.C., 'The Mental Hospital Magazine', *Psychiatric Quarterly*, 17(1963): 243–8.
39. *Speedwell*, Issue 1 (Summer 1959), p.4.
40. Ibid., p.45.
41. Anonymous, *St. Thomas's Hospital Gazette*, 59.1 (1961): 13.
42. *Speedwell*, Issue 1 (Summer 1959), p.14.
43. Ibid.
44. Ibid., p.12.
45. *Rara Avis*, *Speedwell*, Winter 1964, p.36.
46. Ibid., p.40.
47. Ibid., p.36.
48. Ibid.
49. *Speedwell*, April 1968, p.25.
50. Ibid., pp.24–5.
51. *Speedwell*, Autumn 1966, p.20.

52. Ibid., p.20–7
53. Handler, R., 'Erving Goffman and the Gestural Dynamics of Modern Selfhood', *Past & Present*, 203: Supplement 4 (2009): 280–300, p.284.
54. *Speedwell*, April 1968, p.25.
55. Ibid.
56. Mulholland, *To Care Always*, p.59.
57. *Speedwell*, Summer 1959, p.12.
58. Mulholland, *To Care Always*, p.64.
59. Ibid.
60. *Speedwell*, Autumn 1961, p.11.
61. Mulholland, *To Care Always*, p.64.
62. Lerner, A., 'A Look At Poetry Therapy', *The Arts In Psychotherapy*, 24:1 (1997): 81–9.
63. *Speedwell*, April 1968, p.15.
64. *Speedwell*, Autumn 1972, pp.10–11.
65. *Speedwell*, Christmas 1966, p.36.
66. *Speedwell*, Christmas 1972, p.29.
67. *Rara Avis, Speedwell*, Winter 1964, p. 41.
68. Ibid., p. 42.
69. Mulholland, *To Care Always*, p. 68; DHSSPS(NI) Mental Health Services in NI, VFM Review (Belfast: DHSSPSNI, 2002) available at http://www.dhsspsni.gov.uk.mental_health_services_in_ni_vfm_review_regional_summary.pdf [accessed 28 November 2011].
70. Doroshow, J., 'Performing a cure for schizophrenia: insulin coma therapy on the wards', *Hist. Med. Allied Sci.*, 62 (2007): 213–43, p.213.
71. Doroshow, 'Performing a cure', p.213.
72. Stein, G. and Greg Wilkinson (eds), *Seminars in General Adult Psychiatry*, 2nd edition, (London: Royal College of Psychiatrists, 2007), p.215.
73. *Rara Avis, Speedwell*, Winter 1964, p.40.
74. Ibid., p.39.
75. Moncrieff, J., 'An investigation into the precedents of modern drug treatment in psychiatry', *History of Psychiatry*, 10: 40 (October 1999): 475–90, p.475.
76 Goffman, *Asylums*, p.68.
77. Ibid.
78. Ibid., p.69.
79. Mocellin, G., 'Occupational Therapy and Psychiatry', *International Journal of Social Psychiatry*, 25: 29 (1979): 29–37, p.31.
80. Ibid., p.29
81. NIHA, 14th *Annual Report* 1960 (Belfast: NIHA, 1961).
82. Mulholland, *To Care Always*, p.76.
83. Wandsworth N. and A. Miles, 'Industrial Therapy in Psychiatric Hospitals', A King's Fund Report (London: Ministry of Health, 1969), p.9.
84. Clough, R., *Speedwell*, Christmas 1967, p.41.
85. L. McK., Ward F. 3A, *Speedwell*, Summer 1966, p.40.
86. *Rara Avis, Speedwell*, Winter 1964, pp.3–6.
87. Greeley, H., *Bird's Nest Soup* (Dublin: Figgis and Co., 1987), p.98.
88. Rara Avis, *Speedwell*, Winter 1964, p.39.
89. NIHA, 17th *Annual Report* 1963 (Belfast: NIHA, 1964), p.43.
90. Mulholland, *To Care Always*, p.76.
91. Ibid., p.80.
92. Ibid., p.82.
93. *Speedwell*, Christmas 1970, p.29.
94. William R. Carney, Jr., 'Personal Accounts: My Experiences as a Psychiatric Patient in the 1960s', *Psychiatric Services*, 56: 12 (December 2005): 1499–500; Greeley, *Bird's Nest Soup*; Goffman, Asylums.
95. NIHA, 13th *Annual Report* 1960 (Belfast: NIHA, 1961), p.40.
96. *Speedwell*, Christmas 1962, p.34.
97. *Speedwell*, December 1968, p.29.
98. *Speedwell*, Spring 1972, p.29.
99. *Speedwell*, December 1968, p.28.
100. *Speedwell*, Autumn 1965, p.40.

101. *Speedwell*, December 1968, p.29.
102. *Speedwell*, Christmas 1962, p.34.
103. Ibid.
104. *Speedwell*, Autumn 1965, p.40.
105. *Speedwell*, Summer 1967, p.33.
106. *Speedwell*, December 1968, p.28.
107. *Speedwell*, Summer 1971, p.20–1.
108. *Speedwell*, December 1968, p.29.
109. *Speedwell*, Autumn 1963, p.32.
110. Goffman, *Asylums*, p.68.
111. *Speedwell*, Spring 1972, p.28.
112. Goffman, *Asylums*, p.94.
113. Hinshelwood, R.D., *Suffering Insanity: Psychoanalytic Essays on Psychosis* (Hove, England/New York: Brunner-Routledge, 2004), p.15.
114. Mulholland, *To Care Always*, p.83.
115. Ibid., pp.83–4.
116. *Speedwell*, Spring 1972, p.28.
117. Ibid.
118. Mulholland, *To Care Always*, p.86.
119. O'Reilly, D. and M. Stevenson, 'Mental Health in Northern Ireland: Have "The Troubles" Made It Worse?', *Journal of Epidemiology and Community Health*, 57: 7 (2003): 488–92, p.488.
120. *Speedwell*, Easter 1973, p.35.
121. The author is 'R', and is probably Robairt Clough, *Speedwell*, Easter 1973, p.18
122. *Speedwell*, Spring 1972, p.28.
123. *Speedwell*, Christmas 1973, p.5.
124. Ibid., pp.16–17.
125. Mulholland, *To Care Always*, p.82.
126. *Speedwell*, Spring 1969, p.29.
127. Mulholland, *To Care Always*, p.82.
128. NIHA, 25th Annual Report 1971 (Belfast: NIHA, 1972), p.29.
129. NHSSB, 'Centre Voices: A Qualitative Study of the Experiences of People Who Have Been In-patients in Tobernaveen Centre, Holywell Hospital', (Ballymena: NHSSB, 1998), p.21.
130. Ibid.
131. Ibid.
132. NHSSB, 'Centre Voices', p.22.
133. DOH, 'Department of Health guide on provision of adult acute in-patient care' (London: DOH, 2002).
134. Rex Haigh, 'Acute wards: problems and solutions Modern milieux: therapeutic community solutions to acute ward problems', *Psychiatric Bulletin*, 26 (2002),pp.380–2.

4

Mental Health Services in Ireland, 1959–2010

Dermot Walsh

The Report of the Inspector of Mental Hospitals for the year 1959 recorded that there were, on the 31 December 1959, 19,590 patients under care in the district and auxiliary mental hospitals compared with 20,046 in the preceding year.[1] These patients resided in 18 district and three auxiliary hospitals. Four of the district hospitals had almost 2,000 patients, Ballinasloe, Cork, Grangegorman and Portrane. In addition, there were another 1,019 resident in private mental hospitals. This represented a small decline on those of 1958 that were the highest ever recorded in the 26 counties (the Republic of Ireland).[2]

The 1959 report returned the diagnoses of those under care, with 10,670, or exactly half, suffering from schizophrenia disorders. These were followed by 2,782 or 13 per cent with manic-depressive reaction. The only other group of any size comprised of people diagnosed with 'mental deficiency', numbering 2,242 or 11 per cent. The number of admissions had risen from 5,877 in 1950, of which 31 per cent were voluntary, to 11,742 in 1959, of which 58 per cent were voluntary. Schizophrenia and manic-depressive reaction, when taken together, accounted for 54 per cent of admissions (in almost equal measure) and alcoholism for 5 per cent of admissions. A detailed breakdown of the occupation of admitted and resident patients for the year was also provided in the 1959 report.[3]

The Inspector of Mental Hospitals, Dr. Dolphin, noted a change in the 'the machinery for administering the mental health services'. This was the result of the Health Authorities Bill 1959, which broke down the statutory barriers between mental health services and other health services. The aim was to integrate psychiatry more closely into general health services, by removing them from separate administration by county councils and transferring their administration to the new health authorities in the larger catchments. Inter alia, it was hoped that this transfer of responsibility to a wider health administration would break down the stigma of mental illness.

Because of overcrowding at Grangegorman and Cork, elderly patients were transferred from both hospitals to former tuberculosis sanatoria in mountainous areas – to Crooksling in Co. Dublin and Heatherside in Co. Cork. In 1959, outpatient clinics continued to grow, with 5,442 patients making 14,264 attendances. Outpatient clinics had been provided for by the Mental Treatment Act of 1945 and, as the Inspector declared in his 1956 report, were 'regarded by many as the greatest single advance in the treatment of mental disease in this country in recent years'.[4]

At that time, the cost of the mental health service was defrayed by the county and county boroughs from their rateable income. Through the provisions of the Health Services (Financial Provisions) Act 1947, each authority was reimbursed to the extent of 50 per cent of revenue expenditure from the Central Fund. This arrangement, which must have disadvantaged those authorities with the lowest rate income, led to a non-capital expenditure from central sources, and therefore half of total expenditure, for the year to the 31 March 1960 of £1,877,500.[5] In addition to the district mental hospitals and their auxiliaries, the Central Mental Hospital at Dundrum, Dublin, as it was to be known following the Mental Treatment Act 1961, was administered and funded by the Department of Justice. On 31 December 1962 there were ninety-nine patients resident. These patients came from two sources, first by transfer from the prisons of prisoners believed to be suffering from mental disorder and, secondly, by powers of section 207 of the Mental Treatment Act 1945, from psychiatric hospitals of involuntary patients who, following a sitting of the District Court in the relevant hospital, were found to have committed an indictable offense. The patients of private hospitals, prior to the establishment of the first national private medical insurance scheme, the Voluntary Health Insurance, in 1957 were responsible for their own expenses, apart from some who were members of groups paid for through their own schemes, such as the Gardai and firms such as Guinness.

THE COMMISSION OF ENQUIRY ON MENTAL ILLNESS, 1961

Despite these changes and the influence of the Mental Treatment Act 1945, in introducing voluntary admission and the limited impact of outpatient clinics, there was a general consensus that matters in the mental health services were not quite what they might be. This was the case despite the aspirations outlined in the duties and responsibilities of personnel employed in the service as laid out in the Mental

Hospitals (Officers and Servants) Order of 1946,[6] which was an accompaniment of the 1945 Mental Treatment Act. The service remained largely institutionalised, there were no specialised services for children, general practice was largely uninvolved in psychiatric care and all inpatient care was in nineteenth-century mental hospitals, with the exception of the only purpose-built hospital of the twentieth century, that at Ardee, Co. Louth. Additionally the service comprised almost exclusively of psychiatric nurses and doctors, with no general nurses, psychologists, social workers or occupational therapists. And, more particularly, the hospitalisation rate per 100,000 of the population was the highest in the world.[7] It is difficult to determine exactly the origin of the concern that resulted in the setting up (by Warrant) of the Commission of Enquiry on Mental Illness in 1961. However, a seminal impetus had come from an analogous situation in England and Wales, where a report had indicated the need to reduce numbers of inpatients through extension of community services.[8] The Report itself, without any ministerial introduction, did not give a rationale for its *raison d'être*. The Commission held its first meeting on 31 July 1961.

Perhaps the same concern (at the size of the inpatient population) underlay the holding of a Conference of Managers and Medical Superintendents, convened by the Department of Health in December of the same year. Addressing the Conference, the minister stressed the need to improve and expand the treatment services and to reduce drastically the number of inpatients. The big mental hospitals in Dublin, Cork and Ballinasloe received particular attention. Conference participants were requested to prepare concrete plans for the improvement of their services.[9] Meanwhile, in 1960, the former sanatorium at Ballyowen, was transferred to the mental health services in Dublin and henceforth became known as St. Loman's Hospital, and the former sanatorium at Newcastle was approved as a district mental hospital for Co. Wicklow. During the same period, similar concern surrounded the care of the intellectually disabled, as a separate Commission of Enquiry had been set up, also in 1961, to examine the problems associated with the care and treatment of 'mentally handicapped' persons.

The Commission of Enquiry was charged 'to examine and report on the health services available for the mentally ill and to make recommendations as to the most practicable and desirable measures for the improvements of these services'. Membership of the twenty-six-person Commission comprised a legal chair, Irish and UK psychiatrists, a psychologist, managers, representatives of the nursing body, lay members and a journalist who had previously written about the state of services in a national newspaper. Four witnesses, including the present writer and a representation from the Irish Division of the Royal College of Psychiatrists, gave evidence to the Commission.

The Commission, in its summary, having noted the extremely high rate of hospitalisation, expressed the view that 'it will be clear that, in Ireland, mental illness poses a health problem of the first magnitude.' As to the hospitals, it opined that

> [T]here are still too many barrack-like structures, characterised by large wards, gloomy corridors and stone stairways. Too many also have inadequate facilities and services and lack the purposeful activity and therapeutic atmosphere that are necessary in a modern mental hospital. In the Commission's view, a pattern of services confined to the traditional type of mental hospital would leave unfilled the need to diagnose and treat as widely as possible incipient mental illness, to provide in whole or in part, treatment in the home or in surroundings akin to the patient's normal mode of living, to provide adequate community services, and, in particular, it would leave unbridged the gap between psychiatry and general medicine.[10]

The Commission was nothing if not diligent and obviously took its responsibilities very seriously. It met on thirty-eight occasions and most meetings were two-day affairs. In addition, it set up a number of committees and these held seventy-two meetings. Finally, in 1966, the Department of Health published the Commission's Report, which ran to 224 pages. As a cardinal reference point,

> The Commission's recommendations indicate that radical and widespread changes will have to be made, if these services are to be brought up to the desired standard. In brief, these recommendations postulate a combination of community services and short-time and long-term hospital care.[11]

It went on to recommend home care, day hospitals, hostels, family care, domiciliary consultations and the use in the community, not only of psychiatrists, but also of general practitioners, nurses, psychiatric social workers, voluntary organisations and public health personnel. It also recommended research into the reasons why the numbers in hospitals were so great and recommended that the nascent Medicosocial Research Board undertake this work. This work was eventually undertaken and found no evidence to support the thesis that there was more serious mental illness in Ireland than elsewhere.[12]

The Commission recommended the setting up of short-term units in general hospitals to deal with acute illness requiring inpatient care, to work in close collaboration with the general hospital which 'would be a valuable step towards creating a link between psychiatry and other forms of medicine'.[13] It envisioned special services for certain classes such as children and adolescents and others. It also advised intensive rehabilitation services while stressing the preventive and early diagnostic role of the general practitioner and stressed 'that he is most likely to have the first opportunity of seeing the patient and diagnosing his problems'.[14] On medical education, it was of the view 'that the curricula of medical schools were inadequate to enable doctors in general and general practitioners in particular, to take their proper part in the services'. It advocated wide programmes of public education to overcome stigma and enable persons to come forward early for treatment as it considered that 'in this way best outcomes are most likely'.[15]

For the general purpose of advancing its recommendations, the Commission recommended the setting up of a small expert National Advisory Council which, on its own initiative or at the request of the minister, would provide advice on any matters relating to mental health services. This recommendation was to be re-echoed, forty years later, in the Report of the Expert Group *A Vision for Change*. The detailed statement of the 1966 Commission's recommendations ran to over thirty pages. In its understanding of the defects of the service of the time the Commission was particularly acute and its recommendations so visionary that they are hardly bettered in principle or in spirit by its successors, *Planning for the Future* in 1984 and *A Vision for Change* in 2006.[16]

The chief problem concerning the 1966 Commission report was its very comprehensiveness at the expense of detail. No mechanism of implementation was broached and no costing was attempted. In consequence, it is difficult to evaluate the impact it had on mental health services.

CATCHMENTING AND SECTORISATION

During this period, some initiatives were emerging at local level. Dr. Ivor Browne, Professor of Psychiatry at University College Dublin and Clinical Director of St. Loman's, Ballyowen, and subsequently of St. Brendan's, Grangegorman, together with the present author, were encouraged by the example of 'sector psychiatry' which had been the subject of a World Health Organisation demonstration project in the 13th arrondissement of Paris.[17] In their opinion, the subdivision into smaller catchment areas seemed a sensible way of breaking up the highly centralised model of care delivery in the Dublin area, where the 2,000 bedded Grangegorman Hospital was the only public inpatient base for a population of close to a million persons. The principle, in practice, involved the breaking up of such large areas into smaller catchments, each containing populations of around 100,000, with their own inpatient base. These catchments could be subdivided further for the purposes of delivering community care into sectors of about 30-35,000 in population, each of these served by its own multi-disciplinary team of professionals.[18]

Already, the seeds of this development had been laid down with the St. Loman's Hospital at Ballyowen, serving a catchment involving the postal districts of Dublin 10 and 12 and the surrounding area of County Dublin. At first, in 1962, it was decided that the hospital, a former sanatorium with vast areas of glass and completely open in terms of access, would only accept patients who had already been admitted to St. Brendan's and had proven their docility – and only female patients at that! Accordingly, such patients were transferred out to a hospital remote from their urban origins and their visiting relatives had to make their way to rural County Dublin to visit them. Eventually, around 1965, since nothing catastrophic had occurred despite the absence of locked doors, direct admissions were introduced and, soon afterwards, male patients were accepted.

By now, the former sanatorium at Newcastle, Co. Wicklow had been allocated to psychiatry[19] and without waiting for its conversion to psychiatric purposes, a medical superintendent and matron had been appointed and they began a community and domiciliary service on the basis of GP referral. At first, inpatient care was sought in St. Brendan's, but reasonably quickly, following some adaptations, the hospital began to cater for its own inpatients.

The quest was now on for inpatient bases to serve the other newer and smaller catchments. This was to prove quite fruitful. In South Dublin, a former nursing home, Cluain Mhuire was acquired to provide the centre of community-based services in Blackrock/Dunlaoire and the Dublin Health Authority, which had replaced the earlier city and county administration, contracted with the neighbouring St. John of God Hospital, which also received private patients, to fund a number of beds for the public service from the Cluain Mhuire catchment. A relatively new fever hospital in Clonskeagh was persuaded to make a unit available for inpatient care for the catchment of Dublin South East, comprising Ringsend, Donnybrook and Milltown and Rathmines. Now attention was turned to Dublin South Central where a unit of the former St. Kevin's Hospital was made available for that sector of south inner city Dublin.[20] This unit was subsequently demolished and replaced by a new modern unit in the hospital that was now called St. James.

In North Dublin, St. Ita's Hospital, Portrane, which up to this point had not admitted patients directly, was provided with an admission unit for the sector of North County Dublin and surrounding parts of the north city. A nineteenth-century building in Dublin North East, St. Vincent's Fairview, which had been established by the Dublin Catholic Archdiocese for the care of female religious, was induced to provide inpatient care in a newly constructed unit funded by the Eastern Health Board (which by now had replaced the Dublin Health Authority) for the surrounding area and sectors, later to be supplemented by a smaller unit in the Mater Hospital with fifteen beds. The James Connolly Hospital, a former sanatorium, made available a unit for the Dublin North Central catchment area serving Castleknock and Blanchardstown. Two adjoining sectors of this catchment, Finglas and Cabra remained dependent for inpatient care on St. Brendan's until 2010, but eventually transferred with the other sectors, to a new, recently constructed unit on this campus.

These individual catchments each appointed a clinical director, a consultant psychiatrist equivalent to the old resident medical superintendant (RMS), and efforts were made to recruit multi-disciplinary teams so that most catchments had individualised teams serving each sector (three or four in each catchment). A similar initiative followed in Cork, where a catchment based on a local hospital in Skibereen, serving the catchment of West Cork, had been in operation since the 1970s. This would later move to the General Hospital at Bantry. New catchments were created in North Cork, based on two admission units in the former sanatorium, Sarsfieldscourt, at Glanmire. For East Cork County and City, the North Lee catchment was created, based on a unit at Shanakiel in the grounds of the large Our Lady's Psychiatric Hospital, the Cork equivalent of Grangegorman. This inpatient base would later move to a unit in the Mercy Hospital, freeing up the Shanakiel unit, now renamed Carraig Mor, to undertake specialised intensive care and rehabilitation. For West Cork City and adjoining county areas (to the junction with the West Cork catchment), a unit was provided in Cork Regional, later to become Cork University, Hospital.

The creation of these individual catchment area services led to the eventual closure of Our Lady's Psychiatric Hospital, Cork in 2002.

IMPORTANT DEVELOPMENTS IN THE 1970s AND 1980s

The Aborted 1981 Act

In 1981, the Health (Mental Services) Act was passed with the purpose of 'making further and better provision for the regulation of the care and treatment of persons suffering from mental disorders'. Inter alia, it proposed the abolition of the certification distinction embodied in the 1945 Act, whereby two medical recommendations were required for a private patient as against one for a public patient. The detention period was to be of twenty-eight days, but could be extended following a separate examination by two medical practitioners. The Act established boards for the review of detention, consisting of a legal, medical and lay member. Although enacted, the Act never came into force because of the belief in some quarters that it was logistically too difficult to implement.

Planning for the Future, 1984

Despite forward moves in services, by 1981, the projection of the Commission that, if its proposals had been implemented, beds would have fallen to 8,000, was not fulfilled and on 31 March of that year there were still 13,984 inpatients. Whether, as a consequence or not of this failure to reach the target, in October 1981 the then Minister for Health, Mrs Eileen Desmond, set up a Study Group on the Development of the Psychiatric Services. This resulted in a report published in December 1984 entitled The *Psychiatric Services – Planning for the Future.*[21] This group was home grown, with a predominantly medical and civil service composition, with one nurse, but with no representatives from other health professionals or from service users or carers. As a generalisation, the Report in its summary of main findings conceded that:

> At present the psychiatric hospital is the focal point of psychiatric services in most parts of the country. Large numbers of patients reside permanently in these hospitals. Many of them have lived there for years in conditions which in many cases are less than adequate because of overcrowding and capital underfunding. In addition staff and public attitudes have tended to concentrate effort on hospital care as a result of which community facilities are relatively undeveloped.[22]

The Study Group met on 27 occasions, including one two-day meeting. In summary, its recommendations stressed that the service should be comprehensive across a wide range of provision, including day care, community-based residences and rehabilitation. It should be community-orientated, it should be sectorised, and acute inpatient services should be based in psychiatric units in general hospitals. Each unit should establish admission policies, and patients currently residing in psychiatric hospitals should be accommodated in community-based housing. Attention was also given to children and adolescents. Each health board should draw up successive five-year plans. In considering the cost implications of its recommendations, on the basis of 0.5 beds per 1,000 of the population for acute and medium stay patients in general hospital units, the requirement would be for 1,700 beds nationally. This was calculated to cost thirty-four million Irish pounds.[23] For long-stay patients a guideline of 0.5 beds per 1,000 of the population was estimated, of which 0.4 would be in community residences and 0.1 in units for continuing care for persons with severe behavioural problems arising from dementia. The cost of this provision was estimated at twenty-three million Irish pounds. An additional 1,420 day places, to bring the total to 2,000, would be required at a cost of eight million Irish pounds. Somewhat confusingly the report estimated the total capital cost of its recommendations as coming to fifty million, despite the total from the component parts, as itemised, totalling sixty seven million. It suggested that the cost be spread over a period of 10-15 years. Curiously, despite recommending other services, such as child psychiatric teams, the Study Group felt there was no need to increase or critically examine the existing revenue budget which it deemed sufficient for the task in hand.

Trying to Close Hospitals

Shortly afterwards, in 1987, the Minister for Health, Barry Desmond, made the shock and largely unexpected announcement, that he was going to close two hospitals – St. Dympna's, Carlow and St. Patrick's, Castlerea. No reason was given for this choice, although it was true that for some time, services for North Kildare had been removed from the Carlow service and allocated to St. Loman's, Ballyowen, because towns such as Celbridge, Leixlip and Maynooth were nearer to Ballyowen than they were to Carlow. Ironically, St. Dympna's had become something of a showcase for Irish mental health services due to the energies and vision of its Resident Medical Superintendent, Dr. Bertie Blake, who had been committed to community care and had reduced bed numbers substantially through developing community services. In addition, he had brought other medical services into the hospital so that it was now more of a medical centre than a psychiatric hospital per se. By the time of the closure announcement, he had retired. Officials from the Department of Health and the Inspector of Mental Hospitals were dispatched to negotiate the closure with the two services involved. Needless to say, the local reaction in these two communities and from the nursing unions was one of anger and outrage. Accordingly, the Department personnel were not greeted very amicably. In the case of Carlow, alternatives to using the hospital as an inpatient location were explored, including the conversion of a small maternity unit which was on the St. Dympna's campus to provided acute inpatient care. Carlow had received attention before Castlerea, although departmental staff visited there too in the context of the proposed closure. Eventually, in the face of local opposition and a change of government, the whole idea fizzled out and both hospitals survived the crisis, although Castlerea was later to succumb to closure, in the face of the provision of an inpatient unit at Roscommon General Hospital in 1997, with the former St. Patrick's becoming a prison.[24] Carlow provided inpatient care for elderly long-stay patients in a vestigial fashion and day services and a mental health centre for the two Carlow sectors of the new combined Carlow/Kilkenny Mental Health Service until November 2011, when it finally closed.

Psychiatry in General Hospitals

On the wider front, progress, if slow, was being made. A number of general hospital psychiatric units opened. The original unit in Waterford Regional Hospital, which was the very first in the country, opening in the 1960s, had been replaced by a new modern unit. A psychiatric unit had been built and opened in Cork Regional Hospital and, similarly, in the 1970s and '80s, units opened in Limerick, Tralee, Galway and Letterkenny. These units were provided within the fabric of the general hospital. Separate psychiatric admission units on the campus of general hospitals but not within the fabric of the hospital were established at Clonmel, Castlebar and Bantry Hospital. At the Mater Hospital, Dublin, fifteen beds in a basement ward had been made available for psychiatry, analogous to a similar arrangement in St. Vincent's Hospital, Elm Park, Dublin. Despite this progress, in no instance did the initiative lead to the concurrent closure of the parent mental hospital, although, in later years much of St. Mary's Castlebar was given over to third-level educational purposes. Later, integrated units were opened at the Mercy Hospital Cork, Castlebar, Portlaoise, Kilkenny and a new purpose-built unit, Elm Mount, replaced the former St. Camillus ward at St. Vincent's, Elm Park, together with a new unit at James Connolly Hospital, Blanchardstown. As a result of these initiatives, by 2010, the majority of admissions to inpatient care in the public sector were to general hospital units rather than to psychiatric hospitals built in the nineteenth century. As a consequence, the old hospitals at Cork, Castlebar and Ballinasloe had closed and most of the remaining hospitals were vestigial by the standards of their halcyon days. However, in 2006, they still contained 1,180 long-stay patients in generally unsatisfactory accommodation.[25]

Community Care

Slowly and incrementally, long-stay and other patients, such as those who were homeless, were accommodated in community residential accommodation. These varied in the level of support provided by staff. In the so-called high support residences of 10-15 patients or residents, there was 24-hour nursing cover; in the medium support residences, day cover; and in the smaller 4-5 person, low support residences, occasional call-ins by mainly nursing staff was provided. The search for suitable houses to buy or rent was a feature of services in those days and engendered a deal of enthusiasm and challenge. I can recall Department of Health personnel and officials from the Clare service, setting out on one dark November day to view the 'canon's house' a disused parochial house in West Clare, buffeted by the Atlantic gales with faded photographs of a diocesan pilgrimage to Lourdes in the 1930s on the walls. In the event, the house was left to its windy devices and the search continued elsewhere. Later the larger of these community residences were criticised as constituting mini-institutions and lacking rehabilitation initiative towards independent living.

Premises were also sourced for day hospitals, either in hospital property or by rental or other arrangement. As far as possible, their location was selected so that there was one in each sector. Some doubled as mental health centres as well, out of which the sector team operated. There was also recognition that in some hospitals there was an inappropriate placement of elderly and, particularly, of intellectually disabled patients, in general adult wards. Accordingly, a programme of 'de-designation'was introduced whereby these patients were moved to inclusive accommodation where their special needs were more appropriately met and provided for. In many instances, such as in Sligo, Waterford, Monaghan and Ballinasloe, intellectually disabled patients were moved to existing residential care designated for their disability. In others, such as Portlaoise and Mullingar, they were moved to self-contained accommodation within the parent hospital. One adverse consequence of all of this was that, being no longer 'on the register' of the hospital, they then ceased to come under the remit of the Inspectorate of Mental Hospitals, with no alternative arrangements for inspection in place.

Overall, progress towards moving to community care was patchy and uneven. Some services, such as those of St. Loman's, Ballyowen and Cavan/Monaghan, had substantially implemented community provision as indicated by low admission and residence rates and by very few patients becoming long-stay in institutional care. The latter in particular was often quoted as an exemplar, not alone because of what had been achieved but also because of the administrative and clinical arrangements, particularly those of rehabilitation through multi-disciplinary teamwork, which had been responsible for the changes wrought. On the other hand there were some services where little had changed from the 1960s.

Mental Health Information Systems

Throughout the nineteenth century, the data supplied in the annual reports of the Inspectors of Lunacy on patients admitted and resident in asylums were comprehensive. They included details on their demography and medical conditions in the diagnostic categories prevalent in that century, supposed cause of illnesses, duration of illness prior to admission and much else besides. These extensive data mostly disappeared in the twentieth century reports. However, in 1958, a survey of mental illness in accordance with the International Classification of Diseases was carried out on all patients admitted, departed, deceased and resident during that year. This survey related solely to diagnostic categories. The Inspector's Report of 1959, which contained the results, was less than optimistic with the outcome:

> While an effort was made to ensure that the classification of illnesses would be carried on a uniform basis in all institutions, the wide variation in the returns from similar types of institutions suggest that different criteria may have been applied in deciding on classification.[26] Nevertheless half of the patients resident in psychiatric beds were returned with a diagnosis of schizophrenia and a quarter of admissions were returned with a diagnosis of

schizophrenia, with another quarter returned with a diagnosis of manic-depressive reaction.

Faced with the very high psychiatric hospitalisation rate in Ireland the 1961, the Commission stated that it was unable, because of paucity of data, to decide whether this reflected more mental illness in Ireland than elsewhere. However, it recommended that the question should be addressed by the Medico-social Research Board (MSRB), which had just been established by statutory instrument. The new board acceded to this request. As a first step, it analysed and published the returns from the 1963 Census of psychiatric hospital residents which had been set up by the Department of Health. In 1973, it established the National Psychiatric Inpatient Reporting System which, starting with a census, published thereafter detailed annual reports on admissions, discharges and deaths. This series is continued by the Health Research Board (HRB), the successor to the MSRB, and also involved decennial censuses which have now become triennial. Because the information in these reports is cross-sectional only and relates solely to inpatient care, psychiatric case registers were set up by MSRB in certain services to follow patients throughout their clinical careers in all phases of care, outpatient, day care etc. Unfortunately, this endeavour faltered through resource limitation. Nonetheless, certain regional services, in Limerick and Cluain Mhuire in Dublin, did succeed in establishing patient management systems with longitudinal follow-through information. More recently, HRB in association with the Health Service Executive (HSE) embarked on a very ambitious information system, entitled Wisdom, but this has been shelved because of the substantial resource implications arising from the complexity of the system.

Equally unsatisfactory has been the lack of comprehensive information on budgeting and expenditure in psychiatric services. There have been suspicions that lack of transparency has been a deliberate feature of health funding and expenditure, so that funds are available for transmission to politically sensitive demands as occasion arises, irrespective of priority and need. Not surprisingly 70-75 per cent of non-capital expenditure is now accounted for by wages and salaries.

THE GREEN PAPER ON MENTAL HEALTH, 1992

Cumulatively by the end of March 1991, service initiatives had reduced the inpatient population to 8,207. In June 1992, the Department of Health published a Green Paper on Mental Health.[27] This came on the initiative of the then Minister for Health Dr. John

O'Connell who in his foreword declared that 'I have been concerned for many years with the quality of services we provide for persons suffering from mental illness and the legal provision which underpins these services.' The paper was in two parts. The first dealt with the services and progress made since *Planning for the Future* and the second with mental health legislation. The paper reported that 'Figures suggest that while facilities for the care of the mentally ill are increasingly to be found in the community, our services are still heavily reliant on hospital beds.'[28] However, it did note that the number of admissions had fallen from 28,330 in 1984 to 22,118 in 1990.[29] On the other hand, Irish rates of hospital residence were twice as high as those of France, Denmark and England and Wales and, although the rates of referral for consultation to psychiatric services were low, once patients came to the service, they were retained there, rather than being referred back to their general practitioners. The Green Paper noted the increase in day hospital and day centre places and the fact that the number of patients becoming 'new long-stay', i.e. passing to more than one year in continuous inpatient care, had substantially reduced.

In an extended review and re-iteration of the recommendations of *Planning for the Future*, the Green Paper stated that 'the momentum to provide additional community facilities must be maintained particularly in areas which are still far from meeting the norms for community services recommended in *Planning for the Future*' and 'as many of existing long-stay patients as possible be transferred to alternative community settings'.[30] The bulk of this part of the Paper was essentially a review of 'the service developments which are under way … and the improvements which will be needed to make the services fully comprehensive and community orientated'.[31] A page and a half of the Green Paper was devoted to the private hospitals. While acknowledging the role that these hospitals played in care provision, the paper pointed out the difficulties inherent on their current inability to provide community care for their clientele. However, it did not discuss the funding required to bring about the improvements it advocated.

Part Two of the Green Paper, dealing with legislation, stressed that there should be statutory obligation to provide services and 'to integrate further the psychiatric with health services in general'. Having reviewed the international law and principles in relation to mental disorder, the paper first occupied itself with definitions of mental disorder and mental health centres. It then dealt with issues concerning the applicant for a person's detention, the nature of the medical recommendation, the duration of detention and the review of detention by a mental health review board. Next for attention was the issue of the legal framework for consent to treatment, legislation for mentally ill offenders, supervision orders or community treatment orders and legal representation for detained and other patients in the psychiatric system. This part of the paper was essentially a set of proposals for reform and discussion of proposals based on an acknowledgement that the current legal safeguards as provided by the 1945 Act (as amended) did not conform to international standards of protection for people with mental disorders.

The consequence of the discussion surrounding the Green Paper was the publication, in 1995, of a White Paper by the Department of Health entitled *A New Mental Health Act*.[32] This set out in some detail a more formal presentation of the 1992 proposals dealing with the main issues discussed in the Green Paper, with chapters concerning criteria for involuntary admission, procedures for voluntary admission, duration of detention, review of detention orders, consent to treatment and the mentally disordered offender but did not consider community treatment orders. These subjects and the manner of accommodating them formed the basis of the Mental Health Act 2001 and the Criminal Law (Insanity) Act of 2006.

THE INSPECTORATE OF MENTAL HOSPITALS

In 1987, a new Inspectorate of Mental Hospitals was installed. Unlike previous inspectorates, where the personnel were full-time staff members within the Department of Health, this new initiative consisted of an inspector who was a clinical director of area services, an assistant inspector who was likewise a clinical director and a director of psychiatric nursing. All three were part-time and combined their inspectorial and advisory roles to the minister and the Department with their service commitments to their respective health boards. This inspectorate carried out the annual statutory inspections in some detail, hospital by hospital and ward by ward, and included all community services as well. Annual reports were published on a yearly basis between the years 1988 and 2003. During this time, there were joint promotional meetings between the Inspectorate, departmental officials, clinical directors and administrators and professionals of the health boards to plan and advance improvements. On the whole, these efforts were successful and stimulating. There was, too, an added advantage in that there existed a separate programme and programme manager for mental health within each of the eight health boards, which had been established in 1970, replacing the former local administrations such as the Dublin Health Authority. In the Dublin area, the single health board later mutated into three, making ten in all. These were dissolved with the setting up of the Health Service Executive (HSE), with national responsibility for health and social care and without dedicated representation for mental health. Mental health policy had become anonymous within the larger health and social care framework of service delivery.

In its report for 1993, the Inspectorate noted that the new general hospital units had virtually eliminated transfer of patients from them to the old hospitals but pointed out that this was not so in the case of the Unit at Galway Hospital, where patients from West Galway, in relatively large numbers, were still being transferred to St. Brigid's in Ballinasloe.[33] The report noted that hospitals in Letterkenny, Sligo, Waterford and Castlebar had transferred all their intellectually disabled patients ('mentally handicapped' was the terminology of the time) to appropriate specialised community or residential facilities, but that this was not the case in Ballinasloe or Clonmel. The Inspectorate was concerned at conditions in St. Brendan's and St. Ita's and with the admission facilities in Vergemount Unit, Clonskeagh and hoped that this latter would be replaced by a unit for this catchment area at St. Vincent's, Elm Park, Dublin. St. Loman's in Mullingar had a high admission rate and admission facilities were unsatisfactory. An admission unit for Carlow/Kilkenny was planned in St. Luke's, Kilkenny, as was one for Leix/Offaly at the general hospital in Portlaoise, where the admission facilities in St. Fintan's, the nineteenth-century hospital, were deemed unsatisfactory. Both these units opened in the first years of the twenty-first century. The Inspectorate deplored the lack of capital funding and pointed out the poor furnishing and decoration of health board hospitals contrasted with the higher standards, in this regard, in some private hospitals. It was to be remembered that in the 1970s and 1980s, there had been a minor capital programme operated by the Department of Health, which allowed for the disbursement of not insubstantial sums for urgent capital works with a minimum of formality. Unfortunately this scheme had ended. The Inspectorate advised services to draw up practice and procedural manuals dealing with the handling of various occurrences and emergencies embracing such matters as the use of seclusion, special nursing, and patients who were absent on leave. It, too, was concerned with issues such as privacy, personalised clothing, and the wearing of identity badges by staff. In 1998, the Inspectorate published a manual dealing with these and other issues, entitled *Guidelines on Good Practice and Quality Assurance in Mental Health Services.*[34]

TRAINING AND STAFFING OF MENTAL HEALTH SERVICES

The staffing and the training of staff in the psychiatric services had long been a concern in Ireland. There was a particular issue with multi-disciplinary staffing. As far back as the time of the Report of the Commission of Enquiry in 1966,[35] the absence of social workers, psychologists and occupational therapists had been an issue. Although there had been some improvement in recruitment, the matter was still quite unsatisfactory even as late as the 1990s, and teams with a full multi-disciplinary complement were the exception. Traditionally, the service had been a doctor/nurse one (at its highest point, the psychiatric nursing complement nationally had reached almost 8,000) and there was a reluctance or failure to appreciate the complementary rule and special skills of other disciplines. Insecurity of work tenure and the threat of having one's role supplanted were behind this passive, sometimes active, resistance to working with other health and social care professionals. This was augmented by the reluctance of these other professionals to join psychiatric services because of the professional isolation caused by their numerical disadvantage in these services – a problem that persists to this day.

The training of psychiatric nurses had moved considerably from the old 'keeper' role to something more professional, and the great majority of nurses had received general nurse training as well as mental health training. Increasingly, they assumed the managerial roles that had proliferated in the services. They were represented by the Services Industrial Professional and Technical Union (SIPTU) and by the more vocal Psychiatric Nurses' Association (PNA), a powerful body not affiliated to the Irish Congress of Trade Unions, which, while it was successful in advancing the welfare of its members, often slowed down advances in service provision in pursuit of its own objectives. This sometimes had the effect of delaying progress, such as the opening of new facilities, due to disputes over staffing levels.[36]

Mental hospital doctors had become a strong professional body. Those in Ireland were affiliated to the Irish Division of the Royal Medico-Psychological Association, based in London. In the 1970s, it became the Royal College of Psychiatry and Irish psychiatrists continued as members. The College had modernised post-graduate psychiatry by introducing procedures for the recognition of training courses. In Ireland, a body called the Irish Postgraduate Training Committee, which was recognised by the Irish Medical Council, formally supervised the implementation of the British programme. However, it initiated little that hadn't come from Britain.

As time passed, it became obvious that this training arrangement with Britain was increasingly incongruous, given the different legal and administrative systems under which British and Irish services were constituted and delivered. Accordingly, in 1993, an effort was made to create a separate Irish College of Psychiatry (for training and other purposes) by some forward-looking Irish psychiatrists, but this was resisted by the more conservative elements. It was easier to allow others to do for you what you should be doing for yourself! In the early 2000s, a rival indigenous organisation, called the Irish Psychiatric Association, was formed with the objective of eventually becoming an indigenous Irish College. Whether it would have succeeded, at least in the short or medium term, is unclear, such was the reliance of some reactionary elements on the link with the British College. However, the situation was resolved in 2005 when the Royal College decided to call a moratorium on the existing situation and informed the Irish members that it was no longer appropriate to continue the existing arrangement. From this, the College of Psychiatry of Ireland was born and formally initiated in 2008. It now is recognised by the Medical Council as the professional training and representative body for psychiatrists in Ireland. During this time, the number of academic appointments of professors and lecturers in psychiatry proliferated and whereas most of the resources were provided by the service provider, this was not always reflected in the accompanying service input. Psychiatrists were encouraged to undertake research and much was accomplished in epidemiological and genetic research. Research on mental health services was also undertaken and later supported by the Mental Health Commission.

Other disciplines such as social work, psychology and occupational therapy had for some years incorporated a mental health module in their didactic training and psychiatric service placements in their practice training. This they continue to do.

TREATMENTS

The search for effective treatments in psychiatry began in earnest in the 1960s.[37] Prior to this, there had been few treatments of proven value. The treatment of general paralysis of the insane (GPI) had been effected by the placing of patients, with this condition – there could be as many as 200 of them, mainly males, in a hospital as large as Grangegorman – so that they could be bitten by a mosquito (brought in from a mental hospital in England) in order to induce malaria. This came about because a German doctor had claimed that soldiers with syphilis (the cause of GPI) improved when they contracted malaria. Indeed in the 1940s, there was a lively correspondence between Dr. John Dunne, resident medical superintendent (RMS) at Grangegorman and the Department of Health on whether or not separate premises should be built for the accommodation of the mosquitoes and the patients under treatment. In the event, premises were not built and soon the mosquitoes became dispensable, having been replaced by the injection of blood taken from a patient already infected with malaria. Ultimately, the introduction of penicillin made the malarial treatment redundant.

On doubtful evidence, epileptic-type fits were introduced as a treatment for some symptoms of mental illness. These fits were at first brought about by the injection of a substance to patients who were depressed, allegedly with some improvement. In the late 1930s, these injections were replaced by electrically induced fits devised by two Italians, Cerletti and Bini in 1938.[38] At first, these fits were induced 'straight', that is to say the patients were awake and their muscles were unrelaxed, so that the procedure was both terrifying and painful. Later, the procedure was given under anaesthesia and a relaxant drug administered, so that the muscular spasms were minimal. It was claimed, with some justification, that in severe and psychotic depression, the results were very satisfactory. However, the use of the treatment was widespread and the indications for its deployment quite unclear. The result was that, during the early 1960s, upwards of 60 patients were on the electro-convulsive treatment (ECT) list thrice weekly in Grangegorman – 30 in the male house and 30 in the female house. Clearly, it was given somewhat indiscriminately, without clear indications for suitability in particular cases. As time wore on and anti-depressants were introduced, its administration became ever more curtailed and by 2006, its use was negligible.[39] The Mental Health Act 2001 tasked the Mental Health Commission to issue rules for its administration including the reporting of its use in each instance to the Commission.[40]

Until the early 1960s, insulin coma treatment for schizophrenia was still in vogue. This consisted of injecting insulin into a patient who then went into coma to be awakened a little later by the oral administration of glucose. Special units were set up for patients (mostly first episode) on this treatment. These units were highly staffed and with a major emphasis on occupational and social activities. Such units existed at Grangegorman and elsewhere in Ireland only to be abandoned in the mid-1960s, when a controlled trial indicated no specific benefit from this treatment.[41]

By the late 1950s, the pharmaceutical industry had become interested in the potential reservoir of profit that lay unexploited in mental hospital populations and in those afflicted by mental illness generally. Thus, the introduction of major tranquillisers such as chlorpromazine and reserpine, drugs whose calming effects had been observed in anaesthesia, began. Many patients, who had been neglected in the 'back wards' now found themselves subjects of interest, if only because they were now the recipients of attention three times daily to have a tablet popped into their mouths. The major tranquillisers were followed by minor tranquillisers and then by anti-depressants. As time progressed, the marketing of these substances became more sophisticated and, as in the car industry, newer drug products came to market and were increasingly prescribed by a medical work force compliant with the marketing influence but uncritical about the underlying science. Thus, by the 1990s, first generation anti-psychotics had been replaced by second generation or 'atypical' anti-psychotics. Similarly, the earlier anti-depressants were replaced by ever newer drugs for depression, the main characteristic of which was that they were more expensive in the face of doubtfully more efficacious effect, not to mention side effects.[42] By 2003, the drug bill in psychiatry was claiming up to 30 per cent of revenue expenditure.[43]

THE TWENTY-FIRST CENTURY

In 2005, by powers of the Health Act 2004, the health boards were abolished and replaced by a single organisation called the Health Service Executive (HSE). Mental health policy was to be catered for by a centralised directorate of mental health services, thus abolishing the separate regional programmes existing under health boards. Service providers complained that there was now only a local generic administration catering for all social and health services in each area and that mental health fared badly in this competitive situation. And even then, local agents had little decision-making autonomy with relatively trivial issues having to be approved centrally. By 2001, numbers in psychiatric hospitals and units had fallen to 4,321, a reduction of 47 per cent on 1991, and constituting a rate per 100,000 of the population of 119 compared to 62 in England, 74 in Wales, 179 in Scotland and 70 in Northern Ireland.[44] Of the 4,321, 83 per cent were voluntary patients, but 53 per cent were in hospital continuously for one year or more compared to 29 per cent in England. The statistics revealed a number of characteristics of this population. The unskilled and those with schizophrenia had highest rates, 38 per cent were aged 65 and over and 69 per cent were single. The majority, or 3,125, were in health board hospitals (that is old psychiatric hospitals), 614 in general hospital psychiatric units and 582 in private hospitals. In that same year, there were 24,446 admissions to hospital, of which 70 per cent were re-admissions. Depression accounted for 30 per cent of these admissions and schizophrenia for 20 per cent. Fourteen per cent of admissions to health board psychiatric hospitals were involuntary as were 10 per cent to general hospital units and 4 per cent to private hospitals. Twenty-two per cent of discharges from health board hospitals and units were within a week of admission compared to 9 per cent from private hospitals. There were considerable variations in admission rates between health boards, which differed by a factor as high as two. Of all admissions to public hospitals, almost half were now to general hospital units.[45]

By 2001, there were 237,667 attendances at 254 outpatient clinics, 2,498 places in 104 day centres and 1,145 places in 63 day hospitals. Finally there were 3,077 places in 404 community residences, of which 1,345 were high support.[46] Throughout the later years of the twentieth century, the Central Mental Hospital in Dundrum had about 80–90 patients, the great majority males, from its two sources and under separate legislation for each – prisoners and involuntary inpatients sent from psychiatric units and hospitals. Those in prison could be transferred by the courts through the powers of the Criminal Law (Insanity) Act 2006, which commenced in the same year and allowed for a review of detention by a Review Board and for a temporary release with conditions which could not be enforced (this omission was later amended). The Mental Health Act 2001 allowed for the transfer from hospitals and units to Dundrum, but only on a ministerial order on the recommendation of a mental health tribunal. With the decision to build a new prison in north Co. Dublin, the government proposed the building of a new central mental hospital on the same site as a replacement for the now obsolete Dundrum building. However, due to the credit crunch and to opposition from many organisations, the plans are in abeyance.

The Last Report of the Inspectorate of Mental Hospitals

The last report of the inspector of mental hospitals, for the year 2003, noted that there were 3,701 patents in inpatient care compared to 11,114 when the Inspectorate had commenced operation and that 55 per cent of these were long-stay patients. The report deplored a number of 'black spots', such as at Clonmel, Mullingar, Killarney and all of St. Brendan's. The Inspectorate was not happy with the old building at Ballinasloe, but this subsequently closed. It was also unhappy about some of the smaller private hospitals catering for elderly patients in small rooms spread out over several floors. It commented on the reduction in the proportion of national health expenditure which was allocated to mental health – falling from 24 per cent in the 1960s (reflecting the cost of maintaining the large institutions) to 13 per cent in 1988, and to under 7 per cent in 2003, even though the absolute expenditure had risen from 165 to 612 million euro between 1988 and 2003.[47]

The 2001 Mental Health Act – The Mental Health Commission

The 2001 Mental Health Act set up the Mental Health Commission, with responsibility for protecting and safeguarding the civil rights of persons coming in contact with mental health services and, in the case of persons admitted involuntarily, of reviewing their detention through the setting up of mental health tribunals. The Commission became a physical reality in 2003, operating from premises in central Dublin. In 2004, the new Inspectorate of Mental Health Services created under the Act became operational and Regulations followed in 2006. The Commission was empowered to draw up Rules relating to the administration of electro-convulsive therapy and psychosurgery and Codes of Practice on such issues as the admission of children. This was a strengthened Inspectorate, multi-disciplinary in composition and with a more whole-time commitment.[48] Meantime, the commencement of Part 2 of the Act (concerning the setting up of tribunals) was in abeyance, pending negotiations with consultants who were taking a stand against implementation until more consultants were appointed. This was a reaction to the consultant staffing proposed in the Hanly report in 2003.[49] This report had looked at the implementation of an EU directive on the working hours of non-consultant hospital doctors and recommended the regionalisation of acute hospital services to a number of geographic centres, each with a psychiatric unit aligned to these general hospital catchment areas. This would lead to the closure of smaller general hospitals – something which in fact had been recommended as far back as in 1968, in the Fitzgerald Report on the *Future of the Hospital System*.[50] In effect, Hanly was proposing a consultant-delivered service. To date, Hanly still languishes in a semi-limbo. Part 2 of the Act eventually commenced on 1 November 2006 and one salutary consequence was that, by 2008, the national rate of involuntary admission, which had been in decline for many years, had fallen further to around forty five per 100,000 of the population, which was in accord with best international practice.[51]

The Private Sector

Private psychiatry in hospitals has had an honourable role in Irish psychiatry from its earliest days in the eighteenth century, although the number has decreased in recent times. In 1959, it accounted for 1,019 residents, 5 per cent of all residents nationally and for 3,023 admissions, 26 per cent of the total. By 2010, the numbers resident in private hospitals had fallen to 551 but now represented 20 per cent of resident patients. Thus, while the proportion of residents decreased substantially in the public sector as a consequence of community care, this was not a private hospital option. On the other hand, the numbers and the proportion of admissions increased in the private sector to 4,305 by 2010, constituting 22 per cent of admissions. Of these, the acute sector, comprising St. Patrick's, St. Edmundsbury and St. John of God Hospitals comprised 4,238 or 98 per cent of admissions. These hospitals provide some limited capacity for special categories of illness to the public sector on contract terms.

Non-acute private hospital care is provided by a number of providers registered for this purpose as approved centres by the Mental Health Commission. This care mainly concerns elderly persons with organ illnesses such as dementia. In 2010, the number of places was limited to ninety-three and admissions to sixty-seven. In addition to private hospital care, a number of private psychiatrists, without hospital affiliations, practice in clinics in the larger urban centres.

With approximately half of the Irish population covered by private health insurance by the year 2000, providing generous inpatient coverage for mental illness and somewhat more limited cover for addictions, it was not surprising that the two main acute mental health care providers, St. Patrick's Hospital/St. Edmundsbury and St. John of God Hospital, should continue to attract an increasing inpatient clientele. The stigma of public care, aggravated by some not always warranted adverse media publicity, helped to maintain a two-tier system of inpatient care.

Despite the general consensus that, for obvious reasons, acute psychiatry should be provided in a general hospital setting, these private services continued to operate in an isolated, stand-alone mono-speciality setting, and strangely, given a patient clientele limited to private patients, in the case of St. Patrick's, acquired university designation from Trinity College. This was despite the exclusion of half the needier proportion of the Irish population and the obvious difficulty of hospitals centralised in Dublin in providing community-delivered care to patients from the four corners of the country. In an attempt to remedy this shortcoming, St. Patrick's has recently established what it has called Dean Clinics for private consultation outside Dublin thus reduplicating services in local areas. In contrast to the public sector, where in 2010, the proportion of admissions that was involuntary was 10 per cent, that for private psychiatry was much lower, at 1.6 per cent. A possible interpretation for this may be that the public sector patient clientele comprises of persons with more serious illnesses. Another interpretation may be that the relative lack of treatment-based options other than hospitalisation (in the private sector) has resulted in a certain but as yet unquantified drift from private to public sector care for those patients, the impairments of whose illness endure and require more comprehensives and continuous care in community settings.

A Vision for Change

In 2003, an Expert Group on Mental Health Policy was appointed by the Minister of State at the Department of Health and Children to 'review long-standing policy in this area and to formulate a blue print for a modern comprehensive world class service to meet the mental health challenges facing our society'.[52] While the Group was multi-disciplinary as in the case of *Planning for the Future* there was no private service representation. The Report entitled *A Vision for Change* was published in 2006.[53] The Group entered a consultation process with consumers and stakeholders as a preliminary exercise. In the report itself, the fruits of this were evident in the ethic of service providers working in partnership with service users and their families towards recovery and reintegration by the provision of accessible, comprehensive and community-based services. The report repeated much of the recommendations of the two earlier reports, that of the Commission of Enquiry in 1966 and *Planning for the Future* in 1984, and gave emphasis to specialist services for particular groups of disorders. It recommended fourteen catchment areas, with the amalgamation of smaller catchments which could not provide specialist services because of their small population size. More than the previous reports, it emphasised the administrative and organisational structures that needed to be put in place to bring about change. Central to this was the establishment of a National Mental Health Directorate (as had been recommended in 1966 by the Commission of Enquiry) and, in detailed annexes, set out the physical requirements for the proposed service, together with the staffing required for each element and projected costs.

A Vision for Change set out a time scale for implementation of the recommendations and the setting up of a Monitoring Group to report on change on a yearly basis with a more formal review in seven years. Up to 2008, this Monitoring Group had been highly critical of the failure of the health service to advance any of *Vision's* recommendations and in particular the failure of the Health Service Executive (HSE) to appoint the National Directorate as recommended.[54] These disappointments were echoed in a number of publications by the newly formed College of Psychiatry of Ireland, which bewailed the failure of appropriate funding and alleged the siphoning away from mental health services of funding that was allocated to it.[55] The slow progress in reducing the inflow of new long-stay patients to the inpatient system[56] and the failure to alter the 'revolving door' phenomenon, whereby over three quarters of admissions were re-admissions[57] were particular points of disappointment. Although the HSE presented no detailed intelligible plan of progressing *A Vision for Change*, it became clear that some changes were to hand. In the face of the condemnation of the admission wards in St. Senan's Hospital, Enniscorthy, it closed to admissions in Spring 2011, with admissions now proceeding to the psychiatric unit in Waterford Regional Hospital, but without continuity of care, as the Wexford consultants do not follow their patients to Waterford. The HSE has similarly been attempting to close the St. Michael's Unit at Clonmel for the same reason as in Enniscorthy, with the intention of providing admission services for south Tipperary in the Kilkenny Unit and those for the north of the county (bizarrely) in Ennis rather than the more appropriate and nearer unit at Limerick. There is still no psychiatric unit at Beaumont Hospital in Dublin to replace the unsatisfactory admission wards at St. Ita's in Portrane, despite the Beaumont Unit first being discussed and planned over thirty years ago. However, it has been promised for 2013.

In 2009, the Health Service appointed fourteen executive clinical directors, all being consultant psychiatrists, presumably with the intention that these would work towards the establishment of the

fourteen catchments for psychiatry, based on the Hanly regionalisation model and with the objective of amalgamating existing
catchments.[58] However, no very clear job description or responsibility
was ever enunciated nor were the mechanisms through which these
goals were to be achieved.

Sale of Property to Progress Change

In early 2010, the Minister of State at the Department of Health
and Children announced that his Department was going to embark
immediately on a programme of sale of former psychiatric service
properties, of lands and buildings associated with the old mental
hospitals, to fund the provision of new facilities to accommodate those
patients still in the old hospitals in order to allow them to close.
Concurrently, new mental health centres, day hospitals, community
residences, child inpatients units, rehabilitation units and a replacement Central Mental Hospital were to be provided through the capital raised – and all of this would be achieved by 2013. In all, sales would
contribute over fifty million euro to new projects.[59] The cynics pointed
out that in the present deep recession, few would contemplate buying
land for development or building and that there were 350,000 vacant
and unwanted residential units in the country already.

The 2010 Psychiatric Unit and Hospital Census

On 31 March 2010, there were 2,812 persons resident in Irish psychiatric units and hospitals, a reduction of almost 500 since 2006, and of 83
per cent since the first MRSB census of 1963. Of these, 715 were in
general hospital units, 1,309 in old psychiatric hospitals, 551 in private
hospitals and 99 in the Central Mental Hospital. The genders were
almost equally represented, with schizophrenia the largest diagnostic
group, in contrast to admissions where affective disorders (depression
and mania) had overtaken schizophrenia. The number of long-stay
patients (those hospitalised continuously for more than one year)
was 669, and it was calculated that at the current rate of long-stay
decrement and rate of patients entering the long-stay category, it will
take up to 2030 before all are discharged and the last of the nineteenth-
century public mental hospitals can close.[60]

CONCLUSION

Between 1959 and 2010 there has been considerable changes made to
the delivery of mental health services in Ireland. Most strikingly,

numbers in mental hospitals have declined from around 20,000 to fewer than 3,000, and community services have been put in place in all publicly funded health and social care services. General hospital psychiatric units have proliferated and the majority of admissions are now to these units in the public service. Admissions in the acute, independent (private) service (for the 50 per cent of the population with private medical insurance) continue to be to free-standing psychiatric hospitals, based in Dublin and, for the most part, without community services. Services have become more specialised, with dedicated services for children, older people and forensic patients, rehabilitation for those with enduring illness, and liaison services to general hospital wards and accident and emergency departments, as well as services for persons with intellectual disabilities with accompanying psychiatric illness. The Mental Treatment Act of 1945 has been replaced by the Mental Health Act 2001 which, inter alia, has established the Mental Health Commission, with responsibility for safeguarding the civil rights and the quality of service delivered to persons coming in contact with psychiatric services. In the case of persons admitted and detained involuntarily to inpatient care, the Commission has the legal duty of setting up mental health tribunals to review all cases of involuntary detention. A new Criminal Law (Insanity) Act 2006 now governs those found 'not guilty by reason of insanity' and amends the law relating to unfitness to plead.

On the negative side, some 1,500 long-stay patients languish in the remnants of those large, older mental hospitals that have not yet closed and, in some cases, these hospitals still admit acute patients to surroundings that are no longer fit for purpose. In addition, the physical resources available for the delivery of community care are seriously deficient in some instances – lack of suitable premises for day hospitals, community mental health centres, community residences, rehabilitation units and intensive care secure community-based units. Residential units for children and adolescents, although in existence, are still insufficient and there are reportedly long waiting lists in child services. Many sector-based general adult and specialised teams are still far from being multi-disciplinary and in the present recessionary climate, a moratorium on staff recruitment is a compromising element in this scenario, with 800 nurses reported as leaving the service in 2010. Overall the reduction in recent years, from 11 per cent to 6 per cent of the health budget on mental health services expenditure, is constraining further development, although this is not to say that more efficient and effective use could not be made of what is currently available.

NOTES

1. The author was the Inspector of Mental Hospitals and psychiatric advisor to the Department of Health (Ireland) 1987–2003. Most of the information in this chapter is from these reports which he wrote, with additional statistics from his private paper containing notes from his daily work.
2. DH, *Report of the Inspector of Mental Hospitals for the Year 1959* (Dublin: The Stationery Office, 1960).
3. Ibid.
4. DH, *Report of the Inspector of Mental Hospitals for the Year 1956* (Dublin: The Stationery Office, 1957).
5. DH, *Report of the Inspector of Mental Hospitals for the Years 1961–2* (Dublin: The Stationery Office, 1963).
6. Department of Local Government and Public Health, 1946.
7. DH, *Report of the Commission of Inquiry on Mental Illness* (Dublin: The Stationery Office, 1966).
8. G.C. Tooth and E. Brooke, 'Trends in the mental hospital population and their effects on future planning', *Lancet*, 1 (1961): 710–3.
9. DH, *Report of the Inspector of Mental Hospitals for the Years 1961–2* (Dublin: The Stationery Office, 1963).
10. DH, *Report of the Commission of Inquiry on Mental Illness* (Dublin: The Stationery Office, 1966), p.xiii.
11. DH, *Report of the Commission of Inquiry on Mental Illness* (Dublin: The Stationery Office, 1966), p.xv.
12. N. Ni Nuallain, A. O'Hare and D. Walsh, 'Incidence of Schizophrenia in Ireland' , *Psychological Medicine*. 17; pp.943–8.
13. DH, *Report of the Commission of Inquiry on Mental Illness* (Dublin: The Stationery Office, 1966), p.xv.
14. Ibid.
15. Ibid.
16. DH, *Planning for the Future* (Dublin: The Stationary Office, 1984); DHC, *A Vision for Change* (Dublin: The Stationary Office, 2006).
17. WHO, *Mental Health Services in Pilot Study Areas* (Copenhagen, Denmark: World Health Organisation: Regional Office for Europe, 1987).
18. I. Browne and D. Walsh, *Mental Health Services in Dublin* (unpublished document, 1966).
19. DH, *Report of the Inspector of Mental Hospitals for the Years 1961–2* (Dublin: The Stationery Office, 1963).
20. I. Browne and D. Walsh, *Mental Health Services in Dublin* (unpublished document, 1966).
21. DH, *The Psychiatric Services – Planning for the Future* (Dublin: The Stationery Office, 1984).
22. Ibid., p. xi.
23. Statistics are from the author's personal papers.
24. Department of Health and Children, *Report of the Inspector of Mental Hospitals for the Year 1997* (Dublin: The Stationery Office, 1998).
25. A. Daly and D. Walsh, *Irish Psychiatric Units and Hospitals Census 2010*. HRB Statistics Series 12 (Dublin: Health Research Board, 2011).
26. DH, *Report of the Inspector of Mental Hospitals for the Year 1959* (Dublin: The Stationery Office, 1960).
27. DH, *Green Paper on Mental Health* (Dublin: The Stationery Office, 1992).
28. Ibid.
29. Ibid.
30. Ibid., p.18.
31. Ibid.
32. DH, *White Paper: A New Mental Health Act* (Dublin: The Stationery Office, 1995).
33. DH, *Report of the Inspector of Mental Hospitals* (Dublin: The Stationery Office, 1994).
34. Department of Health and Children, *Guidelines on Good Practice and Quality Assurance in Mental Health Services* (Dublin: The Stationery Office, 1998).
35. DH, *Report of the Commission of Enquiry* (Dublin: The Stationery Office, 1966).
36. Department of Health and Children, *Report of the Inspector of Mental Hospitals for the Year 1997* (Dublin: The Stationery Office, 1998).
37. D.K. Henderson and I.R.C. Batchelor, *Henderson's and Gillespie's Textbook of Psychiatry*, 9th edition (London: Oxford University Press, 1962), pp.334 ff.

38. L. Bini and U. Cerletti, 'Un nuovo metodo di shockterapia: ' L'electroshock'. *Boll. R. Accad. Med. Roma*, 64 (1938): 136–8.
39. Mental Health Commission, *Annual Report including the report of the Inspector of Mental Health Service* (Dublin: Mental Health Commission, 2007).
40. Mental Health Commission, *Rules Governing the Use of Electro-convulsive Therapy* (Dublin: Mental Health Commission, 2006).
41. B. Ackner, A. Harris and A.G. Oldham, *Lancet*. I (1957): 607.
42. J. Moncrieff and I. Kirsch, 'Efficacy of anti-depressants in adults', *British Medical Journal*, 33 (2005): 155–7.
43. Author's personal papers.
44. Health Research Board, *Irish Psychiatric Hospitals and Units Census 2001* (Dublin, Health Research Board, 2002).
45. Health Research Board, *Irish Psychiatric Hospitals and Units Census 2001* (Dublin, Health Research Board, 2002).
46. Ibid.
47. Department of Health and Children, *Report of the Inspector of Mental Hospitals for the Year 2003* (Dublin: The Stationery Office, 2004).
48. Mental Health Commission, *Annual Report including the report of the Inspector of Mental Health Service* (Dublin: Mental Health Commission, 2007).
49. Department of Health and Children, *Report of the National Task Force on Medical Staffing* (Dublin: The Stationery Office, 2003). (The Hanly Report.)
50. Department of Local Government and Public Health, *The Future of the Hospital System* (Dublin: The Stationery Office, 1948) (The Fitzgerald Report.)
51. H.J. Salize and H.E. Dressing, 'Epidemiology of involuntary placement of mentally ill people across the European Union', *British Journal of Psychiatry*, 184 (2004): 163–86.
52. Author's private papers.
53. Department of Health and Children, *A Vision for Change* (Dublin: The Stationery Office, 2006)
54. Department of Health and Children, R*eport of the Monitoring Group on The Vision for Change* (Dublin: The Stationery Office, 2008).
55. V. O'Keane, D. Walsh and S. Barry, *The Irish Psychiatric Association Report on the Funding Allocated to Adult Mental Health Services: where is it actually going?* (Dublin: Irish Psychiatric Association, 2005).
56. A. Daly and D. Walsh, 'An audit of new long-stay inpatients', *Irish Journal of Psychological Medicine*, 26 (2009): 3.
57. A. Daly, D.T. Doherty and D. Walsh, 'Reducing the revolving door phenomenon', *Irish Journal of Psychological Medicine*, 27.1 (2010): 27–34.
58. Department of Health and Children, *Report of the National Task Force on Medical Staffing* (Dublin: The Stationery Office, 2003). (The Hanly Report.)
59. Department of Health and Children, Dublin. Press Release, January 2010.
60. A. Daly and D. Walsh, *Irish Psychiatric Units and Hospitals Census 2010*. HRB Statistics Series 12 (Dublin: Health Research Board, 2011).

5

Voices of Mental Health Service Users –
Poetry and Prose

Stillness

Mental illness knows no borders
and crosses all divides.
She is rude, crude, polite, sophisticated
Her abodes are thoroughly complicated.
Her's the silent cry for help or vicious screams,
Mental illness is a terrible mistress
and seldom what she seems.
Friend, fear God, not mental illness
Gods grace gives the longed for stillness.

Psychiatric Admission

Dread, bed, meds.
Coke, smoke, joke.
Ill, pill, through the mill.
CD, TV, ECT.
TLC?
Professionals treat patients
but people need people.

Mental Illness (a glimpse)

Mental illness,
What is it like?
Ever been self-conscious?
How do I appear?
I rub my nose.
I look at the toes of my shoes.
I look to the right.
I look to the left.
I look up, down, around.
Perhaps a little too hot under the collar.
Perhaps a little redder in the cheek.
Perhaps a little too casual.
Perhaps a little too neat.
Is my voice too loud?
Is my voice too soft?
Am I being overheard?
Perhaps a little too everything!
Mental illness is like self-consciousness, only worse
And self-consciousness is like hell.

Am I Enough?

Am I enough
When I move away
When I sit with myself
And I hear it say 'stay'

Am I enough
With my fears and my tears
My doubts about life
My yearning for strife

Am I enough
When it calls me back
To ease all my pain
Take all the strain

Am I enough
When I give up the fight
When I let it all go
And stand upright

Am I enough
When I say 'just for today'
I've got all I need
The prisoner has been freed.

Behind the Wall

Behind the wall there lies a girl
So vulnerable and weak
From time to time a brick comes loose
And we get a peek

Inside her world of confused thoughts
Of distrust and of pain
When help arrives
They must try to build her up again

Protected by this man-made wall
She keeps the world at bay
In her mind she cannot find
The words she needs to say

'I'm not okay, I'm feeling trapped
Trapped by my own mind'
But help has come and so begins
A journey of a kind

So bit by bit the wall comes down
As rescuers ensure
To tell the truth about the world
Albeit somewhat obscure

Of what it takes to live a life
And face its fears and pain
In order that she may know
The pleasure there's to gain.

Just a Thought

At thirteen years as thoughts emerged
I kept them deep inside
Until one day on paper they
Could no longer hide

To write about the things I saw
And share it if I dare
The ups and downs, smiles and frowns
Of people are never rare

Then suddenly the music came
And stories turned to song
Emotions freed, good times recalled
And pictures that live on

Through song and dance and poetic chance
A light shines brightly on
The beauty in a complex world
And knowing I belong.

© Tara Marie Hogan (2012). All rights reserved.

Rabbit's Lament

The sun shines oh so brightly
Upon the distant green
My little ball sits whitely
Upon its little tee
But all that well known fairway
Is not much use to me
The heather sprouts so strongly
And bravely blows the whin
But in spite of all my efforts
I'm nowhere near the pin

The flag it waves so pretty
And verdant is the green
But aren't the bunkers gritty?
And deeply flows the stream
Those flags are outward yellow
And inward they are red
But though they are inviting
I never lay it dead
If I try to play it forward
I only make a slice
And when I'm extra careful
I hook it off the splice!
Though my woods are growing rotten
And my irons rusty red
The good shots aren't forgotten
And I'll be playing when I'm dead.

© Robairt Clough (Published in *Speedwell*, Easter 1973)

Night Nurse

Silent and swift as a silver moth
She comes and goes. Seldom she sits
In the green circle of the table lamp
But when she does, pondering, pen in hand
How best to phrase a patients pain
So that tomorrow, when the day is sane
It may be eased, I watch her pensive face
Courage has firmed the jaw, compassion arched
Deep lines of mute concern above her brows
In the soft welling of her watchful eyes
Is understanding, and when she comes
Soft as a whisper to stand beside the bed
In the stiffness of her apron, there is hope.

(Written by M.E., a patient in Holywell. Published in *Speedwell*, April 1969)

Alone

I looked from my window
And saw the young moon
Surrounded by stars
And heard through the trees
The fresh wind sighing
Like dreamy music
Suddenly away in the distance
I heard a girl singing
Softly, so softly –
Perhaps, to a child
I looked and I saw the stars
The wind and the singing were one
And I was alone.

(Written by an anonymous patient in Holywell. Published in *Speedwell*, Spring, 1962)

EXTRACTS FROM ARTICLES WRITTEN BY PATIENTS AND STAFF FOR
SPEEDWELL, THE HOLYWELL HOSPITAL MAGAZINE IN THE 1960S

From the recreation hall (Speedwell, Autumn 1963)

Now in the midst of preparing the winter programme, it seems no
time at all since we were discussing the summer programme. Time
certainly does fly! As the weather during the so-called summer was
so unsettled, the weekly dance and film show and, at the request of
the patients, the weekly whist drive, continued throughout. The
outdoor games, such as tennis, putting and cricket, didn't always
materialise, owing to the weather. However, with Mr. J. and his staff
organising the evening football match, especially the full week
when they hit it lucky with the weather, this proved most enjoyable
to both male and female patients.

* * * * *

From the recreation hall (Speedwell, Summer 1967)

- Hospital challenge: A competition in light entertainment
  between psychiatric and special care hospitals in Northern
  Ireland. This year it was held at Gransha Hospital, Derry,
  and eight hospitals participated. The judges were Mr. Mc C.,
  TV critic, *Belfast Telegraph*, Mr. F., Manager of the Embassy
  Ballroom. Muckamore Abbey was the winner, second place
  was taken by Omagh, and Derry and Holywell tied for third
  place. Holywell gave a splendid half hour of variety. The
  same half hour variety show was presented to our own
  patients at the request of the Friends of Holywell at their
  annual party.
- As a treat for the patients taking part in the Christmas Play
  and the Challenge Competition, seats were booked at the
  Odeon in Belfast to see the magnificent colour musical film
  The Sound of Music. This was much appreciated by all the
  patients who attended.
- Monthly dances: The Royal Accordion Band and the Green
  Angels Dance Band attended our patients' dances. We are
  greatly indebted to all these people for giving of their time
  and talent to come along and entertain our patients.

* * * * *

From the recreation hall (Speedwell, April 1968)

It was with much regret that during the outbreak of Foot and Mouth disease, quite a number of concerts arranged for patients had to be cancelled. However, this did not interfere with the usual patient activities, dancing, whist drives, social club, badminton, bingo and bowls.

* * * * *

From the recreation hall (Speedwell, December 1968)

- Debating club: The Club got off to a fine start last Thursday, with a 20 Questions programme, the Student Nurses opposing the patients from Ward F. 5, with Mr. J. (CMN) as Chairman. The evening proved very enjoyable. The ladies from Ward F. 5 were the better team and won the contest. *Tall Stories*, true or false, is the contest next week and as far as I can hear from some of the contestants eager to enter, we shall be hearing some really good ones.

* * * * *

From the recreation hall (Speedwell, Christmas 1970)

- Indoor bowling: Matches between psychiatric and special care hospitals are still proving very enjoyable. So far this season, Holywell has won two matches, one against Eastern Special Care and one against Tyrone and Fermanagh, but lost at Derry, with five more matches to play. I am sure they will enjoy them all, win or lose! The team looks forward to the away games, as they enjoy the travelling and it is another days outing. A friendly match took place at Craigy Hill Presbyterian Hall, Larne, on Saturday, 5th December, and the Saturday night out was much enjoyed by all concerned.
- Mackie cup football competition for psychiatric and special care hospitals: This competition took on a new look and was played on a one day, seven-a-side knock out system. Teams were composed of three patients and four staff. The competition took place at Purdysburn on 1st October 1970. Congratulations to the team for bringing back the Mackie Cup to Holywell after so long. Holywell were the winners of this trophy in 1957, 1958, 1959, 1960, 1961 and now again in 1970. The trophies and medals were presented to winners and runners-up at a social evening, which was held in the

recreation hall, Purdysburn – a most enjoyable ending to a very busy and successful day.

* * * * *

From the recreation hall (Speedwell, Spring 1972)

It was with much regret that a number of concerts and bowling matches had to be cancelled, owing to the 'troubles', especially Patients Prize Giving Day, which was to be held for the first time at the Downshire – this was indeed a bitter disappointment to our patients. They were looking forward to a get together with all the other psychiatric hospitals taking part in the prize giving. It was also a great disappointment not being able to be presented with the trophies and plaques they had won, namely NIHA Mackie Cup and Indoor Bowls Competition. Still, one keeps on hoping that times will return to normal soon, and we will be able to travel and take part in the usual competitive games.

- Film Show: Lately, there has been a very poor attendance at the Film Show in the evenings. On making enquiries, it was discovered that TV was the enemy and the nursing staff found it difficult to get patients to attend.
- Dances: Numbers have also fallen away, but those who do attend really enjoy themselves. We are very fortunate in having our own dance band and hail, rain or snow, they are always present – we are greatly indebted to them.
- Social Club: The patients Social Club is still going strong and Saturday evenings are spent in a singsong and games. The members of the Club presented Alan M. with a very nice travelling case on his discharge from the hospital. Allan was a very helpful member of the Club and acted as Treasurer for many years. The members are now looking forward to the summer, when they can arrange their outings.

* * * * *

From the recreation hall (Speedwell, Spring 1973)

In the Autumn issue of *Speedwell*, details were given regarding the Arts and Crafts Inter-hospital competition. This was the first competition of this kind and was held at Gransha Hospital, Londonderry on 21 September, 1972. The competition was organised by the NIHA

Recreation and Entertainments Committee. It proved to be a great success, with seven hospitals taking part and 296 individual entries. The results of the competition were as follows:

1st Prize   Downshire Hospital
2nd Prize   Gransha Hospital
3rd Prize   Tyrone and Fermanagh Hospital

- Patients outings: Approximately 150 male and female patients were taken out weekly from the beginning of June until 18 October. These picnics were thoroughly enjoyed, especially when the Sister and Charge Nurse accompanied patients. Special lunches were prepared with plenty of sweets, cigarettes and fruit and favourable weather all went a long way to help give as much pleasure as possible. When the weather got colder, hot stew was provided in hot containers and was indeed enjoyed. My sincere thanks to Mr. A., Catering Officer, and all his staff who prepared the meals to take out daily, and also to the drivers who were always willing to help in the dishing out of meals, especially Jimmy T., who has been off sick recently. We are now looking forward to the summer when the outings will commence again.

* * * * *

I'M VERY FOND OF HOLYWELL, BUT … A CONSTRUCTIVE CRITICISM

By *Rara Avis* – a patient (published in *Speedwell*, Winter 1964)

On the relationship of patients to staff

How easy it is to forget that the patient is the most important person in any hospital. The sting is in the fact that we usually forget what we don't want to remember, and hence the role, the true role, of the patient has been conveniently sacrificed on the altar of something approaching hero worship for the staff, and for the medical staff in particular.

At Holywell and elsewhere, every whim and fancy of the staff is usually vented upon the patients, and particularly those inclined to servility. One is certainly not reminded of behaviour becoming a hospital ward when a crabbit dictatorial and domineering nurse of whatever calibre literally gulders a patients surname, and does not request, but commands him to undertake some menial task, such as washing out lavatories, sweeping and polishing floors, hauling and pulling furniture from one end of the hospital to the other – and not forgetting the doctor or nurse who likes to take advantage of the fact that he can have his car washed and polished for nothing. *Quid nunc?* Such nurses, of course are the exception rather than the rule, but the types of work to which patients are driven seldom varies from what, in effect, is free and forced manual labour.

I need hardly remind my readers that brave men have fought and died to prevent this kind of abuse, and the Hospitals Authority should make it part of the practice to ensure that the medical staff of any hospital where this so-called Occupational Therapy takes place, must see to it that such therapy is undertaken voluntarily by patients and is not allowed to deteriorate into a farce, a masquerade, a sham and an excuse for the real thing. This point about Occupational Therapy is being made here so as to highlight more pertinently some of the flaws that can arise in the relationships between staff and patients, when members of the former fail to exercise due care in treating the latter.

Here, let it be said that the offences are few, and that the vast majority of nurses at our hospital could be numbered among natures gentlemen at heart – kindly, considerate in all things, only too willing to help if humanly speaking possible at any time, and completely uncontaminated by the ignorance of their more idiotic brethren. Let us for the moment leave behind the cheek of the odd nasty nurse. After all, we have the compensation of their vastly superior colleagues, numerically and otherwise.

On psychiatry

Readers will have to excuse the dogmatic tenor of my remarks, when I say it is my considered opinion that there is little or nothing in this general and rather vague psychiatry, and those who profess it are well paid for practising what amounts to nothing more than routine.

Whilst on this matter, may I ask why there is not, and never has been, to my knowledge, a psychotherapist at Holywell? That would be a pig with a different snout, and I venture to suggest that a one thousand bed hospital should not be without its complement of them.

Psychiatry has at least proved itself in a great many cases, but it is a difficult art, and naturally we attempt to avoid the difficult. I had better make it clear that I say this despite being a convinced Adlerian, by and large, and whilst I think the apostle of freedom said more that was important than either of the other fathers of psychology, Adler's premises are by no means incompatible with Freudian psychoanalysis. Freud may have scored on the psychopatho-genetical end, but it doesn't make sense without Adler's aetiology, if indeed the whole thing makes sense at all.

It is nothing short of amusing to see certain patients delivering tea or coffee to the doctor(s) in mid-morning. They have to have a special tray, nicely laden with specially decorated china, and sweet-meats that a patient need never hope to see. The goods are usually handed in by some servile mug, roped in as a kitchen-boy, who puts on his best smile – albeit artificial. It is a wonder that there is not a fanfare of trumpets! Of course, you will always get people who will sell their birthright for a mess of pottage.

Holywell Debating Club (written by J. B. L. for *Speedwell*, June 1959)

The Holywell Debating Club came into being on 28th November 1958. At the time, opinions differed as to the possible length of its life – the pessimists gave it a month, while those of a more optimistic nature gave it six or seven weeks! However, it has proved itself to be a lusty infant, and has gone on from strength to strength. Its initial membership of forty five has increased to about 100 and it has proved very popular among the patients, though one feels that the staff might give it greater support.

Since its formation up to the 10th April, the Club has met every Friday evening and the programme has included debates on 'Space Travel'; 'the Colour Bar'; 'Amateurism vs. Professionalism in Sport'; 'Television'; and 'Town Life vs. Country Life'. There have been talks on 'Life in the USA'; 'The Running of a Modern Airport'; and 'My Rugby Tours' by Dr. Jack Kyle. Then there were two 'Problem Nights' run on the lines of the BBC programme 'Is this your problem?', at which a panel of experts discussed and answered problems sent in by both patients and staff. This, by the way, proved no easy task, especially when our learned friends were confronted with something as subtle as 'How to eat my cake and have it?' Another enjoyable evening was based on the TV programme 'What's my Line?', and the miming of some of the challengers equalled anything the BBC could produce! In fact, it had to be seen to be believed.

Altogether, we feel that this has been a most successful and rewarding session. At the time of going to press, we have plans in hand for monthly outings, during the summer, to places of interest, including Nutt's Corner Airport, Rowallen Gardens, and Carrickfergus Castle.

We hope to re-open for the winter session on Friday 2nd October. We already have quite a few ideas for the programme for next winter, but we would welcome any suggestions or criticisms, in fact, we are almost anxious to have them. So do send yours in to the Honorary Secretary or any member of the Committee. Remember, this is YOUR Club, so pull your weight in it and help to make it a really lively and vital feature of our hospital life.

PART TWO
NINETEENTH CENTURY

6

Irish Immigrants in a Colonial Asylum during the Australian Gold Rushes, 1848–1869

Elizabeth Malcolm

In 1886 Dr. John Springthorpe, a young English-born doctor, testified before a Royal Commission established by the parliament of the colony of Victoria, which was conducting a lengthy investigation into lunatic and inebriate asylums.[1] Springthorpe had worked in one of Victoria's goldfields lunatic asylums during the early 1880s and he had strong opinions on the subject of madness. He gave his evidence only about fifty years after the beginnings of European settlement in Victoria, yet he argued that it was the nature of the colony's short history that was behind its high rates of mental illness. According to Springthorpe:

> One very important cause I consider to be the past history of the whole colony. You may call it our fevered past – the time of the gold fields – the distinct nervous tendency inherited from those times, the excited natures that came out and which have been transmitted to their descendants.[2]

Springthorpe had been born in 1855 in Staffordshire. He arrived in Sydney with his parents as an infant and in 1872 moved to Melbourne to study medicine.[3] Gold was first discovered in Victoria in 1851, so he had no direct personal experience of the 'fevered past' that he referred to. However, his suggestion that gold fever unsettled the nerves and created an unhealthy excitement was not a new one, for such a view had been expressed repeatedly at the time of the rushes themselves during 1850s and 1860s. Nor was his claim that this 'distinct nervous tendency' could affect the children of those who had taken part in the rushes particularly novel either. In 1852, John Bede Polding, a Lancashire-born Benedictine, who was Catholic archbishop of Sydney from 1834 to 1877, had delivered a Lenten sermon in which he warned the present generation that its obsession with the pursuit of gold was calculated to corrupt the beliefs and morals of the next generation.[4] Archbishop Polding had in mind the bad example set by parents for their children, but more than thirty years later, in a period increasingly convinced that heredity played a major role in madness, Dr. Springthorpe was arguing that the fevered mental state precipitated by the lure of gold could actually be inherited by the children of those who had flocked in their thousands to the Victorian gold diggings during the 1850s and 1860s.

Three years after Springthorpe gave evidence to the Zox Royal Commission, an influential Australasian inter-colonial medical congress was held in Melbourne. The psychology section of the gathering was chaired by Dr. Frederick Norton Manning, who since 1876 had held the position of Inspector of the Insane in New South Wales (NSW). Manning was widely regarded as the country's leading alienist.[5] His keynote address to the congress highlighted the link between madness and migration. He quoted statistics on the origins of the inmates of Australian and New Zealand asylums in 1887, which tended to suggest that Springthorpe's fears about the mental health of the children of the gold-rush generation were exaggerated. For, according to Manning, only 23 per cent of those in Australian asylums had been born in the Australian colonies, the rest having come from overseas. The largest ethnic group in both Australian and New Zealand asylums in 1887 were the Irish born: they made up 27 per cent of inmates in Australia and 28 per cent in New Zealand. In Victoria in 1887, according to Manning's figures, the asylum population was 25 per cent Irish born, with 22 per cent of male inmates being Irish and 29 per cent of female inmates. Indeed, Irish women were particularly numerous in Victorian asylums for, whereas men formed the majority of the overall asylum population (54 per cent), among Irish inmates women were in the majority (53 per cent).[6]

By the 1880s and 1890s there was concern, not only in Australia, but in most of the main countries of the Irish diaspora, as well as in Ireland itself, about the apparently high rates of mental illness amongst Irish-born people.[7] Yet, while there has been a good deal of study of mental health in Ireland during the second half of the nineteenth century and some investigation of Irish mental health in the United States and Britain, very little study has been undertaken of the Irish who were committed to lunatic asylums in colonial Australia.[8] Most histories of Australian mental institutions that deal with the nineteenth and early twentieth centuries have ignored the

Irish, and often the whole field of immigrant mental health.[9] This is very surprising, given that during the period most asylum inmates were immigrants. Only Mark Finnane and Trevor McClaughlin have produced articles specifically addressing the mental health of nineteenth-century Irish immigrants in Australia, while Stephen Garton's important study of insanity in NSW during the period 1880–1940 makes passing reference to the large numbers of single Irish men in psychiatric institutions.[10]

Patrick O'Farrell, in his standard history *The Irish in Australia*, devoted only one paragraph to the topic of health. High rates of Irish psychiatric committal in NSW during the early 1880s were evidence, he argued, that some immigrants 'must have been isolated, friendless, unable to cope'. But he also accepted contemporary allegations that Irish families 'deliberately dispatched to Australia relatives with mental problems, to relieve themselves of that burden'.[11] O'Farrell stressed social and economic deprivation in both Ireland and Australia as the root cause of Irish mental 'collapse'. He claimed that 'it is often impossible to disentangle mental illness and poverty', and portrayed asylums as essentially 'pauper institutions'. However, at the same time, he acknowledged that there was an 'absence of research'. Although definitive conclusions may have been impossible at the time he originally wrote his influential book in the early and mid-1980s, nevertheless, O'Farrell's stress on deliberate Irish efforts to export lunatics and on the poverty of the Irish in Australia has been influential.[12]

One broad aim of this chapter is to begin the task of filling in some of the large gaps in our knowledge of the mental health of Irish immigrants in Australia. More specifically, the chapter also aims to consider the impact of the gold rushes on Irish asylum committals. The colony of Victoria is an appropriate site for such a study as it witnessed the most substantial of the mid-nineteenth-century Australian gold rushes and it was home to a significant population of recent Irish immigrants, some attracted by the prospect of easy wealth. While the Irish scattered widely throughout Australia, the majority settled in the eastern colonies, especially in Victoria and NSW. According to the 1891 census, 38 per cent of Irish-born immigrants were living in Victoria and 33 per cent in NSW, with 19 per cent in Queensland.[13] As we shall see, Victoria in fact had a significant Irish-born population from the beginnings of European settlement in the 1830s, and this population soared during the gold-rush era of the 1850s and 1860s.

The 1891 census also showed that Victoria had the highest rate of psychiatric committal among the Australian colonies. The Victorian rate was 3.33 per 1,000 of population; the comparable rate in NSW was 2.62; and in Queensland it was 2.90.[14] The English hospital administrator Henry Burdett, in his massive 1891 study of hospitals and asylums of the world, noted when he came to Australia and New Zealand that: 'For some reason which is not easy to determine, lunacy is more general in Victoria than in the other Australasian colonies...' His figures for the years 1887–9 showed that Victoria's five asylums had 3,632 inmates; the five NSW asylums had 2,821; while the two in Queensland had 925.[15]

VICTORIA, 1850s: GOLD FEVER

Before looking at the Irish inmates of Victoria's main public lunatic asylum, it's important to describe briefly what life was like in the colony during the gold-rush era and how its asylum system evolved, since these developments had significant implications for Irish immigrants and their mental health.

From the mid-1830s European settlers began arriving in substantial numbers in the region, then known as the Port Phillip District and still officially the southern part of NSW, governed from Sydney. The district was constituted a separate colony called Victoria in July 1851 and was granted limited self-government in November 1855, with Melbourne as its capital. Growth was rapid in the 1840s: a population of about 11,800 in 1841 had jumped by 1851 to 77,300. A census in 1846 revealed that men born in Ireland made up 25 per cent of the male population, while Irish women made up 32 per cent of the female population.[16] However, the population growth of the 1840s was as nothing compared to that which occurred after the discovery of gold in various parts of the new colony in July 1851.

The population of Victoria soared by a massive 206 per cent in the three years between 1851 and 1854, by an additional 104 per cent in 1854–61, and by another 35 per cent during the less prosperous years from 1861 to 1871. On the goldfields themselves, the population leapt by 120 per cent between 1854 and 1857 to reach nearly 150,000. Thus, in 1891, only a little over fifty years after white settlement began, Victoria contained more than one million people, and was the largest Australian colony in population terms. Irish immigration also increased substantially, though given the high cost of the passage to Australia, many Irish immigrants were assisted.[17] From nearly 10,000 in 1846, the Irish population of Victoria had climbed to nearly 40,000 in 1854, to nearly 65,000 just three years later in 1857, and by 1861 it had reached a little over 88,000. The 1871 census recorded an Irish population peak in Victoria of 100,500. However, between 1854 and 1861 the Irish-born proportion of the total population remained fairly steady at 16 per cent, and by 1871 it had actually fallen slightly to 14 per cent.[18]

The tens of thousands of Irish who made the long voyage to Victoria between the 1830s and 1870s were thus entering a new and rapidly expanding British colony. Opportunities for acquiring farming and grazing land, for developing successful businesses and trades, for securing well-paid jobs and, most importantly, for making their fortune through mining were considerable. This was a fluid pioneering society where traditional barriers and divisions were much less restricting than they were in contemporary Ireland. Yet, at the same time, Victoria was a demanding and unpredictable place in the mid- and late nineteenth century, and this unpredictability took a considerable toll on the mental health of those who immigrated there with high expectations of economic and social betterment.[19]

When gold was first discovered, the authorities were alarmed at the potentially destabilising effect of a gold rush on the new colony. This destabilisation was perceived not only in political, social or economic terms, but even more fundamentally in psychological terms. When first reporting the discovery to London, Lieutenant Governor Charles La Trobe referred to the 'mania' already sweeping Melbourne.[20] Later writers frequently employed metaphors that made a specific link between the lure of gold and madness. John Sherer, who arrived in early 1852 and proceeded to the Ballarat diggings, described Melbourne as full of rumours about new gold discoveries that 'produced a species of bewildering excitement to the mind'; 'golden dreams ... day and night, were continually haunting the imaginations of the victims of the prevailing mania'.[21] On the diggings themselves, Sherer was struck by the frenetic atmosphere:

> ...the sudden transitions which sometimes take place from gloomy despondency to joyous success is [sic] far too much for the size of the brain which the heads of some of the diggers carry above their shoulders. Many have run mad. Two went so in our neighbourhood in one day. The one threw himself from a rock ... the other took to the woods ... It would have been far better for them if they had never heard of the diggings ...

where the mind is constantly racked and fevered, and hardly ever at rest.[22]

Charles Gavan Duffy, who arrived from Ireland in 1856 and swiftly entered colonial politics, rising to become premier of the colony in 1871–2, remarked in his memoirs, on the 'mad recklessness', the absolute 'frenzy', created by gold during the 1850s.[23] In his pioneering 1887 history of the Irish in Australia, the journalist and later Home Rule MP, J.F. Hogan, used the word 'delirium' to characterise the rush, describing successful diggers as 'bereft of their ... senses'.[24]

Letters written by immigrants to their families tell us much about the initial excitement of the rushes, about the often unrealistic expectations of those left behind in Ireland and also about the hardships many Irish diggers endured. Noah Dalway, formerly a Belfast bank clerk, wrote to his mother from the Victorian diggings in December 1854 comparing his lifestyle to that of a convict: 'I feel as though I were transported for I work hard from five in the morning until nine in the evening.' Dalway went on: 'This Australia, dear mother, is most falsely represented ... thousands come thinking to get a fortune in a few months but alas what a mistake they make ... [for they end up] barely making a living ...'[25] Irish immigrants were under particular pressure in that they were expected to remit money to help support their parents and siblings back in Ireland.[26] One Irish observer commented that while English diggers spent their money on 'comforts' and Scottish diggers put what they acquired into a bank, the Irish, regarding themselves as 'almost the trustee of [their] family and connexions', remitted most of their earnings back to Ireland.[27] When money was not forthcoming families complained, not understanding that, as Dalway explained to his mother, most diggers in fact were barely able to make a living. Geoffrey Serle has estimated that only about 20 per cent of diggers made anything like a profit from their endeavours.[28]

The gold rushes certainly had a major impact in dramatically boosting the colony's population, while many at the time believed that the high expectations generated and the hardships and disappointments that characterised miners' lives had a detrimental effect not just on their physical health, but on their mental health as well. The rushes also had a marked impact on the building and management of institutions to house those regarded as insane.

VICTORIA, 1840s–70s: ASYLUM BUILDING AND LUNACY COMMITTALS

The mid-nineteenth century in Britain and Ireland, and also in many British colonies, was a period of lunatic asylum building. The prevailing discourse of 'moral management' dictated that the insane should be removed from their families and communities and cared for in therapeutic institutions. The colonists in the Port Phillip District began campaigning for an asylum as early as 1841 – that is a decade before the discovery of gold. This eventually resulted in the opening in 1848 of a small institution known as Yarra Bend Asylum, which was situated just north of Melbourne on high ground above a bend in the Yarra River.[29] By the mid-1850s, it was over crowded, with many patients living in tents, huts and later cottages in the hospital's extensive grounds, while large numbers of other lunatics remained confined in the colony's gaols. From housing just twenty-five inmates when it opened in October 1848, fifteen years later in November 1863 Yarra Bend was home to nearly 900.[30]

Two new asylums were eventually opened on the colony's goldfields in 1867: one at Ararat in the southwest and the other at Beechworth in the northeast. Planning for another large asylum to serve Melbourne started in the late 1850s, but there were numerous delays and the asylum did not begin to receive patients until 1871.[31] It was on the other side of the Yarra River at Kew, within sight of Yarra Bend Asylum. By 1889, less than twenty years after opening, Kew Asylum – with over 1,000 patients – was the largest hospital of its kind in Australasia.[32]

Asylums in Victoria were designed according to mid-nineteenth-century English ideas about asylum architecture, but much of the legislation under which they operated actually followed Irish practices.[33] From 1843 committals in Victoria were regulated by the Dangerous Lunatics Act (7 Vic. No. 14), passed when the district was part of NSW. In 1867 this act was superseded by the Lunacy Statute (31 Vic. No. 309). As its title suggests, the 1843 act was modelled on the Irish Dangerous Lunatics Act, 1837 (1 Vic. c. 27), which was revised in 1867 (30 & 31 Vic. c. 118).[34] Unlike comparable English legislation, which essentially treated lunatics as non able-bodied paupers and linked asylums to workhouses, the mid-nineteenth-century Irish and Australian legislation treated lunatics as criminals and linked asylums to gaols.[35] The 1837 Irish act had been passed just before the introduction of a poor law system, while the Australian colonies never introduced a poor law comparable to the English and Irish ones.

In NSW and Victoria, as well as in Ireland, suspected lunatics had to appear before two magistrates and until the 1870s were normally committed to gaol in the first instance before being assessed for transfer to an asylum. From 1843 police were empowered to arrest those they suspected of being mad and likely to use violence either against themselves or others.[36] The documentation involved in committal not only had to include certificates issued by doctors and magistrates, but also a police report. Thus the police played a major role in determining who was to be sent to an asylum. In 1882 fully 73 per cent of Melbourne asylum committals were instigated by the police, and in 1892 this figure was still 56 per cent.[37] In this context it is important to note that, up until the 1880s, the majority of Victoria's police force were Irish born. In the early 1870s, for example, while only about 12 per cent of the colony's male population was Irish born, fully 82 per cent of its 1,000 policemen were.[38] In many cases the police were first alerted by family or friends that a person was acting strangely or violently, and so they did not actually initiate the committal process.[39] However, it is possible that Irish families felt more confident in approaching Irish policemen with such problems, and possibly also Irish doctors. Many Irish doctors worked on the goldfields and a number were visiting medical officers at Yarra Bend, certifying large numbers of those committed.[40]

The fact that during the goldrush era Irish-style lunacy legislation was being enforced in Victoria often by Irish policemen and that large numbers of Irish people were committed to colonial asylums, on the basis of medical certificates frequently signed by Irish doctors, raises all sorts of intriguing questions as to the precise nature of Irish influences. But, before addressing these, it's important to investigate whom Irish asylum inmates were and exactly why they were committed.

THE IRISH IN MELBOURNE'S YARRA BEND ASYLUM

In April 1853, Sligo-born William Kelly arrived in Victoria to investigate and write about the gold rushes. Kelly had already published a successful book about the earlier Californian rushes and now he wanted to compare them with those occurring in Australia.[41] But he had only been in Melbourne a short time when he was attacked by a naked mad man. Passers-by rescued Kelly and handed over his attacker, whom Kelly believed was suffering from *delirium tremens*, to the police. Despite this frightening initial experience, Kelly praised the colony and especially its many Irish inhabitants. He was impressed with the way the Irish had bettered themselves economically and was of the opinion that 'Irishmen constituted a very small proportion of the loafing population, or of the criminal crowd that filled the gaols and asylums', while the 'proverbial chastity of the Irish female was nobly sustained ...'[42] But if Kelly had had access to the admission registers of Yarra Bend Asylum, he would have been forced to amend at least part of this statement, if not all of it. For of those committed to Yarra Bend during the year 1853, 35 per cent were Irish born – a figure that was around double the proportion of the Irish in the colony's population.

Indeed, right from the outset the Irish had formed what seemed on first glance a disproportionate number of the asylum's inmates in terms of their numbers in the general population. As reported in Melbourne's *Argus* newspaper, the first ten patients to enter the new Yarra Bend Asylum were loaded onto carts at various prisons in which they were being temporarily held and driven to the institution in early October 1848.[43] Of the ten, seven were women. But what was not noted by contemporary newspapers – nor indeed by subsequent researchers – was that seven were also Irish born: five of the women and two of the men. Thus, at the outset of institutional care for the mentally ill in what would soon be the colony of Victoria, 70 per cent of patients were Irish. This majority was not to endure, especially after the discovery of gold in 1851. Nevertheless, throughout the rest of the century the Irish born would remain a noticeably large group among the inmates of Victoria's asylums.

Only by looking very closely at those committed to Yarra Bend during the 1850s and 1860s, both as a group and as individuals, can we hope to explain why so many people born in Ireland ended up in such an institution. An analysis of nearly 1,200 admissions to Yarra Bend Asylum in the period between 1848 and 1869 inclusive allows us to identify a number of key features of the Irish inmates.[44] These include: 1) how many were committed; 2) where they came from in Ireland; 3) numbers of men and women; 4) their marital status and 5) religious affiliations; 6) what jobs they had, if any; 7) their age range; 8) how long they stayed; 9) how many died in the asylum; and 10) what disorders they were diagnosed as suffering from.

1.Numbers Committed

Firstly, it is clear that the Irish born were committed in significant numbers throughout the period, forming a larger proportion of the asylum population than they did of the general population. In 1848–56, for instance, the Irish composed 38 per cent of admissions; in 1863–4 they were 35 per cent of female admissions; while in 1868–9 they were 25 per cent of male admissions (Appendix 6, Table 6.1). During the 1850s, as we have already seen, whereas the absolute numbers of Irish were increasing, their proportion of the colonial population remained steady at 16 per cent, and by the end of the 1860s there had been a slight decline to 14 per cent.

However, comparing asylum populations to general populations is not as straightforward as it may at first appear. There is a need, for instance, to consider both the age and class structure of the general population. Very few children were committed to asylums, so general populations with many children in them are likely to have lower committal rates than populations containing far fewer children. The Irish tended to migrate as young, single adults rather than as family groups so, on arrival and during initial settlement there were fewer children in the Irish immigrant cohort. Similarly, public lunatic asylums were largely pauper institutions. Yarra Bend did accept some paying patients, but a small private asylum called Cremorne opened in Melbourne in 1864, and it was especially patronised by those better off.[45] The Irish were largely working class, more so than English and Scottish immigrants, and therefore we would expect to find more Irish in Yarra Bend as it catered specifically for their class. By being both predominantly adult and working class, Irish immigrants increased their statistical chances of asylum committal. Thus we must be wary about jumping to conclusions on the basis of the apparent disproportionate representation of the Irish born in colonial asylums – in part at least this is probably a reflection of both the nature of the Irish general population and the character of the asylum.[46]

2. Place of Birth

During the 1850s place of birth was simply identified as 'Ireland' in Yarra Bend's patient registers, but during the 1860s sometimes county or town was also recorded. Of the Irish women admitted in 1863–4, for example, around half were just listed as born in Ireland, but of those for whom a county or town was included: 35 per cent were from Munster, 33 per cent from Ulster, 31 per cent from Leinster and none from Connacht. Of men admitted in 1868–9, again around half were just listed as born in Ireland; of the rest 38 per cent were from Ulster, 27 per cent from Leinster, 19 per cent from Munster and 15 per cent from Connacht. This profile is in keeping with the places of origin of most Irish immigrants to Australia, as they generally came from the southern midlands in Munster and Leinster or from the Ulster border counties.[47]

The overwhelming majority of those committed to Yarra Bend in its early years had been born in Ireland, England, Scotland and Wales; very few Europeans, Americans, Asians or indeed Australians entered the asylum before 1851. That situation began to change swiftly, however, as a consequence of the gold rushes, for they attracted not only far more new settlers to the colony but also a much more diverse range of people. Unfortunately, with admissions rising rapidly from 1853, the asylum's record keeping deteriorated markedly. As a result, information on place of birth and religious affiliation ceased to be regularly entered into the admissions registers. But in 1853 patients were committed who had been born in Italy, Germany, Austria, Poland, Egypt, China and the United States (Appendix 6, Table 6.2). All of these patients were men. During the mid- and late 1860s, when record keeping had improved, it is evident that male patients were still coming from a more diverse variety of ethnic backgrounds than were female patients. While the women remained predominantly Irish and British born, among the men were increasing numbers of Australians and New Zealanders, plus Europeans, Americans and Chinese (Appendix 6, Tables 6.4 and 6.6). This doubtless reflects the fact that the gold rushes attracted far more men from different countries than they did women. By 1868–9 Irish men made up 25 per cent of male admissions, yet in 1863–4 Irish women made up 35 per cent of female admissions. Again this difference is a reflection of the composition of the general population, for there were more women among the Irish than among any other immigrant ethnic group.[48]

3. Sex Ratio

During the period 1848–56, more Irish men than women were admitted to Yarra Bend, with 64 per cent being male and 36 per cent female. However, this pattern of male predominance was not constant throughout these nine years. During its first four years of operation, Yarra Bend actually took in more Irish women than men: admissions were 43 per cent male as opposed to 57 per cent female. Between 1853 and 1856, however, with admissions soaring in the context of a population explosion produced by the gold rushes, the balance of the sexes was reversed dramatically. During these three years, Yarra Bend's Irish admissions were 69 per cent male and only 31 per cent female (Appendix 6, Table 6.3). In this regard the Irish balance had shifted more towards the norm in the general population, for in 1857 the population of Victoria was 64 per cent male and 36 per cent female.[49]

4. Marital Status

Marital status was not recorded in the early years. By the 1860s, however, the majority of Irish men and women in Yarra Bend were single. Yet, in both instances, these were not huge majorities. For example, of Irish women committed in 1863–4, 44 per cent were married, while 3 per cent were widows; of Irish men committed in 1868–9, 36 per cent were married, while 3 per cent were widowers (Appendix 6, Tables 6.5 and 6.7). In other words, nearly half of women were married or had been married, and the same was true of around 40 per cent of men. As already mentioned, historians like O'Farrell, McClaughlin and Garton, have portrayed Irish asylum inmates as isolated, lonely, unmarried individuals, lacking close family ties and support. Doubtless many were, but in Yarra Bend during the 1860s large numbers clearly had spouses in the colony and probably also children.

5. Religious Affiliation

In terms of religious affiliation, the Irish in Yarra Bend were predominantly Catholic, while those born in Britain were predominantly Protestant. In 1863–4, 73.5 per cent of Irish women admitted to the asylum were Catholic, while of Irish men admitted in 1868–9, 79 per cent were Catholic. However, this does mean that there was a sizable minority of Protestant Irish in Yarra Bend during the period. Between 1848 and 1852, for example, one-third of the Irish admitted were Protestants, though this had declined to about one quarter by 1853 (Appendix 6, Tables 6.3, 6.5 and 6.7). Still, these figures contradict assumptions often made at the time and subsequently that all the Irish who ended up in psychiatric institutions in the diaspora were Catholics. Clearly, substantial numbers of Protestant Irish also experienced mental health problems. Similarly, while most of the non-Irish in Yarra Bend were Protestant, a minority was Catholic. Among non-Irish men admitted in 1868–9, whose religious persuasion was recorded, 13 per cent were Catholics, while a further 5 per cent were listed as 'pagans': that is they were Chinese. These non-Irish Catholics remind us that, in terms of nineteenth-century Australia, we should not always assume – as we often do – that Catholic automatically equals Irish.

6. Occupations

Occupations were not systematically recorded during the 1850s; during the 1860s they largely were, although there are still numerous gaps. Among Irish women admitted in 1863–4 whose occupations were listed, 58 per cent were described as servants. Several others were 'needle women', while there was also a dressmaker, a laundress, a bookbinder, an upholsterer, a storekeeper and a nurse. Many of the married women were just categorised as 'housekeepers'. Male occupations were of course much more varied than female ones. Irish men admitted in 1868–9 ranged from a barrister to a seaman, from a schoolmaster to a shoemaker. However, 36 per cent of those with occupations were described as labourers, while a further 18 per cent were classed as miners. A comparison with non-Irish male patients admitted during the same two years suggests there were more labourers among the Irish (36 per cent as opposed to 21 per cent), but around the same proportion of miners (18 per cent for both groups). The large number of servants among Irish women and the higher proportion of labourers among Irish men are almost certainly indications of lower economic status and greater poverty.

7. Ages

There was a notable difference between the sexes in terms of age and length of stay. The Irish men admitted to Yarra Bend throughout the 1850s and 1860s were significantly older than the Irish women admitted, yet it seems that women tended to remain longer in the institution than men. Most men on admission were in their mid-thirties, aged thirty-four or thirty-five; most women were in their late twenties, aged twenty-eight, or thirty at most (Appendix 6, Tables 6.3, 6.5 and 6.7). These average ages suggest that few Irish entered the asylum immediately after their arrival in the colony, as most would have been in their late teens or early twenties when they migrated. Thus it seems that only after a number of years living in Victoria did the Irish succumb to mental health problems. This picture tends to refute claims made later, that Irish families and the Irish asylum authorities deliberately shipped mentally ill people to the colonies or that the long and often hazardous voyage had a detrimental effect on health.

8. Length of Stay

Unfortunately, we don't have figures on length of stay for men during the 1860s, but in the period 1848–56, women consistently spent more years in the asylum than did men. For example, while Irish men admitted in 1849 stayed on average for 8.3 years, women admitted during the same year stayed for 14.0 years; in 1853 the comparable figures were 6.9 and 9.3 years.

It is particularly striking that two of the first Irish women admitted in October and November 1848 were still in the asylum at the beginning of the twentieth century. Sarah Smiley, aged twenty-two and a Protestant suffering from melancholia, was among the first group of patients taken from Melbourne Gaol to Yarra Bend in October 1848. Included in the same group was her brother Samuel. However, whereas Samuel Smiley died in the asylum in 1863, Sarah Smiley didn't die there until 1902, when she was seventy-six years old. But Eliza Armstrong, aged twenty-four and a Catholic suffering from dementia, who was admitted in November 1848, stayed even longer: she died in Yarra Bend in 1912, when she was eighty-eight years old. These are certainly unusual cases, yet they do reflect the general pattern of women being longer-term inmates than men.[50]

9. Mortality Rates

In the early years Irish patients had a very good chance of dying in the asylum; and many, unlike Sarah Smiley and Eliza Armstrong, in fact died soon after admission. Some 38 per cent of the Irish admitted to Yarra Bend between 1848 and 1856 died in the asylum. During the first four years of the institution's existence, the death rate was even higher at 40 per cent. We don't know the rate for men in the late 1860s, but for Irish women admitted in 1863–4 the asylum death rate was 16 per cent (Appendix 6, Tables 6.3 and 6.5). What is also notable is that the death rate among the Irish was higher than that among the non-Irish, while many Irish men died during their first twelve months at Yarra Bend. The year 1853 is fairly typical of this period as regards deaths. Of the Irish admitted, 47 per cent died in the asylum; the comparable figure for the non-Irish was 30 per cent. Moreover, 24.5 per cent of the Irish died within twelve months of admission; the comparable figure for the non-Irish was 13 per cent. In addition, those who died in their first year were overwhelmingly men.

Such a high death rate, and particularly so soon after admission, suggests there may have been significant health problems among the Irish. Little research has been undertaken on this topic. However, Janet McCalman's history of Melbourne's Royal Women's Hospital, which was established in 1856 by Limerick-born Dr. Richard Tracy, an unsuccessful gold miner, provides much evidence of the poor general health of Irish women. Initially called the Melbourne Lying-In Hospital, this was a pauper maternity institution, and during 1857, 56.5 per cent of those admitted were Irish born. Moreover, Irish women suffered more than others from physical problems that made birth difficult. In the late 1850s and early 1860s, for instance, there was a high incidence of pelvic deformities, probably caused by malnutrition, among Irish patients.[51]

10. Nature of Illness

With regard to mental illness, Yarra Bend's doctors employed a fairly limited nosology, and sometimes the diagnoses recorded did not accord with any recognised disorder. Of the Irish women admitted in 1863–4, 53 per cent were diagnosed as suffering from some form of mania and 23 per cent from melancholia. Of the Irish men admitted in 1868–9, it was melancholia that was the most common diagnosis, followed by various forms of mania, then intemperance and delusions. But 'vagrancy', 'not under control', and 'noisy and disruptive' were also included. Most mania cases in the 1860s tended to be categorised as 'chronic' or 'sub acute', suggesting they were not serious or that little could be done to cure them. However, as we shall see, when the asylum first opened in 1848 it received far more cases that were labelled as 'acute' and 'dangerous'.

CASE STUDIES: DISAPPOINTMENT, INTEMPERANCE AND ISOLATION

These statistics give us a general picture of whom the Irish were who were committed to Yarra Bend during the gold-rush era. But in order to put a little flesh on these rather anonymous bones, we need to look at smaller groups and at individuals.

In its first three months of operation, in late 1848, Yarra Bend received twenty-five patients, mainly from Melbourne gaols, thirteen of whom were Irish born. This group offers a snapshot of the diversity of the asylum's pre-gold rush Irish population and highlights some important factors. More than half were labelled as 'dangerous'. They had been committed under the 1843 NSW

Dangerous Lunatics Act, but the word may have carried real meaning as regards a threat of violence for not all inmates were so labelled even when committed under the same act. The asylum had a special ward for 'dangerous' patients, so they were obviously segregated from other less difficult cases. Also four of the Irish were said to be suffering from 'acute mania', while one was afflicted with 'raving madness'. Before the opening of Yarra Bend, lunatics had to be sent to the Tarban Creek – later renamed Gladesville – Asylum near Sydney, which had been established in 1838, and they could be held in gaol for considerable lengths of time while their passages to Sydney were being arranged.[52] It is likely, therefore, that the first thirteen Irish inmates of Yarra Bend had been living in prison conditions for many months, if not years. This may be partly why nine of them remained in the asylum for more than ten years and eight of them died there.

Of the eight women, four were diagnosed as suffering from disorders related to childbirth. Ellen Biddle and Susan Carroll, aged twenty-six and thirty-two respectively, had four children each; neither was 'dangerous'; and, unlike the rest of the Irish committed in 1848, both had been brought directly to the asylum by their families, without apparently spending time in gaol. Both were labelled as suffering from 'melancholia' but, while Biddle was released as 'cured' within a year, Carroll remained until 1865 when she was released as 'improved'. The third puerperal case was 38 year-old Bridget Robinson. Unlike the other two, she had been in gaol and was suffering from 'incoherence'. She had given birth to three children, but all had died, and her illness was said to be due to fright, which had led to a 'premature confinement'. She died in Yarra Bend in 1868. The fourth case was 35 year-old Mary Jones, who was diagnosed as suffering from 'acute mania' and was 'dangerous'. She had two children and childbirth was listed as a cause of her illness. However, at the same time it was noted that she had twice been admitted to Clonmel Asylum in Co. Tipperary and once to Tarban Creek in Sydney. She died in Yarra Bend from tuberculosis in 1860.

While postnatal depression figured largely in the first Irish female admissions to Yarra Bend, there was another case that hints at rather different issues. The patient said to be suffering from 'raving madness' was Ann or Emily Passmore, a 26 year-old Protestant, who had arrived in the colony in 1841 on the ship *Theresa*. Passmore was accused of having 'intemperate', 'dissolute' and 'bad' habits, and in 1871, she was transferred from the over-crowded Yarra Bend to the newly-opened Kew Asylum. The remarks on her 'habits' of course suggest moral as much as medical judgments. But an official investigation into Yarra Bend in 1852, which led to the replacement of the lay manger by a medical super-intendent, found that Passmore had been provoked by at least one of the male attendants, Irish-born Catholic Daniel O'Donovan. Called upon to restrain Passmore, it was alleged by other attendants that he had taunted her into exposing herself, and seemed to take pleasure in doing so.[53] We can only wonder if the fact that they were both Irish, though one a female Protestant inmate and the other a male Catholic attendant, played any role in their clashes.

Of the five Irish men committed in 1848, at least one was a former convict. John Burns, aged thirty-four, and suffering from 'acute mania', had arrived in Sydney in 1830 on the *Hercules*. It was reported that he cried on being transferred from Melbourne Gaol to the new asylum. Perhaps, given his background, he had become used to prison life and dreaded an unfamiliar institution.[54] He died in Yarra Bend in 1855. Samuel Smiley, aged twenty-six and a Protestant, was committed with his sister, Sarah, who has been mentioned already. Suffering from 'dementia', he died in the asylum in 1863. The cause of his illness was listed as repeated injuries to his head due to falls.

Difficult births, the deaths of children, intemperance and physical injuries were to figure regularly amongst the causes of illness in succeeding years. Such problems are all understandable in terms of the lifestyles of the new settler society that was developing at Port Phillip in the late 1840s and early 1850s. But individual cases also highlight other significant factors.

Bridget Ferry, a 17 year-old Irish Catholic 'pauper', was committed to Yarra Bend in April 1851. She had not spent time in gaol and was described as a 'congenital idiot'. Yet she was released 'cured' only eight months later. The case notes record that she was an 'orphan' and had arrived on a ship, the *Lady Kennaway*, in 1850. Ferry was in fact one of the so-called 'famine orphans': a little over 4,000 girls sent in 1848–50 from Irish workhouses overcrowded with Famine victims to the Australian colonies, in order to supply the largely male population with domestic servants and hopefully also with suitable wives. The *Lady Kennaway* was the first of the 'orphan' ships to reach Melbourne, and it arrived in December 1848, not in 1850.[55] Ferry was from Dunfanaghy, Co. Donegal, and was only fourteen at the time of her voyage to the colony. Like all the 'orphans', she was apprenticed to an employer on arrival.[56]

Another Irish 17 year-old committed to Yarra Bend in 1851 and identified as an 'orphan' was Eliza Armstrong.[57] She too was not committed through the prison system and was described as a 'pauper'. She was suffering from 'paralysis' and 'dementia', and her case notes state that she was insane for four to five years before leaving Ireland and during the voyage, yet within ten months she too was released as 'cured'. Armstrong, who was from Enniskillen, Co. Fermanagh, had arrived in the colony on the 'orphan' ship *Diadem* in January 1850, having spent nearly five months in the Enniskillen workhouse in 1849. She was put to work for six months in South Yarra for Charles Forrest, whom her case notes identify as a publican, but within a month of her arrival in the colony she was admitted to Yarra Bend.[58]

In reaction to savage contemporary attacks on the 'orphans' as paupers and prostitutes, there has been a strong tendency in recent Irish–Australian discourse to celebrate them as 'mothers of the nation' and to portray them as successfully overcoming prejudice and hardship. However, Trevor McClaughlin's invaluable lists of the women record many who succumbed to illness or who quarrelled with their employers and were sent 'up country' as punishment. In the cases of Bridget Ferry and Eliza Armstrong, it's hard to be sure if they did have a genuine mental illness. Their difficult lives could well have led to one. Yet, the fact that both were 'cured' of supposed 'congenital' and long-term disorders in just a few months suggests otherwise: that perhaps they were using the asylum as a means of escape from intolerable living conditions. But some 'orphans' certainly did have genuine mental health problems. A fellow passenger on the *Diadem* with Eliza Armstrong, who also came from Enniskillen workhouse, was 16 year-old Protestant Alice Ball. On arrival in Melbourne, she was apprenticed to a sail maker for twelve months, but a little over three months later she committed suicide.[59]

In the early years, the divide between the asylum's patients and attendants was by no means absolute. Some of the first 'servants' or 'keepers' employed at Yarra Bend were ex-convicts and some were former 'turnkeys', who had already looked after lunatics in Melbourne Gaol. But at least one of the first attendants was a former patient in Sydney who went on to become a patient in Melbourne as well. Daniel Wellesley O'Donovan, a 50 year-old Irish

Catholic, who, as already noted, was accused of mistreating female patients, was committed to Yarra Bend in April 1850 suffering from 'moral insanity'. The case notes record that he had formerly been in Sydney's Tarban Creek Asylum. After seven months, O'Donovan was released as 'cured'. However, in March 1851, he was re-admitted from gaol, and again released as 'cured' six months later. O'Donovan was unusual in being significantly older than most Irish male patients and also in being re-admitted – re-admissions were infrequent at this time. He was even more unusual in that when Dr. Patrick Cussen, the new asylum's Irish-born visiting medical officer, appointed the first six members of staff in 1848 O'Donovan was among them. He was the only one who wasn't married, as Cussen, like many of those running asylums at the time, preferred to employ married couples. What is particularly interesting is that despite being committed twice, O'Donovan remained employed. In 1852, however, critics of the running of the asylum engineered a select committee enquiry, at which the continuing employment of O'Donovan, whose 'moral insanity' took the form of 'beastly' drunkenness, violence and sexual harassment, became a major issue. Fellow attendants testified against him and the committee condemned him as 'reckless' and totally 'unfitted' for the job. In her study of Yarra Bend's attendants, Lee-Ann Monk speculates that, as most of the asylum's male staff had resigned in 1851–52, presumably to go to the diggings, O'Donovan was not sacked because of a shortage of men willing to do the job.[60]

If true, this is one of the first indications of the impact of the good rushes on Yarra Bend. But the most obvious effect of the rushes on the asylum was not so much the high turnover of staff as the dramatic jump in the number of patients being committed, and especially male patients. Whereas thirty-nine patients were committed in 1852, only seven of them were Irish, and Irish women outnumbered men six to one; in 1853, 145 patients were committed, fifty-one of them Irish, of whom only nine were women. From 1852 onwards references to the diggings also begin to appear in case notes. One of the women committed in 1852, Jane Murphy, a 26 year-old Catholic mother of one, was said to be suffering from 'monomania' due to grief on hearing of the supposed death of her husband at the diggings. Presumably her husband had not died because after one month at Yarra Bend she was released 'cured'.

In 1853–4, there are further references to patients living and working at the diggings. A word that occurs a number of times in the medical notes during these two years, before the records become much sparser, is 'disappointment'. This is sometimes linked with 'intemperance' and also 'isolation'. For example, Patrick Ryan, a Catholic, who was admitted in August 1853, worked as a grocer on the McIvor diggings. He had three children, one of whom, according to the medical notes, was 'at home' – presumably meaning in Ireland. Ryan was diagnosed with 'chronic mania' and he remained in Yarra Bend until 1892, when he was transferred as 'cured' to the Castlemaine Benevolent Asylum. The cause of his condition was listed simply as 'disappointment'. Alexander Miller, an Irish-born Presbyterian, was admitted on the same day as Ryan. He was an unmarried carpenter, who had arrived on the ship *Cowrie* in 1849. Like Ryan he was diagnosed as suffering from 'chronic mania', but unlike Ryan he died in the asylum in 1861. The cause of his illness was just given as 'isolation'.

Though 'isolation' could be a problem, socialising on the diggings also carried risks. Heavy drinking was widespread, with illicit spirits of dubious quality often being sold. Contemporary observers worried that many diggers were being 'poisoned' in 'sly grog' tents largely run by women.[61] 'Intemperance' certainly figured in a significant number of Yarra Bend committals. John Patterson, an Irish Protestant committed in December 1853, was a long-term resident of the colony, having arrived in 1839. He was an unmarried labourer living on the diggings who was suffering from *delirium tremens*. In 1855 Patterson escaped from Yarra Bend, but his body was later recovered from the Yarra River and he was buried in the asylum's cemetery. Another Irish man admitted from the goldfields due to 'intemperance' was 34 year-old Owen McCulla. He was an unmarried blacksmith working on the Bendigo diggings, whose brother, Michael, ran a pub near Kilmore, an area in which many Irish settled.[62] Owen McCulla was diagnosed as suffering from 'chronic mania', yet he was released as 'cured' in 1855.

Some miners entered Yarra Bend in complex ways. James Bollard, an unmarried Irish Catholic labourer, had arrived in the colony in 1851 on board the *Lady Elgin*, presumably attracted by the lure of good. But his hopes were to be quickly dashed. He was working on the diggings when he was convicted of horse stealing and sentenced to five years' hard labour. If drunkenness was endemic on the goldfields, so also was theft.[63] In September 1853 Bollard was transferred from gaol to Yarra Bend suffering from 'chronic mania'. He died in the asylum in 1862.

The asylum's doctors, as well as often noting where patients were born and when they arrived in the colony, also frequently included information on their families or if they had no family. 'Isolation' as a cause of illness was usually employed when the patient was single and had no relatives living locally. Andrew Davidson, an Irish Presbyterian, was transferred from gaol with a group of others to the asylum in March 1853. He was diagnosed as suffering from 'mania', and it was noted that he had spent a long time in prison. Although a Presbyterian, he prayed to 'the Virgin Mary'. The cause of his disorder was given as 'isolation', but there was presumably some more serious malady involved for Davidson died after only two months at Yarra Bend.

That life was hard for miners in the gold fields and also for labourers is evident in the number of cases where physical injury was identified as the cause of madness. Michael Slathery (Slattery?), a Catholic, was admitted from gaol with Andrew Davidson in March 1853. He was a gardener with 'no family' and his 'monomania' was ascribed to severe head injuries sustained in a fall from a horse several years earlier. He remained at Yarra Bend until 1871 when he was transferred to Kew Asylum. Edward Sweeney, who was also admitted in March 1853, was a 39 year-old suffering from 'chronic mania'. He was said to have had his skull fractured in a windlass accident some years before. When Sweeney died in Yarra Bend in 1892, the inquest recorded that he had an old brain injury.

AFTER THE RUSH: MELANCHOLIA

Disappointment at the failure to strike it rich, physical injuries sustained while working, separation from family and friends, and excessive reliance on the comforts of 'sly grog' – all these problems are very evident in the medical records of the Irish men committed to Yarra Bend Asylum during the early years of the Victorian gold rushes. But, what about later? In the initial rushes of the early and mid-1850s, an individual miner could, potentially, dig up a fabulously rich nugget or make good money by panning for gold in rivers and streams. By the 1860s, however, mining had developed into an industry. As surface and alluvial gold was exhausted, deep shafts had to be sunk, which required expensive equipment and large, organised workforces. Thus many diggers faced the alternatives of becoming employees of mining companies or of heading off to join new rushes in other colonies.[64] That increasing numbers of

Irish men were admitted to Yarra Bend in the late 1860s suffering from 'melancholia' is probably significant. One case from this period perhaps encapsulates the experience of many of the Irish diggers who had arrived full of hope in the early 1850s, but found themselves fifteen or twenty years later leading an increasingly unsustainable lifestyle.

John Bresnan was fifty-five when he was admitted to Yarra Bend in December 1868 suffering from 'melancholia'. He was an unmarried Catholic from Limerick, who had arrived in the colony in 1852 to join the gold rush. Prior to immigration Bresnan had served for sixteen years in the Irish Constabulary. Like many miners, he followed a semi-nomadic way of life, moving from one digging to another. He had no family in Victoria. Two brothers had immigrated to the United States, but their exact whereabouts were unknown. Bresnan had not made many friends either, but he did have one 'intimate' friend. This was John Stewart, whom he had known since 1859 and who by 1868 was a mining manager at Golden Point, Blackwood. Stewart presumably began as a digger, but, as he got older and mining changed, he was able to shift into management. For whatever reason, Bresnan was not so successful. At fifty-five, he was still a digger. He did not drink, but the long years of hard work had obviously taken a physical toll.

Bresnan had come to Stewart in late 1868 in search of work, and Stewart had not only provided it, but had also offered accommodation in his own house. According to Stewart, when Bresnan arrived he was 'unsettled in his mind about his own position'. He had been 'unfortunate in a mining speculation' and tended to 'brood' over this. He went to work 'breaking quartz and filling coppers', but after five or six days it became clear that 'he was not strong enough for the work'. It seems that Bresnan then tried to commit suicide by jumping into a river or pond. Stewart was alarmed and consulted both a doctor named Plews and a local Irish policeman, Constable Kiernan. The doctor warned Stewart that Bresnan was 'bad in his mind' and he would either 'have to give him up or take the responsibility of looking after him'. At first Stewart agreed to care for his friend, but when Plews visited again he warned Stewart that he was 'running a risk' – presumably the risk that Bresnan's next suicide attempt would be successful. As a result, Stewart went immediately to Kiernan, who 'came and took him [Bresnan] in charge'. In response to questions, Stewart stressed Bresnan's sobriety and the fact he had never detected in him any 'weakness of intellect', but of late there had certainly been a 'marked change in his general manner'. That Bresnan was suffering from clinical depression seems clear, but at his age, with no family in the colony, few friends, no money and being no longer physically able to work as a miner, he had a lot to be depressed about.

Other Irish miners, who were not committed to an asylum, had similar experiences to Bresnan and some of them looked upon medical institutions as a form of refuge. Sampson Lawrence from Coleraine joined the gold rush with his brother, Charles, in 1853. Neither of them made any money, and Charles died a pauper in a Melbourne hospital in 1869. When writing to an Irish cousin in 1877, Sampson, who was still living on the Castlemaine diggings, acknowledged he was 'much poorer than at the beginning'. By 1878, he was in hospital suffering from dysentery, but reassured his cousin that becoming an inpatient was 'more comfortable with plenty of attendants and attention than my hut'. Some of the patients were 'of respectable families at home', while the surgeon, Dr. McGrath was a 'North of Ireland man' and the 'cleverest doctor in Castlemaine'.[65] Two other brothers, William and Ezekiel Dysart from Derry, arrived on the Victorian diggings in the late 1850s. Not meeting with much success, William followed the lure of gold to New Zealand in the early 1860s. Back in Melbourne in 1877, he wrote after many years' silence to another brother in Ireland, explaining his failure to remain in contact. He felt shame at his lack of success. But he had also been ill with fever, his back had been 'crushed' in a mining accident, and he had a kidney complaint. He had lost contact with his brother and advertised for him in country Victorian newspapers. As a result, he discovered that Ezekiel had died of fever in a Melbourne hospital in 1863. William informed his surviving brother that: 'Dying in the hospital here is no disgrace, as it is the only place a single man can go and a man with no money … and if he dies he is buried in a respectable manner …'[66] While Lawrence and Dysart were talking about general hospitals, it is possible that for some aging Irish miners suffering from mental health problems Yarra Bend was also 'more comfortable' than a 'hut' on the diggings and offered the prospect of burial in a 'respectable manner'.

CONCLUSION

Post-natal depression, grief at the deaths of children, alcoholism, head injuries and poor physical health, which are all very evident in

Yarra Bend Asylum's patient records, were problems precipitating committal to many lunatic asylums during the mid-nineteenth century, not only in Australia, but in Ireland, Britain, and the United States as well. However, the records of Yarra Bend do offer some evidence that 'gold fever' did play a role in the high committal rates evident in colonial Victoria, as contemporaries alleged. The rushes certainly left many 'disappointed': very few achieved the wealth that they had dreamt of. Most of course overcame their disappointment, married, and moved on to other jobs or to other places – even, in the case of the perennially optimistic, to other rushes. But for a number the disappointment was too devastating for them to be able to transcend it. Perhaps this was especially true of those Irish men who had no family in the colony, but parents and siblings back 'home' with high expectations of a regular flow of remittances. The fact that the Irish who immigrated to Australia between the 1840s to the 1870s would have been familiar with asylums, as Ireland's public asylum network was established as early as the 1820s, and that Irish policemen and doctors played a major role in the committal process may also have been factors tending to increased numbers of the Irish born who were committed to Victoria's Yarra Bend Asylum during the gold-rush era.

APPENDIX 6

ADMISSIONS TO YARRA BEND ASYLUM, MELBOURNE, 1848–69

Sources: Yarra Bend Asylum Patient Admission Registers and Case Books, Public Record Office Victoria, Melbourne (PROV, VA 2839: Admission Registers VPRS 7556/P/0001 (1848–51); VPRS 7556/P/0002 (1852–4); VPRS 7556/P/0003 (1855); VPRS 7416/P/0001 (1856); VPRS 7400/P/0001 (1863–4); VPRS 07556/P/0001 (1868–9); Case Book VPRS 7417/p1/1a)

TABLE 6.1: TOTAL AND IRISH ADMISSIONS TO YARRA BEND ASYLUM, MELBOURNE, 1848–56, 1863–64, 1868–69.

Years	Total Admissions	Irish Admissions (% of Total)
1848–56	742 Male/Female	286 (38)
1863–4	249 Female	88 (35)
1868–9	191 Male*	47 (25)
Total	1,182	421 (36)

* This is a sample of admissions in these years, covering 8 months of 1868 and 7 months of 1869.

TABLE 6.2: PERCENTAGE OF ADMISSIONS TO YARRA BEND ASYLUM, MELBOURNE,
BY PLACE OF BIRTH, 1848–53.*

Year	Ireland (%)	England &Wales (%)	Scotland (%)	Other (%) ^	Not Known (%)	Total Admissions
1848	52	36	12	0	0	25
1849	35	35	18	6	6	34
1850	53	33	7	0	7	15
1851	49	29	7	5	10	41
1852	18	46	23	5	8	39
1853	35	35	13	7	10	145
1848–53 Average	40	36	13	4	7	50

* Place of birth was not regularly recorded in 1854–6.
^ Of the 16 'Others' admitted in 1848–53: only 1 was a woman, who had been born in India and was admitted in 1849; 3 men born in the United States were admitted in 1849, 1852 and 1853 respectively; 2 Australian-born men were admitted in 1851; 1 Italian was admitted in 1852 and another in 1853; while the remaining 8 men were all admitted in 1853 and included 3 Germans, 1 of whom was Jewish, 2 Poles, 1 of whom was Jewish, and 3 men born in Austria, Egypt and China respectively.

TABLE 6.3: IRISH ADMISSIONS TO YARRA BEND ASYLUM, MELBOURNE, 1848–56.

Years	Irish Admissions (% of Total)	Male/Female % of Irish	Catholic/ Protestant % of Irish	Average Age on Admission in Years M/F	Average Stay in Years (% Died in Asylum)
1848–52	60 (39)	43/57	67/33	35/30	7.8 (40)
1853–6	226 (38)*	69/31	75/25 ^	34/26	6.3 (36)
1848–6	286 (38)	64/36	71/29#	34.5/28	7.0 (38)

* Irish admissions in 1854–6 are estimates based on Victorian births, deaths and marriages indexes, as place of birth was not regularly recorded.
^ These figures apply to 1853–4 as religion was not regularly recorded in 1855–6.
# These figures apply to 1848–4.

TABLE 6.4: PERCENTAGE OF FEMALE ADMISSIONS TO YARRA BEND ASYLUM,
MELBOURNE, BY PLACE OF BIRTH, 1863–4.

Year	Ireland (%)	England & Wales (%)	Scotland (%)	Australia (%)	New Zealand (%)*	Other (%)	Not Known (%)
1863	38	31	12	2	0	2	15
1864	33	28	16	6	0	5	12
1863–4	35.5	29.5	14	4	0	3.5	13.5

* Of the 8 'Other' women admitted in 1863–4: 3 had been born in the West Indies, 3 in Germany, 1 in Spain and 1 was a Polish-born Jew.

TABLE 6.5: IRISH FEMALE ADMISSIONS TO YARRA BEND ASYLUM, MELBOURNE, 1863–4.

Years	Irish Admissions (% of Total Females)	Catholic/ Protestant % of Irish Females	Married/ Single/Widow % of Irish Females	Average Age on Admission in Years	Average Stay in Years (% Died in Asylum)
1863	45 (38)	68/32	39/59/2	28.5	5.9 (11)
1864	43 (33)	79/21	50/47/3	31	4.2 (20.5)
1863–4	88 (35.5)	73.5/26.5	44/53/3	30	5.0 (16)

TABLE 6.6: PERCENTAGE OF MALE ADMISSIONS TO YARRA BEND ASYLUM, MELBOURNE, BY PLACE OF BIRTH, 1868–9.

Year	Ireland (%)	England & Wales (%)	Scotland (%)	Australia (%)	New Zealand (%)	Other (%)*	Not Known (%)
1868	26	24	7	8	3	12	20
1869	24	32	7	3	0	16	18
1868–9	25	28	7	5.5	1.5	14	19

* Of the 27 'Other' men admitted in 1868–9: 6 had been born in Germany, 5 in China, 5 in the United States, 3 in Italy, 3 in Norway and 1 each in Denmark, Switzerland, the West Indies, India and Ceylon (Sri Lanka).

TABLE 6.7 IRISH MALE ADMISSIONS TO YARRA BEND ASYLUM, MELBOURNE, 1868–9.

Years	Irish Admissions (% of Total Males)	Catholic/ Protestant % of Irish Males	Married/ Single/Widower % of Irish Males	Average Age on Admission in Years	Average Stay in Years (% Died in Asylum)*
1868	23 (26)	84/16	35/65/0	35	N/A
1869	24 (24)	74/26	38/57/5	35	N/A
1868–9	47 (25)	79/21	36/61/3	35	N/A

* Dates of discharge or death for male patients admitted in 1868–9 were not regularly recorded.

NOTES

1. I would like to thank the Australian Research Council for funding the research upon which this article is based. I would also like to thank my colleague, Dr. Dianne Hall, who collected much of the data concerning the inmates of Yarra Bend Asylum.
2. Quoted in J. Damousi, *Freud in the Antipodes: a Cultural History of Psychoanalysis in Australia* (Sydney: UNSW Press, 2005), pp.15, 338–9.
3. B. Egan, 'Springthorpe, John William (1855–1933)', *Australian Dictionary of Biography*, Vol. 12 (Melbourne: Melbourne University Press, 1990), pp.38–9.
4. D. Goodman, *Gold Seeking: Victoria and California in the 1850s* (Sydney: Allen & Unwin, 1994), p.57.
5. D.I. McDonald, 'Manning, Frederic Norton (1839–1903)', *Australian Dictionary of Biography*, Vol. 5 (Melbourne: Melbourne University Press, 1974), pp.204–5.
6. In 1887 in Western Australia, 34 per cent of asylum inmates were Irish born, while in Queensland the comparable figure was 33 per cent. F.N. Manning, 'President's Address: Psychology Section', *Intercolonial Medical Congress of Australasia: Transactions of Second Session Held in Melbourne, Victoria, January 1889* (Melbourne: Stillwell & Co., 1889), p.818, Table IV.
7. D.H. Tuke, 'Increase of Insanity in Ireland', *Journal of Mental Science*, 40, 171 (1894), pp.549–61.
8. The seminal work on Ireland remains M. Finnane, *Insanity and the Insane in Post-Famine Ireland* (London: Croom Helm, 1981). For the United States, see J.W. Fox, 'Irish Immigrants, Pauperism and Insanity in 1854 Massachusetts', *Social Science History*, 15 (1991), pp.315–36; A. Vander Stoep and B. Link, 'Social Class, Ethnicity and Mental Illness: the Importance of Being More than Earnest', *American Journal of Public Health*, 88 (1998), pp.1396–1402. For England, see E.L. Malcolm, '"A most miserable looking object" – the Irish in English Asylums, 1851–1901: Migration, Poverty and Prejudice', in J. Belchem and K. Tenfelde (eds), *Irish and Polish Migration in Comparative Perspective* (Essen: Klartext Verlag, 2003), pp.121–32.
9. M. Lewis, *Managing Madness: Psychiatry and Society in Australia, 1788–1980* (Canberra: Australian Government Publishing Service, 1988); C. Coleborne and D. MacKinnon (eds), *'Madness' in Australia: Histories, Heritage and the Asylum* (Brisbane: University of Queensland Press, 2003).
10. M. Finnane, 'Asylums, Families and the State', *History Workshop*, 20 (1985), pp.134–48; T. McClaughlin, '"I was nowhere else": Casualties of Colonisation in Eastern Australia during the Second Half of the Nineteenth Century', in T. McClaughlin (ed.), *Irish Women in Colonial Australia* (Sydney: Allen & Unwin, 1998), pp.142–62; S. Garton, *Medicine and Madness: a Social History of Insanity in NSW, 1880–1940* (Sydney: UNSW Press, 1988), pp.102–5.
11. For evidence that some of the female inmates of Dundrum Central Criminal Asylum were encouraged by Dublin Castle to emigrate on release, see P. Prior, 'Emigrants or Exiles? Female Ex-Prisoners Leaving Ireland, 1850–1900', *Australasian Journal of Irish Studies*, 8 (2008/9), pp.30–47.
12. P. O'Farrell, *The Irish in Australia, 1788 to the Present*, 3rd edition (Sydney: UNSW Press, 2000), pp.169–70.
13. D. Fitzpatrick, *Oceans of Consolation: Personal Accounts of Irish Migration to Australia* (Ithaca, NY, and London: Cornell University Press, 1994), p.6.
14. Lewis, *Managing Madness*, p.29.
15. H.C. Burdett, *Hospitals and Asylums of the World: their Origin, History, Construction, Administration, Management, and Legislation*, Vol. 1 (London: J. & A. Churchill, 1891), pp.303, 309, 313.
16. G. Serle, *The Golden Age: a History of the Colony of Victoria, 1851–61* (Melbourne: Melbourne University Press, 1963), pp.1–8; J. Boyce, *Van Diemen's Land* (Melbourne: Black Inc., 2009), pp.244–50; W. Vamplew (ed.), *Australians: Historical Statistics* (Sydney: Fairfax, Syme & Weldon Associates, 1987), p.10.
17. Between 1848 and 1859, nearly 30,500 Irish assisted immigrants reached Victoria. In a colony that was 60 per cent male in 1851, some 69 per cent of these Irish immigrants were young women. Fitzpatrick, *Oceans of Consolation*, pp.12–13.

18. O. MacDonagh, 'The Irish in Victoria, 1851–91: a Demographic Essay' in T. D. Williams (ed.), *Historical Studies VIII* (Dublin: Gill and Macmillan, 1971), pp.82–4; Vamplew (ed.), *Australians: Historical Statistics*, pp.10, 26, 29.

19. G. Bolton, 'The Gold Discovery 1851–80 and Ireland' in C. Kiernan (ed.), *Ireland and Australia* (Cork: Mercier Press, 1984), pp.23–33; M. Murphy, 'The Irish in Australian Mining History' in S. Grimes and G. Ó Tuathaigh (eds), *The Irish-Australian Connection* (Galway: University College Galway, 1989), pp.81–90.

20. Quoted in Goodman, *Gold Seeking*, p.194.

21. J. Sherer, *The Gold-Finder in Australia: How He Went, How He Fared, How He Made his Fortune*, reprint (1853; Harmondsworth: Penguin Books, 1973), p.9.

22. Ibid., p.73.

23. C.G. Duffy, *My Life in Two Hemispheres*, colonial edition, Vol. 2 (London: T. Fisher Unwin, 1898), pp.156, 158.

24. J.F. Hogan, *The Irish in Australia* (London: Ward & Downey, 1887), pp.14, 16.

25. Quoted in P. O'Farrell, *Letters from Irish Australia, 1825–1929* (Sydney and Belfast: NSW University Press and the Ulster Historical Foundation, 1984), pp.44–5.

26. Fitzpatrick, *Oceans of Consolation*, pp.169–70.

27. W. Kelly, *Life in Victoria, or Victoria in 1853 and Victoria in 1858*, reprint, Vol.1 (1859; Kilmore, VIC: Lowden Publishing, 1977), p.369.

28. Serle, *The Golden Age*, pp.85–6.

29. For the background to the building of Yarra Bend Asylum during the 1840s, see L.A. Monk, *Attending Madness: at Work in the Australian Colonial Asylum* (Amsterdam and New York: Rodopi, 2008), pp.24–7; R. Bonwick, 'The History of Yarra Bend Lunatic Asylum, Melbourne' (unpublished M. Med. thesis, University of Melbourne, 1996). The asylum closed in 1925 and some of its buildings were later used as a hospital and a prison; the grounds are now a golf course.

30. Report of the Melbourne Lunatic Asylum for the month ending 30 November 1863 (Public Record Office Victoria [hereafter PROV], VPRS 3991/P/0000/37/D10428).

31. E.L. Malcolm, 'Australian Asylum Architecture through German Eyes: Kew, Melbourne, 1867', *Health and History*, 11, 1 (2009), pp.46–64.

32. According to Burdett's figures, in 1889 Kew had 1,092 inmates, compared to Yarra Bend's 860, while in 1887 Parramatta in NSW had 1,031 and in 1888 Woogaroo in Queensland had 1,021. Burdett, *Hospitals and Asylums of the World*, Vol.1, pp.303, 309, 313.

33. Malcolm, 'Australian Asylum Architecture through German Eyes', pp.50–1.

34. Finnane, *Insanity and the Insane in Post-Famine Ireland*, pp.87–113.

35. P. Bartlett, *The Poor Law of Lunacy: the Administration of Pauper Lunatics in Mid Nineteenth-Century England* (London and New York: Leicester University Press, 1999), pp.81–102.

36. C. Coleborne, 'Passage to the Asylum: the Role of the Police in Committals of the Insane in Victoria, Australia, 1848–1900' in R. Porter and D. Wright (eds), *The Confinement of the Insane: International Perspectives, 1800–1965* (Cambridge: Cambridge University Press, 2003), pp.129–48.

37. D. Wilson, *The Beat: Policing a Victorian City* (Melbourne: Circa, 2006), pp.122–6, 143.

38. R. Haldane, *The People's Force: a History of the Victoria Police* (Melbourne: Melbourne University Press, 1986), p.82; E.L. Malcolm, '"What would people say if I became a police-man?" The Irish Policeman Abroad' in O. Walsh (ed.), *Ireland Abroad: Politics and Professions in the Nineteenth Century* (Dublin: Four Courts Press, 2003), pp.95–107.

39. C. Coleborne, *Madness in the Family: Insanity and Institutions in the Australasian Colonial World, 1860–1914* (Houndmills, Basingstoke: Palgrave Macmillan, 2010), pp.59–61, 72–3, 86–7.

40. K.M. Bowden, *Goldrush Doctors at Ballarat* (Mulgrave, VIC: The Author, 1977), pp.106–20. A number of Yarra Bend's first visiting medical officers, who certified many patients, were Irish. When Limerick-born Dr. Patrick Cussen, the first visiting medical officer, died in 1849, he was replaced by the colonial surgeon, Dr. John Sullivan. When Sullivan died in 1853, he was replaced by the colony's chief health officer, Belfast-born Dr. William McCrea, who served until 1879. Tarban Creek Asylum in Sydney also had a long-serving Belfast-born medical superintendent during this period: Dr. Francis Campbell, who was appointed in 1848 and replaced by Dr. F.N. Manning in 1868. B. Gandevia, 'Cussen, Patrick Edward (1792–1849)', *Australian Dictionary of Biography*, Vol.1 (Melbourne: Melbourne

University Press, 1966), pp.272–3; D.M. O'Sullivan, 'McCrea, William (1814–99)', *Australian Dictionary of Biography*, Vol.5 (Melbourne: Melbourne University Press, 1974), p.138; D.I. McDonald, Francis Rawdon Hastings (1798–1877)', *Australian Dictionary of Biography*, Vol. 3 (Melbourne: Melbourne University Press, 1969), pp.345–6.

41. W. Kelly, *A Stroll through the Diggings of California* (London: Simms and McIntyre, 1852).
42. Kelly, *Life in Victoria*, pp.114–5, 139–40.
43. *Argus*, 6 October 1848.
44. See the Tables in the Appendix for details of the patient sample used in this analysis. Unless otherwise stated, patient data is taken from Yarra Bend's admission registers and case books covering the years 1848–69, held in the Public Record Office Victoria, Melbourne (PROV, VA 2839: VPRS 7556, 7416, 7400, 07556, 7417).
45. I would like to thank my colleague Dr. Dolly Mackinnon, who is studying Australian private asylums, for information about Cremorne.
46. The same statistical qualifications apply to the apparently disproportionate number of Irish found in Australian colonial prisons. M. Finnane, 'The Irish and Crime in the Late Nineteenth Century: a Statistical Inquiry' in O. MacDonagh and W.F. Mandle (eds), *Irish-Australian Studies: Papers Delivered at the Fifth Irish-Australian Conference* (Canberra: Australian National University, 1989), pp.77–98.
47. Fitzpatrick, *Oceans of Consolation*, pp.14–6.
48. In 1861, whereas there were 109 Irish men for every 100 Irish women in Australia, there were 168.6 English men for every 100 English women and 152.5 Scottish men for every 100 Scottish women. Vamplew (ed.), *Australians: Historical Statistics*, p.11.
49. Ibid., p.10.
50. For a study of women in Victorian asylums, including Yarra Bend, see C. Coleborne, *Reading 'Madness': Gender and Difference in the Colonial Asylum in Victoria, Australia, 1848–88* (Perth: Network Books, 2007).
51. J. McCalman, *Sex and Suffering: Women's Health and a Women's Hospital. The Royal Women's Hospital, Melbourne, 1856–1996* (Melbourne: Melbourne University Press, 1998), pp.5, 18–19, 22–4. Professor McCalman is currently engaged in a large 'Founders and Settlers' project, studying the health of the 73,500 convicts sent to Dan Diemen's Land in 1803–53 and the health of their descendants up to World War I. This study will doubtless yield much valuable information about the health of the Irish in Australia.
52. D.I. McDonald, 'Gladesville Hospital: the Formative Years, 1838–50', *Journal of the Royal Australian Historical Society*, 41, 4 (1965): 273–95.
53. Monk, *Attending Madness*, p.51.
54. Ibid., p.23.
55. Patients are often identified in case notes by the ship on which they arrived in the colony. This probably reflects the fact that it was easier for people, especially if they were illiterate, to remember the name of the ship on which they had spent months at sea rather than the exact date at which they finally reached Australia.
56. T. McClaughlin, *Barefoot and Pregnant: Irish Famine Orphans in Australia* (Melbourne: Genealogical Society of Victoria, 1991), p.161.
57. This Eliza Armstrong, who spent only ten months in Yarra Bend in 1851, is a different Eliza Armstrong from the woman already mentioned, who was committed in 1848 and died in the asylum in 1912.
58. McClaughlin, *Barefoot and Pregnant*, p.192.
59. Ibid.
60. Monk, *Attending Madness*, pp.27–9, 35, 49–53.
61. M. Anderson, 'Mrs Charles Clacy, Lola Montez and Poll the Grogseller: Glimpses of Women on the Early Victorian Goldfields' in I. McCalman, A. Cook and A. Reeves (eds), *Gold: Forgotten Histories and Lost Objects of Australia* (Cambridge: Cambridge University Press, 2001), pp.234–5; Goodman, *Gold Seeking*, pp.199–200; M. Sturma, *Vice in a Vicious Society: Crime and Convicts in Mid Nineteenth-Century New South Wales* (Brisbane: University of Queensland Press, 1983), pp.149–50.
62. During the 1850s and 1860s the Kilmore electoral district had the highest proportion of Irish settlers in the colony. In 1857, for example, 32 per cent of the district's inhabitants were Irish born, while in 1871 the figure was 26 per cent. McDonagh, 'The Irish in Victoria', pp.86, 88.

63. J. Sadlier, *Recollections of a Victorian Police Officer*, reprint (1913; Harmondsworth: Penguin Books, 1973), pp.38–56.
64. G. Serle, *The Rush to be Rich: a History of the Colony of Victoria, 1883–9* (Melbourne: Melbourne University Press, 1971), pp.1–2.
65. O'Farrell, *Letters from Irish Australia*, pp.46–8.
66. Ibid., pp.49–50.

7

Transnational Ties to Home: Irish Migrants in New Zealand Asylums, 1860–1926

Angela McCarthy

In her recent study of the colonial asylum in four Australasian settings, Catharine Coleborne explores the connections between families and insanity. In finding evidence of the family in case notes, correspondence, visitors books, and maintenance payments, she examines how the family sought to explain and respond to the insanity of their kinsfolk, how they interacted with asylums, how they grappled with demands for maintenance, and how they coped with patients who returned to the family environs.[1] In doing so, Coleborne builds upon other works relating to asylums and the family beyond Australasia. Notable here is work by Mark Finnane who argues for 'the asylum's role as the arbiter of social and familial conflict'. In other words, families admitted 'those whose demeanour, behaviour, antagonism, resistance or withdrawal failed to fit their immediate context'.[2]

Despite the pertinent insights offered by the broader literature on the family and insanity, there are two significant omissions in such studies. First, just who constitutes the family is rarely discussed explicitly, at least not in detail or quantitatively. We get no idea, for instance, whether the family comprises spouses, siblings, parents, children, or other extended family members. Such omission is surprising in light of David Wright's reflections on this very issue more than a decade ago, querying for instance whether nuclear or extended families undertook committal.[3] It is also critical in light of an influential atomisation thesis put forward by historian Miles Fairburn that 'most colonists … had already severed their links with place, family, friends, community in the great uprooting that led them to New Zealand'.[4] Moreover, the family connections explored in studies of the asylum are predominantly confined to the country in which the asylums are located. The operation of transnational communications between home and abroad is strikingly absent.

In light of this manifest neglect, this chapter seeks to contribute to the historiography in two ways. First, it examines the family networks that existed for Irish patients in New Zealand asylums. Does the evidence support recent research based on alternative sources which demonstrates the robust existence of ties of family and friends, or were Irish migrants in New Zealand asylums atomised and devoid of wider kin networks? Second, the chapter looks at the connections between home and abroad, with a particular emphasis on efforts to restore family networks.

OVERVIEW OF THE IRISH BORN IN NEW ZEALAND ASYLUMS

While overall statistics still elude us, annual data from asylum admissions in New Zealand when compared with published census data demonstrates the significant over-representation of the Irish-born compared with their counterparts from Europe (see Table 7.1). This echoes international analyses of the differences in the ethnic composition of lunatic asylums which also identify the disproportionate representation of Irish migrants. A number of theories have been posited to explain this. Contemporary claims alleged that Ireland exported its insane while others suggested that the Irish were inherently predisposed to insanity.[5] Scholars such as John Fox, meanwhile, in his study of the Irish in Massachusetts, argued that 'higher rates of insanity among the Irish were a result of their higher rates of pauperism and not their ethnicity.'[6] Prejudice and the supposed isolation of Irish migrants are also proffered as explanations for mental illness among twentieth-century migrants.[7]

TABLE 7.1: PERCENTAGE OF IRISH-, SCOTTISH-, AND ENGLISH-BORN PATIENTS IN NEW ZEALAND ASYLUMS AND THE OVERALL COLONIAL POPULATION AS A PROPORTION OF THE FOREIGN-BORN POPULATION, 1878–1906.

CENSUS YEAR	IRELAND-BORN		SCOTLAND-BORN		ENGLAND-BORN	
	CENSUS (%)	ASYLUM (%)	CENSUS (%)	ASYLUM (%)	CENSUS (%)(	ASYLUM (%)
1878	18.2	29.0	20.0	21.9	44.3	38.5
1881	18.5	31.7	19.8	18.3	44.7	36.8
1886	18.5	32.1	19.7	17.9	45.2	37.9
1891	18.3	33.0	20.0	18.1	45.0	37.8
1896	17.6	31.0	19.3	18.1	44.5	38.0
1901	17.0	29.7	18.6	19.0	43.6	38.1
1906	15.0	28.4	16.9	17.7	41.3	38.6

The analysis of records emanating from the Dunedin and Seacliff asylums attests to this over-representation of the Irish born.[8] Data relating to a sample of all patients admitted to these asylums in every third year between 1864 and 1909 reveals the admission of 1,384 patients, 755 of whom we have information relating to birthplace. Of this total, 136 (18 per cent) were born in Ireland, 124 (16.4 per cent) in England, 200 in Scotland (26.5 per cent), and 210 (27.8 per cent) in New Zealand. Taking the 1881 Census as a mid-range guide, the share of these groups among Otago's total population was: Ireland (9.2 per cent), England (16.5 per cent), Scotland (21.6 per cent), and New Zealand (42.4 per cent). So while the English were admitted in similar proportions to their representation in Otago, and the New Zealand born under-represented, the Irish and the Scots were over-represented, the Irish the most significantly so.

Of the sample of 136 Irish-born patients admitted to the Dunedin and Seacliff asylums between 1863 and 1909, the gender profile is relatively balanced: seventy Irish women and sixty-six Irish men. Analysis of other ethnic groups in the asylums, by contrast, shows a male over-representation with seventy-three English males admitted compared with fifty-one females, and 123 Scottish men compared with seventy-seven women from Scotland. This rough gender parity of the Irish presumably reflects the tendency of Irish women to migrate in numbers similar to that of Irish men, whereas other European nations losing populations were predominantly male.[9] Irish-born admissions to Dunedin's public asylums were also distinctive in relation to their religious beliefs with eighty-six (around two-thirds) Irish-born patients recorded as Catholic. It is difficult to determine how representative this is of the larger Irish migrant flow, for there are no firm statistics for the religious leanings of Irish migrants in New Zealand, although a Census-based estimate equating Catholics in New Zealand as Irish estimates three-quarters of Irish migrants were Catholic.[10] The findings from the Dunedin and Seacliff asylums, however, replicate a study of patients admitted to the Auckland asylum in the early twentieth century in which one third of the Irish born were Protestant.[11] Most English-born and Scottish-born migrants in New Zealand, as well as patients in the colony's asylums, were Protestant. Meanwhile, in terms of age, almost half the Irish born were admitted to Dunedin's public asylums between the ages of thirty and forty-nine, while just over half were married or widowed.

NETWORKS IN THE COLONY

Studies of insanity in New Zealand have predominantly focused on gender issues, with the family only recently being incorporated into the analytical framework.[12] Yet were foreign-born asylum patients likely to be without networks of family and friends in the colony, reinforcing historian Miles Fairburn's claim that 'Bondlessness was central to colonial life'?[13] Analysing casebook entries provides some insight into the issue with a range of family connections evident, comprising parents, siblings, spouses, children, and extended kinsfolk. All told, the presence or absence of kin connections was explicitly established for ninety-seven of the sample of 136 Irish patients in the Dunedin public asylums. These casebooks were examined together with other sources relating to insanity which reveal family networks such as the correspondence kept by the asylums' medical superintendents, visitors' books, and official government reports and correspondence relating to the migration of insane migrants. They reveal the following findings.

A significant characteristic of the Irish flow to New Zealand, as elsewhere, was its composition of young, single adults.[14] While this feature might suggest an absence of family networks, evidence suggests that Irish migrants moved with or to siblings, often making use of nominated and assisted schemes for their passage.[15] Of Irish patients in the Dunedin and Seacliff asylums, twenty-two were known to have a sibling in the colony. Such connections were also found more widely throughout the colony.[16] Bridget O., confined to the Auckland asylum on arrival, was one of those voyaging to New Zealand with a sibling, her brother Michael. According to George Goode, the Surgeon Superintendent of the *British Empire* in 1875, Bridget 'is of unsound mind, the symptoms of which manifested themselves during the greater part of the voyage'. Throughout the journey Bridget was 'forcibly bathed', while 'Her screams were dreadful, frightening and keeping awake all those in the compartment.' Confined in the ship's hospital, Bridget broke the door and when 'locked up in the bath room and she twisted and broke off the strong lead pipe for conveying water to the bath'. George Goode believed 'the conduct of her brother, who came in the S.M. compartment, highly culpable. He acknowledged in presence of several of the girls that she was bad in this way before.' As Goode continued:

> Some of the girls say that her brother told her in presence of several of the girls nearly six weeks ago that he would have her

put into an asylum when he got to New Zealand. He also asked me just before the Commissioners came on board to get them to send her to some asylum. He evidently wants to get her off his hands. The mystery is why he should have brought her here. He says her mother is alive in Ireland, and that they have three brothers in Australia who are doing well. I saw her this morning at the Depot, and, although quieter, her manner & speech are still far from rational. She said this morning she wanted to go to her friends in Australia. ... If he can be punished for bringing this girl to the colony I consider he will richly deserve it.[17]

Two days later the Commissioners Report noted that Bridget was committed to the provincial asylum. The Commissioners reported that her brother Michael denied any knowledge of her mental state prior to emigration, though 'there is only too much reason to believe that he was not altogether ignorant of the girls [sic] condition, and that she was liable to at least occasional mental derangement prior to embarkation.' They went on to regret 'that there are no available means provided by law for the punishment of frauds of this description by which the colony is subjected either to heavy permanent charges for maintaining such persons for life, or put to the serious cost of returning them again to the Mother Country.'[18]

If true, Michael's actions suggest a more unsavoury motivation for migration, to relinquish responsibility of an insane family member to the state. Indeed, this issue was of deep concern for authorities in New Zealand who expressed alarm that patients previously admitted to home asylums or showing 'insane tendencies' were shipped to New Zealand to escape 'the burden of their maintenance at home'.[19] In Britain and Ireland, for instance, maintenance of the insane was a local charge with central government only providing some financial relief after 1874.[20] In New Zealand, by contrast, care of the insane was provided by the general government, though attempts were made to secure financial support from the families of those committed.[21] The resultant Maintenance Books and Registers such as those for the Auckland asylum provide some insight into the diverse formation of family members supplying financial contributions. More useful for a quantitative analysis in determining family relationships, however, are asylum Visitors Books which note the visitor's name, address, and relationship to the patient. While a longitudinal study would prove most instructive, a cursory examination of 518 patients in the Auckland asylum who were visited between October 1891 and January 1893 reveals that most visitors were wives (109), friends (97), mothers (78), and sisters (55). The gender dimension is also striking with figures for sons (26), fathers (21), and husbands (8) comparatively low, presumably a reflection of their work commitments preventing men from asylum visits, and also that most patients in asylums were male.[22]

Eliza C., a 20 year-old Catholic domestic servant from Londonderry, also migrated with her brother and 'During the voyage she became insane and was taken here. She says she was very badly treated by the other girls on board.'[23] For most Irish migrants, however, mental illness seemingly developed several years after arrival. Jane A. from Armoy in County Antrim, for instance, was committed to the Dunedin asylum in 1879, seventeen years after she voyaged to New Zealand with her brother who had recently drowned under the suspicion of suicide.[24] Other migration pathways included migrants following siblings already settled in the colony such as Luke O., a labourer from Cavan, whose 'brothers had been here before him & sister'. An uncle was also resident in New Zealand, with Luke living with him for two years.[25] Despite the existence of such connections, some Irish migrants sought to keep their condition private, such as 31 year-old Catherine N., a single domestic servant from County Clare who did not want her sister, also resident in the colony, knowing of her mental condition.[26]

Further insights into family connections in the colony arise as a result of the asylum authorities' concerns with heredity, an alleged family predisposition to insanity. In relation to 26 year-old Catholic domestic Kate G., confined at Seacliff in 1900, 'Her sister [*name deleted by author*] is at present a patient here, so there is evidently [*erased*: an] insane tendency in the family.'[27] Catholic labourer Michael E., meanwhile, 'is not even aware of the fact that his two sisters are in the Asylum though they have been here for many years'.[28] And a cousin of 34 year-old Catholic farmer John G, originally from Letterkenny, informed medical authorities that John's brother had committed suicide in Wellington after a period in the asylum there.[29] It was also reported of 65 year-old Church of England retired hotelkeeper Alexander H., originally from County Tyrone, that his brother died at Seacliff.[30] Apart from siblings, hereditary observations were also made in relation to parents and children in the colony with Cork-born Patrick F.'s son also in the asylum as well as two sons of 73 year-old Malachi M., a Catholic labourer at Milton.[31] Mention of parents (and one mother-in-law), however, appeared in just nine cases of known Irish migrants in the Dunedin and Seacliff asylums.

While the dominant flow of young, single Irish men and women was often undertaken without parents, alternative family networks comprising uncles and aunts, nephews and nieces, were present in the colony.[32] All told these sibling, parental, and wider kin and friend connections were apparent for thirty-eight Irish patients, comprising almost 40 per cent of those for whom family networks were explicitly established. Moreover, various studies focusing on the correspondence of migrants and asylum patients reveal the character of these family relationships, in harmony and discord.[33] Among those who moved to a wider family network was 20 year-old Mary Ann B., a single domestic servant from County Kerry who was committed to the Seacliff asylum in 1893. According to her uncle, 'She has been depressed since landing here.' He attributed her condition to 'absence from her family in Ireland' and her case note supports this indicating that 'At first she was very cheerful on board ship, but after a few weeks she became sullen. On landing in N.Z. she at first refused to speak to her uncle, who met her & took her by train to his residence.' The lengthy medical report certainly indicates that Mary Ann was distressed during the passage to New Zealand: 'She admits that she was dull and wretched on the voyage out' and that she missed life at home. Yet the medical report reveals a further dynamic, showing that a range of reasons contributed to her condition: 'Says she tried to escape from her uncle's place because her aunt was cruel to her.' As her case note entry also divulged:

> She speaks very highly of her uncle (her father's brother) who she says would have sent her back to her friends in Ireland months ago if his wife had not stood in the way. She says she was very happy at home and saw plenty of people. She had four younger sisters and had enough to keep her going in house work milking doing shopping &c. They always danced at home on Sunday after the cows were milked. She was never at any time dull or melancholy before she left home.[34]

An uncle also paid the passage of Maria B and her sister from Ballygar, Galway, but upon arrival they allegedly found the uncle ill and the aunt drunk and unkind.[35]

The single most prevalent family connection present in the analysis of Irish migrants in the Dunedin public asylums was spousal relationships, with thirty-eight individuals in the asylums visited by a husband or wife, sometimes accompanied by their offspring. Children visiting alone, meanwhile, were evident in eighteen cases.

Indeed, the combined total (fifty-six) of spousal and child relations supplied 58 per cent of the kin connections apparent for the Irish in the Dunedin and Seacliff asylums. Some marital unions were formed prior to migration such as Charles M. from County Cavan who voyaged with his new wife in 1893 on the *Oruba* via Australia. According to Charles' wife, 'his mind was troubled on board ship by his protestant fellows jeering him about religion.' She stated that he had 'No cause [*erased*: unless] for grief unless leaving home and parting with friends. He was very anxious to get to NZ and never showed any sign of grief.' She continued, noting that 'He was not strange or essentic [eccentric] only he began talking about religion and as pious as the people were at home compared to the people in the ship he commenced talking about piety ten days before he got insane.'[36] Other marriages were formed after arrival. Indeed, acquiring a marriage partner abroad was presumably a factor for some Irish migrants in light of 'The rigidity and growing inefficiency of the post-Famine marriage system'.[37]

As with other relationships, these spousal unions were not always harmonious. For instance, Catholic woman Mary Ann M., presumably of Irish descent, wrote to her husband, 'you are nothing to me so don't dare to ever come to see me any more, not ever you Blazon rotten old liar of an Irish Fenian, Brazon looking Irish Fenian.'[38] That medical authorities vetted the writings of patients has resulted in the survival of such letters deemed too volatile to send to family and friends and now often lodged in casebooks or case files. Meanwhile, Thomas B., who 'says that all Irish men are mad', refused to recognise his wife when she called to see him in 1901 after a two-year lapse in visitation.[39] Violent or aggressive actions were also cited in asylum correspondence. John Adams, for instance, wrote to the Public Trustee in Dunedin about Thomas D., a patient from Blacklion, Ireland, admitted to the asylum in 1891. According to the police report at the time, 'I beg to report that the man is a small farmer and resided at Fortrose. He has a wife and family of nine children but they are so much afraid of him that they left him about three years ago and live away from him. He has been living in a small hut by himself since then. His family do not go near him.'[40]

Bridget N. of Tipperary was another patient seemingly suffering domestic abuse. Asked by Medical Superintendent Dr. Truby King in 1905 if her husband ever hit her, Bridget responded, 'Yes, many a time, and dragged me down to the gate by the hair of the head. If I ask him any question lately he hits me and then I run out screaming.'

She also claimed her husband assaulted one of their children, an act Bridget also admitted to. As well as undertaking an extensive question and answer session with Bridget, King wrote at length about her, concluding more broadly that the domestic surroundings of patients required fuller investigation:

> Her account of her husband, her family, and neighbours, convey the fact that whatever they may be she is herself narrow, ignorant, and unaccommodating, and has her mind centered on the wrongs she has suffered and the harshness and cruelty with which she has been treated by her husband. On the other hand she is rather convincing in the matter of her husband's harshness. The one thing clear is that their home is a miserable one for every member of it, and the children are the most to be pitied. In my opinion this is a class of case in which a more thorough investigation should be made locally by the certifying doctors and by the police before a person is committed as insane. The woman is not sound in mind, is narrow, ignorant, and eccentric, and probably almost impossible to live with, but one would like to know more about how her husband has been in the habit of treating her, and how far her present condition and conduct may be the outcome of brutality, tyranny, and general ill-usage.

Also evident from King's interview with Bridget is her isolation, both in New Zealand and from family and friends in Ireland: 'A searching examination of the patient reveals the fact that according to herself her parents in Tipperary were harsh and brutal, especially her father. She became sick of the old home, emigrated, married, and has kept up no communication with Ireland, and formed no friends in the colony.'[41] Bridget N. therefore appears to typify Fairburn's atomised migrants. A smattering of other cases similarly suggests that family ties were non-existent after the process of migration, and perhaps even beforehand. According to the wife of John P. from Antrim, 'he left home young and I do not think he had much communication with any of his relations.'[42] Thomas S.'s wife also indicated that her Cork-born husband had no relations in the colony, though she did note: 'herd him speek of his Brother drinking hevely at home'.[43] The absence of such connections were explicitly noted for three Irish patients; a further five patients were seemingly without such links as reported by their wives.

TRANSNATIONAL CONNECTIONS

While some Irish migrants were seemingly cut off from ties to home, others maintained robust bonds, often demonstrated through the exchange of personal letters.[44] But Fairburn, too, acknowledges these ties to home, albeit linked to his atomisation thesis, arguing that 'colonists remained emotionally tied to the Old World because their atomised society could not satisfy the human need for gregariousness.'[45] Yet Fairburn fails to consider records connected to lunatic asylums or the broader issue of mental illness in his analysis, focusing instead on loneliness, drunkenness, and interpersonal violence as the social problems arising from a 'deficient framework of association'.[46] Analysis of various sources connected to asylums, particularly correspondence but also case notes, provides us with illuminating insight into the existence of transnational ties.

As with the wider historiography of Irish migration, asylum records demonstrate the efforts of some families to reunite abroad. In 1876, Thurlow Astley, an immigration agent at Dalkeith, sought the reunification of Irish woman Ellen W.'s family in New Zealand. It transpired, however, that Ellen's father had been confined at the Richmond Hospital in Dublin, suffering from 'Melancholy Madness', seemingly brought on by an inability to find work in Dublin. Astley emphasised that the father was discharged nine months earlier and that 'the voyage, coupled with the certainty of his getting some little employment out there as a porter or messenger &c would entirely cure him and would be the very best thing for them both.' Astley continued by contending 'although his state of health might prevent his being of any great value to the Colony, still there were sons and daughters all going and not yet in their prime … whose services and power of labour would of the greatest use in the Colony.' He finally queried that if Ellen nominated her siblings would her father be able to migrate also?[47] The Agent General for New Zealand in London replied this was not possible and after a further exchange of correspondence informed Astley, 'the Government cannot prevent the arrival of any person who pays his own passage to the Colony, but it is one of their objects to discourage the emigration of persons in whose family indications of insanity are known to exist.'[48]

Indeed, in cases where passengers paying their own passage to the colony were found to have been previously admitted to an asylum or to have arrived in a state of insanity, attempts were made to ship the insane person back to the homeland. If the captain or owner of a vessel refused, then specific legal acts, such as the Imbecile Passengers Act, were enforced against the ship's owner or captain requiring them to pay a bond of £100. If a passenger was then admitted to an institution within five years the bond was taken as payment for their maintenance.[49]

Asylum authorities in New Zealand also needed to take care in discharging patients who sought to leave the colony. For example, in August 1900 Truby King wrote to the Managing Director of the Union Steamship Company challenging the belief that 'an attempt has been made to deport a lunatic to another Colony from this Asylum whether with or without any sanction.' The case concerned 51 year-old single Kerry woman Hannah L. who came to New Zealand from Melbourne six months prior by the Union Steamship Company. She had first arrived in New Zealand some twenty years earlier before spending some years in San Francisco before moving to Melbourne and then Dunedin. Having spent about six weeks at Seacliff she desired to return to relations in Australia. Seemingly, the Union Steamship Company feared the legal repercussions of her being transported to Australia. As King made clear, 'I have no power or responsibility with regard to a person who happens to have been in the Seacliff Asylum after the patient has been legally discharged by a magistrate. In Miss [*name deleted by author*] case this had been done some ten days before she left the colony and I had no reason to suppose she would become insane although of course a person who has been insane previously is more liable to mental disease than one who has not had the same experience.'[50]

Like Hannah L., other patients sought to relocate elsewhere, their efforts in this regard reported in their case notes. In some instances, migrants indicated that their family and friends in New Zealand were putting procedures in place to facilitate a return home. According to 27 year-old John C. in 1903, who had arrived in the colony as a 2 year-old, 'My friends are making all arrangements for me to take a trip Home to Ireland [*erased*: who were] immediately I leave here, where I was born & where all my friends are. I will stay there when I go Home, & not come back to this country again.'[51] Meanwhile of Denis M. from 'Lisbelnagroah' [*Lisbellanagroagh*], County Antrim, 'A younger brother of his was somewhat eccentric in manner though not that way before coming to New Zealand & on account of this they sent him home again as he did not like living in this country.'[52]

For some patients, 'anxiety' was a key term associated with the desire to return home. According to single Catholic servant Ellen G. from the north of Ireland in 1892, there was 'anxiety to be back home again. Have worked in New Zealand away from all my relations for thirteen yrs.'[53] Eight years later she was transferred to the Porirua asylum. Norah F., a 27 year-old single Catholic servant from 'Corrindoolla' [*Corrandulla*] in Galway, had spent a similar period away from Ireland, with her brother reporting, she 'Has always been anxious to return to the Old Country'. Admitted to Seacliff Hospital in 1897 for five months before being discharged, she was readmitted within two weeks.[54] The language of emotions that appeared in letters and casebooks has received consideration,[55] but it is also important to recognise the practical agendas, such as arranging return migration, which generated the deployment of such language.

Among those medical superintendents in contact with family members to arrange, where possible, a return home was Truby King. In 1889, for instance, King was in contact with Rose M., a sister of Bridget M., who was residing in New York, providing her with a letter from Bridget who wished to visit. According to King:

> If she had enough money to pay her passage I should not hesitate to send her away at once for she is mentally fit to leave and a good worker, but I do not think it would be well for her to go from here to stay in Dunedin because she would be better among friends & a struggle to earn a living directly she left might make her health break down again. On the other hand the sea voyage & prospect of soon being with you will be sure to act beneficially. Bridget has applied to you for fifteen pounds & I think it would be well if you could spare that sum, but if you cannot do so send her <u>twelve</u> which I think would just enable her to reach you though it would not leave her much money in her pocket for an emergency. The money should be made payable to the Superintendent of Seacliff Asylum unless you wish to send it to Bridget.[56]

As well as communicating with networks of family and friends at home and throughout the Irish diaspora in arranging a return passage, asylum authorities also responded to requests from home for updates on a patient's condition. Writing in 1902 to Ballycastle, Ireland, King's communication not only provides an account of the patient's health, but also reveals the range of family members present in New Zealand:

> I find an old letter of enquiry concerning a Mrs [*name erased by*

author] and as there is no evidence of any reply having been sent to you I am now writing to tell you about the patient. She was admitted from Dunedin about 6 years ago suffering from Delusional Insanity and she has never recovered. She has her reasoning faculties in most matters but has many delusions. Her health is good & she is not unhappy. She is 69 years old and is visited from time to time by her husband her brothers. Her daughter has not been here of late and I do not know where she is living ...'[57]

The following year King wrote to Clough in County Down about the patient Margaret B., revealing her admission to the asylum in May 1885 and her physical and mental state: 'She has suffered from recurrent attacks of mania, but the attacks become less severe as she gets older. Her present mental state is one of partial mindlessness, and for the last three years she has been quiet and doing useful work in the kitchen. She has abundant outdoor exercise, and our asylum is on the midst of a large estate. Margaret is quite contented, her memory is poor but she never expresses any desire to go away from the institution.'[58] Her case note reveals that in 1903, eighteen years after her admission, she 'wrote to her brother in Ireland on this day informing him that she is well'. No further correspondence with her brother was commented upon and Margaret died in May 1906.[59]

One of the most extensive exchanges of correspondence between home and abroad relates to Belfast seaman Samuel who in 1911 the Australasian Federated Seamen's Industrial Union of Workers 'discharged from one of our steamers on account of mental derangement'.[60] Admitted to the Auckland asylum, early letters from his wife and sister, resident in the north of Ireland, sought information on his whereabouts. Both his wife and sisters sought the intervention of their local church ministers: the Reverend Edwin E. Wilson at Belfast, and the Reverend Alexander Cuthbert of the Manse at Carrickfergus. According to Wilson, 'His wife is very anxious to have him brought home if he could be allowed to come, as he a few years ago suffered from a derangement of the mind and she was able to nurse him successfully at home.'[61] Letters from Samuel's wife also alluded to his past attack, wondering 'if his mind is completely gone or does he ever mention the child or myself or his Sisters as he was very fond of them. I cannot rest thinking about him so far away from home so you be so kind as to let me know what way he is affected [erased: h]is he quiet or outrageous. He was slightly affected before but was very quiet ... that is about ten years ago.'[62]

Similar letters wondering about Samuel's health and interest in his family continued to be sent from his wife and sisters. By August 1912, his wife sought financial aid: 'you said in your last letter his case was Moreless Hopeless. When he left Belfast he had a few pounds in the post office Savings Bank in his own name it is a long time since I got any money from him as you know how long he is in the Hospital and I have myself and child to support would you kindly ask the Doctor to send me a line about his condition to enable me to draw they money as I am in need of it.'[63] In January 1913, Samuel's wife wrote a local missionary explaining that her daughter 'cries often for her Father and she was only nine months old when he went away but I expect it is me always talking to her about him. Do you think he is ever in his right mind that he would be able to read a letter if I could send him one … I wrote several times to Avondale but never got an answer.'[64] A photograph of his daughter was sent in April 1913, in an effort to bring 'his memory back to think of home'.[65]

In response to these ongoing enquiries, the asylum's response was devoid of hope: 'I regret that your husband is still an inmate of this Hospital, and that in my opinion he is likely to remain so. I think now that he has no prospects of recovery. The letter which you wrote and photograph which you sent were delivered to him, but he has made no reference to the matter since. He never makes any inquiry about any relative.'[66] Scattered letters continued to arrive from Samuel's wife until 1917 and from his sisters into the early 1920s. One dated January 1925 from his sister Sarah revealed that his wife had been remarried six years. The last surviving letter from February 1926, five years before Samuel's death, revealed that a friend of Samuel's sister was to visit, an event noted by the Auckland medics: 'I regret your brother Samuel [*surname deleted by author*] does not show any mental improvement and I am afraid he is unlikely to recover. His general health is fairly good. He was visited Recently by some friends from Ireland.'[67]

A further way in which transnational contact was undertaken related to the financial maintenance of patients and, apart from letters, maintenance registers also give some insight into the practice. For instance, it was noted of Arthur, admitted to the Auckland asylum in 1876, that 'he is reputed to belong to a wealthy and distinguished Irish family.' In 1892 there were indications that Arthur would 'be entitled to considerable property at the death of his mother' but in the meantime he was obliged to repay a significant loan. It was therefore suggested to watch the mother's life and 'appeal to the family pride'. Arthur, however, died in 1896.[68] The Maintenance Register reveals the geographical extent of such communication, including correspondence with family in England, Scotland, Australia, Finland, Austria, Hungary, and Italy. The family of Irish patients were therefore not unusual in the maintenance of such exchanges.

CONCLUSION

A comparative approach to issues of transnational ties and asylums reveals that the Irish born were not the only patients who maintained such connections. Where the Irish born may differ from other ethnicities, however, relates to the type of kin linkages found in the colony. While the broader historiography suggests that the Scots born were similar to the Irish in the range of family networks operating, English migrants may have been less inclined to have this range of ties, though in the absence of sustained investigation such an hypothesis is only tentative. As this chapter has shown, rather than adhering to an overarching portrayal as atomised beings, many Irish migrants confined to the public asylum in Dunedin moved within networks of family and friends. While parental connections in the colony were often absent for those Irish moving as young adults, they could avail of the presence of siblings and extended networks comprising aunts, uncles, and cousins. Such connections were explicitly noted for at least 40 per cent of Irish patients. Most relationships, however, were those of spouse or offspring. This, however, does not mean that those Irish patients were without other wider networks in the colony; simply that this was the prime relationship noted in the documentation. We should bear in mind, however, that no information about family or friends was made for one-quarter of the sample of Irish migrants in the Dunedin or Seacliff asylums. Furthermore, this reflection on the presence of family networks is simply a snapshot in time. Alternative evidence reveals, for instance, that some migrants moved to the colony with or to join family and friends, but in these connections were not always maintained.[69] Where they were, such ties were both harmonious and discordant. Ongoing research into the diverse ethnicities found in asylums will hopefully clarify a number of these issues.[70]

NOTES

1. Catharine Coleborne, *Madness in the Family: Insanity and Institutions in the Australasian Colonial World, 1860–1914* (London: Palgrave Macmillan, 2010).
2. Mark Finnane, 'Asylums, Families and the State', *History Workshop Journal*, 20 (1985), pp.135, 136.
3. David Wright, 'Getting out of the Asylum: Understanding the Confinement of the Insane in the Nineteenth Century', *Social History of Medicine*, 10:1 (1997), p.150.
4. Miles Fairburn, *The Ideal Society and its Enemies: The Foundations of Modern New Zealand Society, 1850–1900* (Auckland: Auckland University Press, 1989), p.94.
5. Elizabeth Malcolm, '"A most miserable looking object": The Irish in English Asylums, 1851–1901. Migration, Poverty and Prejudice', in John Belchem and Klaus Tenfelde (eds), *Irish and Polish Migration in Comparative Perspective* (Essen: Klartext-Verlag, 2003), p.123.
6. John W. Fox, 'Irish Immigrants, Pauperism, and Insanity in 1854 Massachusetts', *Social Science History*, 15:3 (1991), p.331.
7. Malcolm, in *Irish and Polish Migration in Comparative Perspective*, p.125.
8. The Dunedin asylum was founded in 1863 with its larger replacement, Seacliff, opening in 1877. All patients were eventually transferred from the Dunedin asylum to Seacliff by 1884. For histories of the asylums, see chapters by Jeremy Bloomfield, Cheryl Caldwell, and Caroline Hubbard in Barbara Brookes and Jane Thomson (eds), *'Unfortunate Folk': Essays on Mental Health Treatment, 1863–1992* (Dunedin: University of Otago Press, 2001).
9. David Fitzpatrick, *Irish Emigration, 1801–1921* (Dundalk: Irish Economic and Social History Society, 1984), p.7.
10. Donald Harman Akenson, *Half the World From Home: Perspectives on the Irish in New Zealand, 1860–1950* (Wellington: Victoria University Press, 1990), pp.65–6.
11. Angela McCarthy, 'Ethnicity, Migration, and the Lunatic Asylum in Early Twentieth-Century Auckland, New Zealand', *Social History of Medicine*, 21:1 (2008), p.53.
12. The main works on gender and insanity in New Zealand are: Barbara Brookes, 'Women and Madness: A Case-Study of the Seacliff Asylum, 1890–1920', in Barbara Brookes, Charlotte Macdonald, and Margaret Tennant (eds), *Women in History 2* (Wellington: Bridget Williams Books, 1992), pp.129–47; Barbara Brookes, 'Men and Madness in New Zealand, 1890–1916', in Linda Bryder and Derek A. Dow (eds), *New Countries and Old Medicine: Proceedings of an International Conference on the History of Medicine and Health, Auckland, New Zealand, 1994* (Auckland: Pyramid Press, 1995), pp.204–10; Bronwyn Labrum, 'Looking Beyond the Asylum: Gender and the Process of Committal in Auckland, 1870–1910', *New Zealand Journal of History*, 26 (1992): 125–44.
13. Fairburn, *The Ideal Society*, p.11.
14. Akenson, *Half the World From Home*, p.43. See also Fitzpatrick, *Irish Emigration*, p. 8.
15. Lyndon Fraser, *To Tara Via Holyhead: Irish Catholic Immigrants in Nineteenth-Century Christchurch* (Auckland: Auckland University Press, 1997); Lyndon Fraser, *Castles of Gold: A History of New Zealand's West Coast Irish* (Dunedin: Otago University Press, 2007); Angela McCarthy, *Irish Migrants in New Zealand, 1840–1937: 'The Desired Haven'* (Woodbridge: The Boydell Press, 2005).
16. This total is confined to those cases where a sibling was the only family member mentioned. Three cases demonstrate siblings visiting with other family members: brothers visiting with mothers (2); and siblings visiting with an uncle (1).
17. Archives New Zealand Wellington Regional Office (hereafter ANZ WRO), George Goode, Surgeon Superintendent, British Empire, to the Immigration Commissioners, 12 October 1875, IM/5/29*4/22.
18. ANZ WRO, Commissioners Report on British Empire, 15 October 1875, IM/5/29*4/22. No casebook survives for the period of Bridget's admission at Auckland but she appears in the Register of Admission (1869–79), the cause of her insanity being attributed to 'Change of country', in Archives New Zealand Auckland Regional Office (hereafter ANZ ARO), YCAA/1017/1, 505. Bridget died in the asylum on 18. November 1877. Her file is in ANZ ARO, Committed patient case files (1875–6), YCAA/1026/10, 505.
19. Appendices to the Journals of the House of Representatives, 1884, H-7, p.1.
20. Mark Finnane, *Insanity and the Insane in Post-Famine Ireland* (London: Croom Helm, 1981), pp.54–9.
21. See, for instance, Coleborne, *Madness in the Family*, Ch. 5.
22. ANZ ARO, Visitor's Book, 1891–1911, YCAA/1075/1.

23. Archives New Zealand Dunedin Regional Office (hereafter ANZ DRO), Dunedin Lunatic Asylum Medical Casebook (1876–1913), DAHI/D264/19956/38, case 121.
24. ANZ DRO, Dunedin Lunatic Asylum Medical Casebook (1877–1913), DAHI/D264/19956 /39, case 194.
25. ANZ DRO, Dunedin Lunatic Asylum Medical Casebook (1877–1913), DAHI/D264/19956/ 39, pp.250, 163.
26. ANZ DRO, Dunedin Lunatic Asylum Medical Casebook (1876–1913), DAHI/D264/19956/ 38, p.4.
27. ANZ DRO, Seacliff Hospital – Medical Casebook (1899–1900), DAHI/D264/19956/51, case 3340.
28. ANZ DRO, Dunedin Lunatic Asylum Medical Casebook (1877–1913), DAHI/D264/19956 /39, p.222.
29. ANZ DRO, Seacliff Hospital – Medical Casebook (1897–8), DAHI/D264/19956/49, case 3093.
30. ANZ DRO, Seacliff Hospital – Medical Casebook (1903), DAHI/D264/19956/56, case 3743.
31. ANZ DRO, Seacliff Hospital – Medical Casebook (1906–07), DAHI/D264/19956/60, case 4163; and Seacliff Hospital – Medical Casebook (1905–06), DAHI/D264/19956/59, case 4097.
32. For an example of an extensive family migration of this type, see Seán G. Brosnahan, *Kerrytown Brosnahans* (Timaru: R.J. and H.P. Brosnahan, 1992). Six Irish migrants were known to have connections of this type.
33. McCarthy, *Irish Migrants in New Zealand*, Ch. 6; Coleborne, *Madness in the Family*, Ch. 4.
34. ANZ DRO, Seacliff Hospital Medical Casebook (1893–4), DAHI/D264/19956/45, case 2651.
35. ANZ DRO, Dunedin Lunatic Asylum Medical Casebook (1877–1913), DAHI/D264/19956/39, p.193.
36. ANZ DRO, Seacliff Hospital Medical Casebook (1893–4), DAHI/D264/19956/45, case 2718.
37. Fitzpatrick, *Irish Emigration*, p.40.
38. ANZ DRO, Seacliff Hospital Medical Casebook (1892–3), DAHI/D264/19956/44, case 2571.
39. ANZ DRO, Seacliff Hospital – Medical Casebook (1896–7), DAHI/D264/19956/48, case 3038, and (1897–8), DAHI/D264/19956/49, case 3052.
40. ANZ DRO, John Adams to the Agent, Public Trustee, Dunedin, 13 May 1893, Outwards Letters (13 February 1893 – 28 December 1893), DAHI/D264/5b. Also see Thomas's case note in ANZ DRO, Seacliff Hospital Medical Casebook (1890–91), DAHI/D264/19956/42, case 2440.
41. ANZ DRO, Examination of Bridget Nolan, 25 July 1905, Outwards Letters (10 November 1904 – 28 October 1905), DAHI/D264/11b.
42. ANZ DRO, Seacliff Hospital – Medical Casebook (1894–5), DAHI/D264/19956/46, case 3802.
43. ANZ DRO, Seacliff Hospital Medical Casebook (1891–2), DAHI/D264/19956/43, case 2473.
44. McCarthy, *Irish Migrants in New Zealand*.
45. Fairburn, *The Ideal Society*, p.203.
46. Ibid., p.12.
47. ANZ WRO, Thurlow Astley, Dalkeith, 4 March 1876, Individual Immigrants, IM/3/3*1/3 (1875/1524-1876/980).
48. ANZ WRO, A. O. Ottywell, London, 22 March 1876, to Thurlow Astley, Dalkeith, Individual Immigrants, IM/3/3*1/3 (1875/1524-1876/980).
49. Adrienne Hoult, 'Institutional Responses to Mental Deficiency in New Zealand, 1911–1935: Tokanui Mental Hospital' (MA, University of Waikato, 2007), p.17.
50. ANZ DRO, Truby King to the Managing Director, Union Steamship Company, Dunedin, 17 August 1900, Seacliff Hospital Medical Superintendent Outwards Letters (25 January 1900 – 2 April 1901), DAHI/D264/9a. Also see her case note in ANZ DRO, Seacliff Hospital Medical Casebook (1900), DAHI/D264/19956/52, case 3375.
51. ANZ DRO, Seacliff Hospital Medical Casebook (1903), DAHI/D264/19956/56, case 3807. Also see DAHI/D264/19956/45, case 2721.
52. ANZ DRO, Seacliff Hospital Medical Casebook (1892–3), DAHI/D264/19956/44, case 2631.
53. ANZ DRO, Seacliff Hospital Medical Casebook (1891–2), DAHI/D264/19956/43, case 2537.
54. ANZ DRO, Seacliff Hospital Medical Casebook (1897–8), DAHI/D264/19956/49, case 3046.
55. Coleborne, *Madness in the Family*, Ch 4.
56. ANZ DRO, Truby King to Miss Rose M., Brooklyn, 6 August 1889, Outwards Letters (2 October 1888 – 8 January 1890), DAHI/D264/3b, p. 414. Bridget was admitted to the asylum in 1887: ANZ DRO, DAHI/D264/19956/40.
57. ANZ DRO, Truby King to Mrs. S., Toberbilly, Ballycastle, Ireland, 4 April 1902, Outwards Letters (1 Jan 1882 – 2 October 1888), DAHI/D264/10a, p.132. The 1911 Census for Toberbilly reveals that the correspondent was resident there. Jane was admitted to the

asylum in 1896: ANZ DRO, DAHI/D264/19956/47.

58. ANZ DRO, Sydney S. Allen to William B., Drumcaw, Clough, County Down, Ireland, 20 August 1903, Outwards Letters (22 December 1902 – 29 October 1903), DAHI/D264/10b, p.577. The 1911 Census for Drumcaw confirms the correspondent's residence there.

59. ANZ DRO, Dunedin Lunatic Asylum and Seacliff Hospital Medical Casebook (1863–c.1920), DAHI/D265/19956/1, p.342, and DAHI/D264/19956/40, p.57.

60. ANZ ARO, Australasian Federated Seamen's Industrial Union of Workers to Dr. Beattie, 10 May 1911, Committed Patient Case Files, YCAA/1026/12, no. 4124.

61. ANZ ARO, Reverend Edwin E. Wilson (Belfast), 6 July 1910 [sic], in Committed Patient Case Files, YCAA/1026/12, no. 4124.

62. ANZ ARO, Mrs. Sarah H. (Belfast) to Asylum, 18 July 1911, in Committed Patient Case Files, YCAA/1026/12, no. 4124.

63. ANZ ARO, Mrs. Sarah H. (Belfast) to Asylum, 7 August 1912, in Committed Patient Case Files, YCAA/1026/12, no. 4124.

64. ANZ ARO, Mrs. Sarah H. (Belfast), to Captain William Bazeley, Missioner of Sailors Society, 30 January 1913, in Committed Patient Case Files, YCAA/1026/12, no. 4124.

65. ANZ ARO, Mrs. Sarah H. (Belfast), to Asylum, 22 April 1913, in Committed Patient Case Files, YCAA/1026/12, no. 4124.

66. ANZ ARO, Asylum to Mrs. Sarah H. (Belfast), December 1913, in Committed Patient Case Files, YCAA/1026/12, no. 4124.

67. ANZ ARO, Asylum to sister Sarah (Whiteabbey, Co. Antrim), 25 March 1926, in Committed Patient Case Files, YCAA/1026/12, no. 4124.

68. ANZ ARO, Maintenance Book (1890–99), YCAA/1044/1, p.77–78.

69. See, for instance, the opening story of Bessie Macready in McCarthy, *Irish Migrants in New Zealand*, pp.1–2.

70. Royal Society of New Zealand Marsden funded project, 08-UOO-167 SOC.

8

The 'Chaplaincy Question' at Belfast District Asylum, 1834–1870

Pauline M. Prior and David V. Griffiths

The 'chaplaincy question' refers to a public dispute between the Board of Governors of the Belfast District Lunatic Asylum and the Lord Lieutenant of Ireland in the mid-nineteenth century.[1] The Governors were so opposed to the Lord Lieutenant's wish to appoint asylum chaplains that they entered into successful litigation in a Dublin court. This chapter investigates the motives that inspired the Board to defy such a powerful opponent. Documents of the period reveal a solid network of social support for the Belfast Governors, based on a deep-seated resentment of colonial administration; opposing views on the role of religion in the treatment of the insane; and professional rivalry between Dr. Francis White, inspector of lunatics, and Dr. Robert Stuart, resident medical superintendent (RMS) of Belfast Asylum. The examination of the incident is divided into four sections. The first introduces the conflict and its main protagonists, the second sets it within its historical context, the third concludes the narrative, and the final discussion reflects on the wider issues underlying the dispute.

THE PROBLEM EMERGES

When Belfast Asylum opened in 1829, a Board of unpaid Governors was nominated by the Lord Lieutenant of Ireland, to assist in the administration and management of the asylum. In March 1834, the Governors assembled to discuss the regulation of divine worship. The catalyst for the discussion was a letter from the commissioners for the erection of lunatic asylums in Ireland, enquiring (for the information of the Lord Lieutenant) whether or not chaplains had been appointed. No reply was sent to the commissioners, though the Board members decided unanimously to take matters into their own hands. The Board passed a resolution which was formulated to cover all possibilities. This resolution is long and the language is legalistic, but it is worth quoting in full, as this formed the basis for the legal battles that followed.

> That whereas for some convalescent patients who could not be suffered to attend public worship, it may, under proper regulations, be useful and consolatory, and not likely to be detrimental to hear the reading of the Holy Scriptures and the offering up of prayers on their behalf by a minister of religion, ordered that, on a wish being expressed by a patient to receive such professional visits, the manager of the asylum, if he is of opinion that such visits are not likely to produce an injurious excitement in the patient, but are likely to be beneficial to him, be authorised to request the attendance of a clergyman of the Established Church, whether the parochial clergyman, or, with his permission, the clergyman of the parish to which the patient belonged before this admittance, or of the minister of such other denomination as the patient may have belonged before his admittance, if he should give a preference to such other minister, subject however to the same local limitation as in the case of the clergyman of the Established Church ... that the Manager report the application and the results at the next monthly meeting of the Governors and that no nurse or any other person connected or unconnected with the asylum, be suffered to introduce any minister of religion to a patient without the knowledge and express permission of the Manager.[2]

Rather surprisingly, the Board's action did not incur the immediate disapproval of central government. Eleven years later, the Governors received a letter from the inspector general of prisons – also responsible for asylums during the first half of the nineteenth century – requesting the names and salaries of chaplains appointed to the asylum. According to the minutes of the Board meeting held on 6 October 1845, there was a lengthy discussion on the request from the inspector, after which the Governors agreed to reply that 'no such offices were attached to the establishment'.[3] This was a highly significant step for them to take. Board members were in no doubt that the inspectorate of prisons was requesting information that could easily have been obtained from routine financial returns and that the request was a formal reprimand. As had happened in

1834, the Board again ignored the request for information and instead recommended that the Lord Lieutenant appoint the resident medical superintendent, Dr. Robert Stuart (the first medical manager to be appointed to a district asylum in Ireland), to the new position of inspector of lunatics in Ireland.[4] The recommendation of the Board was ignored by the central authorities and Dr. Francis White, until then inspector of prisons with responsibility for asylums, was appointed to the new position. The Board had no legitimate objection to the appointment of White, who had an established academic reputation and considerable experience in the treatment of lunacy.[5]

The next clash came in 1847, when Dr. White proposed that each asylum in Ulster should be enlarged and another asylum constructed at Omagh, Co. Tyrone, to accommodate 500 incurable lunatics. The Belfast Asylum Board of Governors was highly critical of the proposal and contested that, according to statistical evidence drawn from Dr. White's report, the Belfast Asylum alone would require increased accommodation for 250 patients and that a central asylum of 500 beds would be inadequate to meet the needs of Ulster.[6] The Board expressed the 'repugnance of the Grand Juries of Antrim and Down in contributing funds to an asylum (Omagh) over which they would exercise no control'. It also stressed that its objection to Dr. White's proposal was based on humanitarian considerations, as the labelling of people as incurable was unacceptable.

> ... such a removal, passing as it would the sentence of incurable upon them, would be as regards their friends unkind, as regards themselves injurious, and as regards the dealings of Providence presumptuous.[7]

However, the Board was not consistent in its argument. In the same year, it proposed a new building on the Belfast site capable of holding an additional 500 patients and designed 'to embody the curative system of moral management', recommending that the existing building be assigned to 'incurable lunatics, idiots and epileptic patients'.[8]

This dispute, though it does not relate directly to the chaplaincy issue, shows the Board's reluctance to yield control over the asylum to a central authority. Within a few years of being appointed as inspector of lunatics, Dr. White abandoned his proposals for a special asylum at Omagh. However, he continued to champion the appointment of chaplains to asylums through the annual reports of the inspectorate. In 1945, he wrote:

> The appointment of chaplains we look upon to be a most

necessary regulation, and we need only refer to some of our reports, to prove that their attendance on the patients and the celebration of Divine Service, has been productive of good effects.[9]

In the following year, 1946, he wrote:

It is hoped that religious consolation and instruction will soon be secured for all the district asylums; but in the meantime, the occasional service of the parochial clergy are afforded.[10]

Dr. White knew that the Belfast Governors opposed the appointment of chaplains, but he was confident that they would eventually adopt his way of thinking. It is clear from the annual asylums report for 1851, that Dr. White completely underestimated the strength of opposition among the Governors and did not anticipate the impending crisis.

As remarked in our last report, there existed some difficulties with regard to the appointment of chaplains to two northern asylums, from the variety of persuasions within them. We trust, however, they are now surmounted and that the majority of creeds will have their respective clergy to attend them.[11]

This statement seems especially naïve in the light of the events that followed. In September 1851, the Governors of Belfast Asylum received plans from the Board of Public Works for proposed new buildings. As was standard practice in other asylums in Ireland, such plans included a chapel. Following considerable discussion, ten members of the Board supported the motion that 'the system of religious instruction adopted on 3 March 1834 and which hitherto has been so successful, should be continued' and that the 'erection of a chapel and the appointment of chaplains and probable introduction of religious controversy and excitement among the patients is inexpedient'.[12] Minutes were sent to the Lord Lieutenant, the Board of Public Works and to Dr. White, inspector of lunatics. The response was swift and to the point. The undersecretary of state for Ireland wrote immediately, stating that Lord Lieutenant Clarendon could not concur with the opinion of the Board. In December 1851, in spite of Dr. White's personal intervention, a motion was passed stating that 'the Board's resolution of 6 October last be re-affirmed by this meeting and that the statement now submitted, assigning reasons for its adoption, be transmitted to the Lord Lieutenant.'[13] The dispute was now formal and public. Later in the same week, the

Belfast Daily Mercury and the *Northern Whig* ran short editorials, praising the decision of the asylum Governors. In a sober account, the Mercury reported:

> (T)he Board of Governors, after mature reconsideration of the matter, resolved that it was not desirable to make such appointments ... We learn that the unfortunate patients include members of seven religious denominations. For upwards of twenty years, this establishment has been conducted with distinguished success, and it is greatly to be feared that if religious distinctions were to be introduced among a society of the kind, the effects would be most prejudicial ... We trust that Government will no farther press for a deviation from a course which has been pursued so long, with the greatest success, under the present superintendent, Dr. Stuart.[14]

This article embodied the crux of the Governors' stated position, highlighting their fear of disturbance due to religious differences and their confidence in the resident physician, Dr. Stuart. The *Northern Whig*'s editorial expressed a more extreme view.

> There seems to be something eminently absurd – and we will add mischievous – in the notion of appointing a chaplain to a number of insane persons, whose mental condition renders them utterly incapable of appreciating the teachings and practices of religion. Everybody knows that lunatics, when strongly seized with the religious idea, become often dangerously and hopelessly mad. Religious discourse ... excites the most alarming displays in the insane, and in such cases, fearful results, murder or suicide, frequently follow.[15]

The *Whig*'s editorial could be dismissed merely as an example of early sensational journalism, had not its arrogant and self-righteous tone seemed so accurately to express the attitude of the majority of the Board of Governors. However, the Board's decision was not unanimous – the Right Reverend Bishop Denvir (Bishop of Down and Connor and Dromore), Reverend J.B. Mountsel, and Reverend Dr. Edgar, did not support the motion. Furthermore, Bishop Denvir had proposed an amendment at the October meeting of the Board, but it was defeated by a majority of ten:

> That, inasmuch as the appointment of chaplains in other hospitals for the insane has been found beneficial to the inmates and has not been found to produce any injurious

effects, we resolve to express our approbation of his Excellency's intention to appoint chaplains in the Belfast Hospital for the Insane.[16]

In his evidence to the 1858 Commission of Inquiry into Lunatic Asylums, Bishop Denvir explained that he had joined the Board of Governors in 1851, during the early discussions on the chaplaincy issue. He told the commission that it was clear to him that 'there was a strong opinion as to the disadvantage of chaplains in general institutions, where there was a mixed community' and that he 'felt reluctant in giving a decided opinion, without taking some pains to get ... better acquainted on the matter'.[17] To accomplish this goal, the bishop sent a circular letter to all of the asylums in Ireland, requesting information on the effects of the appointment of chaplains. Without exception, the replies were positive, and the bishop based his subsequent and unwavering support for the appointment of chaplains to the Belfast Asylum on this evidence. The following reply from Mr. D. Cluff, manager of the Londonderry Asylum, was typical of the responses received by Bishop Denvir.

> Respecting the effect religious worship has on the patients in the asylum; in reply, I beg to state that it has been most beneficial in many respects. There never has been any unpleasantness caused by Divine Worship being performed here, but to many it gives much comfort, they being insane on other points, not on religion. It was the opinion of the physician that it would have bad effects before it was tried, but he has changed his opinion on seeing the good effect it has produced.[18]

THE WIDER CONTEXT

Ireland was one of the first countries in Europe to establish a centrally controlled network of asylums for the lunatic poor. At the beginning of the nineteenth century, the lunacy problem drew the attention of two powerful Irish MPs, Sir John Newport and Thomas Spring Rice, who had the ear of the newly appointed chief secretary, Robert Peel. In 1817, the Select Committee on the Relief of the Lunatic Poor in Ireland was appointed and, in 1821, the Lunacy (Ireland) Act (1&2 Geo. iv c. 33) provided the legal basis for the establishment of a network of district asylums throughout the country.[19] Before the end of the decade, four asylums had been built – at Armagh (1824), Londonderry (1827), Limerick (1827) and Belfast (1829). Historian,

Mark Finnane, attributes the speed at which the asylum system expanded to a combination of factors.

> ... the absence of a Poor Law in Ireland; the scarcity of any special confinement for lunatics; and finally, the state of rural Ireland itself, its economic weakness, the poverty and vulnerability of its rapidly growing population, the affront that these conditions gave to those who wished to improve Ireland and the challenge that they offered to the maintenance of social order.[20]

The first asylums were small institutions, serving 100 to 150 patients and proclaiming a new humanitarian approach to insanity.[21] In the previous century, magical and mystical explanations of lunacy predominated, and physical control and cruelty characterised treatment. The new approach to treatment, attributed to Philippe Pinel in Paris, incorporated the positive techniques of moral management pioneered by William Tuke in the York Retreat in England. Distinct differences between the theories of Pinel and Tuke were relevant to the chaplaincy question. Pinel was a qualified doctor, who sought to transform the treatment of the insane within established hospitals such as the Bicètre and the Salpetrière in Paris. Pinel maintained a scientific approach to his work and stressed the need for controlled experimentation and careful observation of results. He also believed that religious activities should be restricted because they 'promoted dangerous ecstasy'.[22] Tuke, on the other hand, made no claims to medical expertise but, as a Quaker philanthropist, offered an alternative to the cruelty of existing asylums. Tuke and his followers 'claimed that the new approach was little more than an application of common sense and humanity'.[23] At York Retreat, religious activity was a central element in the process of recovery.

As in England, the struggle for dominance between lay managers and the medical profession was evident in Ireland.[24] By the middle of the nineteenth century, it had become apparent that Irish asylums were not fulfilling their curative role. Asylums were overcrowded, and the confinement of lunatics in workhouses and prisons continued to disrupt the functioning of these establishments. When Dr. Francis White was appointed as the first inspector of lunatics in 1845, he found himself in a position of great power. In addition to his duties of inspecting existing asylums, he was highly influential in guiding decisions about the location of new asylums and the extent of accommodation to be provided. As the inspector of prisons, Dr.

White had campaigned energetically for the establishment of a medically trained lunacy inspectorate to monitor and guide lunacy policy. In the year prior to his new appointment, he was instrumental in drafting the first Privy Council rules for the regulation of asylums, which limited the role of lay superintendents to asylum management, and placed responsibility for the treatment of patients in the hands of a visiting physician. In the years following White's appointment, the post of asylum superintendent/manager was invariably given to a doctor. Therefore, there were no obvious grounds for dispute between White and the Belfast Asylum, which regarded itself as being at the forefront of medical treatment.

Dr. Robert Stuart, appointed as manager of the Belfast Asylum in 1835, was Ireland's first resident medical superintendent. Like Dr. John Connolly and Dr. W.A.F. Brown, acknowledged world experts in moral treatment, Stuart was educated in Scotland and was influenced greatly by Robert Cleghorn and the work at the York Retreat.[25] His claim to expertise in treating insanity was widely accepted in Ireland and elsewhere in the British Isles. Stuart enjoyed the support of his medical colleagues and of the Board of Governors, and Dr. White often waived rules to allow Stuart to take responsibility for the moral as well as the medical regime in the asylum. Like Pinel, Stuart believed that religious practice was a potential source of dangerous ecstasy. In 1853, he wrote in the *Dublin Quarterly Journal*: 'It is well known that, of all the exciting causes of insanity, religious enthusiasm is one of the rifest; that its effects are the most lasting, and the prospects of the sufferer the most hopeless.'[26] It seems ironic, therefore, that before the chaplaincy question became public, Stuart often assembled the patients to read portions of the scriptures, and described religion as 'the never failing consolation and ... ultimate resource of the Christian of sound mind'.[27] Before the 1858 Commission of Inquiry, he denigrated the appointment of chaplains, but justified his own ministry.

> ... my not being a clergyman ... had, of course, a different effect upon them, for they look upon the head of this place as their father, so to speak. It was more just as a family prayer than a distinct service, or worship, gone through by a professional minister.[28]

Stuart's paternalistic attitude is entirely in keeping with moral management. Historian, Elaine Showalter describes this approach as the 'domestication of insanity' with the manager taking the role of a strict father and controlling the household accordingly.[29] Dr. Stuart was undoubtedly powerful in his own right, but with the backing of the Board of Governors, he was a formidable opponent.

The Board of Governors for district asylums were drawn mainly from 'the principal nobility and gentry in the several counties and dignitaries of the several churches, as well as clergymen of different persuasions'.[30] However, commitment to duty by the Board members varied throughout Ireland, and the 1858 Commission of Inquiry found that Governors' meetings were 'infrequent and poorly attended', book-keeping 'unsatisfactory', and asylum inspection and other duties 'often neglected'.[31] None of these criticisms could be levelled at the Belfast Asylum Board of Governors. Even a cursory examination of the minute books reveals a good representative attendance at regular monthly meetings; monthly inspections of the asylum and meticulous recording of events, purchases and plans. For Governors who took the job of representing local ratepayers seriously, such as those in Belfast, decisions made by central government were often unwelcome. The 1858 Commission of Inquiry found general discontent among Governors throughout the country, so Belfast was no exception. In his evidence to the Commission, Reverend Henry Montgomery complained that central government

> ... makes a Board of gentlemen the mere tools and slaves of the Board of Works, however respectable the members of the Board ... We have to pay the money and I think we should have some voice in the expenditure of that money. I have put before you this evil which is patent to everyone.[32]

Perhaps the dispute over chaplains was simply a manifestation of the general feeling of powerlessness in local affairs that was being felt by Boards of Governors.

LITIGATION

Though the chaplaincy question had become a matter for public debate in 1851, it was not until 1856 that the legal confrontation took place. Between 1851 and 1853, three different members of the British nobility held the post of Lord Lieutenant of Ireland, and the Belfast Asylum Board of Governors was optimistic that each might be persuaded to reverse the decision of his predecessor. The best surviving example of their attempts at persuasion is found in their first memorial to Lord Lieutenant the Earl of Clarendon, dated 1

January 1851. This document claims brevity but, in fact, is a detailed account of the objections of the majority of the Governors to the appointment of chaplains, with arguments to support their opinions.

> Since the opening of the asylum ... there has not been a complaint either from a friend or a patient or a member of the Board, as to the want of sufficient religious instruction and consolation in this establishment ... On the 10th October 1851, there were patients of no fewer than seven religious persuasions. On an inspection of the annual reports, it will be found that this asylum stands in a most high position with regard to the treatment of the patients, both to the numbers cured and relieved ... we are convinced that no advantage would accrue from the proposed change.[33]

The memorial continues by referring to reports of the English Commissioners of Lunacy, which seem to support the position of the Belfast Asylum Board of Governors. However, the argument is poorly presented and the selected quotations sometimes confirm the benefits derived from professional religious ministration. For example, the memorial quotes Lord Ashley, Chairman of the Metropolitan Commissioners of Lunacy (England) as follows:

> The patients are said frequently to look forward to the service with pleasure, and to consider exclusion from it a privation. Considering religious exercise in lunatic asylums merely as medical aids and conducive to good order, they are of most important use. So long, at least, as the service lasts, they occupy the patients' minds and set before them an example of quiet and decorum. The prayers of the church are eminently calculated to produce a soothing influence upon even the insane hearer.[34]

In contrast, the Governors of Lincoln Asylum support the arguments of the Belfast Governors:

> Prayers are read every evening by the house surgeon or matron, and the aid of a chaplain for family prayers is contrary to the general custom of families and quite unnecessary. It must not be forgotten that patients belong to various sects of religion, and that some of the patients have been brought to their unhappy condition by fanatical excitement.[35]

The Belfast Asylum Governors were convinced that dissension was inevitable:

> In an asylum where there is but one chaplain and one persua-
> sion, the judicious clergyman may be permitted to visit without
> restriction; he may converse with them in the ward rooms and
> have free intercourse with them collectively. How different
> would be the case here. There are in this house seven religious
> persuasions, three of them of considerable number. Are the
> different persuasions to be separated into different ward rooms
> on the visit of each chaplain? Are the chaplains to be allowed at
> all times the free range of the house and grounds? This, in
> either event, we are decidedly of the opinion would promote
> that controversial tendency and discussion which ought to be
> most particularly guarded against in any asylum.[36]

The Governors obviously hoped that the Lord Lieutenant would
overrule the inspectorate, but to their chagrin, the Earl of Clarendon
referred the memorial to Dr. White. Although his views were already
well documented, Dr. White wrote a lengthy reply, in which he examined the arguments and provided counter arguments that effectively
destroyed those put forward by the Belfast Board. This erudite piece
was published (as the official response) alongside the Governors'
memorial to the Lord Lieutenant in the inspector's annual report on
asylums of 1853. Dr. White not only used the sources provided by the
Governors to his own advantage, but he also reflected on the irony of
the situation:

> Were the inspectors doubtful of the results of their own experi-
> ence, or afraid to rely on their own observations, they could not
> select a much more satisfactory or favourable argument in
> favour of the appointment of chaplains to lunatic asylums than
> the following paragraph, though cited in opposition by the
> memorialists themselves.[37]

Dr. White demonstrated that the Governors had no doubt as to the
benefit of prayers and religion within the asylum and suggested that
their memorial was tantamount to an agreement, in principal, to the
appointment of chaplains. He proposed that the difficulty of minis-
tering to a variety of creeds could be overcome by appointing three
chaplains – Protestant, Roman Catholic and Presbyterian – rather
than by resorting to the Lincoln Asylum solution.

> … the selection of the Lincoln Asylum as a model was rather
> infelicitous. The Report from which the memorialists quote,
> being in answer to certain charges made against it by the

Commissioners of Lunacy for various errors and moralities, which, possibly, might not have occurred had there been a regular chaplain in attendance.[38]

Dr. White gave ample evidence of the benefit of chaplains in asylums, not only in England, but also throughout Europe and, having established that a combination of chaplains from different dominations was desirable, he went on to provide evidence that it was also feasible. White included a letter from Dr. Rogan of Londonderry Asylum, who initially had opposed the appointment of three chaplains on grounds similar to those of the Belfast Governors, but who, after a trial period of more than a year, had declared that their attendance was 'productive of unalloyed good'.[39]

As one might expect, given the weakness of the arguments put forward by the Belfast Asylum Governors and the strength of those provided by the lunacy inspectorate, the Lord Lieutenant ordered the appointment of three chaplains to Belfast Asylum. The appointment was delayed and at the beginning of 1852 (the following year), the Board asked the new lord lieutenant, the Earl of Eglington, to reconsider the case. His decision to uphold that already taken by his predecessor inspired heated debate in the Belfast Asylum Board room on 29 December 1852. Based on a majority vote, the Board resolved to discontinue 'ineffectual remonstrances against a measure forced against them in opposition to their own convictions' and at the same time expressed a determination to take no part in the appointment of chaplains 'or otherwise carrying out an arrangement of which they decidedly disapproved'.[40] Though the Board of Governors had written directly to the Lord Lieutenant in 1851 and 1852, it was not until February 1853 that a deputation of five Governors went to meet the new incumbent to the position, the Earl St. German. The meeting, which was also attended by Dr. Francis White, lasted for four hours but did not resolve the dispute.[41] The Earl St. German agreed with the decision of his two predecessors. The Board was neither appeased nor silenced. On the contrary, at the next meeting, the majority passed a number of resolutions that effectively empowered Resident Medical Superintendent Dr. Stuart to obstruct the chaplains who had, by then, been appointed by the inspectorate. In evidence presented to the Commission of Inquiry on Lunatic Asylums in 1858, two of these chaplains reported that they were denied entry to the asylum for a full twelve-month period after officially commencing their duties.[42]

The next development occurred in December 1853, when the

Board's attention turned to a letter from the Lord Lieutenant ordering payment of salaries, equalling £50 per annum, to three appointed chaplains. The Governors decided to postpone discussion to the next meeting, in order to call all members of the Board to attend for the express purpose of deciding what to do about the order. The meeting, which took place in January 1854, was fraught with tension, as the minority made a last but futile attempt to change the course of action proposed by the majority of Board members. The outcomes in a great number of proposals, amendments and counter amendments, were identical, in that all were either carried or defeated by a majority of ten to four. Ultimately, the majority (ten members of the Board) refused to conform to the order from the Lord Lieutenant and therefore, would not agree to amend the estimates to provide for the salaries of the chaplains who had been appointed without the approval of the Board. The minute book recorded the following statement:

> We consider it scarcely necessary to record the fact that the reso-
> lutions of the Board of Governors have not been influenced by
> any degree of political or sectarian feeling. They have been
> arrived at on a deliberate consideration of the subject, and from
> an intimate knowledge of local circumstances which, in the
> judgement of the majority, make the proposed experiment
> more dangerous here than elsewhere; and they have been
> supported by the great majority of the Governors, including
> various shades of political and religious opinion and they have,
> as we feel assured, the approval of the great mass of the
> educated and intelligent portion of the community.[43]

Public opinion supported the Belfast Asylum Board of Governors in its task of managing the asylum and in defending its right to make decisions relating to its management, particularly decisions involving expenditure. In a lengthy memorial to support the Board's deputation to the Lord Lieutenant, the Earl St. German in 1853, the grand juries of County Antrim and County Down suggested that asylum governors should have increased responsibilities for local fiscal and employment issues.

> This arrangement would remove the offensive anomaly com-
> pelling counties to pay unlimited salaries to officers in whose
> appointment they have no concern and over whose conduct
> they have no control.[44]

There is no further evidence of internal disputes among the Belfast Governors after the meeting in January 1854, so the viewpoint of the majority prevailed. Litigation began in June of that year, when writs were received from the Queen's Bench, demanding payment of the chaplains' salaries. Meticulous to the end, the Board immediately arranged that the outstanding money be set aside in a separate, ring-fenced, account, after which solicitors were appointed to prepare a legal defence.[45] Meanwhile, the unpaid chaplains were allowed limited access to the asylum.[46]

Brought in the name of a Protestant chaplain, the case of Reverend John Carroll v the Governors and Directors of Belfast Lunatic Asylum, was heard before the Queen's Bench at Dublin in December 1855. The judgment, on 21 January 1856, found in favour of the Governors, awarding them full costs. Their sense of triumph was echoed in an article in the *Belfast Daily Mercury*.

> We have learned, with the greatest possible satisfaction, that the unjustifiable attempt of the Governors of Ireland to overrule the Governors of the Belfast Lunatic Asylum, for the purpose of perpetrating a mischievous job appointing chaplains to that establishment, was yesterday completely frustrated by the Lord Chancellor. It had been demonstrated, beyond all doubt, that to send in a troop of chaplains of various creeds would be to expose the unhappy inmates to great risk of being agitated and disturbed; and the clearest evidence was shown of the satisfactory manner in which the institution had worked in a moral and religious point of view ... The law was appealed to and the result, we rejoice to say, has been that the Government and their two favoured Inspectors have been opposed, not only to all propriety, but the law besides, and that the integrity and authority of the Board of Governors have been vindicated.[47]

The *Belfast Newsletter* reproduced lengthy extracts of the Queen's Bench judgment revealing that the judgment had nothing to do with the agitation of the asylum inmates or an assessment of the institution's workings from a moral and religious point of view. The decision of the judges rested on the legality of the Lord Lieutenant's appointment of chaplains and the subsequent demand that they be paid by the Belfast Board. The judges found that, under the Act of 1821 (1&2 Geo. iv c. 33), he had no such rights. However, the ruling would have gone against the Board had it not introduced its own system of religious instruction in 1834.

LOCAL VERSUS NATIONAL INTERESTS

The story of the chaplaincy question at the Belfast Asylum illustrates a number of important areas of potential conflict in nineteenth-century Irish life. On the surface it appears to be a dispute about religion. Certainly an increase in religious excitement at the time of the Belfast revival in 1859 provided evidence of a possible link between religiosity and mental disorder.[48] When placed alongside obvious problems caused by having a patient population derived from at least six church groups, the logic Dr. Stuart used in his opposition to the appointment of official chaplains is clear, if not convincing. Religious differences among patients and managers in nineteenth-century Ulster asylums presented special problems not paralleled, or indeed understood, in other parts of Ireland.

However, this dispute was not only about religion. It was also about an alliance between the two elite interest groups – the medical profession and the gentry. The Belfast Asylum Governors represented the interests of local ratepayers and, although they were not averse to spending money on either expanding the asylum or engaging in legal proceedings, they objected to the manner in which the government, operating from Dublin, dictated the direction and amount of that expenditure. The British government was more successful in implementing lunacy provisions in Ireland than in England, due largely to the highly centralised and powerful administration in Dublin Castle. During the first half of the century, there was general agreement that the sick poor (including the insane) needed publicly funded care and treatment. But, by the 1850s, it was clear that plans to expand the system were underway; that decisions about this expansion were being made largely by Dr. Francis White and hi colleague at the lunacy inspectorate; and that local grand juries, involved only peripherally in drawing up plans, were expected to bear the financial burden. The chaplaincy question was the public face of an ongoing power struggle between local landed interests and colonial rulers. The financial burden of asylums was not allevi-ated until 1875, when a central government per capita grant (in aid of local taxation) was introduced.[49] However, the financial burden of asylums on local ratepayers was not completely resolved until the twentieth century, when asylums were integrated into cen-trally funded health care systems in both parts of Ireland.

Returning to the nineteenth century, the Belfast Asylum Board of Governors would not have entered into litigation had it not had the utmost confidence in the professional opinion of Dr. Robert Stuart, the resident medical superintendent. Stuart's career spanned periods in which the medical profession recognised the positive elements in moral management, combined them with medical science, and became experts in moral treatment, thus establishing medical dominance in the management of insanity. Both Dr. Robert Stuart and Dr. Francis White (of the lunacy inspectorate) were exemplars of what has become known as the 'medicalisation of madness'.[50] Dr. Stuart did not attain the international reputation enjoyed by his former contemporaries Dr. W.A.F. Brown and Dr. John Connolly, but he was a pioneer of moral treatment and was well respected within his profession throughout the British Isles. Stuart was a founding member of the Medico Psychological Association (later to become the Royal College of Psychiatry) and held the office of honorary secretary for Ireland for twenty-five years.[51]

Dr. Stuart was not unique in having reservations about the efficacy of church-led worship in asylums, but by the mid-nineteenth century, most medical superintendents in Britain and Ireland were happy to have official chaplains fulfil the role originally carried out by the lay moral manager. In retrospect, Stuart can only be found guilty of making an error in judgment. From the time of his appointment in 1835, he had enjoyed complete professional autonomy, supported not only by the Board of Governors, but also by Dr. Francis White, especially during his time as inspector of prisons with special responsibility for asylums. Rather than yielding on the issue of chaplains, Dr. Stuart allowed the Governors to use his excellent reputation to oppose the Lord Lieutenant and the lunacy inspectorate. As in most disputes, once the issue became public, it gained its own momentum, leading indeed to victory. But the victory was inevitably short lived, as in the next round of legislation, the Lunacy (Ireland) Act 1867 (30 & 31 Vic. c. 118), the Lord Lieutenant was empowered to appoint chaplains, and Governors were obliged to make provision for the payment of salaries.

Resolute to the end, the Governors at the Belfast Asylum took another three years to allow the official Protestant, Catholic and Presbyterian chaplains to hold services in the asylum. Unsurprisingly, fears of an increase in insanity due to religious dissension were unfounded. As the end of the century approached, the issue of religion in asylums became less important as the larger question of the relationship between Ireland and England dominated the political agenda.

NOTES

1. We wish to acknowledge the kind permission of the Irish American Cultural Institute to reproduce an article by Pauline M. Prior and David Griffiths, published in its journal 'Eire-Ireland'. This article appeared as Prior P.M. and D.V. Griffiths (1997) 'The Chaplaincy Question: The Lord Lieutenant of Ireland versus the Belfast Lunatic Asylum', *Eire-Ireland: An Interdisciplinary Journal of Irish Studies*, 33 (2 & 3): 137–53. (Summer/Fall).
2. Minutes of the Belfast Lunatic Asylum Board of Governors meeting, 3 March 1834, contained in files held at the Public Record Office Northern Ireland (PRONI), HOS 28/1/1/1, p.97–98.
3. Minutes of the meeting of Board of Governors, 6 October 1845, PRONI HOS 28/1/1/2, p.71.
4. Ibid., p.73.
5. He had gained this experience as surgeon to the Richmond Asylum in Dublin. See Joseph Reynolds, *Grangegorman: Psychiatric Care in Dublin since 1815* (Dublin: IPA, 1992), p.67.
6. Minutes of the meeting of Board of Governors, 7 August 1848, PRONI HOS 28/1/1/2, p.98.
7. Minutes of the meeting of Board of Governors, 6 October 1845, PRONI HOS 28/1/1/2, p.107.
8. Ibid., p.98.
9. *Asylums Report*, HC 1845 (645) xxvi. 269, p.274.
10. Ibid.
11. *Asylums Report*, HC 1851 (1387) xxiv. 23, p.68.
12. Minutes of the meeting of Board of Governors, (no date) September 1851, PRONI HOS 28/1/1/2, pp.295–6.
13. Minutes of the meeting of Board of Governors, 1 December 1851, PRONI HOS 28/1/1/2, pp.299–301.
14. *Belfast Daily Mercury*, 4 December 1851, p.2.
15. *Northern Whig*, 4 December 1851, p.2.
16. Minutes of the meeting of Board of Governors, 1 December 1851, PRONI HOS 28/1/1/2, p.302.
17. Report of the Commissioners of Inquiry into the state of the Lunatic Asylums and other Institutions for the Custody and Treatment of the Insane in Ireland (with minutes of evidence and appendices)1858, HC 1857–58 (2436) xxvii.1, Evidence, pp.388–9.
18. Ibid.
19. For a discussion on the influence of Newport and Rice, see Arthur Williamson, 'The beginnings of state care for the mentally ill in Ireland', *Economic and Social Review*, 1970, pp.281–90.
20. Mark Finnane, *Insanity and the Insane in Post Famine Ireland* (London: Croom Helm, 1981), p.20.
21. Ibid., p.227.
22. Anne Digby, *Madness, Morality and Medicine: A Study of the York Retreat 1796–1914* (Cambridge: University Press, 1985), p.32.
23. Andrew Scull, *Museums of Madness: The Social Organisation of Insanity in Nineteenth Century England* (London: Allen Lane, 1979), p.114.
24. See Williamson, 'The beginning of state care'.
25. Roy McClelland, 'The Madhouses and Mad Doctors of Ulster', *Ulster Medical Journal*, 57:2 (1988), pp.101–20.
26. Dr. Robert Stuart, *Dublin Quarterly Journal*, xvi (August/November 1853): 375–9.
27. Ibid.
28. *Commission of Inquiry on Lunatic Asylums 1858*, HC 1857–58 (2436) xxvii.1, Evidence, p.322.
29. Elaine Showalter, *The Female Malady: Women, Madness and English Culture 1830–1880* (London: Virago Press, 1987).
30. *Commission of Inquiry on Lunatic Asylums 1858*, HC 1857–8 (2436) xxvii.1, Report, p.6.
31. Ibid., p.7.
32. Ibid., Evidence, p.322.
33. *Asylums Report* for 1853, HC 1852–3 (1653) xli. 353, Appendix, p.374.
34. Ibid.
35. *Asylums Report* for 1853, HC 1852–3 (1653) xli. 353, Appendix, p.375.
36. Ibid., p.376.
37. Ibid.
38. Ibid., p.378.

39. Ibid., p.379.
40. Minutes of the meeting of Board of Governors, 29 December 1852, PRONI HOS 28/1/1/2, p.317.
41. *Asylums Report* for 1853, HC 1852–3 (1653) xli. 353, Main report, p.365.
42. Commission of Inquiry on Lunatic Asylums 1858, HC 1857–8 (2436) xxvii.1, Evidence, pp.363–4.
43. Minutes of the meeting of Board of Governors, (no date) January 1854, PRONI HOS 28/1/1/2, p.384.
44. Memorial to the Lord Lieutenant in PRONI HOS 28/1/1/2, p.476.
45. Minutes of the meeting of Board of Governors, (no date) June 1854, PRONI HOS 28/1/1/2, p.476.
46. *Commission of Inquiry on Lunatic Asylums 1858*, HC 1857–8 (2436) xxvii.1, Evidence, p.363.
47. *Belfast Daily Mercury*, 22 January 1856, p.2.
48. J. Donat, 'Madness and Religion: on the physical and mental disorders that accompanied the Ulster Revival of 1859', in W.F. Bynum, R. Porter and M. Shepherd (eds), *The Anatomy of Madness: Essays in the History of Psychiatry*, Vol. 3 (London: Routledge, 1988), pp.125–50.
49. For a brief discussion on asylum financing, see Pauline M. Prior, *Mental Health and Politics in Northern Ireland* (Aldershot: Avebury, 1993), p.17.
50. For example, see Andrew Scull, *Museums of Madness: The Social Organisation of Insanity in Nineteenth Century England* (London: Allen Lane, 1979); and Andrew Scull (ed.) *The Asylum as Utopia: W.A.F. Browne and the mid-nineteenth century consolidation of psychiatry* (London: Tavistock/Routledge, 1991).
51. Obituary for Dr. Stuart in the *Journal of Mental Science*, xxi (October 1875): 311; See also Rosaline Delargy, *The History of the Belfast Lunatic District Lunatic Asylum 1829–1921*, Unpublished PhD Thesis (Jordanstown: University of Ulster, 2002).

9

A Mystery Malady in an Irish Asylum: The Richmond Epidemic of the Late Nineteenth Century

E. Margaret Crawford

This is the story of a mysterious illness that afflicted many patients and a few staff at Richmond Asylum, Dublin during the mid-1890s.[1] The symptoms were characteristic of an eastern disease known as beriberi,[2] although some key elements then perceived fundamental to the presence of this disease were missing. For instance, beriberi was a common disease among populations subsisting on highly polished rice, and was associated with warmer climates, such as Japan and Indonesia. Neither characteristic applied to the Richmond. Nevertheless the unusual symptoms presented by the sick led to the suggestion of beriberi. And, as the numbers of cases in the Dublin asylum increased, the epidemic attracted attention of the medical profession, civil servants, politicians and newspaper editors at home and abroad.

Beriberi is caused by a lack of the B vitamin, thiamin.[3] The disease presents in two forms – wet and dry. The prominent feature of wet beriberi is oedema. The tissues of legs, trunk and up to the face become water-laden. Dry beriberi, on the other hand, is essentially a polyneuropathy, more simply, inflammation of the nerves. Between June 1894 and 1898, 546 patients and staff in the Richmond Asylum displayed symptoms resembling both wet and dry beriberi. In 1894 the disease affected 127 male and forty seven female patients.[4] Of these, eighteen males[5] and seven females died. The next year, the asylum was free of the disease, but it re-appeared in July 1896 with thirty-one males and seventy-six females plus seven nurses complaining of symptoms. There were eight deaths. The peak year was 1897, when 246 cases occurred: forty-five males, 193 females, plus two male attendants and six nurses. Although the number of cases was high, only eleven people died. Finally, in 1898 there were twelve cases and four deaths, all female. In the first year of the epidemic, male patients outnumbered females, which conformed to the pattern observed where beriberi was a common affliction, but in subsequent episodes the reverse was true.[6]

IDENTIFICATION OF THE DISEASE

The outbreak probably pre-dated June 1894. The resident medical superintendent of the Richmond Asylum, Dr. Conolly Norman, admitted that the 'exact period at which [the disease] began is uncertain, for [he was] satisfied that [he had] overlooked many mild cases at first, and ... misunderstood several of the earlier cases, which were severe enough.'[7] And subsequently it was believed that 'the great number of deaths from paralysis of the heart, which immediately preceded the epidemic ... was only a symptom of the as yet unrecognised beri-beri.'[8]

Dr. Norman was a highly qualified physician[9] with an enlightened approach to mental health. He was well respected within the profession, becoming President of the Medico-Psychological Association in 1894, and was joint editor of the *Journal of Mental Science.*[10] At the time of his death, he was Vice-President and Censor of the Royal College of Physicians, and in 1907, the University of Dublin conferred on him the honorary degree of M.D. 'in recognition of his distinguished professional services'.[11] His appointment to the Richmond occurred in 1886, where he remained until his death in 1908 at the early age of fifty-five years. The writer of Norman's obituary referred to his reforming zeal and his desire to transform the Richmond from 'almost mediaeval inefficiency ... to the very first rank, not in Ireland, merely, but in the world.'[12] But administrative tardiness made this task an enduring struggle. It was claimed that the stress he suffered during the beriberi outbreak was responsible for a weakness of his heart, leaving him with a chronic cardiac condition.[13]

While the Richmond Asylum in Dublin was the only one in Ireland to register cases of beriberi, other institutions in Europe and America had patients displaying similar symptoms at around the same time. Norman examined cases in the Suffolk County Asylum in 1895, and made reference to cases in the Alabama State Asylum, Tuscaloosa, during 1895 and 1896, the Arkansas State Asylum, Little Rock, in 1895, and at the Asylum of Saint Gemmes-sur-Loire, France in 1897.[14] Also from time to time, cases of beriberi were admitted to port hospitals, and so when mariners exhibiting symptoms were admitted to the Seamen's Hospital at Albert Dock and the Hospital for Seamen at Greenwich in London in 1896, Norman's assistant physician and pathologist, Dr. Daniel F. Rambaut, was dispatched to examine them. The patients were from 'the Orient', except one who was 'a Swede'. In Rambaut's judgment 'these cases presented symptoms and signs of a disease … similar in every respect to those … observed in this [Richmond] asylum.'[15]

The unusual nature of the illness generated much discussion. The question underpinning the debate was whether the symptoms observed in the asylum were really those of beriberi. So great was the concern about this mysterious illness, that the matter was raised in Parliament, prompting the Lord Lieutenant of Ireland, Lord Houghton, later the Earl of Cadogan, to order an investigation into its cause. Initially Dr. Norman was blamed for the outbreak. However, reports of the Municipal Dublin Council and Board of Control[16] meetings reveal that the authorities had been unwilling to raise funds sufficiently to increase accommodation for the ever growing lunacy population. It was, moreover, recognised by Norman and the Governor of the Richmond, John Clancy, that there should be additional funds for improvements in the treatment of the insane to bring Ireland in line with the policy implemented in Scotland and England. At a meeting of the Dublin Corporation in November 1894, the Lord Mayor stated that Britain:

> … had long ceased to treat lunatics not as paupers but as people requiring to be treated in hospitals, and having proper places for such treatment provided. Here in Ireland, and especially at the Richmond Asylum, for many years, whilst all over the world great progress had been made in the treatment of the insane, they [the Richmond] stood stock still, and were suffering from want of proper attention.[17]

Clancy accused the Board of Control of 'apathy and remissness', 'perverse inaction and culpable neglect'.[18] He referred to the many pleas of Dr. Norman during the late 1880s and early 1890s, highlighting the defective conditions of kitchens and laundry provision, as well as the overcrowded state of the asylum. His pleas fell on deaf ears. However, two facts brought the issue to a head. The first was the 1893 Richmond death rate of 12.5 per cent, a figure considerably above the average found in other Irish asylums. And second, the appearance of a mysterious disease among the patients in 1894 added fuel to the fire.

The identification of this unusual malady and its cause became urgent. The advice of numerous medical specialists was sought. As early as October 1894, a report was submitted by Brigadier Surgeon Lieutenant Colonel Barry and Surgeon Major Rhodes, of the Army Medical staff, to Surgeon Major General Sir William Mackinnon, Director General of the Army Medical Department at the War Office.[19] It was because of their experience in the Far East, that Barry and Rhodes were asked to see the sick patients in the Richmond, by the principal medical officer for Ireland, Surgeon Major General Colahan.[20] The opinion of Dr. John Mallet Purser, Professor of Physiology at Trinity College Dublin, was also requested. He had gained a reputation as a 'pioneer of the newer therapeutical principles ... (and had) introduced really scientific methods in the treatment of disease', and consequently, 'in difficult cases, his opinion as a diagnostician was much sought after by the leading physicians of his time.'[21] Surgeon Lieutenant Colonel Adye-Curran and Deputy Surgeon General C. Joynt, from the Indian Medical Service, had both witnessed beriberi in the Far East, so they too were consulted. Two professors of medicine, Dr. Walter G. Smith, King's Professor in *Materia Medica* at Trinity College Dublin and President of the Royal College of Physicians of Ireland, and Sir Thornley Stoker, Professor of Anatomy and President at the Royal College of Surgeons, were approached because of their expertise in tropical diseases. Both agreed to investigate the strange disease in the asylum.[22] A noted author on beriberi was Sir Patrick Manson of London.[23] He was contacted because of his personal experience of beriberi when practising, as a medical officer to the Chinese Imperial Maritime Customs, in Formosa (Taiwan), Amoy (China) and Hong Kong.

At an early stage, the opinion of the numerous clinicians consulted was that the disease presented by the asylum patients 'closely resembl[ed] beri-beri, and [was] probably due to causes or conditions similar or identical with those associated with that disease'.[24] However, Barry and Rhodes were more cautious in their diagnosis. They observed 'certain clinical particulars [which] differ[ed] from the Oriental beri-beri'.[25] Several of the doctors consulted pointed out that the climate of Ireland was very different from that of Southern Asia where beriberi was commonly found. More significant, possibly, was a perceived variation in the pattern of the disease among the sane and insane.

With recurrences of the disease in 1896 and 1897, Norman contacted Rear Admiral L.P. Gysberti Hodenpyl, Inspector of Marine

Medical Services in the Netherlands, for advice. Dutch scientists were at the forefront of research into beriberi because the disease was so prevalent in the Dutch East Indies, prompting their government to commission an investigation into the disease. Two Dutch doctors, A.F. Verschuur and G. van Ijsselsteyn, were dispatched to Dublin, both with experience of beriberi while practising in the Far East. They spent six days at the Richmond Asylum in August of 1897, where their remit was to examine the afflicted patients and review the environment of the asylum.

The report of Drs Verschuur and van Ijsselsteyn demonstrated great thoroughness.[26] They examined the fabric of the asylum buildings, which were originally of stone, but were later extended in 1893, 1894 and 1895 using wooden buildings, to accommodate the ever increasing numbers of patients. These buildings were either painted or whitewashed, and arsenic or other poisonous substances in the paint were looked for, but not found. The ventilation, the heating system, iron bedsteads, mattresses, bed clothes, and night attire were all examined. The bath rooms and kitchens were inspected, as also were the sewage system and water supply. The sewage system was quite new, installed in 1887, and the water supply was from the same source as supplied to the city of Dublin. Nevertheless, a sample was taken to be sent to Holland for analysis by a chemist of the Royal Dutch Marine Service. It was pronounced as 'excellent'. Methods of disinfecting within the asylum proved satisfactory and laundry facilities passed inspection. In the kitchen, cooking utensils were examined, and there was no evidence of metallic poisoning from pots and pans. Finally there was food. The provisions stores were viewed and 'gave no ground for criticism', and, 'the quality of the bread, butter, sugar, tea, fresh meat and vegetables was very good'.[27] Rice was one food focused upon, but it was recorded in small quantities, added to soup. 'A dinner at which we [the doctors] were present gave the impression that, both in quantity and quality, the patients' food was excellent.' The two Dutch doctors also added that 'sufficient care has been taken to ensure variety in food'.[28] Their report was sceptical about the presence of beriberi in the Richmond Asylum, and suggested that the medical superintendent, Dr. Norman, had been 'induced to believe [the disease] was beri-beri'.[29]

The gradual realisation that the symptoms presented in the Richmond Asylum might be beriberi is perfectly understandable. It was not a disease doctors would expect to find in late nineteenth-century Ireland, where potatoes were still the mainstay of the diet.

The medical profession was baffled as to its cause, though the asylum symptoms seemed to fit textbook descriptions. Furthermore, during the 1880s and 1890s, a plethora of articles were published on beriberi, many in German and Dutch, and we know from Norman's obituary that he was both widely read and a talented linguist and, therefore, he was likely cognisant of the latest papers on this disease. So, a hypothesis of beriberi was not unreasonable, as the true nature of the disease was not yet properly understood. This understanding did not fully emerge until the early decades of the twentieth century.

EXPLORATIONS TOWARDS THE CAUSE OF BERIBERI

Diet was not identified as important when the search for a cause of the Richmond epidemic was in progress. Norman was aware of the dietary scale prescribed for his patients and he used the opportunity of the 1894 epidemic to make small improvements in the asylum diet.[30] But, in his numerous articles about beriberi, he paid little attention to diet. However, after the epidemic had receded, there appeared a short piece on the 'Etiology of Beri-beri' in the *British Medical Journal* of August 1899, paraphrasing a contribution by Dr. Laurent to the *Archives de Médecine Navale et Coloniale* (March 1899), in which Laurent suggested that 'it would be interesting to know what part fat formed in the dietary of the Richmond Asylum, Dublin before the appearance of beri-beri there.'[31] Norman responded several weeks later and provided the asylum diet. But he remained sceptical of any dietary connection, stating that 'on the whole, I am afraid our experience does not lend aid to the newest any more than to the older notions of the dietetic origin of beri-beri.'[32] This comment was made despite medical reports on a similar epidemic in France, where it had been observed there that patients 'whose dietary was the least nutritious' were the only ones attacked by the disease.[33]

Several doctors in the late nineteenth century favoured the theory that 'a peculiar poison which is distilled ... from the soil, the building, and the surroundings in which the patient lived,' was responsible for beriberi.[34] They reached this conclusion by observing that 'removing patients in the earlier stages of this disease to new surroundings ... [prompted] recovery'.[35] This belief concurred with some of the early theories of the Dutch. However, in another of his articles, published in the same year, Norman wrote that 'No satisfactory cause [had] been assigned for the appearance of beri-beri in the Richmond Asylum.'[36] But he was aware that the disease waxed and waned according to the size of the asylum population. The numbers afflicted with the disease increased when overcrowding was acute and decreased when the number of patients diminished.

The overcrowded conditions in the Richmond had caused disquiet for many years, and the epidemic provided leverage for those who wished to put pressure on the government to address this problem. As early as 1891, the inspectors of lunatics complained in a special report 'that the Board of Control had taken no action to meet in any way the urgent requirements of the institution, with its vast population, for increased accommodation'.[37] There was a strong suspicion that the consequence of this overcrowding was the epidemic, described as 'a loathsome disease hitherto confined to the densely populated and filthy quarters of Chinese and other Eastern cities'.[38] On 18 March 1897, Mr. J.L. Carew, MP for College Green, Dublin, brought the matter to the attention of the House of Commons in London. He asked the Chief Secretary, Gerald Balfour, whether he was acquainted with this problem of overcrowding. Ultimately, in July 1897, the House was told that after consultations between the Board of Governors and the Board of Control, it was decided to build a new larger asylum, and it was already under construction on a site at Portrane, to be completed in about a year.

Whether or not the mysterious illness afflicting so many of the Richmond patients was the catalyst required to prompt action to alleviate overcrowding is a speculative point. Nevertheless, in 1897 the empty Grangegorman prison was transferred to the Board of Control for conversion to accommodation suitable for the mentally ill. Ireland, like many European countries, was grappling with an increasing population of mentally ill people. Between 1851 and 1891, the number of insane in Irish asylums increased over three fold. The annual report from the inspectors of lunatics recorded 3,234 insane in asylums in 1851, 7,141 in 1871, and 11,265 in 1891. The Richmond Asylum was one of the largest asylums in the country and at the time of the epidemic, it catered for the city and county of Dublin, counties of Louth and Wicklow, and the town of Drogheda.[39] It was built to accommodate 1,100 people but from the late 1880s, this number was consistently exceeded, rising to a daily average of over 1,686 patients by 1896. The following graph demonstrates how quickly the asylum population increased during the late 1880s and 1890s, and at the time of the annual inspection on 28 and 29 December 1896, the number of patients on the register of the Richmond Asylum was 1,728 (see Figure 9.1).

FIGURE 9.1: DAILY AVERAGE PATIENT NUMBERS IN THE RICHMOND ASYLUM,
1866–96

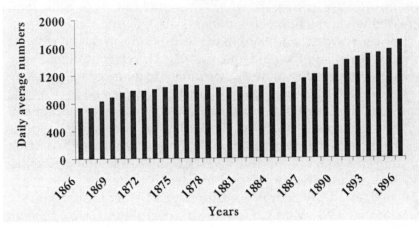

Source: *The Forty-sixth Report of Inspector of Lunatics* (Ireland) HC 1897 (C. 8639) xxxviii, 527,
Appendix F, p.181

While the inspectorate and the medical establishment searched for
causes of the outbreak, newspaper editors focused on the issue of
overcrowding at the Richmond. The packed and unhygienic conditions of the asylum were repeatedly blamed for the appearance of
the strange and unpleasant disease. The Dublin paper, *Freeman's
Journal* and *Daily Commercial Advertiser*, returned time and time
again to the subject, and several English and Scottish newspapers
also reported the Richmond epidemic. Accounts appeared in the
Aberdeen Weekly Journal, Manchester Times, Birmingham Daily Post and
the *Glasgow Herald*. Much further afield, the topic filled columns of
newsprint too. On the far side of the world, the *Nelson Evening Mail*
in New Zealand, picking up the item, suggested that a death on a
'barque' was 'presumably from beri-beri'.[40]

THE SCIENTIFIC INVESTIGATION TO EXPLAIN BERIBERI

By the closing decades of the nineteenth century, the pace of scientific
investigation was accelerating. The link between beriberi and diet,
in particular a diet primarily of rice, was first made by a German-
trained Japanese Naval Surgeon, Takaki, in the 1880s. He concluded
that beriberi was the consequence of a protein deficiency. Pursuing
a dietary connection was correct, but his conclusion was incorrect.
Meanwhile, in Germany, Robert Koch was successful in identifying
bacterial infection as the cause of many killer diseases, prompting a

number of Dutch investigators to pursue a similar line of enquiry as a cause of beriberi. Two scientists, Cornelis Adrianus Pickelharing and C. Winkler, were sent to the Dutch East Indies in 1886–7 by the Netherlands government, specifically to investigate the prevalence of beriberi in the region. In their book on the subject, they concluded that 'beri-beri is caused by a micrococcus which exists in the place where the disease prevails, and which can penetrate into the human body. It is very probable that this micro-organism enters by the organs of respiration with the air inhaled, and that from them, it penetrates into the circulation.'[41] The research of Pickelharing and Winkler was known to the Director General of the British Army Medical Department, Sir William A. MacKinnon and he recommended their work to the Chief Secretary's Office in Dublin when discussing the Richmond Asylum disease outbreak. MacKinnon pointed out that medical treatment did not appear efficacious in curing beriberi. Thus, the perceived wisdom of the day attributed bacteria as the culprit causing beriberi.[42] Sir Patrick Manson also thought a toxin was responsible for beriberi, either harboured in the air or carried by insects.[43] The fabric of buildings, therefore, needed to be inspected because the disease was prevalent where large groups of people were congregated together, such as in prisons, asylums and, in the Far East, among labourers in rubber plantations and in Japanese prisoner-of-war camps.

Once it was realised that a diet of highly polished rice consumed over a long period of time caused beriberi, and that a change to normal brown rice reversed the condition, investigators had a conundrum. Was beriberi induced by a toxic bacterium in polished rice for which an antidote was contained in the outer husk of the rice grain, or was there some special property in the husk essential for preventing the disease?[44] The mystery was further complicated by the observation that beriberi could also occur where excessive amounts of highly milled wheat were consumed.[45]

A disease resembling beriberi had been known for many decades. As early as the mid-sixteenth century, beriberi symptoms were described among non rice-eating people in the Molucca Islands, now part of Indonesia. By the end of the nineteenth century, it was evident that beriberi was not restricted to rice-eating populations or to Asians. Cases were recorded among the fishermen of Labrador on the north-eastern coast of Canada, who subsisted on long fishing trips on fish and little else. The inhabitants of Newfoundland succumbed to the disease in early spring, as their diminishing winter stores were reduced to little more than tea and bread.[46] And further south in Brazil, particularly in the region of Bahia, where sugar production was a cash crop, beriberi was a serious problem. Cassava meal was their staple grain, a food very low in thiamin. The dietary patterns of these wide-ranging geographical locations were very different. None included rice, yet they were all diets low in the vital thiamin, and so placed these populations vulnerable to beriberi.

The discovery that a deficiency of the B vitamin, thiamin, caused beriberi, took many decades and involved many scientists. The breakthrough linking beriberi with the pericarp (outer layer) of the rice husk was the work of Christiaan Eijkman and Adolphe Vorderman during the 1890s.[47] But it was another Dutch scientist, Gerrit Grijns and a Pole, Casimir Funk, who early in the twentieth century recognised that a vital nutrient, an anti-beriberi substance, was the key to understanding the disease.[48] The final stage was the identification of the water soluble B vitamin, thiamin, as the crucial anti-beriberi element. This last piece of the puzzle was fitted only in the 1930s. Thus, the scientific journey to understanding the cause of beriberi as a vitamin deficiency disease was long and tortuous and, unfortunately, the Richmond Asylum epidemics occurred before the sick there could benefit from the unravelling of this nutritional puzzle.

UNDERSTANDING THE NUTRITIONAL DIMENSION

We have already established that thiamin is essential in preventing beriberi. For our investigation to develop further, we must explore two questions. Firstly, what is the function of thiamin? Secondly, did the Richmond asylum diet measure up to the thiamin requirement necessary to prevent beriberi? Thiamin is essential for the metabolism of carbohydrates, it being a component of an enzyme system required to fulfil the breakdown of starch and sugary foods. In short, it liberates energy from carbohydrate foods. The consequence of an insufficiency is an accumulation of lactic acid and pyruvic acid in the blood stream, resulting in muscular weakness, palpitations of the heart and degeneration of the nerves. Early symptoms of thiamin deficiency are subtle. A patient will complain of a vague malaise and loss of appetite. If wet beriberi develops, the dominant features are waterlogged tissues, pain in legs on walking, the calf muscles being tense and tender to touch. As the disease progresses, the heart muscle becomes enlarged from increased cardiac output to maintain circulation, and from a lack of thiamin to nourish this muscle. Sudden death can occur, the result of myocardial failure. Patients with dry beriberi suffer an unpleasant sensation of 'pins and needles' progressing to intense pain, because the nerves are inflamed. Muscles become more wasted and weak, making walking difficult. Foot and wrist drop are common and are the result of muscle tenderness. The patient becomes thin to a point of emaciation.

How do the symptoms described by Norman and others compare with those of beriberi? Norman published two articles in 1899 and 1900 describing the symptoms he observed. These are summarized in Table 9.1 and they are compared with symptoms of beriberi as described in modern nutritional texts.

TABLE 9.1: COMPARATIVE TABLE OF CLASSICAL SYMPTOMS OF BERIBERI AND THE SYMPTOMS DESCRIBED BY DR. CONOLLY NORMAN.

Symptoms described in nutritional texts	Symptoms described by Dr. Norman
Onset insidious	√
Heaviness and weakness of legs	√
Pins and needles	√
Numbness of legs	√
Anaesthesia of skin	√
Anorexia	
Calf muscles tender under pressure	√
Wet beri-beri	Wet beri-beri
Oedema of legs, trunk and face	√
Palpitations	√
Pain in legs on walking	√
Dry beri-beri	Dry beri-beri
Polyneuropathy	√
Muscular wasting	√
Wrist and foot drop	√

Sources: Conolly Norman, 'The Clinical Features of Beri-beri', pp.1–16; Conolly Norman, 'A brief note on Beri-beri', pp.503–11; Davidson, Passmore, Brock, Truswell, *Human Nutrition and Dietetics* 7th Edition (Edinburgh, 1979), pp.284–5.

If the Richmond patients were indeed suffering from beriberi, the thiamin content of their diet is a crucial issue. The foods richest in thiamin are yeast, bran, Marmite, pulses and wholemeal. Moderate sources are fresh fruit, vegetables, meat, pork and, to a lesser degree, milk and eggs, though these foods can become useful contributors if eaten in large amounts. However, thiamin is sensitive to heat, water and alkalis and so considerable quantities of the vitamin are destroyed in cooking processes. Furthermore, thiamin is not a storable vitamin, the body excretes excess, and so daily dietary intake is important.

With the exception of some years during the 1850s,[49] prescribed dietary scales for the Richmond Asylum were published in the *Reports of Inspectors in Lunacy* for four decades, a practice that stopped in 1890. Subsequently, only limited comments on diets were reported by the Inspectors. However, for the years of the epidemic, we can resort to dietary scales published in the *Annual Reports of the Richmond District Asylum.*[50] These diets allow us to assess if a marked nutritional deterioration occurred during the 1890s. For this purpose, the *ordinary* diet of the Richmond Asylum in the years 1844–5, the decade 1873–83, and the year 1895–6 have been selected as snapshots in time.

Before proceeding further, a note of caution – in a large institution caring for mentally ill patients, all or indeed any of the foods recorded in the published menus may not have been consumed. For instance, the food on the plate may not have matched the diet recorded. A good example of a dietary discrepancy was uncovered by Mark Finnane when researching for his book on the insane in post-Famine Ireland. The 'Richmond dietary table indicated that half a pound of meat a day was allowed [to] each patient,' but, 'the stores return … showed an average per patient per day of less than one ounce.'[51] Alternatively, some patients may have chosen not to partake of some or all of the food offered on the plate. Nevertheless, these dietary scales are all we have and they probably provide us with the upper range in food rations.

The following Tables 9.2, 9.3 and 9.4 show the *ordinary* diet for male patients for 1844–5, 1873–83 and 1895–6. The female menu was the same, except that the quantities of some of the foods were smaller.

TABLE 9.2: RICHMOND 'ORDINARY' DIETARY SCALE FOR MALE PATIENTS, 1844–5.

Breakfast:	1 qt Stirabout (oatmeal)
	1 pt New Milk
Dinner: Sun/Tues/Thurs	¾ lb Beef
	2 lb Potatoes
Mon/Wed	1 qt Soup
	3 lb Potatoes
Fri/Sat	3 lb Potatoes
	1 pt New Milk
Supper:	8 oz Brown Bread
	1 pt Buttermilk

Source: *Asylums Report* for 1844, HC 1845(645) xxvi. 269, Appendix No. 3, p.57; *Asylums Report* for 1845, HC 1846 (736) xxii. 409, Appendix 4, p.38.

TABLE 9.3: RICHMOND 'ORDINARY' DIETARY SCALE FOR MALE PATIENTS, 1873–83.

Breakfast:	½lb Bread
	1pt Tea
Dinner: 2 days*	1pt Pea soup; 10oz Bread
5 days	8oz Meat; 1pt soup; 10oz Bread
Supper:	½lb Bread
	1pt Cocoa

* From 1879 one pint of pea soup and coffee was served.

Source: *Twenty-third Report on the District, Criminal, and Private Lunatic Asylums in Ireland*, HC
1874 (c. 1004) xxvii. 363, p.92, and in each inspectorate report for the next 10 years.

A healthier menu plan emerged during the late 1880s so that the inspectors reported in 1892: 'The dietary has been improved by the substitution of soup for coffee on Wednesdays … The patients get beef, potatoes, and soup for dinner on Sunday, Monday, Tuesday, and Saturday, and pork on Thursday … Tea and bread is given for breakfast, and cocoa in the evening.'[52] On the eve of the mysterious illness, dietary scales showed further improvements, as displayed in Norman's correspondence to the *British Medical Journal* in 1894, when responding to a previous enquiry on the fat content of the patients' diet,[53] and recorded in the *Annual Reports* of the Richmond District Asylum, as shown in Table 9.4.

TABLE 9.4: RICHMOND 'ORDINARY' DIETARY SCALE FOR MALE PATIENTS, 1895–6.

Breakfast: –	1pt.Tea, ½lb Bread, ½oz Butter
Dinner: –	1 day: 8oz Bacon; 5oz Bread; 1 lb Potatoes; 1lb Vegetables *
	4 days: 8oz Beef, 5oz Bread; 1 lb Potatoes; 1lb Vegetables
	1 day: 8oz Pork, 5oz Bread; 1 lb Potatoes; 1lb Vegetables
	1 day: 8oz Fish with sauce, 5oz Bread, 1lb Potatoes; 1pt Coffee
Supper: –	1pt.Tea, ½lb Bread, ½oz Butter

•Cabbage, turnip or parsnip were served according to the season, prepared with dripping.

Source: *Annual Reports of the Richmond District Asylum, Dublin* for the Years 1895, 1896, printed
by order of the Board of Governors.

To display changes in the Richmond dietary regimes over time, Table 9.5 summarises menus expressed as weekly food rations.

So, can we push the analysis further, using Food Composition Tables to calculate the thiamin content of the menus?[54] These tables

TABLE 9.5: WEEKLY FOOD RATIONS (RAW WEIGHT) SERVED IN THE RICHMOND
ASYLUM, 1844–5, 1873–1883 AND 1895–6.

	1844–5	1873–83	1895–6
Oatmeal*	49 oz	–	–
Milk	9 pt	1¾ pt**	2 pt
Buttermilk	7 pt	–	–
Potatoes	288 oz	–	112 oz
Beef/Bacon/Pork	36 oz	40 oz	48 oz
Fish			8 oz
Bread***	56 oz	182 oz	147 oz
Butter			7 oz
Soup	4 pt	5 pt	
Pea Soup		2 pt	
Cocoa powder		3½ oz.	
Fresh vegetables root & green		–	96 oz
Sugar for tea/coffee/ cocoa		7 oz	7½oz
Tea		7 oz	7 oz

* Some asylums used 7 oz oatmeal others 8 oz to 1 pt of stirabout.

** As no tea and cocoa recipes were provided by Richmond Asylum, quantities quoted for
another asylum were used.

*** Modern bread is fortified with several nutrients including thiamin and so a flour surrogate
was used for the nutritional analysis.

provide the carbohydrate, protein, fat, mineral and vitamin content
of a large variety of foods. There are, however, pitfalls in applying
modern nutritional techniques to historical data. Retrospective
analyses require certain modifications to the calculations. These
issues are explained in detail elsewhere.[55] Suffice here to point out
that modern food surrogates had to be selected in place of foods no
longer eaten or changed in composition with the passage of time.[56]
Difficulties also occur with 'home-made' dishes, when no recipes
were recorded. Significant weight loss following preparation and
cooking had to be accommodated too, for which the compilers of the
tables provide adjustment figures.[57] Moreover, and as pointed out
earlier, there was no guarantees that the menus recorded in the
Inspectors' reports were precisely translated into food served on
plates of the patients. Such adjustments leave us with a 'best fit'
approach for our nutritional analysis of the Richmond diets.

Table 9.6 shows the results of carrying out an analysis of the
carbohydrate and thiamin contents of three Richmond diets for
1844, 1873 and 1896.

TABLE 9.6: CARBOHYDRATE AND THIAMIN CONTENT OF RICHMOND ASYLUM
DIETS, 1844, 1873 AND 1896.

	CHO	Thiamin
	(g)	(mg)
1844 Menu 1	500.9	2.5
1844 Menu 2	614.3	2.8
1844 Menu 3	617.1	3.0
1873 Menu 1	448.6	0.7
1873 Menu 2	457.2	0.6
1896 Menu 1	403.9	1.3
1896 Menu 2	391.9	0.9
1896 Menu 3	431.5	1.8
1896 Menu 4	422.9	1.0

It is clear that the thiamin content of the 1844 diet was superior to the later menus of 1873 and 1896 and, by implication, the diets of the epidemic years. The traditional Irish foods of potatoes, milk and oatmeal were responsible, as they provided good or moderate sources of thiamin. By the 1870s, these staple foods were either omitted or reduced in quantity, with the result that the thiamin content suffered accordingly. The removal of oatmeal provides a particularly good example of the impact of these changes. The Richmond was one of a handful of asylums that took oatmeal off the patient menu. The majority of Irish asylums still retained oatmeal stirabout in amounts varying between six and ten ounces daily and, in these asylums, this simple and cheap dish provided their patients with approximately one third of their daily thiamin requirement.

The tinkering with the quantities of potatoes and milk also contributed to the decline in thiamin levels in the 1870s menus. Potatoes are a moderate source of thiamin and, when eaten in the large quantities common in Ireland, their contribution to the overall intake of the vitamin was considerable. So, their reinstatement by the late 1880s and early 1890s improved the thiamin content. However, the removal from the menu by the 1870s of fresh cold milk as a drink, to be replaced by hot drinks such as cocoa and tea containing smaller amounts of milk, also reduced the thiamin content of the diet. Moreover, by subjecting these beverages to heat reduced the thiamin levels even further. So, this alteration was yet another step that was detrimental to the nutritional quality of the menu.

The crucial question is, were the menus of the 1890s sufficiently deficient of thiamin to precipitate beriberi? The four menus analysed from the year 1895–6 show a wide span of thiamin contents, ranging from 0.9 mg to 1.8 mg daily. Perhaps a closer look at the carbohydrate and calorie content may shed more light on the question. Here, we enter the complexity of the biochemical function of vitamins. As pointed out earlier, carbohydrate metabolism is dependent on adequate supplies of thiamin, and it has been observed that high levels of carbohydrate accelerated the appearance of beriberi. It has been estimated that in a well balanced diet, approximately 55 per cent of calories comes from carbohydrates, but in the Richmond Asylum diets, this percentage was considerably higher, as demonstrated in Table 9.7.

TABLE 9.7: MEAN CARBOHYDRATE VALUES OF RICHMOND MENUS, 1844, 1873, 1896.

	CHO (g)	kcal. from CHO	Total kcal.	Percentage of kcal. from CHO
Richmond Diet 1844	566.48	2124	3244	65%
Richmond Diet 1873	454.72	1705	2337	73%
Richmond Diet 1896	411.05	1541	2418	64%

Initially scientists reckoned that for every 1000 calories in the diet derived from carbohydrates, 0.6 mg of thiamin was required to prevent deficiency, though more recently this figure has been reduced, with some research suggesting 0.3 mg/1000 kcal, and other investigators preferring 0.4 mg/1000 kcal to ensure prevention of beriberi.[58] Table 9.8 shows the thiamin requirement of the Richmond diets expressed on the basis of their calorie content.

TABLE 9.8: THIAMIN REQUIREMENT OF RICHMOND DIETS, BASED ON CALORIE CONTENT.

	1844–5 diets	1873–83 diets	1895–6 diets
Basis of 0.6mg/1000kcal	1.95mg	1.40mg	1.45mg
Basis of 0.4mg/1000kcal	1.30mg	0.93mg	0.97mg
Basis of 0.3mg/1000kcal	0.97mg	0.71mg	0.73mg

If the published rations served were a true representation of what the patients received, and furthermore consumed, the figures in Table 9.7 reveal that the 1844 menus yielded more than adequate thiamin to prevent beriberi, irrespective of the level calculated. All of the 1895–6 menus met the thiamin requirement at the 0.3 mg/1000 kcal level. When assessed at the 0.4 mg/1000 kcal level, all but one menu met the requirement, though that particular menu was served four days per week. However, the shortfall was very small. At the highest level, only one menu achieved the target. The poorest menus were those of the 1870s and early 1880s. One menu almost made the thiamin requirement at the lowest level of 0.3 mg/1000kcal, the other menu was slightly below and, therefore, both menus failed at the higher levels. Thus, the period when diets had the poorest thiamin content did not coincide with the epidemic of the mid-1890s. This dietary information places serious doubt over the possibility that the sickness suffered by so many of the Richmond patients was beriberi.

CONCLUSION

What conclusions can we draw from this episode of a strange epidemic in the Richmond Asylum during the mid-1890s? Dr. Conolly Norman pursued a diagnosis of beriberi and many of the doctors who examined the afflicted patients were also confident that beriberi was the cause of the sickness. Other physicians, however, were more doubtful. Based on the nutritional analysis we have attempted, an epidemic of beriberi in the Richmond asylum in the mid-1890s was unlikely. The most vulnerable era was during the 1870s and 1880s, when the quality of the diet was poorest. However, as demonstrated in the Japanese prisoner-of-war camps, beriberi is very perverse. Two physicians who worked there made the following observation:

> The uniformity of environment, work, diet and even of type of individual in the camps, emphases the mystery ... why, of a group of apparently similar men, on diets similarly deficient in vitamin B[1], one should get neuritis, another edema, [sic.] a third should die suddenly of heart failure, and a fourth be apparently well, cannot as yet be explained.[59]

If we dismiss an epidemic of beriberi, what alternative explanations can we propose? It was noted by Dr. Norman that a significant number of their alleged beriberi cases were also epileptic, not only in the Richmond, but also in asylums in America. This fact leads one to wonder if the medication being used for that condition had an adverse affect on the metabolism of thiamin or if the long-term use of such medication produced side effects similar to the symptoms of beriberi. From the mid-nineteenth to the early years of the twentieth century, a group of drugs based on bromide salts was used to treat epilepsy. So successful was this drug as an anticonvulsant agent, that it was commonly prescribed in asylums for this condition. However, bromides are highly toxic, causing neurological and gastrointestinal problems. Perhaps further research down this avenue will yield a clearer picture of a cause for the Richmond epidemic.

Apart from the epileptic patients, we do not have information on the length of time patients who succumbed to so-called beriberi spent in the asylum or on the perceived cause of their mental illnesses. As part of their mental illness, some patients may have been suffering from eating disorders, making them vulnerable to multiple sub-clinical or full-blown deficiencies of various nutrients. Other long-term patients may also have exhibited sub-clinical deficiency of thiamin, permitting the progression to full-blown beriberi, though this is unlikely on the scale reputed in the Richmond. These suggestions are no more than speculations, and whatever the disease was that afflicted a sizable number of patients in the Richmond Asylum, and what the cause of the epidemic might have been, we will probably never know. Medical scares, however, develop a life of their own, and there are plenty of examples from our own times, such as the many dietary fads that come and go to explain cause and effect of untreatable diseases. As sizable numbers of the Richmond patients presented a series of unusual symptoms, there was enough uncertainty to make a diagnosis of beriberi plausible. In the technical language of the Dutch doctors:

> Could this disease have been beri-beri? From the point of view that an acutely dilated right heart + anaesthesia of the legs + disappearance of the knee tendon reflex = beriberi; or, if finding on examination, oedemas without renal disease + brown atrophy of the heart muscle + degeneration of some nerves, one says it is beri-beri ... one is almost justified in believing in the existence of beri-beri, at least as regards a great number of the cases. After an investigation of all the symptoms which occurred in the Asylum disease, and those also observed in beri-beri, possibly with many there will remain but little doubt as to the correctness of the diagnosis.
>
> Let us be allowed to state, as our own opinion, that this disease is not beri-beri such as it manifests itself in our colonies [Dutch].[60]

NOTES

1. I am grateful to Mr. Richard Bennett, custodian of the Richmond District Asylum Archives, for searching out documents so valuable in the preparation of this essay.
2. The spelling of this disease has changed over time. In the nineteenth century a hyphen was used, now it is omitted. In this paper the modern version will be used except where the word appears in a nineteenth-century quotation.
3. Thiamin is one of several vitamins which collectively are known as vitamin B complex.
4. *The Forty-fourth Asylums Report*, HC 1895 (C. 7804) liv. 435, p.161 cites 152 patients afflicted by beriberi, whereas in A.F. Verschuur and G. van Ijsselsteyn, translated by Daniel F. Rambaut, in 'The Epidemic Disease in the Richmond District Lunatic Asylum in Dublin', *Dublin Quarterly Journal of Medical Science*, vol. CIX, No. 5 (1900), p.374, higher figures of 127 males and 47 females (making a total of 174 patients) are recorded.
5. Again, there is a discrepancy in figures cited in Parliamentary Papers and those published in medical journals articles. The number of male deaths from beriberi recorded for the year 1894 is 17 in *The Forty-fourth Asylums Report*, HC 1895 (C. 7804) liv. 435, p.160, whereas in Conolly Norman, 'A Brief Note on Beri-beri in Asylums', *Journal of Mental Science*, vol. XLV (1899), p.504, and in Verschuur and van Ijsselsteyn, 'The Epidemic Disease in the Richmond District Lunatic Asylum', p.374, the figure of 18 males is recorded.
6. The disease statistics for years 1896–8 are those cited by Dr. Conolly Norman, in his article 'A Brief Note on Beri-beri in Asylums', pp.504–5.
7. Conolly Norman, 'A Brief Note on Beri-beri in Asylums', p.504.
8. A.F. Verschuur & G. van Ijsselsteyn, 'The Epidemic Disease', p.374.
9. Conolly Norman was a Fellow of both College of Physicians and College of Surgeons.
10. This journal is now the *British Journal of Psychiatry*.
11. Obituary of Conolly Norman, M.D., FRCPI, *British Medical Journal*, 29.ii 1908, p.541.
12. Obituary of Conolly Norman, M.D., FRCPI, in the *Journal of Mental Science*, Vol. LIV, No. 225, April 1908, pp.203–4.
13. Brian O'Shea and Jane Falvey, 'A History of the Richmond Asylum (St. Brendan's Hospital), Dublin', in Hugh Freeman & German E. Berrios (eds.), *150 Years of British Psychiatry, Volume II, The Aftermath* (London: Athlone Press, 1996), p.416.
14. Conolly Norman, 'A Brief Note on Beri-beri in Asylums', p.504.
15. Extracts of the report of Dr. Daniel F. Rambaut were published in the *Richmond District Asylum, Dublin Annual Report for the Year 1896*, pp.12–13, and in the *Freeman's Journal* and *Daily Commercial Advertiser* (Hereafter, Freeman's Journal), Dublin, 5 November 1896.
16. The Board of Control was established under the Lunatic Asylums Repayment of Advances (Ireland) Act, 1855.
17. Report of The Presentments for 1895–6, presented to the Dublin Municipal Council, published in Freeman's Journal, 5 November 1894.
18. *Freeman's Journal*, 5 November 1894.
19. Chief Secretary's Office Registered Papers, 1894, 18 October, NAI CSORP/1984/13918.
20. There are several spellings for this surname – Colahan is used in this paper.
21. Obituary of John Mallet Purser, M.D., D.Sc., F.R.C.P.I., *The British Medical Journal*, 28 September, 1929, p.600.
22. Reports of Dr. Manson, Dr. Smith and Sir Thornley Stoker, *Richmond District Asylum, Annual Report for the Year 1896*, Appendix 1, pp.31–41.
23. Writings include: Patrick Manson, 'Beri-beri' in Andrew Davidson (ed.), *Hygiene and Disease in Warm Climates* (Edinburgh & London: Young J. Pentland, 1893); Patrick Manson, *Tropical Diseases: a manual of diseases of warm climates* (London: Cassell, 1898). See also Reports of Dr. Manson, Dr. Smith and Sir Thornley Stoker.
24. From a report submitted by Dr. Conolly Norman to a meeting of Governors of the Richmond Asylum, Dublin and extracted for *Freeman's Journal*, 10 October 1894.
25. *Freeman's Journal*, 10 October 1894.
26. A.F. Verschuur & G. van Ijsselsteyn, 'The Epidemic Disease', pp.375–80, 446–54.
27. Ibid., p.371.
28. Ibid., p.372.
29. Ibid., p.374.
30. Correspondence: Conolly Norman, 'The etiology of beri-beri', *British Medical Journal*, 19 August 1899; 2 (2016), p.487.
31. 'The etiology of beri-beri', in *British Medical Journal*, 2 (2016), 19 August 1899, p.487.

32. 'The etiology of beri-beri', in *British Medical Journal*, 2 (2019), 9 September 1899, p.686.
33. Conolly Norman, 'A Brief Note on Beri-beri in Asylums', p.509.
34. Cited during discussion of Conolly Norman's paper, 'Clinical features of Beri-beri', and published in *Dublin Journal of Medical Science*, vol. CVII (1899), pp.309–10.
35. Dr. Walter Smith on the discussion of Conolly Norman's, paper 'The clinical features of Beri-beri', read to the Royal Academy of Medicine in Ireland and published in *Dublin Journal of Medical Science*, vol. CVII (1899), p.309.
36. Norman, 'A Brief Note on Beri-beri in Asylums', p.505.
37. Parliamentary Debates, *Hansard*, Fourth Series, vol. LI, 22 July 1897, col. 712.
38. Parliamentary Debates, *Hansard*, Fourth Series, vol. XLVII, 18 March 1897, col. 943.
39. By the end of the 1890s, there were discussions about counties Louth and Wicklow making provision for their own insane. See *The Forty-eighth Asylums Report*, HC 1899 (C. 9479) xl. 501, p.204.
40. *Nelson Evening Mail*, Saturday, 18 January 1896.
41. C.A. Pickelharing & C. Winkler, *Beri-beri: Researches concerning its nature and cause and the means of Arrest, made by order of the Netherlands Government*, translated by Dr. James Cantile (Edinburgh and London: Young J. Pentland, 1893), p.135.
42. Letter from Surgeon-General Sir William A. MacKinnon, KCB, to the Chief Secretary's Office. NAI, CSORP/1894/13918.
43. Patrick Manson, 'The Prophylaxis and Treatment of Beri-beri', *The British Medical Journal*, 20 September 1902, p.834.
44. Roy Porter, *The Greatest Benefit to Mankind: A Medical History of Humanity from Antiquity to the Present* (London: Fontana Press, paperback edition 1999), p.553.
45. Kenneth J. Carpenter, *Beriberi, White Rice, and Vitamin B: a disease, a cause and a cure* (London and Los Angeles: University of California Press, 2000), pp.133–54.
46. Modern flour is fortified with several water soluble vitamins, including thiamin. This did not occur in the nineteenth century.
47. Christiaan Eijkman received the Nobel Prize in 1929 for his work in identifying the outer husk of rice grains as key to explaining the cause of beriberi.
48. Funk gave the anti beriberi element the name 'vitamine' (later referred to as vitamin).
49. In addition to a lack of dietary scales during the 1850s, there is no information on diet for the Richmond asylum for 1861 and 1869 except passing comments on dietary changes. For most of the 1860s, dietary information was presented as annual quantities consumed in each district asylum and therefore not suitable for nutritional analysis.
50. Annual Reports of the Richmond District Asylum, 1892, 1894, 1895, 1896, in the archive of the asylum/hospital, located at St. Brendan's Hospital, Dublin.
51. Mark Finnane, *Insanity and the Insane in Post-Famine Ireland* (London: Croom Helm, 1981), p.203.
52. *The Forty-Second Asylums Report*, HC 1893–94 (C. 7125) xlvi. 369, Appendix F, p.146.
53. Conolly Norman, 'The Etiology of Beri-beri', p.686.
54. In the UK, the tables used are R.A. McCance & E.M. Widdowson, *The Composition of Foods*, Medical Research Council, Special Report Series, no. 297 (London: HMSO, 1960). Fourth revised edition, by A.A. Paul & D.A.T. Southgate (London: HMSO, 1978).
55. L.A. Clarkson and E. Margaret Crawford, *Feast and Famine: A History of Food and Nutrition in Ireland 1500–1920* (Oxford: Oxford University Press, 2001), pp.171–2.
56. An example is bread. The most appropriate approach is to select nutritional values for flour of an extraction rate suitable for the period under study, and reducing the weight of bread by 40 per cent to account for its water content. Flour is now fortified with several vitamins and minerals, one of which is thiamin and so a value of unfortified flour had to be sought. See S. Davidson and R. Passmore, *Human nutrition and dietetics* (Edinburgh: E. & S. Livingstone, 1979), pp.169–71.
57. R.A. McCance & E.M. Widdowson, *The Composition of Foods*.
58. See Kenneth Carpenter, *Beriberi*, pp.163–4 and Donald S. McLaren, *Nutrition and its Disorders* (Edinburgh: Churchill Livingstone, 1981), p.93.
59. D.A. Smith and M.A. Woodruff, 'Deficiency diseases in Japanese prison camps', *Medical Research Council Special Report Series*, no. 274 (London HMSO, 1951), p.170. Cited in Kenneth J. Carpenter, *Beriberi, White Rice, and Vitamin B: a disease, a cause and a cure* (London and Los Angeles, 2000), p.158.
60. A.F. Verschuur & G. van Ijsselsteyn, 'The Epidemic Disease', p.451.

10

Tuberculosis in the Nineteenth-Century Asylum: Clinical Cases from the Central Criminal Lunatic Asylum, Dundrum, Dublin

Brendan D. Kelly

The nineteenth century saw a dramatic increase in the number of institutions dedicated to the care of individuals with mental illness across Europe and the United States, as public authorities moved swiftly to establish large institutions dedicated to accommodating this 'hurried weight of human calamity',[1] providing shelter, food and (later) various forms of 'treatment' for hundreds of thousands of individuals deemed to suffer from mental illness. Historical evidence suggests that, prior to this development, individuals with mental illness in much of Europe tended to live lives of poverty and destitution, generally untouched by changing trends in political thought.[2]

In 1817, a Committee of the House of Commons (of Great Britain, then including Ireland) reported a disturbing picture of the plight of the mentally ill in Ireland:

> When a strong man or woman gets the complaint [madness], the only way they have to manage is by making a hole in the floor of the cabin, not high enough for the person to stand up in, with a crib over it to prevent his getting up. This hole is about five feet deep, and they give this wretched being his food there, and there he generally dies.[3]

The subsequent expansion in asylum populations in the mid- to late nineteenth century was particularly notable in England and Ireland: in England, there were 1.6 asylum inmates per 1,000 of the population in 1859, and by 1909 this had risen to 3.7 per 1,000.[4] In Ireland, there were 3,234 individuals in asylums in 1851, and by 1914 this had risen to 16,941.[5] This expansion in asylum populations was attributable to both governmental concern about the social problems presented by the mentally ill and the philanthropic impulses of nineteenth-century social activists.

This expansion in asylum capacity was underpinned by a belief that rates of mental illness were rising in the population in general. From an epidemiological perspective, it is difficult to establish definitively if such an increase truly occurred, although it is beyond doubt that the perception of such an increase caused considerable alarm in both public and professional circles.[6] Factors contributing to this development included (a) an increased recognition of mental illness by both public and professionals; (b) mutually re-enforcing patterns of asylum-building and involuntary psychiatric committal, fuelled, at least in part, by legislative change; (c) changes in psychiatric diagnostic practices; and (d) possible epidemiological change owing to unidentified biological factors and/or socio-demographic changes.[7]

This chapter aims to examine specific aspects of the phenomenon of tuberculosis[8] in one particular asylum (the Central Criminal Lunatic Asylum, Dundrum, Dublin) through original examination of the archival clinical records of three patients, all of whom died in the asylum and whose deaths were attributed to tuberculosis. The Central Criminal Lunatic Asylum was the first inpatient forensic psychiatry facility established in Great Britain or Ireland.[9] The Lunatics Asylums (Ireland) Act (1845) outlined that the purpose of the institution was to provide 'a central asylum for insane persons charged with offences in Ireland'. Patients were admitted if they were convicted of an offence in court and either found to be 'insane' at trial or developed symptoms of mental illness while in custody. The Central Criminal Lunatic Asylum opened its doors in 1850 and by 1853 there were 40 female and 69 male inpatients.[10]

The three case histories presented in this chapter are drawn from the original medical case-records at the Central Criminal Lunatic Asylum (now called the Central Mental Hospital). In order to maintain patient confidentiality, the patient's names have been changed so as to render them unidentifiable. In all other respects, original language and terminology from the archival records have been maintained; this represents an attempt to optimise fidelity to historical sources and not an endorsement of the broader use of such terminology in contemporary settings.

MR. A.: 'DYING OF PHTHISIS'

Mr. A. was a 21 year-old, single 'servant' from the west of Ireland who was admitted to the Central Criminal Lunatic Asylum in the late 1890s. Mr. A. had been charged with 'wounding and assault' and sentenced to be detained in the Central Criminal Lunatic Asylum 'at the Lord Lieutenant's pleasure' (i.e. indefinitely, at the discretion of the chief administrator of British government in Ireland). Admission notes record that Mr. A, was Roman Catholic, was able to read and write, and presented as 'a case of melancholia'.

Mr. A. had been in prison for one week while awaiting transfer to the Central Criminal Lunatic Asylum, and the prison's surgeon reported that Mr. A. was 'suffering from phthisis [tuberculosis] for a considerable time' prior to his offence. This was also documented in his admission notes at the Central Criminal Lunatic Asylum:

> This man is in an exceedingly delicate state of bodily health. He is suffering from phthisis in an advanced stage, his left lung being chiefly affected. Mentally he appeared slightly depressed but I have not as yet been able to elicit any signs of insanity ... He is utterly unable to work ... I have ordered him extra diet, milk, butter, stout, etc.

A week after admission, Mr. A. was 'confined to bed ... [with] temperature 102 [Fahrenheit; 38.9 Celsius] at night, 100 [Fahrenheit; 37.8 Celsius] in the morning'. Over the following weeks, Mr. A. frequently spent periods of several days in bed, although the 'physician and doctors here consider it well to have him up when possible'. While staff saw 'no delusions or any signs of insanity', their assessment of his physical health was not optimistic:

> There is little to be done for this patient. He has extra diet of all kinds and takes it fairly well, but the disease in his lungs progresses too rapidly and he cannot live very long.

As his physical health deteriorated, his mental health also declined:

> Patient fancies that everyone in the asylum is trying to annoy him; that they work machines on him at night and prevent him from sleeping; that there is a wholesale conspiracy against him. He is in a very delicate state of bodily health. We try to get him up and about as much as possible, but he is difficult to manage owing to his delusions and we are obliged to give him practically his own way.

Three months after admission, Mr. A. was staying 'in bed about five days in the week', had 'lost strength considerably', and was, clearly, 'dying of phthisis'. Mr. A. remained in this weakened state for many months and, nine months after admission, was still 'dying slowly':

> This patient has no pain whatever, but is dying slowly. Nothing more can be done for him. Both his lungs are very largely diseased, especially his left, and his heart is now very weak. He takes his nourishment sometimes fairly, but other times he refuses everything and is not an easy patient to treat ... I wrote some days ago and informed this patient's brother that this man could not last much longer; he answered my letter but is not coming to see him.

Mr. A. continued to deteriorate and, although staff ordered 'him anything he has any fancy for', he remained 'very weak and appears to be nothing but skin and bone'. Ten days later, just over ten months after admission, at twenty-two years of age, Mr. A. 'saw the priest this evening at 6.45pm and died at 10.30'. Three days later, an inquest was held and 'the jury found that [Mr. A.] died from tuberculosis'.

MR. B.: 'HIS LUNGS ARE ATTACKED BY TUBERCULE BACILLI'

Mr. B. was a 47 year-old, married 'painter' from Dublin who was transferred from a Dublin prison to the Central Criminal Lunatic Asylum in the late 1890s. Mr. B. had been convicted of 'manslaughter' three years earlier and sentenced to 'ten years penal servitude'. Admission notes record that Mr. B. was Roman Catholic and unable to read or write.

Admission notes at the Central Criminal Lunatic Asylum recorded that Mr. B. 'looks in delicate health' and described him as a case of 'dementia' which admission notes attributed to 'drink'. There was also some information from the prison:

> The prison surgeon gives no detailed report but states that the patient suffers from melancholia with a suicidal tendency and loss of memory. He has been observed while in prison quietly crying by himself without apparent cause.

Mr. B. was described as 'a quiet, harmless man who looks considerably older than his stated age' and while 'his bodily health is feeble ... there is no definite disease present'. One month after admission, however, Mr. B. 'complained of shooting pains in his legs and weakness. His knee jerk was greatly increased and his pupil reacted to accommodation, but not to light.' These physical symptoms receded over the following weeks however, and, although Mr. B. was 'much depressed and takes little interest in anything', notes recorded that he 'works daily in his ward'.

Six months later, however, Mr. B.'s 'weakness' returned and he was 'confined to bed'. His condition deteriorated rapidly over the following month:

> His condition is critical and I have little hope of his recovery … His heart is very weak and his lungs are attacked by tubercule bacilli. He is getting digitalis, liquid strychnine, whiskey, milk, beef tea.

Four weeks later, Mr. B. had 'made much improvement', was 'allowed up for some few hours', and had apparently 'made a wonderful recovery'. Four months later again, however, Mr. B. was 'confined to bed' and was 'so feeble that he is scarcely able to stand and has now to be fed by an attendant three times daily'. He was soon incontinent of both urine and faeces, 'completely paralyzed in his lower extremities', and 'unable to move himself at all'.

Mr. B. remained in this state for several months, 'sinking slowly' and being 'fed by an attendant'. Twenty months after admission, however, he began to deteriorate more rapidly: he was 'sinking fast' and although 'he takes his milk and brandy still', it was apparent that 'nothing can be done for this man to prolong his life'. A few days later, just over twenty months after admission, at forty-eight years of age, Mr. B. died.

MR. C.: 'DEATH FROM GENERAL TUBERCULOSIS'

Mr. C. was a 21 year-old, single man who was transferred from a prison in the north of Ireland to the Central Criminal Lunatic Asylum in the mid-1890s. Mr. C. had been charged with 'manslaughter' and sentenced to be detained 'at the Lord Lieutenant's pleasure'. Admission notes record that Mr. C. was Protestant and able to read and write. On admission, Mr. C. was diagnosed as a 'congenital imbecile' with 'chronic mania with dementia'. The prison surgeon had described him as a 'quiet harmless lunatic' who had two previous admissions to his local asylum. On admission to the Central Criminal Lunatic Asylum, Mr. C. was 'quite unable to give an account of himself; has no notion of where he is, or for what reason he is here'. Three weeks after admission, there was little change, as Mr. C. 'wanders about the yard; takes no interest in anything; [and] is incoherent in his conversation'.

Three months after admission, Mr. C. was in 'delicate health, and takes his food sparingly; does no work ... untidy and slovenly; bad circulation'. He remained in this 'delicate' state of health for the next three years, which saw a slow but steady deterioration in his self-care: three years after admission, Mr. C. was 'unable to do anything for himself' and 'has to be led up and down the yard by another patient for exercise every day'. He 'has to be dressed each morning and again undressed when going to bed ... The only coherent words that this patient speaks are "I want to go home" [and] "I don't know indeed."' Six years after admission, the clinical picture had changed little:

> A congenital imbecile, quite unable to give any account of himself or look after himself in any way. Spends his entire day biting his fingers and pulling at his teeth, nose and ears. His bodily health is fair. He requires constant supervision.

Soon, however, Mr. C.'s physical health began to deteriorate, as he 'lost weight during the month and vomits after eating'. Two months later, Mr. C. was 'confined to bed; temperature raised, night and morning; has lost very considerably in weight; and suffers from diarrhoea'. He was diagnosed with tuberculosis:

> Is suffering from general tuberculosis, but chiefly affecting the intestines. He has also a cough and undoubtedly his lungs are affected. He gets all kinds of medical extras in the way of milk, eggs, beef tea, port wine, etc.

Notwithstanding these interventions, Mr. C. was 'slowly dying' and was 'visited by his sister and brother'. Two weeks later, six years after admission, at twenty-seven years of age, Mr. C. died. The following day, an inquest was held and a 'verdict of death from general tuberculosis returned'.

TUBERCULOSIS IN THE ASYLUM

Tuberculosis was a significant problem in the Central Criminal Lunatic Asylum and most Irish district asylums at the end of the nineteenth century. One of the key contributors to the problem was the chronically over-crowded state of the newly-built institutions. In 1893, the Inspectors of Lunatics (Ireland) expressed concern:

> The accommodation in District Asylums in this country still continues quite inadequate to supply the wants of the insane population. We have again to repeat the statement made in former reports that the overcrowding is rapidly increasing, and that the necessity for further accommodation is becoming more and more urgent.[11]

One of the most worrying consequences of the over-crowding was the high mortality rate: in 1892, 995 patients died in Irish asylums, which, according to the Inspectors, 'gave a proportion per cent to daily average number resident of 8.3%'; i.e. the number of asylum deaths each year was 8.3 per cent of the average daily population of the asylums. The most common cause of death was 'consumption' (tuberculosis) (26 per cent), followed by 'general debility and old age' (13 per cent) (see Table 10.1).

TABLE 10.1: CAUSES OF DEATH IN IRISH DISTRICT ASYLUMS, 1892.

Category	Cause of Death	Males (n)	Females (n)	Total (n)	Percentage
Cerebral and spinal affections	Apoplexy and paralysis	25	19	44	4 %
	Epilepsy and convulsions	47	25	72	7 %
	General paralysis of the insane	19	2	21	2 %
	Exhaustion after mania or melancholia	38	33	71	7 %
	Organic disease	39	21	60	6 %
	Tumours	1	–	1	0.1 %
Thoracic disease	Consumption	113	146	259	26 %
	Inflammation of lungs and membrane	45	72	117	12 %
	Other pulmonary diseases	16	12	28	3 %
	Diseases of heart and arteries	28	22	50	5 %
Abdominal affections	Inflammation of stomach	1	3	4	0.4 %
	Intestines and peritoneum	7	8	15	1.5 %
	Diseases of liver, kidney, etc.	16	9	25	2.5%
	Dysentry and diarrhoea	29	32	61	6 %
Other	Fever and erysipelas	7	4	11	1 %
	Cancer	10	5	15	1.5 %
	General debility and old age	51	76	127	13 %
	Suicide	2	1	3	0.3 %
	Accident	1	1	2	0.2 %
	Diseases of bones	1	7	8	1 %
	Myxoedema	1	–	1	0.1 %
Total		497	498	995	100 %

The problem of tuberculosis was especially acute in the Richmond Asylum in Grangegorman, Dublin (now known as St. Brendan's Hospital), which was established in 1815, to help address the unmet needs of the mentally ill, especially the destitute mentally ill, in nineteenth-century Dublin.[12] The Richmond is particularly interesting because it was one of the earliest asylums to open during this period; was one of the largest residential institutions of any kind in nineteenth-century Ireland; and, arguably, served as a model for the development and management of other psychiatric institutions throughout the remainder of the century.[13]

On 21 November 1907, the medical superintendent of the Richmond, Dr. Conolly Norman, drew the attention of Richmond Asylum Joint Committee to the problems presented by tuberculosis:

> I believe the desirability of isolation as far as possible in cases of pulmonary consumption will now be generally recognised … The present, therefore, seems to be a particularly suitable time to again draw attention to the great prevalence among our patients of tuberculosis consumption and the need that exists for some special provision for isolating sufferers from this disease. No large scheme of new construction or re-arrangement ought to be considered without a special view to this topic.[14]

Earlier that year, at a meeting of the Richmond Visiting Committee (9 May 1907), Dr. Conolly Norman reported that a nurse 'who has recently been appointed, has contracted very serious and acute lung trouble' and, despite medical intervention, 'died of acute tubercular consumption on May 26th'.[15] At this time, 'consumption' (pulmonary tuberculosis) was a common cause of death in all sectors of the Irish population, accounting for almost 16 per cent of all deaths[16] and over 25 per cent of deaths in asylums;[17] similar problems were reported in asylums in other countries.[18]

Notwithstanding the concerns of Dr. Conolly Norman and others, tuberculosis was to remain a significant problem in Irish asylums well into the twentieth century. For example, some three decades after Dr. Conolly Norman's expressions of concern at the Richmond, tuberculosis still presented the largest single medical problem in Ballinasloe Mental Hospital, another large psychiatric institution in the West of Ireland which, in 1939, had some 1,887 inpatients.[19] In that year, the Inspector of Mental Hospitals summarised the tuberculosis problem in Ballinasloe in stark terms:

> One hundred and twenty-two patients died during the year, of

this number 36 died of Pulmonary Tuberculosis, and six from General Tuberculosis. This is rather a high percentage of deaths from tuberculosis, and can scarcely be regarded as altogether unconnected with the overcrowded state of the institution.[20]

Segregation, as recommended by Dr. Conolly Norman in 1907, remained an important element in the institutional management of tuberculosis and, in February 1940, the Committee of Management at Ballinasloe 'agreed that chronic patients would occupy the cream buildings, TB patients in the TB block, and new and recent admissions in the Admission Hospital'.[21] It was to be several more years, however, before the problem of tuberculosis began to decline.

TREATMENT FOR TUBERCULOSIS

One key perpetuators of the problem of tuberculosis in Irish asylums was the paucity of effective treatments. The cases presented in this chapter provide some guidance on treatment strategies in the late 1890s: Mr. A, received 'extra diet, milk, butter, stout'; Mr. B. received 'digitalis, liquid strychnine, whiskey, milk, beef tea' and 'brandy'; while Mr. C. received 'all kinds of medical extras in the way of milk, eggs, beef tea, port wine, etc.'. The role of enhanced nutrition as a medicinal measure has a lengthy history and the dietary 'medical extras' provided in the Central Criminal Lunatic Asylum were aimed at enhancing the general strength and wellbeing of all patients with physical illnesses, including those with tuberculosis.

Mr. B. also received additional, specific treatments, in the form of digitalis and strychnine. Both of these medications were used for a range of purposes throughout the nineteenth century: digitalis was commonly given for 'weak heart', 'shock' and irregular heartbeat;[22] while strychnine was commonly given for 'shock', poor muscle tone, reduced appetite and weak bladder, amongst other indications.[23] Dr. William Hallaran, in his 1810 textbook, had written especially approvingly of digitalis, which he believed acted by 'restraining the inordinate action of the heart and arteries' and demonstrated unrivalled 'merits as an anti-maniacal remedy, on as high a scale as can well belong to any one subject of materia medica'. Dosage was, however, a significant problem, and it was not until the work of Dr. William Withering (1741–1799) that details regarding standardised preparations and dose-response characteristics were established in order to advance the safe and effective use of digitalis.

While it is exceedingly difficult to establish the extent to which these medications benefited or harmed patients at this time, it is reasonable to suggest that there were significant risks associated with their use, owing not least to difficulties establishing and administering appropriate doses, and establishing precise diagnoses in the first instance. Notwithstanding these concerns, clinical records note that Mr. B. 'made a wonderful recovery' following his treatment with 'digitalis, liquid strychnine, whiskey, milk, beef tea' and 'brandy', although four months later he was again 'confined to bed' and 'completely paralyzed in his lower extremities'. This time, Mr. B. continued to decline until it was apparent that 'nothing can be done for this man to prolong his life' and a few days later Mr. B. died at the age of forty-eight, apparently of tuberculosis.

DIAGNOSTIC CHALLENGES

The case of Mr. B. highlights not only the dietary and medicinal treatments used for tuberculosis in the nineteenth-century asylum but also the diagnostic challenges associated with physical illness in this setting. Mr. B.'s clinical notes record quite confidently that 'his lungs are attacked by tubercule bacilli'. This diagnosis was, however, based purely on symptoms and external physical examination, and, notwithstanding the prevalence of tuberculosis in this asylum and others, alternative explanations of Mr. B.'s symptoms appear entirely possible. Syphilis, for example, was a significant problem in asylums throughout Ireland and elsewhere at this time: in Paris, 'general paralysis of the insane' (a form of advanced syphilis affecting the brain, see below) accounted for 30.5 per cent of voluntary and 17.4 per cent of involuntary male admissions to the Sainte-Anne Asylum between 1876 and 1914.[24]

Syphilis results from infection with Treponema pallidum, and can be present from birth ('congenital syphilis'). Sir Jonathan Hutchinson (1828–1913), a British surgeon and venereologist, associated a specific triad of signs with congenital syphilis: 'Hutchinson's teeth', interstitial keratitis (inflammation of the cornea in the eye) and eighth-nerve deafness. More generally, congenital syphilis is associated with stillbirth, failure to thrive, mucous membrane lesions and nasal infections; at later stages, there may be facial lesions (gumma, granulomata), abnormalities of long bones, 'sabre' tibia, 'Hutchinson's teeth' (small, widely-spaced teeth with notches on biting surfaces) and central nervous system lesions (resulting in protean psychiatric symptoms).[25]

Syphilis may also be acquired during life, through close sexual contact, and this results, initially, in hard ulceration (chancre) at the site of inoculation and, four to ten weeks later, characteristic skin lesions (e.g. brown maculopapular rash) and 'snail-track' ulceration of mucous membranes, along with generalised symptoms such as high temperature and arthralgia (joint pain). If syphilis progresses to the more advanced, tertiary stages it may affect the brain (neurosyphilis), resulting in a range of possible clinical syndromes including 'general paralysis of the insane' (GPI). GPI is characterised by progressive dementia, tremor, brisk reflexes, Argyll Robertson pupils (which do not react to light) and, in some cases, epileptic seizures.[26]

Clinical recognition of GPI was a gradual process which gathered pace as the nineteenth century progressed, as GPI was increasingly associated with certain forms of mental illness. This increasing understanding of both GPI and syphilis was one of the outstanding innovations of the late nineteenth century and had considerable implications for the medical diagnosis of mental illness at this time. More detailed consideration of the historical emergence of GPI and syphilis is beyond the scope of the present chapter, which focuses primarily on tuberculosis. Further information on syphilis in nineteenth-century Ireland, with particular focus on forensic complications of neurosyphilis, is provided by Kelly.[27]

Neurospyhilis is associated with myriad psychiatric symptoms including impaired judgement, personality change, delusions of grandeur (10-20 per cent), decreased self-care and dementia.[28] Patients with tertiary neurosyphilis also have a high mortality, with many dying within three years of diagnosis. While tertiary neurosyphilis is relatively uncommon today, it was quite common in the nineteenth century, and presented real problems in the over-crowded, unsanitary asylums of late nineteenth-century Ireland.[29]

In retrospect, many features of Mr. B.'s clinical presentation are suggestive of syphilis in general and neurosyphilis in particular; there was evidence of arthralgia ('shooting pains'), brisk reflexes ('knee jerk was greatly increased'), Argyll Robertson pupils ('pupil reacted to accommodation, but not to light') and myriad, progressive psychiatric symptoms ('dementia … melancholia with a suicidal tendency and loss of memory'). Mr. B.'s deteriorating physical and mental course ('completely paralyzed'; 'unable to move himself at all'; 'sinking fast') are also consistent with the outcome of advanced syphilis in the late nineteenth century, which often resulted in death.

Notwithstanding the careful clinical description of Mr. B.'s psychiatric and physical symptoms, it is readily apparent that accurate diagnosis of physical illnesses was a challenging task in the nineteenth-century asylum. There were no reliable laboratory tests: in the case of syphilis, for example, a diagnostic test was not developed until 1906, when August Paul von Wasserman (a German bacteriologist, 1866–1925) introduced his complement-fixation test. As a result, there was no definitive method for diagnosing syphilis, or, indeed, tuberculosis, when Mr. B. was admitted to the Central Criminal Lunatic Asylum in the late 1890s. Any diagnostic speculation was based on external clinical examination and ultimately, in many cases, post-mortem examination.

It is not clear whether or not making a distinction between tuberculosis and syphilis would have affected the ultimate clinical outcome in a case such as that of Mr. B. Such a distinction would probably, at the very least, have affected treatment choices: whereas Mr. B.'s apparent tuberculosis was treated with digitalis and strychnine, it is likely that a diagnosis of syphilis would have resulted in treatment with blood-letting, mercury and/or potassium iodide. Throughout the nineteenth century, standard treatments for syphilis included rigorous blood-letting, followed by the administration of mercury, the therapeutic effects of which were thought to be mediated by salivation.[30] As the nineteenth century progressed, potassium iodide replaced mercury as the treatment of choice and there is clear evidence that both mercury and potassium iodide were being used at the Central Criminal Lunatic Asylum in the late 1890s, when Mr. B. was a patient there.[31]

CONCLUSION

It is readily apparent that the lives and ultimate fates of the three individuals whose cases are outlined in this chapter were shaped by a variety of factors, some of which were substantially out of their control, including their alleged offending behaviours, the decisions to detain them in the Central Criminal Lunatic Asylum, their mental illnesses (if any), their physical illnesses (most commonly infectious illnesses such as tuberculosis), the role of the asylum environment in alleviating or exacerbating their mental and physical health problems, and the paucity of discharge options following periods of detention in the Central Criminal Lunatic Asylum.

In historical and epidemiological terms, the role of the asylum in structuring the distribution of tuberculosis in the Irish population merits further research and careful consideration. Tuberculosis was, and still is, a potentially fatal illness that is strongly associated with poverty, social disengagement and – in one form or other – institutional detention.[32] Farmer has presented analogous arguments in relation to the spread of HIV/AIDS in Haiti today and speaks of 'structural violence', which is the sum of the ways in which the distributions and impacts of specific illnesses are determined, at least in part, by political, economic and social forces that shape both the landscape of risk for developing the illnesses and the contexts in which health-care is provided.[33] For centuries, tuberculosis has been such an illness, strongly associated with poverty, exclusion and lives spent in institutions. The three lives outlined in this chapter bear eloquent witness to this fact and demonstrate many of the features of a nineteenth-century form of 'structural violence' resulting from a complex combination of societal, judicial, psychiatric and institutional forces that determined their ultimate fates.

A similar argument, again rooted in the concept of structural violence, can be made more specifically in relation to the effects of mental illnesses, such as schizophrenia, on the life of the individual patient and their family. According to this paradigm, despite growing evidence of a substantial biological basis for many mental illnesses, there is also strong evidence that aetiology, clinical features, treatment and outcome are also substantially related to a range of social, economic and political factors. These factors include living in lower socio-economic groups (associated with earlier age at presentation, longer duration of untreated illness and poor outcome), higher rates of homelessness and imprisonment, and the effects of migration, possibly mediated through forced dispersal in host countries and difficulties establishing social capital in smaller migrant groups. The summative effects of these social, economic and political factors, combined with the enduring stigma of mental illness, represent a form of 'structural violence' which greatly amplifies the effects of illnesses such as schizophrenia in the lives of sufferers and their families, and results in their systematic exclusion from full participation in civic and social life.[34]

The three individuals whose cases are presented in this chapter were also subject to this powerful and enduring force: the stigmatising and socially-exclusionary effects of mental illness, even (or perhaps especially) in late nineteenth-century Ireland. This force was combined with their alleged offending behaviour, physical ill-health and lengthy detentions in over-crowded, unsanitary institutions, to produce a toxic combination of circumstances that resulted, inevitably, in their deaths. While their deaths can, on the surface, be attributed to tuberculosis or other physical illnesses, the broader circumstances surrounding their lives and deaths involve a range of adverse and (arguably) disproportionately punitive societal, political and structural forces over which they had little or no control.

NOTES

1. W.S. Hallaran, *An Enquiry into the Causes producing the Extraordinary Addition to the Number of Insane together with Extended Observations on the Cure of Insanity with hints as to the Better Management of Public Asylums for Insane Persons* (Cork: Edwards and Savage, 1810), p.10.
2. E. Shorter, *A History of Psychiatry: From the Era of the Asylum to the Age of Prozac* (New York: John Wiley and Sons, 1997), p.2; Psychiatrist, 'Insanity in Ireland', The Bell, 7 (1944): 303–10: p.304.
3. Cited in Shorter, E., *A History of Psychiatry: From the Era of the Asylum to the Age of Prozac* (New York: John Wiley and Sons, 1997), pp.1–2.
4. E. Shorter, *A History of Psychiatry: From the Era of the Asylum to the Age of Prozac* (New York: John Wiley and Sons, 1997), p.47.
5. D. Walsh, Daly, A., *Mental Illness in Ireland 1750–2002: Reflections on the Rise and Fall of Institutional Care* (Dublin: Health Research Board, 2004), p.21; Williamson, A., 'The Beginnings of State Care for the Mentally Ill in Ireland', *Economic and Social Review*, 10 (1970): 280–91; Kelly, B.D., 'Mental Health Law in Ireland, 1821–1902: Building the Asylums', *Medico-Legal Journal* 2008, 76 (2008): 19–25.
6. Anonymous, 'Increase in Insanity', *American Journal of Insanity*, 18, (1861), p.95; Tuke, D.H. 'Increase of Insanity in Ireland', *Journal of Mental Science*, 40 (1894): 549–58; Torrey, E.F., Miller, J. *The Invisible Plague: The Rise of Mental Illness from 1750 to the Present* (New Jersey: Rutgers University Press, 2001).
7. B. D. Kelly, 'Mental Health Law in Ireland, 1821–1902: dealing with the "increase of insanity in Ireland"', *Medico-Legal Journal*, 76 (2008): 26–33.
8. Acknowledgements: I am very grateful for the assistance and encouragement of Professor Harry Kennedy of Trinity College Dublin and the National Forensic Psychiatry Service, Dublin, Ireland; Quotations from the Minutes of the Proceedings of the Committee of Management of Ballinasloe District Lunatic Asylum and the Minutes of the Meeting of the Commissioner Administering the Affairs of the Ballinasloe Mental Hospital are taken from the Minute Books in the archives at St. Brigid's Hospital, Ballinasloe, Co. Galway. I am deeply grateful to Mr. John Dair, Mr. Adrian Ahern and Dr. Kieran Power for their cooperation and assistance; I am very grateful for the assistance of Mr. Gerry Devine of the Health Service Executive, Dublin and Dr. Richard Duffy of the Mater Misericordiae University Hospital, Dublin.
9. C. Smith, 'The Central Mental Hospital, Dundrum, Dublin' in R. Bluglass and P. Bowden (eds), *Principles and Practice of Forensic Psychiatry* (Edinburgh: Churchill Livingstone, 1990), pp.1351–3.
10. Pauline M. Prior, *Madness and Murder: Gender, Crime and Mental Disorder in Nineteenth-Century Ireland* (Dublin and Portland, OR: Irish Academic Press, 2008); Smith, C. 'The Central Mental Hospital, Dundrum, Dublin' in R. Bluglass and P. Bowden (eds), *Principles and Practice of Forensic Psychiatry* (Edinburgh: Churchill Livingstone, 1990), pp.1351–3.
11. *The Forty-Second Asylums Report for 1892*, HC 1893–94 (C. 7125) xlvi. 369, p.7.
12. J. Reynolds, *Grangegorman: Psychiatric Care in Dublin Since 1815* (Dublin: Institute of Public Administration in association with Eastern Health Board, 1992).
13. B.D. Kelly, 'One Hundred Years Ago: the Richmond Asylum, Dublin in 1907', *Irish Journal of Psychological Medicine*, 24 (2007): 108–14.
14 J. Conolly-Norman, *Richmond Asylum Joint Committee Minutes* (Dublin: Richmond Asylum, 1907), p.540.

15. Ibid., p.308.
16 G. Jones, 'The Campaign Against Tuberculosis in Ireland, 1899–1914', in E. Malcolm and G. Jones (eds), *Medicine, Disease and the State in Ireland, 1650–1940* (Cork: Cork University Press, 1999), pp.158–76.
17. M. Finnane, *Insanity and the Insane in Post-Famine Ireland* (London: Croon Helm, 1981).
18. P. McCandless, 'Curative asylum, custodial hospital: the South Carolina Lunatic Asylum and State Hospital, 1828–1920', in R. Porter and D. Wright (eds), *The Confinement of the Insane: International Perspectives, 1800–1965* (Cambridge: Cambridge University Press, 2003), pp.173–92.
19. Committee of Management of Ballinasloe Mental Hospital. *Minutes of the Proceedings of the Committee of Management of Ballinasloe Mental Hospital* (Ballinasloe: Ballinasloe Mental Hospital), 14 August 1939.
20. Inspector of Mental Hospitals (28 November 1939), quoted in ibid., 8 April 1940.
21. Ibid., 12 February 1940.
22. J.K. Aronson, *An Account of the Foxglove and Its Medical Uses, 1785–1985: Incorporating a Facsimile of William Withering's 'An Account of the Foxglove and Some of Its Uses'* (1785) (Oxford: Oxford University Press, 1985).
23. J. Buckingham, *Bitter Nemesis: The Intimate History of Strychnine* (Boca Raton, FL: CRC Press/Taylor and Francis Group, 2008).
24. In relation to Ireland, see B.D. Kelly, 'Syphilis, Psychiatry and Offending Behaviour: Clinical Cases from Nineteenth-Century Ireland', *Irish Journal of Medical Science*, 178 (2009): 73–7. In relation to France, see Prestwich, P.E., 'Family Strategies and Medical Power: "Voluntary" Committal in a Parisian Asylum, 1876–1914', in R. Porter and D. Wright (eds), *The Confinement of the Insane: International Perspectives, 1800–1965* (Cambridge: Cambridge University Press, 2003), pp.79–99. In relation to Germany, see Dörries, A., Beddies, T. 'The Wittenauer Heilstätten in Berlin: a Case Record Study of Psychiatric Patients in Germany, 1919–1960', in R. Porter and D. Wright (eds), *The Confinement of the Insane: International Perspectives, 1800–1965* (Cambridge: Cambridge University Press, 2003), pp.149–72.
25. M.J.G. Farthing, Jeffries, D.J., Parkin, J.M., 'Infectious Diseases, Tropical Medicine and Sexually Transmitted Diseases', in P. Kumar and M. Clark (eds), *Clinical Medicine*, 3rd edition, (London: Bailliere Tindall, 1994), pp.1–105.
26. C.R.A. Clarke, (1994) 'Neurological Diseases and Diseases of Voluntary Muscle', in P. Kumar and M. Clark (eds), *Clinical Medicine*, pp.871–955; Ances, B.M., Shelhaus, R., Brown, M.J., Rios, O.V., Herman, S.T., French. J.A. 'Neurosyphilis and Status Epilepticus: Case Report and Literature Review', *Epilepsy Research*, 59 (2004): 67–70; Gürses, C., Kürtüncü, M., Jirsch, J., Yeşilot, N., Hanağasi, H., Bebek, N., Baykan, B., Emre, M., Gökyiğit, A., Andermann, F. 'Neurosyphilis Presenting with Status Epilepticus', *Epileptic Disorders*, 9 (2007): 51–6.
27. B.D. Kelly, 'Syphilis, Psychiatry and Offending Behaviour: Clinical Cases from Nineteenth-Century Ireland', *Irish Journal of Medical Science*, 178 (2009): 73–7.
28. H.I. Kaplan, Saddock, B.J., *Concise Textbook of Clinical Psychiatry* (Baltimore: Williams & Wilkins, 1996).
29. B.D. Kelly, 'Syphilis, Psychiatry and Offending Behaviour: Clinical Cases from Nineteenth-Century Ireland', *Irish Journal of Medical Science*, 178 (2009): 73–7.
30. J.F. Fleetwood, *The History of Medicine in Ireland*, 2nd edition, (Dublin: Skellig Press, 1983); Guthrie, D., *A History of Medicine* (London: Nelson, 1945), pp.383–4; Merrit, H.H., Adams, R., Solomon, H.C., *Neurosyphilis* (Oxford: Oxford University Press, 1946); Brown, E.M., 'Why Wagner-Jauregg Won the Nobel Prize for Discovering Malaria Therapy for General Paralysis of the Insane', *History of Psychiatry*, 11 (2000): 371–82.
31. B.D. Kelly, 'Murder, Mercury and Mental Illness: Infanticide in Nineteenth-Century Ireland', *Irish Journal of Medical Science*, 176 (2007): 149–52.
32. S. Keshavjee, Becerra, M.C., 'Disintegrating Health Services and Resurgent Tuberculosis in Post-Soviet Tajikistan: An Example of Structural Violence', *Journal of the American Medical Association*, 283 (2000), p.1201.
33. P. Farmer, 'Ethnography, Social Analysis, and the Prevention of Sexually Transmitted HIV Infections among Poor Women in Haiti', in: M.C. Inhorn and P.J. Brown (eds), *An Anthropology of Infectious Disease* (Amsterdam: Gordon and Breach 1997), pp.413–18; Farmer, P., 'Pathologies of Power: Rethinking Health and Human Rights', *American Journal of Public Health*, 89 (1999): 1486–96; Farmer, P., *Pathologies of Power* (Berkeley: University of California Press, 2003).

34 B.D. Kelly, 'Structural Violence and Schizophrenia', *Social Science and Medicine*, 61 (2005): 721–30; Kelly, B.D. 'The Power Gap: Freedom, Power and Mental Illness', *Social Science and Medicine*, 63 (2006): 2118–28.

11

Overseeing the Irish Asylums: the Inspectorate in Lunacy, 1845–1921

Pauline M. Prior

The Inspectorate in Lunacy was initially situated within the prison system in Ireland, but became an organisation in its own right in 1846, when an Office of Lunacy was set up at Dublin Castle.[1] The first inspector was Dr. Francis White, a man of rich experience as a medical doctor and as an inspector of health services. He worked as the inspector of asylums within the prison inspectorate from 1841, moving to his new office in 1846.[2] He was joined in 1847 by Dr. John Nugent, a man who was well known for his liberal ideas, having been the personal travelling physician to Daniel O'Connell and an 'original member of the Reform Club'.[3] After the tragic death of Dr. Francis White in 1857, due to an accident on one of his tours of inspection,[4] Dr. George William Hatchell joined Dr. Nugent, with whom he worked for a further thirty years (until 1889). These three men were highly influential in guiding the direction of lunacy policy in the second half of the nineteenth century as the number of asylums grew and lay managers were replaced by doctors. In 1890, they were replaced by Dr. George Plunkett O'Farrell and Dr. E. Maziere Courtenay (former inspector of reform schools), who brought the Inspectorate into the first decade of the twentieth century (see Table 11.3).[5] This was a very different era. By then, the asylum system had expanded beyond all expectations, both in terms of the size and number of institutions. It was a costly system, which appeared to have become the permanent refuge for a significant proportion of the population. The early hopes of Dr. Francis White and his medical colleagues in the mid century, that the asylums would function as temporary resting places where those with mental disorders would be cured before returning home safely, had not been fulfilled. By the end of the first decade of the twentieth century, there were two new inspectors in position – Dr. Thomas I.

Considine and Dr. William R. Dawson. They found themselves over-seeing and inspecting over-crowded institutions in need of a huge injection of money to bring them up to a basic standard of care provision. In 1921, Drs Considine and Dawson saw the Irish mental health service split into two distinct administrative systems within the new politically divided Ireland.[6]

THE EARLY YEARS

At the time of the establishment of the Inspectorate in the 1840s, there were major problems facing policy makers at Dublin Castle. The number of publicly funded asylums in Ireland had increased from two in 1817 (the Richmond, Dublin and the Cork Asylum) to eleven in 1845, following the building of nine District Asylums. At the same time, the number of private asylums had increased from one in 1817 (St. Patrick's/Swift's Hospital, Dublin) to fourteen in 1845.[7] In the first report of the Inspectorate, we read that the total number of people with mental disorders in District Asylums in 1845 was 2,555, with an additional 2,957 waiting for admission.[8] In other words, the system, as it stood, catered for under half of the population in need of care. This was quite shocking, as the network of district asylums set up in the first half of the century was intended to cater for the needs of the country as a whole. A closer look at the statistics, on those waiting for asylum admission in 1845, shows that the local workhouses bore the main burden of care. It housed almost 2,000 people with mental disorders (see Table 11.1).

TABLE 11.1: LOCATION OF PEOPLE AWAITING ADMISSION TO DISTRICT ASYLUMS, 1845.

In local asylums	441
In gaols	391
In union workhouses	1,921
Refused admission to District Asylum (lack of room)	231
Total	2,957

Source: *1st Asylums Report*, p.8. HC 1846 (736) xxii. 409.

In this chapter, we will discuss two of the main problems that dominated the agenda of the Inspectorate. The first was the ever growing demand for places on a system that was expanding but never seemed adequate to meet the needs of the population. The second was the ongoing debate on the cost of the asylum system.

Within this context, we will look at the approach of the Inspectorate to the protection of patients from neglect and abuse. These were not the only issues raised in the reports of the inspectors, but they give a flavour of how they approached their work. As might be expected, not everyone agreed with the views of the inspectors, particularly those whose work was being questioned by them. In the bigger asylums, the Boards of Governors, who represented the local elite from landowning classes and churches, often found themselves at loggerheads with the Inspectorate. In some cases, differences of opinion between the Inspectorate and the local interests reached fever pitch, as illustrated elsewhere in this book in the legal dispute over the appointment of chaplains at the Belfast Asylum.

OVERCROWDING DUE TO AN INCREASING DEMAND FOR ASYLUM CARE

Early discussions on the provision of a network of District Asylums in Ireland were based on the assumption that this would end the problem of the misplacement of people with mental disorders in prisons and workhouses. It was also hoped that it would solve the problem of vagrancy caused by 'lunatics wandering at large'. The asylums built in the first half of the nineteenth century had a capacity for 100-150 patients, as it was expected that people would be cured and would move back home after treatment in the asylum.[9] What the planners failed to anticipate was the gradual build-up of patients who did not improve and therefore were not discharged. They were not prepared for a large number of chronic/long-stay patients. In his first report, in 1846, Dr. Francis White was happy to point out that statistics on Irish asylums were very good, when compared with other countries. Based on data from ten Irish District Asylums, twenty-three English asylums, seven Scottish asylums and five American asylums, Ireland had the best recovery rate (at 48.33 per cent) and the second lowest mortality rate (at 8.7 per cent).[10] Even though these figures were good in international terms, they showed that a build-up of long-stay patients was inevitable.

The problem of demand exceeding supply was highlighted in the 1857 report. It pointed out that even after the building of the first nine district asylums in the 1820s and 1830s – at Armagh, Belfast, Londonderry, Carlow, Ballinasloe, Limerick, Clonmel, Maryborough and Waterford – there was still a shortage of beds.

These asylums, expected to be sufficient for the general exigencies of the country, and built for an aggregate of 980 patients, at a cost of £209,085.0.4, were soon found too limited, so much so that in the course of a few years, by interior re-arrangements and appropriations, they were occupied by 1,930 inmates, or about twice the number for which they had been constructed.[11]

In the 1850s, the inspectors attributed the increase in numbers looking for asylum admission to the high quality of the care and treatment available within these institutions.

> With the growing facilities afforded for the treatment of mental disease in its acute forms, and the refuge which it was felt that asylums extended to those long affected with insanity, the numerous cases hitherto latent among the lower classes attracted notice, and the demand upon these institutions increased so steadily that it became necessary to reform districts … and … to erect asylums at Kilkenny, Killarney, Omagh, Sligo, Dublin and Mullingar, for a total of 1,400 lunatics.[12]

The second wave of asylum building, in the mid-century, was aimed at solving the problem of overcrowding caused by the ever increasing demand for admission and the failure to discharge people quickly. The new asylums were much larger than those built in the first half of the century. For example, there was accommodation for 500 patients in Cork Asylum, for 250 in both Killarney and Sligo, and for 300 in both Omagh and Mullingar. All were planned in the 1840s, when Dr. Francis White was the chief inspector, and opened in the 1850s and 1860s.[13]

At that time, the discussion though focused on the need for buildings to accommodate acute cases, also acknowledged the need to house chronic patients, some of whom might require less expensive care. As Kelly observes, there was provision in the 1845 Act (Section 15) to allow for the establishment of any type of asylum in each province, but this power was not used to create less expensive institutions. Therefore, the issue of caring from chronic patients continued to be highlighted by the inspectors.[14] In 1859, the newly appointed inspector, Dr. William J. Hatchell, who was very concerned about the cost of the asylum system, wrote in his report:

> We may … remark that for practical utility, as well as fiscal advantages, the insane, as a body, may be classified under two heads with respect to asylum accommodation; in the first, we would include urgent and curable cases, as well as those,

though not admitting any reasonable hope of recovery, still require particular treatment, whether from dangerous tendencies, violence or peculiarity of habits; in the second, the idiotic, the great majority of epileptics, and the demented, whose mental and corporeal powers, decline pari passu, but who cannot be properly or efficiently looked after except in establishments solely devoted to their use. For the former, a more expensive organization, both in regard to staff, building and several appliances, is required; for the latter, plain, airy, and commodious dwellings, with ample means of occupation both in and out of doors, would be sufficient, and, at the same time, provided at a much more moderate expense.[15]

The argument, put forward here by Dr. Hatchell, backed up by his colleague, Dr. Nugent, that patients suffering from epilepsy, dementia and intellectual disabilities would be more appropriately and most cheaply cared for in separate institutions, continued to be aired frequently throughout the second half of the nineteenth century. In 1864, 'one auxiliary establishment' was opened at Clonmel and was filled very quickly with 147 people, described as 'lunatics belonging to the district'.[16] However, there is no evidence that the idea was taken seriously by other districts, leading Dr. Nugent and Dr. Hatchell to repeat their recommendation in 1873. In support of their argument, they pointed out the example set in England, where auxiliary asylums were in use.

In England, but particularly in London and the metropolitan counties, a similar state of things existed; which, within the last few years, has been materially obviated by the erection of intermediate institutions, between asylums and union workhouses, into which a large percentage of hopeless cases find admission; at the same time, however, though with a lesser number of attendants, a less expensive staff, and an organization not so complex.[17]

The presence of chronic and low-risk patients in overcrowded district asylums was acknowledged in Section 9 of the 1875 Act, which allowed for the legal transfer of these patients to workhouses.[18] However, this was not regarded as a satisfactory solution by either the asylums or the workhouses, and in 1898, Section 76 of the Local Government (Ireland) Act authorised asylums to open auxiliary asylums for patients who were not deemed to present a danger to themselves or to others.[19] By the early twentieth century, two auxiliary asylums were opened – one at Youghal, to take patients from Cork District Asylum, and one at Portrane – to take patients from the Richmond Asylum.[20]

Alongside the debate on the need for accommodation for chronic and harmless patients was one that centred on the question of insanity itself. Was it increasing in Ireland? A special report on the 'alleged increasing prevalence of insanity' was presented in 1894 to the chief secretary of Ireland, John Morley, by the inspectors, Dr. George. P. O'Farrell and Dr. E. Maziere Courtenay. In this report, they concluded that elements of both an increase in insanity and an increase in the demand for care were contributing to the ongoing problem of overcrowding.[21] Almost ten years later, the issue was still under scrutiny and the findings of the 1894 report were summarised by a Dr. J. B. Dougherty, in another special report in 1906 on the 'alleged increase in insanity'.[22]

- The increasing numbers in asylums (were) due to 'accumulation' (not a real increase in insanity).
- The yearly increase in admissions was mainly drawn from the ranks of the 'unregistered insane' as shown by 'the reduction in the number of lunatics and idiots at large, as given in the Census Returns'.
- That, in the light of the fact that the population of Ireland was decreasing, the annual increase in admissions and in the overall population in asylums pointed to some increase in insanity.[23]

In the 1894 report, the main factors said to be contributing to the 'development of occurring insanity' were – 'heredity and consanguineous marriages; innutritious dietary; the immoderate use of certain nerve stimulants and of alcohol; the mental strain and harassing anxieties following in the wake of acute agricultural depression experienced at that time'.[24] These causes were based on the opinions of the resident medical superintendents who had all studied the different reasons for admissions in their own asylums. Whether or not there had been an increase in any of these causes (except for the economic depression in agriculture) was not clear to anyone.

In 1906, the debate on whether or not insanity was increasing continued to rage. A survey by the inspectors showed that only seven (out of twenty-three) of the medical superintendents of district asylums believed that it was increasing, while the others either disagreed with the statement or gave no opinion on the matter to the Inspectorate. However, it was clear that the total number of people designated as insane in Ireland (including those who lived at home or were 'wandering at large') had been increasing steadily since 1851. Each census provided evidence of this increase, as outlined in Table 11.2.[25]

TABLE 11.2 : THE 'INSANE' IN IRELAND, 1851–1901.

Year	'At large'	In Asylums	In prison	In Workhouses	Total	General population	Insane per 10,000 pop
1851	4,635	3,436	186	1,623	9,880	6,552,385	15.2
1861	7,277	5,016	294	1,511	14,098	5,798,067	24.3
1871	6,490	7,551	7	2,457	16,505	5,412377	30.5
1881	5,491	9,443	–	3,479	18,413	5,174,836	35.6
1891	4,970	12,261	–	3,957	21,188	4,701,750	45.0
1901	3,868	17,350	–	3,832	25,050	4,458,775	56.2

Source: Table adapted from similar table, based on census data, in *Special Report on Increased Insanity*, p.9. HC 1906 (Cd. 3126) xxxix.1.

By the second decade of the twentieth century, the situation had changed somewhat. Numbers of mentally ill people in institutions continued to increase until 1914, after which time they began to decrease. According to the inspector's report for 1919, the average annual number of patients in care in the years from 1910 to 1914 was 24,815 (or 566 per 100,000 of population).[26] In the following period, from 1915 to 1919, the average had fallen slightly to 23,842 (or 546 per 100,000 of population). This happened in spite of the fact that the asylums had admitted 790 men (soldiers and sailors) who had fought in the First World War during this period. The only explanation offered by the inspectors that there had been a higher death rate in the asylums between 1915 and 1919.

However, this decrease in the population in institutional care for mental illness was only a short-term blip in a trend that continued upwards during the first half of the twentieth century. Though mental health services in Ireland after 1921 were under two distinct legal and administrative systems, the trend did not really change until the mid-1960s, when the process of de-institutionalisation began to make an impact in both Northern Ireland and the Republic of Ireland.[27] However, the high level of institutionalisation of people for mental health treatment in Ireland continued to be of concern throughout the twentieth century. Like the inspectors of lunacy in the nineteenth century, scholars disagreed as to whether or not this was due to a higher level of mental disorder among the Irish, or to a higher level of tolerance among the Irish for institution-based care. While some academics, such as American anthropologist Nancy Scheper Hughes, argue that there was something in the Irish culture that predisposed people to mental illness, others, such as Mark Finnane, Damian Brennan and Pauline Prior, argue that statistics reflect the high level of institutional provision rather than the incidence of mental illness.[28] According to this second argument, socio-economic and political factors helped to maintain the status quo and impeded the development of community-based mental health services which would have reduced the numbers of people in institution-based mental health care.

TABLE 11.3: INSPECTORS OF LUNATICS, 1850–1921.

Dr. Francis White	1846–1857 (died 1859)
Dr. John Nugent	1847–1890 (died 1899)
Dr. George William Hatchell	1857–1889 (died 1890)
Dr. George Plunkett O'Farrell	1890–1907
Dr. E. Maziere Courtenay	1890–circa 1911
Dr. Thomas I. Considine	1911–1921
Dr. William R. Dawson	1911–1921

THE COST OF THE ASYLUM SYSTEM

The Inspectorate was determined to keep the cost of the asylum system as low as possible, but it was clear from the beginning that institutional confinement was not cheap. As already discussed, early plans for district asylums had been based on projections of size and number that were soon found to be highly inaccurate, both in terms of the numbers of asylums needed and the demand for places in these asylums. As the century progressed, the size of the asylum system continued to grow beyond all expectations. It also became clear that the costs included not only those arising from the needs of patients for accommodation, food and medical treatment, but also those of the staff for accommodation, salaries and some type of superannuation.

As with workhouses, the costs of asylums were borne largely by the areas they served. Every annual report from the Inspectorate contained detailed information on expenditure in each asylum. Some expenditure was anticipated, such as accommodation, food and clothing for patients, and salaries, food and accommodation for staff. Others were not anticipated, such as the cost of long-term care of patients who were not 'cured', or of superannuation for staff. The need for a grant from central government funds for current costs based on a per capita cost was discussed many times but was not introduced until 1898 when the local Government (Ireland) Act (61 & 62 Vic. c. 37) was passed.

Early Costs

The 1845 Report of the Inspector General on asylums noted, with some satisfaction, that the 'industrial exertions' of the patients in 1844 had resulted in a gross profit of £1,881.4s.4d. However, as the total cost of running the asylums in that year was £28,904.12s.6d, with an average cost per patient of £14. 0s. 7d, 'patient industry' could not be regarded as a significant source of income.[29] While statistics like this are interesting, they are difficult to evaluate without knowledge of the overall cost of the system, including capital expenditure. A detailed examination of the substantial capital costs of the asylum system was presented in the 1857 Inspectorate report. These capital costs were covered in the first instance by central government, but they were later repaid by the local Grand Juries of the district covered by the asylum. The 1857 report gives the capital expenditure for each of the district asylums, with details of the repayments from each division of the district served. Only in rare cases were any of the costs borne by central government as was the case in the Cork Asylum.

> The Cork Asylum, commenced under an Order in Council, dated 26th June, 1846, was also completed in 1852, and cost, everything included, £85,828, having accommodation for 500 patients; but in consequence of the liberal remission of £6,013, and a further sum of £1,213 specially granted for improving the ventilation, water-closets &c; without charge to the ratepayers, making a total of £7,226 conceded by the Treasury, the amount to be repaid by the county and city has been reduced to £79,827, the former being assessed for £69,278, and the latter for £10,548.[30]

At this stage, in 1857, the total cost of establishing the asylum system was reckoned to be approximately £660,000, with 'a debt remaining to the Treasury of £340,000'.[31] Local ratepayers bore the brunt of the financial burden placed on each district, a burden which was sometimes uneven. As noted by the inspectors, ratepayers in poorer areas were disproportionately penalised.

The amount of accommodation in District Asylums, and the

expenses of erection allocated to each county (when two or more are associated), being based on the number of inhabitants, tells, unfortunately, against those counties, the population of which bears a marked numerical disproportion to the value of property in them. As a case in point, we adduce Leitrim, the population of which is about the same as that of the more fertile and richer County of Westmeath; the rateable property of the latter being £306,800, or £2. 16s. per head, while that of the former is but £121,000, or £1. 1s.7d. per head. A similar disadvantage takes place in regard to the current expenditure, but we think that satisfactory adjustment might be made so as to equalize the annual levies without loss to the Treasury or inconvenience to the district.[32]

The plea from the inspectors for a review of charges to poorer areas was not heard and the costs of asylum care remained the focus of debate and argument between local rate-payers and central government for many years. As asylums grew bigger and buildings needed constant upgrading, the question of who should fund repairs and improvements was not resolved. This led to building projects being delayed and to a deterioration in physical conditions in most of the publicly funded asylums.

From the questions raised by the Inspectorate, it is evident that current expenditure (expressed as the cost per patient) was the cause of more debate than that of capital expenditure (on buildings and equipment). One of the main arguments put forward by both the inspectors and medical staff was that there were many people in asylums who required only a low level of care due to the nature of their illnesses, i.e. illnesses that did not respond to medical treatment. Some of these, it was suggested, would be better placed in workhouses, which cost a great deal less to run. For example, in the inspectors report for 1858, we read:

> A great majority composed of the idiotic and hopelessly demented require nought beyond simple places of shelter, with a due supply of creature comforts in the way of food, raiment, and the means of healthful occupations, placed solely under the supervision of this department … We have already classified the insane poor under two general heads, viz., those requiring a special and more expensive mode of treatment, and those who, constituting the larger portion, can be supported in less complex buildings but with ample regard to their comfort and condition.[33]

An actual comparison of costs between workhouse and asylum care was put forward in the Inspectorate report in 1865.

> On an analysis of the expenditure hitherto incurred in the erection and furnishing of asylums, and the purchase of land attached to them, we believe that £7 would represent with tolerable accuracy the annual interest thereon for each patient, as against perhaps £1 for the ordinary pauper inmate of a union workhouse. The current yearly maintenance of a lunatic averages £20; that for a pauper, £8; consequently the total charge per annum on the ratepayer may be estimated at £27 and £9 for each, respectively.[34]

However, even though there seemed to be a general acceptance of the fact that asylums were very expensive to run and that some of the patients did not necessarily need to be there, the government was reluctant to sanction a wholesale transfer of people from the asylum to the workhouse or to build auxiliary asylums. The ever increasing burden on local ratepayers continued to be debated throughout the 1880s and 1890s and was partially solved by the Local Government (Ireland) Act 1898 (61 & 62 Vic. c. 37), at which time an agreed per capita grant was introduced for all patients in district asylums. As might be expected, this grant was not generous and it did not take very long for the costs of keeping a patient to exceed the per capita grant. However, it did relieve some of the financial burden on local rate payers.

TABLE 11.4: RECEIPTS FOR DISTRICT AND AUXILIARY ASYLUMS IN IRELAND, 1918–19.

Receipts				£	s.	d.
a) **From Public Funds**						
Local Rates				760,695	11	8
Government Capitation Grant				183,079	14	3
Gov. fees for criminal lunatics etc				15,788	2	5
b) **From Paying Patients**				25,886	13	9
c) **From Miscellaneous sources**						
Cash sales from farm/garden produce	£23,717	2s	5d			
Other receipts	£6,729	10s	11d	30,446	13	4
Total Receipts				£1,015,896	15	5

Source: *69th Asylums Report*, p.xvi. HC 1921 (Cmd. 1127) xv. 165.

In 1921, in the final report of the Inspectorate before Ireland acquired political independence, we get a detailed picture of income and expenditure in the asylum system (see Table 11.4).[35] What is clear from this table is the fact that, while the capitation grant was significant (approximately £183,000), it was less than a quarter of the amount derived from local rates (approximately £760,000). Of interest also is the income from the farm and garden (approximately £24,000) which was almost as much as that derived from private patient fees (approximately £26,000). However, when the expenditure on the farm and garden is examined more closely (in Table 11.5), it becomes obvious that these enterprises are running at a loss, as the expenditure was approximately £61,000 (indicating a loss of approximately £37,000).

In the same report in 1921, the expenditure from all the asylums was also itemised. Of interest here is the expenditure on medicines and surgical appliances (see Table 11.5).[36] In spite of the arguments in the reports of the inspectors, that the high cost of asylum care could be attributed to the specialist attention and treatment received by the patients, the expenditure on medicines and surgical appliances (approximately £5,000) was well below half of that spent on tobacco and snuff (approximately £12,500). However, though medicine did not feature largely in the care of mentally ill patients, the investment in specialist staff is obvious, with the highest level of expenditure going on wages and salaries (approximately £195,000). It would be wrong to assume that staff members were overpaid, as salaries for asylum staff were lower in Ireland than in England, a situation that led to disputes and strikes by nursing staff in the early twentieth century.[37]

TABLE 11.5: EXPENDITURE ON DISTRICT AND AUXILIARY ASYLUMS IN IRELAND, 1918–19.

Expenditure	£	s.	d.
Provisions, necessaries, and clothing	447,300	6	6
Medicines and surgical appliances	4,973	1	11
Tobacco and snuff	12,542	9	0
Salaries and wages	194,697	14	4
Superannuation	17,341	2	5
Furniture and bedding	33,046	17	7
Fuel and light	107,479	5	10
Farm and garden expenses	61,006	13	7
Repairs and alterations	20,444	9	2
Other expenses	40,224	0	7
Total cost of maintenance	939,056	0	11
Loan Repayments for capital charges (erection and equipment of buildings, purchase of land etc)	84,394	3	10
Total expenditure	**£1,023,450**	**4s.**	**9d.**

Source: *69th Asylums Report*, p.xvi. HC 1921 (Cmd. 1127) xv. 165.

The cost of institution-based mental health care continued to be a problem right up until the mid-twentieth century, by which time government policy in both parts of Ireland led to a reduction in patient numbers. In the early years of the Northern Ireland government, efforts were made to change the system of financing asylums/mental hospitals from a block grant (set at the level of the 1921 per capita grant) to a realistic per capita payment based on current costs. This did not happen immediately, but the thorny issue of funding was resolved successfully in 1948, when mental hospitals were absorbed into the general health-care system funded by central government. For the first time since they were built, asylums were no longer a burden on local rates.[38] Similarly, in the Republic of Ireland, the burden of paying for mental hospitals moved from the ratepayer to the taxpayer in the late 1940s, but the costs continued to rise until the patient population decreased in size in the late twentieth century.

PREVENTING ABUSE AND NEGLECT

The possibility that vulnerable people might be subject to abuse in closed institutions is now publicly acknowledged after a spate of highly publicised examples of such abuses in schools, care homes and hospitals. However, as this was not a publicly debated issue until quite recently, it is surprising that it featured so frequently in the reports of the inspectors of lunacy in nineteenth-century Ireland. They were constantly on the alert for any reports that might suggest that patients were being either neglected or abused. The abuse was usually physical and could be inflicted by members of staff or by other patients. The neglect was always blamed on nursing rather than medical staff, although there were some instances in which the management of the asylum came under scrutiny for practices that might have led to neglect or abuse of patients.

As a matter of course, the resident medical superintendent of each asylum was obliged to report any complaints or any instances of what might be construed as neglect or abuse immediately to the Board of Governors and to the Inspectorate. As early as 1815, the rules of the Richmond Asylum stated that 'all violence or ill-treatment of the patients is strictly prohibited, under any provocation, and shall be punished in the most exemplary manner.'[39] These sentiments were repeated in the code of practice for care in district asylums as laid out in the Privy Council Rules. The standards were clear. According to the revised Privy Council Rules of 1874, the general expectation was that the approach to patients would be characterised by gentle encouragement and minimal restraint.

> (Patients) shall be treated with all the gentleness compatible with their condition; and restraint, when necessary, shall be as moderate, both in extent and duration, as is consistent with the safety and advantage of the patient.[40]
>
> They (attendants and servants) are to avoid any harsh or intemperate language to patients, and must, by steadiness, kindness, and gentleness, endeavour to contribute to that system of moral government upon which the value of the Asylum depends.[41]

In addition to a mild and encouraging approach to patients, staff members were given clear instructions as to their duties in situations in which the patient might be at risk of being harmed by another patient or of harming him or herself. In fact, they were expected to supervise the patients at all times. There were also clear lines of authority between the medical and nursing staff in relation to mechanical restraint, seclusion and the use of some 'water treatments'. These were carried out by nursing staff, but were only used following a specific instruction from a member of the medical staff.

> Attendants and servants, both male and female … shall observe habits of cleanliness, order, and subordination, as well as the most unvarying kindness towards the lunatics placed under their charge, or with whom they may come in contact … The attendants shall never absent themselves from their divisions so as to leave the patients unguarded, nor shall they attempt mechanical restraint, seclusion, or the use of the shower or plunge bath, without express directions from either of the Medical Officers. The presence of an attendant or servant, in the case of baths being given, shall be imperative.[42]

While these rules applied to all staff in the asylum, the medical superintendent had the overall responsibility for their implementation. He also had the power to discipline and suspend members of staff who engaged in behaviour that could be seen as neglectful or abusive.

> The Resident Medical Superintendent shall superintend and regulate the whole establishment, and is to be entrusted with the moral and general medical treatment of its inmates, for whose well-being and safe custody he shall be responsible.[43]

He (the Resident Medical Superintendent) shall take care that all the Officers, servants, and attendants of the institution acquit themselves of their respective duties, and in any case of their neglect, he shall report accordingly to the Board at its next meeting. In cases, however, of drunkenness, insubordination, or cruelty, he may suspend any attendant or servant, reporting to the Inspectors within three days the name of the party and the cause of suspension, and at its subsequent meeting to the Board for its decision; and until such decision the offender shall be removed from the Asylum.[44]

While this behaviour sometimes came to light through complaints made by patients or their relatives, it was more often discovered when a patient was injured or when a patient died due to injury or suicide. Reports from the Inspectorate show that while abuse or neglect of patients did not seem to be rampant in any of the asylums, it was not a rare occurrence. As with today, however, it is likely that abuse was under-reported. The kind of problems discussed by the inspectors covered a range of situations, including the injury of a patient by an attendant; the death of a patient due to the neglect or during the absence of an attendant or servant; the abuse or injury of one patient by another in the absence of proper supervision by staff; the involvement of staff in the escape of one or more patients and, finally, evidence of a lax approach by a resident medical superintendent towards staff who transgressed. As with crime in the world outside of institutions, it was more common for male attendants (rather than female nurses) to cause injury to patients and, as the sexes were segregated in Irish asylums, their victims were always male. As early as 1857, an incident at the Maryborough Asylum ended up in court. The facts were summarised by Resident Medical Superintendent Dr. I. Berkely, in the report of the Inspectorate.

A patient, named Richard Ramsbottom, charged an assistant keeper, named Patrick Cashen, with assaulting him, while in bed, and striking him with a stick, whereby a bone in Ramsbottom's right arm was broken. Cashen was tried at quarter sessions, and sentenced to pay a fine of £3, or imprisonment. William Patten, keeper, and Patrick Cashen, assistant keeper, were dismissed; the former for not reporting the circumstances to the manager at the time.[45]

In this instance, the patient had made a complaint directly to the authorities, which was a very unusual occurrence. However, in his case there was clear evidence of injury as he had a broken arm. In other cases, the outcome was somewhat different. For example, in 1875, a complaint by a patient in Kilkenny Asylum, that he was not happy with the treatment he was receiving, was fully investigated, but was found to be 'totally unfounded and unworthy of belief'.[46] While we do not know the essence of the complaint, it is interesting that it was taken very seriously, being the subject of a special meeting of twelve governors, chaired by the local dignitary, the Marquess of Ormonde. The complainant was 'a respectable farmer' and he had the backing of his friends. The Board members concluded that there was no case to answer and 'tendered to the Medical Officers of the asylum and its staff the expression of their unaltered confidence in its management'.[47] One might be forgiven for thinking that this complaint was only taken seriously because of the patient's social position.

Other instances of abuse only came to the attention of the medical superintendent when an unexplained injury or death occurred. Instant dismissal was usually the outcome, with only some cases going to court. In Sligo Asylum in 1862, a male attendant who had 'maltreated a patient, by knocking him down in a moment of passion', was dismissed, although it was thought that the act was not premeditated. In the words of the inspectors, the dismissal was 'a warning to other servants in the establishment'.[48] In 1864, at Ballinasloe Asylum, a male attendant was also dismissed by the inspector and his wages were withheld while the Board of Governors decided whether or not to take the matter to the police.

> Having learned from Dr. Eaton that an attendant, Michael Brennan acted with cruelty towards one of the male patients, by striking him with a bunch of keys on the head, and thereby inflicting a wound; and, further, that he used threatening language towards the head Superintendent in the division, I ordered his immediate dismissal.[49]

This attendant had committed two offences – cruelty and insubordination – both of which were deemed unacceptable. However, we do not know the background to these events and, as modern research on abuse and violence shows, it is likely that the perpetrator had engaged in other acts of cruelty which may or may not have been noticed. From the reports of the inspectors, it appears that resident medical superintendents had some discretion in how they reported and dealt with alleged abuse. In some cases, the inspectors were of the opinion that the approach taken within a specific asylum was too lenient. This happened in Ennis Asylum where a number of incidents that worried the inspectors took place. In May 1870, three men were dismissed for neglect of duties.

> I regret to have to report that I have considered it necessary to dismiss peremptorily three of the officials – the engine man and his assistant, for gross neglect of duty, by which one of the steam-boilers has been, I fear, much damaged; and the shoemaker for having left the premises without permission (having gone over the boundary wall) and returned between two and three in the morning.[50]

However, in August of the same year, 1870, the resident medical superintendent did not dismiss a female attendant, Anne Malone, who had broken a patient's arm. Instead, he accepted her resignation without imposing a fine. Board members were not happy about this and asked for a full report. In it, Dr. W. Dixon, the medical superintendent, said that he and Dr. P.M. Cullinan, the Visiting Physician, had made a full enquiry into the case and concluded that though she may have caused the patient's arm to break, it was not deliberate abuse.

> The head nurse, Ellen Garvey, and her two assistants, one of whom Anne Malone, was in the immediate vicinity of the patient, the other attendants being occupied in another part of the corridor. As far as I could ascertain, the patient was allowing water to run from one of the taps, and, on her not desisting when directed, the girl, Malone, went to remove her from the lavatory, and admitted that in doing so she gave her arm a twist, though she denied having broken it … I wish to observe that the limbs of the woman are abnormally slender, and that a slight force would have probably been sufficient to cause the injury.[51]

The Board members did not disagree with the decision of the medical superintendent, but the inspectors, Dr. J. Nugent and Dr. G. W. Hatchell, were not impressed by what appeared to them to be a rather arbitrary approach to discipline. There were other incidents in the Ennis Asylum that troubled the inspectors in that year, two of which were very serious. In the summer of 1870, a female patient, M.H., who had been transferred from Ennis gaol, where she had been held as a 'dangerous lunatic', became pregnant by another patient. She had been employed in the Matron's kitchen where she was 'allowed a certain amount of liberty'. She admitted that she had gone 'on more than one occasion' to the 'gas-house and had intercourse with a male patient who was employed there'. In his report to the Board members, Dr. Dixon, the medical superintendent, said that 'she was a woman of bad character, and had two illegitimate children in the Scariff Workhouse', a fact that only became known when her current pregnancy was discovered. The disclosure of this fact did not alter the opinion of either the Board members or the inspectors on the lax state of discipline and of supervision in the asylum. As a result of this, the Board 'passed a resolution prohibiting the employment of a patient in any part of the Asylum, except under the strict supervision of some of the attendants'.[52] In other words, women could work with men (or vice versa), but only under supervision.

In December of the same year, there was another incident at Ennis Asylum that indicated to the inspectors that little had changed. On 28 December, a male patient, R.K., died 'from the effects of injuries sustained by reason of his falling from the corridor window' two days previously. The jury at the coroner's court found 'no blame attaches to the attendants' but rather suggested that the windows were so constructed that it was easy for a patient to throw himself out of one, if left unsupervised. However, as the inspectors found out, on the night in question, the female night-watch, who had responsibility for the supervision of patients, was missing. She was later brought before the Board of Governors 'for drunkenness and absence for the night' and fined five shillings and the withdrawal of her pass-out for three months, a punishment that was much too light according to the inspectors. 'We think that in cases where the attendants on the insane are guilty of such gross misconduct, a much heavier punishment should be awarded as a warning to others.'[53] However, on this occasion the medical superintendent was not reprimanded formally, although the views of the Inspectorate were published in the annual report that would have been read widely.

It was possible for the inspectors to recommend the dismissal of a senior member of staff, but it did not seem to have happened very often. There is a record of the dismissal in 1851 of the Visiting Physician at Ballinasloe Asylum for 'a gross violation of confidence'.[54] This was a very serious situation in which it came to light that the visiting physician, Dr. Heise, was responsible for the pregnancy of a patient, Miss I. After offering his resignation to the Board of Governors in 1848, he lost his salary and his job immediately. As shown by Oonagh Walsh in the next chapter, Heise had also been removed in 1830 from his previous position as manager at the Richmond Asylum for failing to raise standards of care. He was given a second chance in 1833 as visiting physician at Ballinasloe, but he found himself at loggerheads with the Board of Governors many times over management issues. In the end, it was his own behaviour that brought about his dismissal – he had sex with a patient and then tried to hide her pregnancy by discharging her.

Suicide and Homicide

Lax management in relation to staff discipline often led to situations not directly linked to individual staff members, but which showed a general lack of patient supervision. This sometimes led to dangerous outcomes such as homicide or suicide. Homicides were a rare occurrence, but they did happen. In 1863, a male patient in Mullingar Asylum, Peter Farrell, strangled another male patient, who was described as 'quiet' and 'harmless'.

> The homicide, Peter Farrell, seeing himself observed by one of the other occupants of the dormitory, made a furious attack on him also, and but for the timely arrival of an attendant, who was attracted by the noise, might have taken a second life. An inquest was held and the facts ascertained, the verdict exonerating the officers of the asylum from all blame, as the jury conceived it was an occurrence which no human care or foresight could have obviated.[55]

The inspectors made their own inquiry into the circumstances of the killing and expressed 'regret' that no post-mortem was carried out. No disciplinary action was taken against the staff, but the patient was transferred to gaol where he awaited trial. He was found 'incapable of pleading' and was sent to the Central Criminal Lunatic Asylum, Dundrum, by order of the Lord Lieutenant. In another case of homicide, in 1872, at the Richmond Asylum, there was not sufficient evidence to bring the matter to court. A female patient, M.D., was found dead in her bed one morning. A post-mortem showed that she had died from 'effusion on the brain attendant on external injuries'.[56] Though they could not work out how the injury was caused, the medical staff and governors were of the opinion that she had been killed by another female patient who had gone missing from her bed that night. There were no witnesses to the incident.

> She (the alleged perpetrator) was found in her proper place on the following morning and from a rambling incoherent statement made by her, it was thought that she might have inflicted the injuries observed upon the deceased.[57]

The inspectors did not blame the asylum staff for this death, as they appreciated the strain under which the Richmond was operating. It was constantly overcrowded, though some of the patients had been transferred to the newly opened asylum at Mullingar. In addition, during the year in question, there had been no suicides, although several attempts at 'self destruction were made, and only one escape was effected'. This was taken as an indication of 'great care and discipline' in the running of the asylum.

In all asylums, there were occasional successful suicide attempts. In some years, there were as many as six suicides in the asylum population as a whole, with a maximum of two in an individual asylum. Most of the suicides were by hanging or by injury caused by a tool stolen from a workshop. Two examples from the Richmond in 1970 were typical of other asylum suicides. Esther Kinsella hanged herself with her apron and John Leonard cut his throat with a chisel. Esther has been deemed a suicide risk when first admitted, but later seemed to improve.

> … all suspicions were lulled about her. She was seen by the nurse in charge at half past seven o'clock a.m. and shortly after the nurse missed her, but as she was in the habit of making her own bed, no further notice of her absence was taken until breakfast time (nine o'clock), when on making search she was found hanging from the banisters leading to the Assistant Matron's room.[58]

While it is understandable how this happened without anybody noticing it, it is more difficult to accept that there was no neglect or lack of supervision in the case of John Leonard. John had just been admitted on 12 June as a dangerous lunatic, but within three days, he was dead.[59]

> On the 15th (June) he cut his throat with a chisel, taken from the tool-case of a carpenter who was at work in the division in which the patient was. An inquest took place and the following verdict was returned: John Leonard died … from the effects of a wound in his throat, inflicted by himself with a chisel, in the bath of the asylum.[60]

As discussed earlier, no patient was supposed to be allowed to have a bath unattended or unsupervised. How did he manage to smuggle a chisel into the bathroom and why was there no supervision? In this case, none of the attendants were found to be at fault, so one must conclude that the rules of supervision of patients were not always observed. This is understandable in the light of the fact that by the 1870s, most public asylums in Ireland were over-crowded and understaffed.

What might appear to us as a lenient approach to members of staff who were careless in their approach to patient supervision or physically cruel to those who did not cooperate with them, might also be explained by the general approach to care and confinement in the mid-nineteenth century. At this time, there was an acceptance of mechanical restraint for patients who were violent. We get a glimpse of what was going on in 1857 from a small study conducted by the inspectorate on the use of mechanical restraint. The short questionnaire, sent to the manager of every asylum, was included in an appendix in the annual report for that year, as were the findings from the study.[61] The methods of restraint included the following: 'leather muffs'; a 'camisole'; 'arm-straps'; 'a leather girdle to which broad soft straps are sewed, which pass before and confine the wrists'; 'strait vest' or 'strait waistcoat'; a 'waist belt by day, confining one arm' or 'wrist band attached to girdle'; and, finally, a 'bed of peculiar construction'. These were used to calm a violent patient in conjunction with or instead of sedatives, or seclusion in a single room with a mattress or straw on the floor. The sedatives were chloroform, morphine, opium and 'tartarised antimony', all administered under the supervision of the resident medical superintendent. Very few asylums had padded cells or separate rooms for these violent patients, though many expressed an interest in special accommodation to prevent disruption to the ward in general. This small study in the late 1850s revealed that all of the asylums used mechanical restraint when necessary and that it was preferred to the use of physical coercion by a staff member. Dr. Thomas Power, the resident medical superintendent at Cork Asylum, was typical in his approach to the topic:

> My opinion is that it cannot be altogether dispensed with ... I would prefer mechanical restraint to that of coercion by attendants, as less irritating to the patient and more safe for both patient and attendants, but would have recourse to seclusion in the padded cell in preference to either. I find mechanical restraint

indispensable in cases determined to remain in an upright position day and night, without clothing, if permitted; in cases when patients have a propensity to knock their heads against the wall; in cases so wild as not to permit of their being allowed at large without danger to the other patients and attendants.[62]

It is not possible to work out if this level of mechanical restraint continued into the late nineteenth century, as this study was not repeated, nor was there any record in the annual report of the inspectors on the use of these methods of controlling violent patients. We know that violence within asylums continued to be a problem into the early twentieth century, as the inspectors continued to report on suicides and 'deaths from misadventure', which covered deaths due to accidental or deliberate injury. The final report of the Inspectorate summarised what happened to nine people who died in asylums in 1919 due to suicide or 'misadventure'. As with the incidents discussed already, some of these deaths showed laxity of supervision, while others reflected the difficulties involved in supervising violent and suicidal patients in institutions that were overcrowded and understaffed. Three of these deaths happened in Ballinasloe and two in Enniscorthy. In all cases, there was an internal inquiry and a report presented to the Committee of Management (formerly the Board of Governors).

> Suicides: In Ballinasloe Asylum, a female patient hanged herself by strips of her chemise fastened to a bar across a window in a water closet. In Castlebar Asylum, a male patient thrust a nail taken out of a mop into his larynx, thereby setting up septic pneumonia from which he died three days later.
>
> Deaths from Misadventure: In Ballinasloe Asylum, a female patient's clothing caught fire, and she thereby sustained severe burns, which proved fatal three days afterwards. In the same Asylum, a female patient was poisoned by eating yew leaves which had been distributed as 'palm' on Palm Sunday, and she died in a few hours. In Enniscorthy Asylum, a male patient during a struggle with three attendants sustained fractures of several ribs, thereby causing congestion of the right lung, to which he succumbed ten days after he had received the injuries.[63]

The final category of deaths shows that violence between patients was a common occurrence. Some of the perpetrators were brought to court and were transferred to the Central Criminal Lunatic Asylum at Dundrum.

Deaths by homicide: In Clonmel Asylum, a male patient was knocked down and kicked by another, thereby sustaining fracture of both bones of his legs. He succumbed to these injuries almost a month afterwards, death being accelerated by maniacal exhaustion. In Sligo Asylum, a male patient died from concussion of the brain, as the result of a fall on his head, caused by a blow from another patient.[64]

One of the interesting features of the Inspectorate reports was the fact that they were published as Parliamentary Papers on an annual basis, making their findings publicly available to anyone who wished to read them. Institutions were named and incidents were reported in a very transparent manner. During the twentieth century this transparency disappeared to some extent as the onus on hospitals to provide detailed information declined and inspectors had to rely on their inspection visits to uncover problems.

CONCLUSION

Though the Inspectorate in Lunacy disappeared in the early twentieth century, its functions continued to be carried out by the inspectors of mental hospitals in the Republic of Ireland, and by Department of Health inspectors in Northern Ireland. In the twenty-first century, each part of Ireland has a Mental Health Commission in addition to procedures for monitoring and inspection within the departments of health for each jurisdiction. Like their predecessors, inspectors and commissioners continue to raise issues and point out problems encountered during their inspections of hospitals and other mental health services throughout the country. Now, as then, their concerns are not always heard. When reading some of these reports, it is clear that each inspector had his own style of writing and that sometimes this style grated on the ear of the reader and did not help the cause of improving mental health services. We will end with a comment made about one of the most acerbic of inspectors, Sir John Nugent, who died in 1899.[65]

Unfortunately, he was one of those men in whom high and low tones are so intermingled as to produce a discord … His subtlety, wire-drawn in later years, together with a natural defect in his powers of expression, which were not developed in proportion to his other capabilities, gave rise to the peculiar, complicated and contradictory style of his official reports, which made the

Irish Lunacy Blue Book for some generations more amusing than instructive.[66]

NOTES

1. Legal basis for inspectorates: *Prisons* (Ireland) Act 1826 (7 Geo. iv. c. 74): and *Central Criminal Lunatic Asylum* (Ireland) Act 1845 (8 & 9 Vic. c. 107).
2. *8th Annual report on the district, criminal and private lunatic asylums in Ireland, with appendices* (Hereafter, *Asylums Report*), p.26. HC 1857 Session 2 (2253) xvii. 67; Dates for appointment of inspectors were drawn from the following sources: Anonymous, 'Changes in the Irish Lunacy Board', *Journal of Mental Science*, xxxvi: 153 (April 1890): 309–10; Other information on dates of appointments are Finnane, *Insanity and the Insane*, pp.52, 55, 68, 69; Kirkpatrick, *History of the Care*, pp.36–7; Robins, *Fools and Mad*, p.92.
3. Obituary for Sir John Nugent. *Journal of Royal Medico Psychological Association (RMPA)*, 1899, p.431. Accessed online at http://bjp.rcpsych.org/cgi/reprint/45/189/431.pdf [accessed 1 December 2011].
4. *8th Asylums Report*, p.26. HC 1857 Session 2 (2253) xvii. 67.
5. *59th Asylums Report*, p.631. HC 1910 (Cd. 5280) xli. 593.
6. *69th Asylums Report*, p.190. HC 1921 (Cmd. 1127) xv. 165.
7. *1st Asylums Report*, p.11. HC 1846 (736) xxii. 409; *8th Asylums Report*, p.4. HC 1857 Session 2 (2253) xvii. 67.
8. *1st Asylums Report*, p.8. HC 1846 (736) xxii. 409.
9. *8th Asylums Report*, p.4. HC 1857 Session 2 (2253) xvii. 67.
10 From research by Dr. Thurnam, York Retreat, quoted in *1st Asylums Report*, p.8. HC 1846 (736) xxii. 409.
11 *8th Asylums Report*, p.4. HC 1857 Session 2 (2253) xvii. 67.
12 Ibid.
13. *8th Asylums Report*, pp.7–8. HC 1857 Session 2 (2253) xvii. 67.
14. Central Criminal Lunatic Asylum (Ireland) Act, 8 & 9 Vic. c. 107; Brendan D. Kelly, 'The Mental Treatment Act 1945 in Ireland: An historical enquiry', *History of Psychiatry*, 19:1(2008): 47–67, p.51.
15. *9th Asylums Report*, p.4. HC 1859 Session 2 (2582) x. 443.
16. *13th Asylums Report*, p.7. HC 1864 (3369) xxiii. 317. Clonmel later lost the designation of 'auxiliary' asylum and became a district asylum.
17. *22nd Asylums Report*, p.7. HC 1873 (c. 852) xxx. 327.
18. Lunatic Asylums (Ireland) Act, 38 & 39 Vic. c. 67.
19. Local Government (Ireland) Act 1898, 61 & 62 Vic. c. 37.
20. *69th Asylums Report*, p.175. HC 1921 (Cmd. 1127) xv. 165.
21. *Special report from the inspectors of lunatics to the chief secretary 1894*, HC 1894 (C. 7331) xliii. 647.
22. *Supplement to the 54th report of the inspectors of lunatics (Ireland), being a special report on the alleged increase of insanity* (Hereafter, *Special report on increased insanity*). HC 1906 (Cd. 3126) xxxix.1.
23. *Special report on increased insanity*, p.7-8. HC 1906 (Cd. 3126) xxxix.1.
24. Ibid.
25. Table adapted from a similar Table, based on census data, in the *Special report on increased insanity*, p.9. HC 1906 (Cd. 3126) xxxix.1.
26. *69th Asylums Report*, p.171, HC 1921 (Cmd. 1127) xv. 165.
27. For trends in the Republic of Ireland, see chapter in this volume by Damien Brennan; For trends in Northern Ireland, see Prior, *Mental Health and Politics in Northern Ireland*.
28. N. Scheper Hughes, *Saints, Scholars and Schizophrenics* (Berkeley: University of California Press, 2001); See chapter in this volume by Damien Brennan; Finnane, *Insanity and the Insane*; Prior, *Mental Health and Politics in Northern Ireland*.
29. *Report of the Inspectors General on the District, local and private lunatic Asylums in Ireland 1844*, p.5, HC 1845 (645) xxvi. 269.
30. *8th Asylums Report*, p.7. HC 1857 Session 2 (2253) xvii. 67.

31. *8th Asylums Report*, p.9. HC 1857 Session 2 (2253) xvii. 67.
32 Ibid.
33. *9th Asylums Report*, pp.5–6. HC 1859 Session 2 (2582) x. 443.
34. *9th Asylums Report*, p.8. HC 1865 (3556) xxi. 103.
35. *69th Asylums Report*, p.xvi. HC 1921 (Cmd. 1127) xv. 165.
36. Ibid.
37. See chapter in this volume by McCabe and Mulholland.
38 For further discussion, see Prior, *Mental Health and Politics in Northern Ireland*, pp.9–45.
39. From 'Rules and regulations to be strictly observed by the Domestics of the Richmond Lunatic Asylum 1815', reprinted in the *8th Asylums Report*, Appendix G, p.64. HC 1857 Session 2 (2253) xvii. 67.
40. Revised code of Privy Council Rules 1874, reprinted as Appendix H in the *23rd Asylums Report*, p.265, section xviii. HC 1874 (c. 1004) xxvii. 363.
41. Ibid., p.277, section xc. HC 1874 (c. 1004) xxvii. 363.
42. Ibid., p.275, section lxxviii and lxxixi. HC 1874 (c. 1004) xxvii. 363.
43. Ibid., p.268, section xxx. HC 1874 (c. 1004) xxvii. 363.
44. Ibid., p.269, section xxxii. HC 1874 (c. 1004) xxvii. 363.
45. *8th Asylums Report*, Appendix G, p.63. HC 1857 Session 2 (2253) xvii. 67.
46. *24th Asylums Report*, p.48. HC 1875 (c. 1293) xxxiii. 319.
47. Ibid.
48. *11th Asylums Report*, p.23. HC 1862 (2975) xxiii. 517.
49. *13th Asylums Report*, p.13. HC 1864 (3369) xxiii. 317.
50. *20th Asylums Report*, p.17. HC 1871 (c. 440) xxvi. 427.
51. Ibid.
52. Ibid.
53. *20th Asylums Report*, p.16. HC 1871 (c. 440) xxvi. 427.
54. *5th Asylums Report*, p.4. HC 1851 (1387) xxiv. 231.
55. *12th Asylums Report*, p.31. HC 1863 (3209) xx. 621.
56. *21st Asylums Report*, p.23. HC 1872 (c. 647) xxvii. 323.
57. Ibid.
58. *19th Asylums Report*, p.26. HC 1870 (c. 202) xxxiv. 287.
59. For a discussion on the implementation of 'dangerous lunacy' legislation, see Brendan Kelly, 'The Mental Treatment Act 1945 in Ireland: an historical enquiry', *History of Psychiatry*, 19:1 (2008): 47–67; Pauline Prior, 'Dangerous Lunacy: The Misuse of Mental Health Law in Nineteenth-Century Ireland', *Journal of Forensic Psychiatry and Psychology*, 14: 3 (2003): 525–53.
60. *19th Asylums Report*, p.26. HC 1870 (c. 202) xxxiv. 287.
61. *8th Asylums Report*, Appendix G, pp.61–4. HC 1857 Session 2 (2253) xvii. 67.
62. *8th Asylums Report*, Appendix G, p.62. HC 1857 Session 2 (2253) xvii. 67.
63. *69th Asylums Report*, pp.xiv-xv. HC 1921 (Cmd. 1127) xv. 165.
64. Ibid.
65. Dermot Walsh, 'Irish College formed for Psychiatrists (at last)', Opinion section, *Irish Medical Times*, 20 January 2009, (no page number). Available online at www.imt.ie/opinion [accessed 1 December 2011].
66. Obituary for Sir John Nugent, Journal of RMPA, p.431. 1899. http://bjp.rcpsych.org/cgi/reprint/45/189/431.pdf [accessed 1 December 2011].

12

A Perfectly Ordered Establishment: Connaught District Lunatic Asylum (Ballinasloe)

Oonagh Walsh

Recent years have seen fundamental alterations in society's attitudes towards medical practice. The rise in alternative therapies, the contested integration of homeopathy into general practice, and a move away from 'illness' to 'wellness' in terms of how the patient is conceived, have challenged the scientific basis of medical practice in the western world.[1] For an older generation of patients and practitioners, this is a large step away from an unswerving faith in laboratory-based medicine, and a belief cherished from the 1950s that in time, all major human illnesses would be delineated and defeated, using the most advanced technologies against the body, and the mind's failings. But today's apparent seismic shift is merely part of an historical continuum that began with Galen.[2] Medicine is nothing if not adaptive, and has been shaped internationally not only by scientific advance, as argued by Whig medical historians, but by complex social and political pressures. Science has determined the environment in which care has been made available, and has underpinned the often dramatic advances in combating disease, but it is less obvious pressures that have shaped its delivery and reception. However, most people would still agree that the physician, in particular the consultant, reigns supreme within the hospital system. If they are less likely to be the God-like figures who swept around the wards trailing students in their wake than they used to be, they are nevertheless the repositories of an expensive and extensive training, and therefore unquestioned in their position at the top of the medical structure.

But this position was hard won, and was neither an automatic entitlement, nor a natural progression as a result of improved medical technique and training. The case of mental health care reflects the general trend towards deferment to the professionally trained, albeit with several unique characteristics. Psychiatry has always been a controversial discipline, historically coming under criticism from within the medical profession itself as well as from former patients. But it has also provided opportunities for individuals as well as groups to shape it in ways that reflect non-medical, in addition to medical, interests and concerns, especially in the nineteenth century. This renders it unique among medical specialisms, as care for the mentally ill did not necessarily have to be delivered in a hospital or sanatorium setting (as the other emergent branches did), nor did it depend in the early years on a scientific, empirical practice, capable of objective measurement. Both the patient and the practitioner were necessarily highly individual. Because of this, psychiatry struggled to establish an etiology for mental illness that paralleled other specialties such as surgery or epidemiology. This chapter will examine the evolution of medical management at the Connaught District Lunatic Asylum (CDLA), later the Ballinasloe Asylum, and look in particular at two of the physicians who served there: the first medical appointee in 1833, Dr. Heise, and one of the most influential, Dr. Fletcher, who presided over the asylum for almost thirty years until his death in 1904. Their respective tenures encapsulate psychiatry's, and indeed medicine's, general move from an hereditary, vocational occupation, to a highly regulated and elite profession, one which both played a part in altering national politics and in reflecting those changes. The challenge posed by middle-class university educated physicians to the ascendancy Board of Governors may not be a straightforward move from a kakistocracy to a meritocracy, in that many of the non-elected Board had a great deal of experience in philanthropic work and a strong sense of their obligations to the com-munity at large,[3] but it does reflect a growing cultural reluctance to adhere to the politics of privilege (For an example of Board members, see Table 12.1). But the history of the CDLA is not exclusively of the elite. Patient experience and the response of the community at large shaped the manner in which the asylum functioned. The dynamics of asylum life were forged by a continual interaction between the principal players: the aristocratic Board, the medical and nursing staff, and the large patient body, with each seeking specific advantages.

Like all the District Asylums, the CDLA was conceived and operated on a strict hierarchical basis, with a top-down model of gradually devolved powers. At the pinnacle of the organisation stood the Lord Lieutenant, with whom lay all power to fund, regulate, and restructure the national system. Each asylum was locally administered by a Board of Governors, which met monthly to pay bills, appoint and discipline staff, recommend admissions and discharges, and attend to the administrative responsibilities of the institution. Required to report to each Board meeting were three key figures: the (lay) asylum manager who was replaced by a resident medical superintendent (RMS) or resident physician in 1859, a visiting physician and a matron.[4] The manager/RMS and matron, who were resident in the asylum, had an intimate knowledge of the organisation and were able to provide detailed information to the Board as to the conduct of the asylum staff and patients. Between these relatively well-paid and privileged employees and the large patient body stood the nurses and keepers, those staff who possessed an intimate working knowledge of the asylum and its occupants. Although firmly under the control of the matron and the manager/ RMS, the nurses exercised a tremendous authority over the patients on the most practical of levels. Despite occupying a somewhat ambiguous professional position, in that they were relatively poorly paid and poorly educated[5] (at least until the latter half of the century), it is likely that if asked who held the reins of power at Ballinasloe, many patients would unhesitatingly have pointed to this group. However, they had limited opportunity to alter the manner in which the asylum functioned, and with the exception of the radical seizure of Monaghan Asylum in 1919 by a combined force of nurses and patients, they were not formal power brokers.[6]

In common with the English model, the Irish District Asylum system was originally conceived by government on firmly non-medical lines, with segregation the primary impulse.[7] Indeed, the two principal concerns of the *Bill to make more effectual provision for the establishment of asylums for the lunatic poor, and for the custody of insane persons charged with offences in Ireland* of 1821, were finance and security. There is little mention of the role of medical officers, who appear obliquely in the Act as potential expenses associated with the institution, and whose role is undefined.[8] In contrast to the situation in Britain, where physicians took swift control in the care of the insane,[9] Ireland's system followed a paternalistic philanthropic model, predicated on the gentry taking the central role in asylum administration. This role was unpaid: indeed it was a condition of taking a seat on the Board that no remuneration be offered for service.[10] Ireland's mental health system was therefore almost feudal in its original conception, with the presumption that the country's elite, however poorly qualified for the job, should govern systems for the care of the mentally ill. But the governing class was no longer what it had been. The Act of Union of 1800 eliminated the Irish Parliament and precipitated the permanent relocation of many Irish landlords to England. Immediately before the establishment of the Irish District Asylums, then, the political system had undergone a fundamental change that boded ill for imaginative and responsible care. There was a loss of funding and investment in those aristocratic power bases, as rents were sent to England, and Irish estates became steadily more decrepit, continually divided and sub-divided amongst a cottier class increasingly dependent on the potato for survival. Many historians believe that the Irish aristocracy who remained after 1800 underwent a similar decline, and a fatalistic attitude prevailed even before the Famine.[11] But it was this class that was expected to drive the asylum system and shape institutions which elsewhere were being created as medical centres.[12] In France, Germany and England, it was medical men who forged systems of care for the insane, and who placed it on what they declared to be a modern, scientific basis.[13] Ireland's initial lack of emphasis on the curative potential of the District Asylums laid the basis for conflict between the state and medical and philanthropic interest groups throughout the nineteenth century.

In Ireland, moreover, lunacy provision was formulated within the rubric of poverty and this had many long-term implications. Perhaps the most important was the principle enshrined in every communication between the asylums and the lord lieutenant's office, that costs be kept to a minimum[14] and that institutions should become self-sufficient as far as feasible. But it also placed the patients into a traditional relationship with the Board of Governors, one of petition and mendacity. Poverty was the determinant for entry, maintaining the established relationship between the ascendancy and the peasantry.[15] The mental state of the patient, although central to the process, in that it precipitated entry to the institution, was in the early years regarded more as a social responsibility rather than as a medical necessity. The second pressing concern was with security. When Robert Peel initiated the commission that led to the establishment of the District Asylums, his prime motivation was to tackle what he described as the 'impropriety' of lunatics wandering at large in Ireland: 'it was not right these unhappy beings should go abroad free from restraint.'[16] The governmental impetus was primarily custodial, not curative, although it was hoped that some of the patients, at least, would recover their reason. Medical opinion was largely absent from the commission, and the evidence given by key

TABLE 12.1: GOVERNORS OF THE BALLINASLOE DISTRICT LUNATIC ASYLUM FOR THE YEAR 1890.*

Name	Title	Position	Address
Armstrong	Elliott G.	Esq	Justice of the Peace (J.P.)	Castlegar
Ahascragh Bagot	Bernard W.	Esq	J.P.	Caranure,Athlone
Grattan-Bellew	Sir Henry	Baronet	Deputy Lieutenant (D.L)	Montbellew
Burke	Sir Henry	Baronet	D.L.	Marble Hill, Loughrea
Clancarty	The Earl of Garbally	Earl	J.P.	Ballinasloe
Comyn	Andrew N.	Esq	J.P.	Ballinderry, Kilconnell
Coote	O.R.	Esq		Larkfield, Athlone
Daly	W.	Esq	J.P.	Dunsandle, Kiltullagh
Davy	P.J.	Esq	J.P.	Woodberry, Kilconnell
Dillon	Hon L.G.	Honourable		Clonbrock, Ahascragh
Duggan	The Most Rev Patrick	D.D.		Bishop of Clonfert
Fowler	Edward W.	Esq	J.P.	Ballinasloe
Gairdner	John	Esq	J.P.	Lisbeg, Ballinasloe
Hynes	John W.	Esq		Woodmont, Ballinasloe
Johnston	Samuel	Esq	J.P.	Fohena
Kelly	James	Esq	J.P.	Johnstown, Athlone
Lambert	J.H.	Esq	J.P.	Lismany,Ballinasloe
M'Dermott	James	Esq	J.P.	Ramore, Killimore
Madden	John J.	Esq		Kilreekel, Loughrea
O'Shaughnessy	J.J.	Esq	J.P.	Birchgrove, Ballinasloe
Palmer	Henry	Esq	J.P.	Forster Park, Galway
Potts	W.T.	Esq	J.P.	Correen, Ballinasloe
Seymour	Walter	Esq	J.P.	Ballymore Castle, Ballinasloe
Ward	John	Esq	J.P.	Ballinasloe
Wigham	The Rev James W.	D.D.		Ballinasloe

*Note: Despite a growing nationalist sentiment at local level, and the imminent reforms of the Local Government (Ireland) Act of 1898, the local gentry (even at the lowest title of Baronet) and the Protestant middle class were over represented on the Board of Governors. Also noteworthy is the predominance of Justices of the Peace. These individuals sat both at the courts that determined whether individuals should be sent to the Asylum under the Dangerous Lunatics Act, and on the Board of the asylum that received them, a worrying conflict of interest.

members of the gentry was firmly influenced by class expectations. Thomas Spring Rice confidently stated:

> It [insanity] is an hereditary malady ... it is connected with scrofulous habits; also hereditary, and therefore advances upon a double principle. It is connected with the habits of lower classes of the people in Ireland, who addict themselves to the use of ardent spirits; and it is connected also with the use of mercury. These four causes are, a priori, sufficient to show that it is on the increase.[17]

In one paragraph, Spring Rice encapsulated an aristocratic anxiety over the poor: they are dirty, inbred, intemperate and reckless. Little wonder then that a national system for their care was based on the presumption that the best that could be hoped for was containment, rather than cure. Class difference also influenced relationships between the Board and the asylum staff at Ballinasloe. The minutes reflect a belief that all employees were literally the Board's servants, and not individuals appointed for their specific skills in dealing with insanity. Although this caused few problems for the nurses and keepers, who were drawn for the most part from the labouring classes, it proved an enduring source of tension for the physicians, particularly in the years preceding a general acceptance of the professional middle classes. The experiences of two of the CDLA's physicians indicate the underlying tensions between the Board and the medical staff, and the significant shift in the asylum as a place of refuge, to a highly medicalised environment, in the course of a few short decades.

Ballinasloe's first medical appointment, Dr. William Heise (occasionally spelled Heisse), was a typical product of the older, vocational physician. A Hanoverian who had served with the British Army in the Peninsular War, he had practiced in Borrisokane, Co. Tipperary for twelve years before being appointed manager of the Richmond Asylum in Dublin in September 1830.[18] With no particular expertise in either management, or the treatment of the mentally ill, his tenure was brief, and he was removed from office in June 1831. He had been appointed with the specific object of raising standards of care in the institution, which had a poor reputation, but Heise seemed content to preside over a regime that had little aspiration towards restoring patients to independent lives. The inspectors of prisons, Major Benjamin Woodward and Major James Palmer, men hardened to minimal standards of care in Irish gaols, were nonetheless shocked by conditions in the Richmond under Heise's authority. There was gross overcrowding – seventy-two patients shared thirty-six beds – extensive use of restraint without record or authorisation, filthy conditions throughout the institution, and a spate of pregnancies amongst patients (asylum tradesmen the putative fathers), all of which Heise declared himself powerless to prevent or control. His defense depended on a shared recognition that Irish asylums in general, and the Richmond in particular, were in appalling states, and he focused rather more on his own perilous finances than the condition of his patients. Pleading for leniency against his dismissal, he declared: 'I have become nationalized by a residence of twenty-five years in these dominions, my years of service in the army included, yet I am a stranger, deprived of interest, of friends and of money, with a large family of a wife and nine children wholly depending on me. They would even be forlorn and destitute without my exertions.'[19] The Board relented sufficiently to supply Heise with a testimonial, which secured him the position of visiting physician at the Connaught District Lunatic Asylum in 1833. The reference contained a significant point: Heise had been appointed manager of the Richmond, with ill-defined medical responsibilities. However, although the Board noted that he had proved an inept administrator ('His removal was considered advisable by the government in order that the situation might be filled by a person more conversant than the doctor appeared to be with the internal economy of a great establishment'[20]), they praised his medical skills: '... it appears that the number of cures which have taken place in the hospital under the administration of Dr. Heise exceed the average of the last six years.'

From the outset, Heise had an uneasy relationship with his Board at Ballinasloe. His appointment predated the important reforms spurred by the *Report of the Select Committee* of 1843, which resulted in the establishment of an Inspectorate in Lunacy, and an increasing emphasis on the medical care of patients. Heise's relative marginal-isation may be seen most clearly in the asylum's official response to the 1843 report.[21] In contrast to the replies from the other major asylums, Heise played no part in the compilation of points, and the focus of the letter (signed by the three most prominent landowning Board members – Clancarty, Ashtown and Laurence) was firmly on the philanthropic and sanctuary aspects of care. They stressed that the true purpose of the institution was to 'accommodate, classify, employ and amuse' the patients, and medical treatment and expertise was unmentioned. Indeed, they spent some considerable time refuting the evidence of medical experts as to the classification of incurables, and the use of prisons during the transfer of dangerous patients unable to reach the asylum directly. The term 'humanity' was used as a means of distinguishing their approach from that of the medical witnesses, with a clear implication that moral governance was more suitable for the insane.[22] However, the determined push towards an increasingly medicalised asylum system is clear from the statements made by Dr. Francis White[23] and others, White even implying a threat of resignation if a system of inspection by physicians was not implemented:

> This [asylum inspections] is a duty totally unconnected with the Inspectorship of Prisons, and which the Inspector General (however competent for his own proper business) cannot fully discharge ... *It would be better to discontinue the present Inspectorship altogether than to have the name of it without its producing the least beneficial results.*[24] (original emphasis)

The asylums in which physicians were charged with preparing the response, emphatically declared in favour of medical governance. Dr. Robert Stewart, RMS at Belfast Asylum, was amongst the most explicit, proposing his own position as an exemplar for the country:[25]

> The governors one and all, feeling it to be a matter of the greatest moment for the good and efficient management of these establishments that none but medical men of the highest moral character and professional attainments should be placed over them as Managers or Superintendents, beg to take the present opportunity of suggesting in the strongest and most respectful manner to the government, that for the future, as vacancies occur amongst the managers, professional gentlemen should alone be selected for so grave and important a charge – an opinion which they have not hastily arrived at, but after very mature consideration, and the good effects of which they have the most constant and satisfactory proof of in this institution.[26]

The steady rise in admissions to Irish asylums helped the case for medicalisation considerably. Added to the growth in the medical profession in the British Isles as a whole, and an increasingly determined effort to expand employment opportunities, the drive to place the physician at the heart of the asylum system proved irresistible.[27]

Heise was appointed as a visiting physician to Ballinasloe Asylum, so his necessarily periodic engagements with the asylum made him a more peripheral figure than the (lay) Manager or Matron. His professional recommendations were often challenged, and an undercurrent of suspicion threads its way through the CDLA minutes. The Board appeared uncomfortable with the key role being assumed by the visiting physician, and turned to a higher authority (one, like themselves, a member of the aristocracy) for support when difficulties arose. In 1845, for example, the Board rejected Heise's protests against the implementation of new regulations governing patients' bed-time.[28] It had previously been 6.30 p.m., but was now changed to 8.30 p.m. on the order of the Lord Lieutenant. Heise argued that it was impossible to get all of the infirm patients to bed at this hour, and that understaffing and the large numbers of patients who needed assistance to prepare for the night, meant that he refused to implement the '11th General Rule'. The Board immediately passed this objection to Dublin Castle, tacitly criticising the action by their own physician. A rebuke from the undersecretary swiftly followed.[29] In a further slight to Heise's authority, the Board sanctioned a wage increase to the keepers and nurses, for the 'extra work' they faced in implementing the 11th General Rule, but left the physician's own salary unchanged. Just two years later, the Board somewhat reluctantly agreed to allow Heise to expand his care of the patients, and granted his request for the purchase of medical equipment 'for the use of the Establishment'. They then sternly added that 'the Board further direct that these instruments should on no account be taken out of the House and that Dr. Heise be appraised of the above order.'[30] The declaration underpins the sinecurial nature of Heise's appointment, at least as far as the Board was concerned, with its presumption that he would operate a private practice outside the institution.[31] In this way, Heise's tenure at the CDLA encapsulates an important moment of transition in Ireland between the physician as a mere support to the asylum, appointed to tend to the inevitable injuries and routine physical illness of the large patient body, to his central role by the end of the century.[32]

Heise's reign at the CDLA came to a dramatic conclusion. At an unusually well-attended Board meeting on March 31, 1848 it was noted:

> That we have this day laid before us the letter of Doctor Heise tendering his resignation as Medical Attendant to the Asylum,

that we have accepted the same and appointed Dr. Patrick Horan to take the temporary charge of the establishment ... The Manager having reported to us the fact of Miss E. I.'s pregnancy and a letter from Dr. Heise acknowledging himself the cause of same – Resolved – that all the letters and documents relating to the case be submitted to the Government and laid by the Manager in person before the Under Secretary and that instructions be requested for the guidance of the local Board – that in the mean time the salary now due to and claimed by Dr. Heise be suspended.[33]

Dammingly, it would appear that Heise had attempted to conceal the pregnancy by discharging the patient:

Resolved – That the letter of Mrs. I. requesting that Miss I.'s discharge pursuant to the Doctor's certificate of 24th of March, be postponed ... after due enquiry from the Manager and temporary Medical Attendant ... we do not consider she should be retained, but that in consequence of the further report from the Governor of her pregnancy, her discharge be postponed till the decision of the Government be received on the case.[34]

At this last moment of Heise's tenure, the Board made an interesting comment, reflective not only of their condemnation of his actions, but indicating a recognition of the reality that medical appointments to Irish asylums were increasingly the norm.

We beg to impress on the Government the great importance of the situation where upwards of 300 patients are under treatment and that we trust in making their appointment of a medical attendant to the Institution, they will select a person of eminent abilities and tried experience in the treatment of mental disease.[35]

The mid-nineteenth century saw a concerted move from 'alienism'[36] to 'psychiatry', and several highly successful individuals had demonstrated that the care of the insane could be as lucrative and high profile as surgery and private practice. Physicians such as William Ellis, knighted for his work at Hanwell Asylum[37] and his successor as superintendent there, John Connolly[38] had worked to place psychiatry on a scientific footing equal to other branches of medicine. Connolly was amongst the first psychiatrists to grasp the importance of publications as a means of transmitting specialist, observational knowledge[39], implicitly placing psychiatry on the

same footing as other medical specialisms and excluding those without formal medical training from the process.[40] Peer spoke to peer,
removing the untrained and indeed those intimately associated
with the effects of madness, namely the family, from the process of
defining insanity.

The early asylum appointees could hardly have envisaged the
powerful position that the RMS would hold by 1900, and the reversal
of status that saw the Board relegated to administration. Once the
RMS became the accepted authority within the asylums, virtually all
elements of institutional life were influenced by his recommendations.
Supported by the medically qualified asylum inspectors, the national
system moved steadily towards the ideal of a curative rather than
custodial system, which was predicated on medical expertise.[41] This
change was resisted by the early asylum Boards. At Ballinasloe, they
prioritised their relationship with the (lay) manager over that with
the Visiting Physician, as the former's status was unproblematically
subservient. The manager was responsible for the smooth running
of the establishment; supervising staff, keeping accounts, processing
tenders and, crucially, reporting any problems amongst the patients
to the Visiting Physician. Thus, he was the first contact for patients,
rather than the Visiting Physician, and his reporting relationship to
the Board ensured that the physician (officially at least) was a
peripheral figure. Yet, the manager had no medical training or
expertise, and his central position in an institution that existed to
cure the insane was galling for the physician, to say the least.
However, Heise and his contemporaries were also part of a more
traditional medical world, in which a system of apprenticeship
played an important role, and the centrality of university training
was still contested. When Dr. Heise was absent from the asylum for
any significant period, he was replaced, with the consent of the
Board, by his son.[42] Despite the fact that in his early years this young
man was not qualified, his intention was to become a doctor, and it
was assumed that he had built up experience sufficient to tend to
the needs of the asylum patients through observation of his father's
practice.

The apparent lack of faith, or perhaps interest, in medically
qualified practitioners, however, did not imply an indifference to the
recovery of asylum patients. On the contrary, the Ballinasloe Board
was sensitive to the broader factors that impacted on mental health, in
a manner that is more reflective of a twenty-first century holistic
approach, than an early twentieth-century medical model. In common

with the inspectors, they recognised the role of poverty in exacerbating mental ill health and, consequently, emphasised the importance of avoiding a workhouse-like atmosphere which might tend to further depress already vulnerable patients.[43] Unlike their counterparts in the workhouse system, members of the Board argued in favour of non-essential facilities such as a library, and requested additional funds for the provision of entertainment and improvements to the décor of the day rooms. Thus, they placed emphasis on maintaining and exceeding standards enjoyed by patients at home and recognised the subtle manner in which individuals might internalise asylum provision. In the Ballinasloe Asylum's response to the Select Committee of Inquiry of 1843, one of the major preoccupations was the question of diet, and the impact that cost-cutting measures might have on patients.

> Upon the ground of humanity, the consideration of which is so much, and in a question of this nature so properly dwelt upon by the committee, it is to be apprehended that a diet inferior in quantity or in quality or perhaps in both to what a lunatic had been accustomed to … would be felt by him as a painful privation. Such a change could not but aggravate the case of a patient who is thenceforward hopeless of that recovery, the prospect of which had previously compensated to him for loss of liberty and removal from his friends. It is impossible to visit an institution of this kind and not be struck with the importance of hope to the support of the patience and cheerfulness of even the most indigent class of patients.[44]

The drive towards a medical model was whole heartedly supported by asylum medical staff, but this is not to say that it was a unanimous approach by the medical profession as a whole. There is evidence from the Ballinasloe records that there was often tension between the dispensary district medical officer, whose signature was required to process a patient to the asylum under the Dangerous Lunatics Act (DLA), and the receiving physician in the asylum. In theory, the dispensary doctor conducted an examination of any patient charged under the DLA and, on the basis of his medical expertise, decided whether the patient was a fit subject for admission. In practice, the dispensary district medical officer called on in these cases merely rubber-stamped a decision already made by the magistrates, with the support of the community, and processed the patient onwards. The fact is that in most instances, the patient was unknown to the doctor,[45] who accepted not merely the circumstances presented to him as credible reasons to commit, but also repeated the accusations made by relatives and others as evidence of insanity, providing a medical imprimatur that was in these circumstances untrue. Uncorroborated testimony thereby received a medical endorsement, despite the lack of first-hand information on the part of the doctor confirming the committal. Moreover, the speed of the process was such that there was no time for independent observation or assessment, with the doctor required to make an evaluation of sanity on the spot. The willingness of district medical officers to participate in the process may have two origins. The first is relatively straightforward – he received a fee for each patient examined.[46] The salaries received by dispensary doctors varied widely, but were generally very poor.[47] The fee for examination was therefore an important contribution to their income, and one not likely to be rejected. Equally, they were unlikely to spend a great deal of time in evaluating patients whom they did not know and who were being sent on to the asylum. The second may lie in the tensions between branches of an increasingly specialised medical profession itself.[48] There is evidence to suggest that there were social, if not professional, rivalries between the medical officers endorsing the committals and the receiving physicians in the asylums, who were required by law to accept any person presented to them under the DLA. Joseph Robins argues that:

> Those doctors who took up full-time salaried posts in the asylums were regarded by some of their profession as placing themselves in an inferior position ... [They were seen as] doctors of 'the hack class', professional mediocrities lacking not only the medical skills but the social distinction of the independent practitioner.[49]

This appears to have been a particular problem in the early years of the system, when 'mad doctors' became so by virtue of an interest in insanity, or perhaps, more cruelly, when they took up positions as resident medical superintendents, with no particular interest in the job, but because of a lack of success in establishing a profitable private practice. And there is evidence to suggest that this was indeed the case, particularly in the early years of the system. The professional discourtesy with which many district medical officers treated their asylum colleagues was noted by the Ballinasloe Board, which ordered the clerk on several occasions to send reminders to the examining physician of their obligations to assess prospective patients carefully.[50]

From the 1845 reforms onwards, the position of the resident medical superintendent in the District Asylum altered considerably, and the career of one such appointment at the Ballinasloe Asylum encapsulates the changes that took place throughout the later years of the nineteenth century. The first doctor to be appointed as manager, or resident medical superintendent, at Ballinasloe Asylum was Dr. Richard Eaton, who held the position from 1859 to his death in December 1874. Dr. Robert Vicars Fletcher, who had been the visiting physician since September 1872, was appointed as his replacement immediately following Eaton's death. As RMS at Ballinasloe for almost thirty years, Dr. Fletcher's career demonstrates the professional and political changes being wrought in Irish asylums towards the end of the nineteenth century. His early career suggested significant professional ambition. He trained as a young man at Steeven's Hospital in Dublin and then moved to Edinburgh, where he received his L.R.C.S. in 1865. In 1879, he became a Fellow of the Royal College of Surgeons in Ireland, and was appointed First Assistant Medical Officer at Downpatrick Asylum at the relatively early age of 29. As his obituary notes, he had 'turned quite early in his career to psychology', a significant statement, indicating faith in the potential that psychiatry held for an ambitious young physician.[51] It also indicates that by the second half of the nineteenth century, psychiatry was no longer a specialism of last resort.

A demonstrable shift in medical emphasis may be seen through the records of the institution, with Fletcher's medical model achieving increasing dominance. It was during his tenure that patient case notes began to be kept for the first time,[52] with the asylum records reflecting a greater interest in the physical as well as mental conditions of the patients. From the 1890s onward, the initial consultation with the patient now involved the completion of a two-page form with headings that attempted a comprehensive overview of the subject's physical as well as mental health. They included under 'Personal History' headings on Syphilis, Fevers, Other Diseases, Injuries and so on, and under 'On Admission' categories such as Expression, Reflexes, Ears and Hearing, Handwriting, Common Sensibility, and 'Ethical', a category that embraced 'Idea of Duty to self and others', 'Value of Property' and 'Habits' (orderly, filthy, destructive, indecent).[53] A limited drug therapy was introduced, with opiates used to calm manic individuals, as well as in an attempt to control epilepsy, with large doses given to overcome the patient's state of excitement.[54] From the 1870s onwards, detailed records of physically ill patients were maintained, together with records of the medical interventions (diet, medication, and surgery) utilised in their treatment. Fletcher advanced the boundaries of care in two other significant ways – he operated extensively on patients, treating long-standing physical injuries and impairments and took a proactive stance in the treatment of patients.[55] This stands out in sharp contrast to the reactive position of visiting physicians such as Heise, who simply treated patients as they fell ill or were injured. Fletcher sought to demonstrate the importance of a professionally trained asylum physician, and this aggressive approach ensured that his authority extended much further into all areas of the institution. The minutes of the meetings of the Board of Governors reflect the expansion of his spheres of influence, as he intervened in non-medical matters such as the acceptance of tenders to the institution, the expansion of the farm, and even the attendants' uniforms. Where prior to 1859, the (lay) manager had reported to the Board on diet, clothing, accommodation, the discipline of keepers and nurses, and the organisation of work parties, now the RMS did so, as each of these areas became part of the active treatment process. Fletcher prescribed tailored diets for certain classes of patients and altered the required tenders as a result. He required the nursing staff to report directly to him on patient progress, responsibilities previously held by the (lay) manager and the matron. Thus, from a position where the physician had concerned himself only with ill-health, with little input to the general running of the asylum, he now directed almost every element on the basis that these areas all contributed to the recovery of patients.

One of Fletcher's key innovations was the use of post-mortem examinations of patients, as a means of classifying the progress of mental disease. Without the benefit of a laboratory (he had only the 'dead house' in the asylum grounds in which to operate), his investigations were necessarily limited, but they met with praise from the Inspectors of Lunacy, who lauded his efforts to advance medical knowledge. However, this practice flew in the face of cultural attitudes towards the dead, including the respect accorded to the deceased. It also interfered with the wake, an essential part of the highly ritualistic process of death, where the corpse was traditionally in plain sight of the mourners from death until burial.[56] Fletcher was especially interested in evidence of disease in the brain, a highly intrusive element in the examination, and one least likely to be permitted by relatives under normal circumstances. But the asylum, like the workhouse, had large numbers of long-stay patients, many of whom were eventually buried by the institutions. Despite the punctilious sending of a standard letter to the last known address of the nearest relative on the occasion of a serious illness and death, many bodies went unclaimed.[57] Otherwise, it is highly unlikely that many would have agreed to a post-mortem, particularly when the cause of death was known. At the time, there was a general public repugnance over what was regarded as a violation of the dead through post-mortem. In 1904, the Dublin Coroner, Mr. Friery, attacked the reluctance of physicians to ascribe a cause of death without the benefit of a post-mortem.

> I am sorry to say that there is a practice springing up amongst some members of the medical profession of refusing to give an opinion in cases such as this [sudden death] as to the cause of death except they hold a post-mortem. I am strongly opposed to such an unjustifiable practice, and I certainly will not give any instructions to have this poor fellow's body cut up. I have been twelve years now acting as coroner, and I must say that this is the first case in my experience where I have found that a doctor declines to give an opinion as to the cause of death. If the doctor is not able to give an opinion I will give an opinion myself, and that is, that this man has died from heart disease. The circumstances you have heard detailed show beyond a shadow of doubt that the diseased has for a considerable time past been attending the dispensary of this hospital, and there is no reason in the world why any medical man should have any hesitation in stating his opinion as to the cause of death. It is a monstrous thing to think that a post-mortem examination should be held in such a clear case as this, and I am determined, so far as I can, to have an end put to the practice in my district.[58]

Fletcher's post-mortem rates were very high, far in excess of those routinely recommended in modern hospitals, and reflect the authority that the RMS had in the nineteenth-century asylum and the degree of latitude he was permitted in the interpretation of his duties. But did these medical interventions provide tangible results in terms of cures or recoveries? The answer is ambiguous. On the one hand, there is no doubt that the physical health of many of the patients improved greatly under Fletcher's direction, and outbreaks of endemic and epidemic disease were less frequent and more rapidly controlled. There is also a clear connection in many cases between an improvement in physical health and recovery of mental health, a factor that both Fletcher and the Board agreed were inextricably linked. The therapeutic regimes in place at Ballinasloe under Fletcher's regime were indeed a significant advance on those that prevailed when Dr. Heise was the visiting physician, not least because they operated on a system of constant surveillance and of deductions based on observation and personal interaction. Fletcher intervened aggressively in patient care and used his extensive experience to modify treatments for particular groups, such as 'puerperal maniacs'.[59] However, although the annual reports, and indeed the Board of Governors' minutes, attest to the benefits of medical therapy, many of the cured and recovered cases stem more from patient responses to old-fashioned moral therapy than to modern medicine. Regardless of age, gender and, to a significant degree, diagnosis, a regime that facilitated rest and a gradual return to willing and productive work, resulted in discharge. 'Cured', 'Recovered', and 'Discharged Unimproved' rates remained steady over the course of the century at an average of 30 per cent, although there were many other variables that affected the discharge of patients.[60] Those who appeared to embrace moral therapeutic principles fared best. Thus, patients who were 'useful and willing workers', who took advantage of the rest permitted for certain cases, who 'eat well' and were 'regular' in their habits, were the individuals with the best outcomes.[61] This approach is clearly reflective of the philosophy of the original Board, who were firm believers in beneficent supervision and of class and gender-appropriate occupational therapy.

As the nineteenth century advanced, the asylum became an increasingly accepted element in local community life, with large numbers depending on it for employment as well as health services. The senior medical staff became significant figures in the locale, forming part of the social elite, and commanding a good deal of respect.[62] But even with this rise in the status of the physician, both in and out of the asylum, there also emerged a consistent level of resistance on the part of certain patients to the authority of the RMS, regardless of his increasingly powerful position. This is one of the most important, yet neglected, aspects of the asylum story, which has tended to confirm a narrative of unalloyed power on the part of the medical profession and asylum authorities. Establishing an accurate picture of patient response to therapy and indeed to the asylum itself is problematic, given the paucity of first-hand testimony.

Although the nineteenth-century Irish asylum records are rich in detail, the patient statements that they contain are often mediated through a third party.[63] The case notes, for example, frequently record direct speech and, while the liveliness and individuality of encounters between the patient and the physician suggest an accurate account of engagements, from this distance it is impossible to know whether, or in what manner, the dialogue has been edited or deleted.[64] One also relies on testimony from relatives, supplied by letter to the physician and, crucially, in the committal warrants, for evidence relating to the patient experience. Patients led a highly structured existence, their lives regulated by the asylum bell which determined when they rose, ate, exercised, worked and slept. However, many refused to follow the rigid schedule and defied the nursing and medical staff through non-cooperation, a strategy that the institution and its officers were often helpless to counter. The District Asylums, in fact, offered a unique space in which such authority could be contested. In other medical settings, such as hospitals, the potential for conflict was significantly reduced. Patients seeking treatment at a dispensary, for example, or requesting admission as a hernia case to a hospital, were more likely to assume a deferential attitude in order to access the treatment they sought. Indeed, the custom of issuing tickets that could only be secured on application to the local elite cast the sick person in a disadvantaged position, one in which an appropriate gratitude, if not obsequiousness, was required.[65] But patients in the asylums, very many of whom had been admitted as much for social as medical reasons, and who were often less inhibited by virtue of behavioral peculiarities, were often entirely coherent in their resistance to Fletcher's authority. The following case is not unusual.

A 22 year-old male, admitted in 1894, engaged with a modern medical discourse to secure his position within the CDLA, and challenge the authority of the RMS. Confidently stating that 'he had water on the brain since he was a little infant', this auto-diagnosis forced Fletcher to assert his own medical expertise through the case notes. 'He has not a hydrocephalic head but one of very small cranial capacity and a sottish unintelligent face with an internal strabismus alternating in each eye [cross-eyed].'[66] But owing to a lack of classifiable criteria, the man was never diagnosed with any mental illness, the principal manifestation of his condition being an uninhibited sexuality. Indeed, Fletcher attributes a high degree of cunning to the patient and the case notes are themselves an eclectic flow of observations with limited medical assessment. He is described as 'very troublesome, annoying helpless and aged patients with monkey like ingenuity [1899] ... is troublesome treacherous and obscene: shouts filthy language from dormitory windows: delights in annoying and irritating helpless patients [1901].' Capable of instruction, he did not seek approval: 'he assumes a responsibility towards the other patients as to their keeping in ranks when exercising etc: he is on the whole rather indifferent to his surroundings but steals tobacco and is very fond of music.' As the patient's stay extended, Fletcher became increasingly concerned with his aberrant sexuality, but could only attempt to modify it, using an unreliable system of punishment. Thus 'he has lately owing to debased habits been blistered, with excellent effect [1895]'.[67] The patient's behaviour had however a more troubling element: Fletcher noted that 'he delights in an opportunity of injuring a helpless patient, and besides music, perhaps nothing pleases him more than teasing idiots of that class ... he is very troublesome at times fighting with and annoying other patients and has been reasonably suspected of sodomy and frequently caught in the act of masturbation until severely blistered on the pupice. He is vicious and treacherous. [1897]' The danger that he posed to vulnerable patients was consistently noted, but the asylum could find no medical solution and followed a largely unsuccessful policy of containment: 'Has had on one or two occasions to be blistered on pupice for indecent practices ... controls himself easily on the threat of a blister. [1899]' By 1906, the notes record with a certain grim satisfaction that he 'has entirely lost use of OD [the right eye] owing to recurrent attacks of inflammation for which he would have no treatment and to blows which he is constantly bringing on himself by his habit of irritating helpless patients and others whom he thinks will not be able for him.' The patient's sole contribution to the running of the asylum was the inefficient polishing of boots ('he never works beyond getting a few boots blacked') but the medical staff seemed at a loss as to how to cure, restrain or re-train him. In English asylums, self-abuse was routinely 'treated' with the use of gloves or a modified manacle,[68] but in this case, and many others at Ballinasloe, punishment and persuasion were the norm.

This case is one of many involving patients who were not appropriate cases for residence in the asylum, but who nonetheless stayed for extensive periods of time, often for life. It stands in sharp contrast to the rapid turnover of patients in the charitable and public hospitals and demonstrates the relative freedom of authority of the asylum

RMS to retain and release patients. Contrast, for example, the case above with that of Joseph Merrick, the so-called 'Elephant Man'. Found in a debilitated and utterly destitute state on his return from the continent in 1886, by the illustrious surgeon Frederick Treves, he was taken to the London Hospital and nursed back to relative health. However, because he was a chronic case, Treeves had no right to admit Merrick and certainly no authority to offer him long-term shelter, despite his obvious need.[69] It was only Merrick's extraordinary physical condition and an extensive media campaign, which secured funds for his support and ensured his continued residence in the hospital. The District Asylums, funded by the counties and central government had, in theory, stringent conditions laid on expenditure, yet in reality offered far more leeway than the general hospitals, with their huge patient turnovers and constant review. Although asylums have been popularly read as sites of involuntary residence, they provided in many instances a haven for those with no resources. Individuals who might find it difficult to gain full expression in the 'outside' world could partially express themselves when inside the asylum.

> There is a remarkable instance of an adult male patient in this division, who, from an early period in life, feigned himself a female, who dresses alike and whose general habits and manner partake altogether of the female character; he presents a very odd, grotesque appearance, on first entrance into the day-room, seeing him sitting amongst a group of men on the floor, just like a woman.[70]

The authority of the RMS within the asylum structure was well established by the end of the nineteenth century. Visiting physicians continued to be appointed, but their power and influence declined as their duties were reduced.[71] The RMS, as chief medical officer and manager of the asylum, had immense authority, not only over treatment, but over expenditure. In addition, the asylums themselves were affected significantly by politics outside their walls. From a position where they ran as proto-fiefdoms of the ascendancy, with little interest on the part of the Catholic Church or local power brokers in their operation,[72] they were recognised as important power bases in local areas, and in concert with a rising nationalist politics, entered the arena, rather unwillingly, of political power struggles. On Robert Fletcher's death, one may see the explicit manner in which power had moved from ascendancy hands into the rising nationalist middle-class, with a worrying implication for the freedom of the physician. In a heated meeting, the Board of Governors discussed the merits of the two candidates for the post of RMS, Dr. Mills and Dr. Kirwan. Mills had been the senior resident medical assistant under Dr. Fletcher, and would ordinarily have expected to secure the position. However, the debate took place almost exclusively in the context of politics and religion, with little mention of either the professional capacity of the candidates, or the medical needs of the patients. Dr. MacCormack, the Catholic Bishop of Galway and Board Chair, proposed Kirwan, a Catholic, and the seconder stated that:

> 97 per cent of the patients were Catholics, and where they had a candidate of equal merits, it behoved them as a committee almost entirely composed of members of the religious belief of the patients, to elect a man of the same faith. If they did not do so they would be less than men.[73]

Arguing that 'the question of religion should not enter into the matter … [Mr Galvin, proposing the Protestant Mills] … asked the governors to give fair play, and to reward merit in the interest of the public service.' Kirwan was elected by seventeen votes to five, and the editor of the *BMJ* commented:

> The result of the election is an illustration of the influences which operate in elections to public offices in Ireland. It is manifest that no devotion to service or ability in the discharge of duty will count when candidates of different creeds are applicants for appointments. The one essential is the form of religious belief. The appointment is worth £620 a year.[74]

The dawn of the new century ushered in a rapidly changing political and medical environment, with the promise of fresh starts for staff, patients, and the country as a whole. But the ominous signs of clerical and party political interference evident in the 1904 asylum election contained the potential for stagnation that came to characterise Irish asylum history for the coming decades.

NOTES

1. Homeopathy's origins are contemporaneous with institutional psychiatry, with German physician Samuel Hahnemann first defining the basic principles in 1796. Despite the damming criticism of homeopathy's efficacy in the House of Commons Science and

Technology Committee's 2010 Report, it continues to be funded on the NHS, confirmation of the power of patient choice in modern medicine.

2. Galen's influence remained strong in western medicine until the 1860s, and is still detectable in psychiatric practice in the latter half of that century. The emphasis on 'moral' causes of mental illness, and the necessity for 'disease histories', remain a central part of the medicalising process in Irish asylums. W. Riese, 'The Structure of Galen's Diagnostic Reasoning' in *Bulletin of the New York Academy of Medicine* 44: 7 (1968): 778–91, p.782.

3. Many of the CDLA's Board of Governors had extensive systems of charity on their own estates, principally for the care of their tenants. See Conor McNamara, 'The Monster Misery of Ireland: Landlord Paternalism and the 1822 Famine in the West', in L. Geary & O. Walsh (eds), *Philanthropy and Nineteenth-Century Ireland* (Dublin: Four Courts Press, 2013).

4. The first RMS in Ballinasloe was Dr. Richard Eaton, appointed in 1859. Dr. Fletcher, the second RMS, appointed in 1874, had been the visiting physician at Ballinasloe from 1872.

5. J.F. Sweeney, 'The role of the Irish Division of the Royal Medico-Psychological Association in the Development of Intellectual Disability Nursing in Ireland', *Canadian Bulletin of Medical History*, 28:1 (2011): 95–122.

6. The extraordinary moment, at which the nurses and patients took over the asylum, and established Ireland's first soviet, provoked questions in the House of Commons. The action was subsequently copied nationally, although not at other asylums, and became a key element in the Anglo-Irish War. *Hansard*, HC Debates 20 February 1919, PPI 1919, Vol. 112, pp.116–17. PPI refers to *Irish Parliamentary Papers*, Irish University Press Series, published by Irish Academic Press, Dublin (Hereafter, PPI).

7. Once the system was established in England, the possibilities for mass observation, and experimentation in therapeutic techniques, became clearer. Thus research was a consequence of the institutional system, not a cause. Roy Porter, *A Social History of Madness: stories of the insane* (London: Phoenix, 1996), p.18.

8. HC 358, PPI 1821, Vol. 3, p.1603.

9. As early as the eighteenth century, English physicians had dominated the emergent asylum system, placing the lay asylum boards in an unambiguously administrative position. Jonathan Andrews and Andrew Scull, *Customers and Patrons of the Mad-Trade: the management of lunacy in eighteenth-century London* (London: University of California Press, 2003), Chapter 1.

10. 'That every person that shall be appointed to be a Governor or director of any such asylum ... shall act without any salary, fee, reward or emolument whatsoever.' HC 358 in PPI 1821, Vol. 3, p.1603.

11. Terence de Vere White famously remarked that no Anglo-Irish library contained a book worth reading after 1800. It is true that many families who remained in Ireland struggled to build on, or even retain, the economic, political and cultural position of the late eighteenth-century. *The Anglo Irish* (London: Gollanz, 1972), Introduction.

12. A typical instance of aristocratic decline may be seen in the fate of one of the CDLA's governors, Walter Laurence. Heir to the once magnificent Bellevue mansion in Lawrencetown, East Galway, which had an extensive eighteenth-century Italian art collection, the estate was heavily encumbered, and large portions of land were sold to tenants throughout the nineteenth century. By 1912, the art treasures were all sold, along with the remainder of the land. The house was demolished in the 1930s.

13. German physicians were instrumental in the admission of patients from the eighteenth century. Christina Vanja, 'Madhouses, Children's Wards, and Clinics: The Development of Insane Asylums in Germany' in N. Finzsch & R. Jütte (eds), *Institutions of Confinement: Hospitals, Asylums, and Prisons in Western Europe and North America, 1500–1950* (Cambridge: Cambridge University Press, 1996), p.122.

14. 'As officers to whom is committed a responsibility both in reference to the management and maintenance of lunatics, we have always endeavoured to attain the double object of combining efficiency with the least possible expenditure.' *Sixth Asylums Report*, HC 1852–53 (1653) xli. 353, p.4.

15. Ironically, it was to the small number of private asylums that the ascendancy and middle-class turned for the care of their mentally ill relatives, a system in which they had little direct control. See Alice Mauger, 'Confinement of the Higher Orders: the social role of private lunatic asylums in Ireland, c. 1820–60' in *Journal of the History of Medicine and Allied Sciences* (forthcoming, 2012/13).

16. *Select Committee on the Lunatic Poor in Ireland 1817*, HC 1817 (430) viii. 33, p.46.
17. Ibid., p.33.
18. Heise's formal title was 'Moral Governor'. Joseph Reynolds, *Grangegorman: Psychiatric Care in Dublin since 1815* (Dublin: Institute of Public Administration, 1992), pp.46–50.
19. Letter of Appeal from Heise to the Richmond Board of Governors, in Reynolds, *Grangegorman*, p.49.
20. Cited in Reynolds, *Grangegorman*, p.49.
21. The Lord Lieutenant's office had requested a response from every asylum manager in Ireland to the Report, and this correspondence was published in 1844 as *Copy of Correspondence between the Irish Government and the Managers of Irish District Lunatic Asylums on the subject of the Report of the Select Committee of the last Session on the State of the Lunatic Poor* (Hereafter, *Copy of Correspondence* 1844). Ballinasloe's is one of the most extensive replies.
22. *Copy of Correspondence* 1844, p.13.
23. White had been a surgeon to the Richmond Asylum, who became an Inspector of Prisons. He fought a swift and successful campaign to establish a separate Inspectorate of Lunatic Asylums, staffed with physicians. This move heralded the medicalisation of Irish asylums, with the increasing dominance of the RMS underpinned by successive asylum inspectors, all of whom were medically trained. See 1845 Act, 8 & 9 Vic. c. 107, sections 23, 24.
24. *Copy of Correspondence* 1844, p.10.
25. Stewart was both resident physician and manager, and the Belfast asylum was often held up by Dr. Francis White as an example of a well-run medical establishment.
26. Dr. Stewart's high opinion was echoed by Dr. Flynn of the Clonmel Asylum, also a physician manager, *Copy of Correspondence* 1844, p.3.
27. See Anne Digby, *Making a Medical Living: Doctors and patients in the market for medicine in England, 1720–1924* (Cambridge: Cambridge University Press, 1994).
28. Board of Governors' Minutes, 2 April 1845.
29. Board of Governors' Minutes, 7 May 1845.
30. Board of Governors' Minutes, 16 January 1847.
31. Fees from private practice were an important part of a publicly appointed physician's income; Greta Jones estimates that it could add up to £150 per annum to a doctor's income. 'Strike Out Boldly for the Prizes that are Available to You': *Medical Emigration from Ireland, 1860–1905*, in *Medical History* 54 (2010): 55–74.
32. Ballinasloe did not appoint its first doctor as manager/RMS, until 1859.
33. Board of Governors' Minutes, 31 March 1848.
34. Ibid. The patient was eventually discharged (classed as 'recovered') on 24 May and there is no further record of her, or her baby, in the asylum records. Register of Discharge and Deaths, Schedule II, 1848.
35. Board of Governors' Minutes, 31 March 1848.
36. The term 'psychiatry' was first coined in Germany by the physician Johann Christian Reil in 1808, and swiftly adopted by medics specialising in the care of the insane, to distance themselves from mere custodians of the mentally ill. It did not find general acceptance in Ireland until the late nineteenth century.
37. 'Ellis, Sir William Charles (1780–1839)' in the *Oxford Dictionary of National Biography* (Oxford: Oxford University Press, 2004).
38. Andrew Scull, 'A Brilliant Career? John Connolly and Victorian Psychiatry' in *Victorian Studies* 27: 2 (Winter 1984): 203–35.
39. Connolly co-founded the *Quarterly Journal of Practical Medicine* in 1836, with the specific purpose of disseminating medical knowledge.
40. This informal erection of barriers between the university-trained and the apprenticed practitioner, reflected the slow but steady move towards regulated medical training in Britain. By the end of the century, the latter had largely been eliminated from the profession. Toby Gelfand, 'The History of the Medical Profession' in *Companion Encyclopedia of the History of Medicine* (London: Routledge, 1993), pp.1134–5.
41. There was one stumbling block to the absolute authority of the RMS within the asylum, however, and that was the operation of the Dangerous Lunatics Act. Despite their protests, the Acts, with their extraordinary powers of lay committal, remained the almost exclusive means of admission to Irish asylums, and overrode medical expertise in evaluating insanity. See Oonagh Walsh, 'Lunatic and Criminal Alliances in Nineteenth-Century Ireland' in P. Bartlett & D. Wright (eds), *Outside the Walls of the Asylum: Historical Perspectives on Care in the Community in Modern Britain and Ireland* (London: Athlone Press, 1999) pp.132–52.

42. Board of Governors' Minutes, 30 June 1842.
43. There was a developed sense of the impact of poverty on asylum patients and, although the Board did not use terms such as 'stress', the admission documents both officially as a diagnosis, and frequently as an explanation, employed terms such as 'reverse of fortune' to explain the onset of mental illness.
44. *Copy of Correspondence* 1844, p.11.
45. The accused was examined by the 'Medical Officer of the Dispensary district in which the Justices shall be at the time ... [or] ... the nearest available Medical Officer of such District. If there is no Medical Officer or no available Medical Officer of the Dispensary District in which the Justices shall be at the time, the nearest available Medical Officer of any neighbouring Dispensary district is to be called by the Justices to their assistance.' Declaration, Committal Warrant of a Dangerous Lunatic or a Dangerous Idiot.
46. Until 1851, doctors had been paid for each patient assessed. After the Medical Charities Act 1851 (14 & 15 Vic. c. 68), this duty was taken into consideration when setting the salary of the medical officer of each district, and those doctors who regularly certified patients for the CDLA ensured that this responsibility was specifically noted on appointment.
47. Larry Geary notes that 'the average annual salary paid to dispensary and fever hospital doctors was slightly less than £72' in 1840, and was in many cases considerably less than that sum. *Medicine and Charity in Ireland, 1718–1851* (Dublin: UCD Press, 2004), p.135–6.
48. Tensions within the profession and with allied branches of the Poor Law in Ireland, were commonly expressed through struggles to exert control over specific areas of medical administration. The importance of medically trained inspectors of lunacy was consistently emphasised in the Poor Law reforms of mid-century, as the profession sought to assert its exclusive right to adjudicate on matters of public health. Ronald D. Cassell, *Medical Charities, Medical Politics: the Irish Dispensary System and the Poor Law, 1836–1872* (Rochester, NY: Boydell Press, 1997), pp.83–90.
49. Joseph Robins, *Fools and Mad: a history of the insane in Ireland* (Dublin: Institute of Public Administration, 1986), p.96.
50. 'Directed: that a note be sent to Dr. Henry Laingstaff, Athlone, drawing his attention to the necessity of a comprehensive medical examination of patients sent under his authority to Ballinasloe, several of whom have proved to be unfit subjects for admission to this institution, being not insane.' Board of Governors' Minute Book, 1 April, 1851.
51. *Journal of Mental Science*, 50 (1904): 358.
52. In common with many of the other District Asylums, case notes began at Ballinasloe in the early 1890s, with retrospective case histories drawn from observation, and the original committal warrants.
53. See for example, the Male Case Book, April to November 1897.
54. In response to the 1857 enquiry into the use of mechanical restraint, it was noted at Ballinasloe that they lacked padded cells in which violent or epileptic patients could be held. 'Such cases have been frequently benefited by sedatives, as morphine or full doses of opium (after due preparation). Small doses appear to only stimulate and make them more restless; they generally bear larger doses of medicine than others.' *Ninth Asylums Report*, HC 1857, Session 2 (2253) xvii. 67, Appendix G.
55. See Oonagh Walsh, 'The Designs of Providence: Race, Religion and Irish Insanity' in J. Melling & B. Forsyth (eds), *Insanity and Society: The Asylum in its Social Context* (London: Routledge, 1999), pp.223–42.
56. Laurence J. Taylor. 'Bas In Éirinn: Cultural Constructions of Death in Ireland'. In L. J. Taylor (ed.), *The Uses of Death in Europe*, in *Anthropological Quarterly*, 62: 4 (1989): 175–88.
57. A standard letter was sent to the address of the relative who had signed the admission form indicating when a patient was seriously ill and unlikely to recover. On death, a notice was sent asking relatives to claim the body within three days, otherwise the asylum undertook the burial.
58. 'The Coroner Again' in *The British Medical Journal* April 16, 1904, p. 914.
59. Oonagh Walsh, '"Danger and Delight": conceptualising the insane in nineteenth-century Ireland' in M. Preston and M. Ó hÓgartaigh (eds) *Gender and Medicine In Ireland*, 1700–1950 (Syracuse: Syracuse University Press, 2012).
60. The presence of large numbers of incurable cases, that included epileptics, the intellectually disabled, the demented, and those in the third stage of syphilitic infection, ensured that recovery rates were lower as a percentage of total cases than should have been the case.

61. These phrases appear in all of the case notes and denote patients who are most likely to be discharged cured or recovered.

62. Fletcher was a keen huntsman and fisherman, and entertained lavishly at home. Little wonder that his obituary noted that 'Personally, Dr. Fletcher was a very popular man, and his funeral was attended by a large number of representatives of all classes.' *Journal of Mental Science* (1904) 50: 358.

63. In the early years at Ballinasloe, there is often a further layer: many of the patients were monoglot Irish speakers, so their testimony was both recorded by the clerk after translation by him.

64. The often unflattering assessments of the physician by his patients suggest that many of the case notes are accurate reflections of their meetings.

65. The position in England was even more fraught with class tension. With a system of subscribers tickets that was gradually augmented by partial payments, the working-class person who was ill had a complex system to negotiate in order to secure treatment at a voluntary hospital. See George C. Gosling's unpublished PhD thesis, *Charity and Change in the Mixed Economy of Care in Bristol, 1918–1948* (Oxford Brookes University, 2011), chapters 4 & 5.

66. Male Case Notes, no. 3524, p. 149.

67. Although blistering was used in a variety of treatments, in this case it appears to have been exclusively for punishment. 'Blisters are used as counter-irritants. By exciting a disease artificially on the surface, we can often remove another which may be at the time existing internally.' Robley Dunglison, *A Dictionary of Medical Science* (Philadelphia: Henry C. Lea Publisher, 1868), p. 132.

68. This use of blistering was reflective of Dr. Richard Bucke's innovation of 'wiring' male patients at the London Asylum in Ontario, Canada, a procedure that he claimed trained male patients to abandon masturbation forever. See Peter Rechnitzer, *The Life of Dr. R. M. Bucke* (Minneapolis: Quarry Press, 1997).

69. Indeed, only by representing Merrick as a divine reminder of how fortunate others were to enjoy unblemished forms, could an appeal to their Christian consciences be made. The Master of the Temple, Dr. John Vaughan, preached an Advent sermon that was an oblique appeal on Merrick's behalf: '… one of the Creator's objects in permitting men to be born to a life of hopeless and miserable disability was that the works of God should be manifested in evoking the sympathy and kindly aid of those on whom such a heavy cross is not laid.' Quoted in Michael Howell and Peter Ford, *The True History of the Elephant Man: the definitive account of the tragic and extraordinary life of Joseph Carey Merrick* (London: Allison & Busby, 1980), p. 96.

70. *Report of the Inspectors-General on the District, Local and Private Lunatic Asylums in Ireland for 1844*, p. 28, HC 1845 (645) xxvi. 269.

71. Two Visiting Physicians worked amicably alongside Dr. Fletcher – Dr. Dominick Burke 1874–85 and Dr. William Rutherford from 1885.

72. The relative lack of interest on the part of the Catholic Church to the operation of the District Asylums stands in sharp contrast to their aggressive involvement in mainstream medicine and in education.

73. 'Ballinasloe District Asylum' in *The British Medical Journal* April 16, 1904, p. 914.

74. 'Ballinasloe District Asylum' in *The British Medical Journal* April 16, 1904, p. 914.

13

Voices of Doctors and Officials

The following extracts are taken from a variety of reports and articles written in the nineteenth century in relation to care and treatment of mental disorder in Ireland. As such, they represent some of the views on mental illness and its treatment as articulated by doctors and officials involved in the asylum system at the time.

RICHMOND LUNATIC ASYLUM 1816: DIRECTIONS TO BE STRICTLY OBSERVED BY THE DOMESTICS OF THE INSTITUTION

- To allow every patient all the latitude of personal liberty consistent with safety.
- To proportion the degree of coercion to the obvious necessity of the case.
- To use mildness of manner or firmness, as occasion may require.
- Every cause of irritation, real or imaginary, is to be avoided.
- The requests of the patients, however extravagant, are to be taken graciously into consideration, and withheld, under some plausible pretext, or postponed to a more convenient opportunity.
- All violence or ill-treatment of the patients is strictly prohibited, under any provocation, and shall be punished in the most exemplary manner.
- The mild acts of conciliation are to be the constant practice in this hospital.
- These laws are of fundamental importance and essential to the prudent and successful management of this Institution.

Source: 'Rules and regulations to be strictly observed by the Domestics of the Richmond Lunatic Asylum 1815', reprinted in the 8th Asylums Report, Appendix G, p.64. HC 1857 Session 2 (2253) xvii. 67.

* * * * *

DIARY/NOTEBOOK ENTRIES OF THOMAS TOBIN, ATTENDANT AT DUNDRUM, 1884–9

Thomas Tobin worked as an attendant/male nurse at the Central Criminal Lunatic Asylum, Dundrum for approximately five years during the 1880s, at the time when Dr. Ashe was the resident medical superintendent. This short extract tells us a great deal about life in Dundrum at the time. From it, we can glean that attendants in addition to having their uniform supplied, also received an annual allowance for boots. As an attendant, one of his duties was to accompany patients to their local District Asylum to which they were often sent after being discharged from Dundrum. The journey referred to here was to accompany the patient Michael Harrington from Dundrum to Cork. This involved a train journey and car hire and probably took a full day. After Tobin emigrated to Australia in 1889, he worked for a short while with the prison service in Fremantle, escorting prisoners between gaols.

The longer extract from the diary describes a violent incident that happened after one patient (Thomas Wilson) attacked another. He had managed to smuggle a knife from his place of work (the shoe making department) and another patient (Kelly) had sharpened a spoon into a lethal weapon. The fight between the two men, according to Thomas, had something to do with religion. It resulted in punishment for the men involved in the fight, and an injury to the doctor who tried to intervene. Violence was not unusual in Dundrum and it could lead to solitary confinement or a transfer to prison for anyone deemed dangerous.

Work related – Dundrum State Asylum

I Thomas Tobin started on duty in Dundrum State Asylum, on the 6th day of November 1884.

Doctor Ashe the Governor told me, the 6th day of March 1885 that he received my appointment from the Lord Lieutenant   *T. Tobin*

Wednesday 11th March 1885
I was supplied with uniform slop suit & top coat   *Thomas Tobin*

March 4th 1886:   Received my boot money   *T. Tobin*
March 4th 1887:   Received my boot money   *T. Tobin*

Received the sum of 17s. from Doctor Ashe on the 7th July 1888
For third class Railway tickets   5s.10d

Escorting Michael Harrington to Cork D. Asylum: Railway Ticket to Cork
-1 pound 19 shillings and 1 penny; Car hire 2.0 shillings

On Thursday the 18th of November their was a scerious encounter between
the Patients at the hour of 1.30. A Patient be the Name of Thomas Wilson
brought a Knife out of the shoe-makers shop, and in the act of going to dine
he attacked a patient be the name of Fox alis Kelly. It seems this Kelly had
the handle of a spoon sharpened Which was equaly as bad as the knife. All
the Attendants that could be availble was their but owing to the interference
of the other Patients the Attendants couldn't part them untill the patient
Kelly got four or five stabs of the Knife on the Neck and face. Of course their
was a search made for the weapons amongst the patients & all of them was
procured.

Wilson of course was confined to cells for some days, then he was allowed
out in the air-ing yard after the other patients going to the Ball-court, with
his hands confined by means of A Strap, the house was very orderly consid-
ering the excited state of the patients as you must understand it was a
Religious matter got up Between them. Untill Saturday the eleventh of
December when Wilson came out after the other patients to the air-ing court
the excitement raised immediately amongest them. The doctor had to be sent
for & the upshot of it was He got struck twice in the face.

Source: This extract from the diary of Thomas Tobin was transcribed
and supplied by his grand-daughter, Denise Shine (nee Tobin). See
the fictional account of the life of Thomas Tobin, written by Denise –
The Undertakers' Mother (Killaghy Publishing, 2012).

* * * * *

REVISED PRIVY COUNCIL RULES 1874 (EXTRACTS)

By the Lord Lieutenant and council of Ireland, Spencer
(Given at the Council Chamber in Dublin, the 23rd day of
February, 1874)

Admission, treatment and discharge of patients: (extracts only)

xvii. Patients, except where special reasons to the contrary may exist, are to be clad in the dress of the institution, and their own clothes are carefully to be laid by, to be returned to them on their discharge xviii. The patients shall, on admission, be carefully bathed and cleansed, unless the Resident Medical Superintendent shall otherwise direct. They shall be treated with all the gentleness compatible with their condition; and restraint, when necessary, shall be as moderate, both in extent and duration, as is consistent with the safety and advantage of the patient.

xix. Strict regularity shall be observed with respect to the hours for rising in the morning and retiring for the night; that for rising being fixed at six o'clock from the 1st April to the 30th of September, called the Summer months, and for retiring at an hour not earlier than half-past eight o'clock nor later than nine for the same period. During the Winter six months, the patients shall rise at seven, and retire not earlier than seven nor later than eight o'clock.

xx. The like regularity must be observed with respect to meals; in no case shall the ordinary number of meals be less than three, and they shall be supplied during the Summer six months at the following hours, viz.: breakfast at eight o'clock; dinner at one o'clock; and supper at six o'clock; and – during the Winter six months at the following hours, viz.: breakfast at nine o'clock; dinner at two o'clock; and supper at six o'clock; but patients actively employed in or out of doors may have an additional allowance of food between the usual meals by direction of the Resident Medical Superintendent.

Resident Medical Superintendent (extracts only)

xxx. The Resident Medical Superintendent shall superintend and regulate the whole establishment, and is to be entrusted with the moral and general medical treatment of its inmates, for whose well-being and safe custody he shall be responsible; and he shall at all times devote his best exertions to the efficient management of the institution.

xxxi. He shall, before one o'clock, p.m., and also occasionally at other times, inspect the whole establishment, daily – dormitories, dining rooms, kitchen, laundry, stores, and other places. He shall go through all the divisions, and see that they are orderly, clean, well ventilated, and of a proper temperature. He shall carefully examine each patient who may seem to require his advice, or to whom his attention may be directed. When going around the female divisions he shall be accompanied by the Matron or Head Nurse of the division, who shall direct his attention to any matter worthy of notice.

xxxii. He shall take care that all the Officers, servants, and attendants of the institution acquit themselves of their respective duties, and in any case of their neglect, he shall report accordingly to the Board at its next meeting. In cases, however, of drunkenness, insubordination, or cruelty, he may suspend any attendant or servant, reporting to the Inspectors within three days the names of the party and the cause of suspension, and at its subsequent meeting, to the Board for its decision; and until such decision, the offender shall be removed from the Asylum.

xxxiv. He shall also visit the male divisions after the patients have retired to rest, and satisfy himself that they are safely and comfortably located for the night.

xxvi. He shall never be absent from the Asylum at the same time with the Matron, nor every for the night without special leave from a Board of Governors or the Inspectors, and upon every such absence he shall enter in the book the date and period; and inform the Consulting and Visiting Physician, who for the time shall exercise a general supervision over the establishment: and in case of protracted absence of the Resident Medical Superintendent of any Asylum in which there is no Assistant Medical Officer, a duly qualified substitute shall be provided, who shall reside in the Asylum during such absence.

Consulting and Visiting Physician (extracts only)

xlii. The Consulting and Visiting Physician shall attend at the Asylum three days in the week, and on every day in those Asylums where the number of patients shall exceed 200; the regular hour of attendance being in the interval of from ten to one o'clock, unless otherwise arranged, by mutual consent, between the Medical Officers. On his arrival he is to communicate with the Resident Medical Superintendent, in company with whom he shall visit all patients labouring under bodily disease, and any who are in seclusion, or under restraint. He shall also see such patients as may have been admitted since his preceding day of attendance, and any others whom he may desire to visit.

xliii. He shall attend at all times when called on by the Resident Medical Superintendent, and afford such advice and assistance as may be required of him, whether to patients, officers, or servants, and he shall afford such advice daily in cases of acute illness, and accidents of a dangerous nature. He shall once, at least, in each fortnight, examine with the Resident Medical Superintendent, into the mental condition of every patient in the Asylum, who is under special medical treatment.

xliv. He is on every day of attendance to enter in the Morning Statement Book the hour and duration of his visit.

The Matron (extracts only)

lv. She shall reside in the Asylum, and shall exercise immediate superintendence over the female department, but in position and authority subordinate to the resident Medical Superintendent, to whom she is to report daily its condition, and any irregularity or misconduct that may occur within it.

lvi. She shall take care that cleanliness, both in person and dress, is strictly attended to, and shall have particular regard to the rooms in which sick, refractory, or idiotic patients are confined.

lvii. She shall employ the female patients as advantageously as possible to themselves and to the establishment, and in every way endeavour to promote their comfort and well being.

lxiii. The Matron is to consider herself an officer of great trust, and must sedulously watch over the good conduct and becoming demeanour of the female servants and attendants. She shall not absent herself from the Asylum at the same time as the Resident Medical Superintendent; nor at any time by night without the special permission of the Board or the Inspectors.

Attendants and Servants (extracts only)

lxxviii. Attendants and servants, both male and female, in their various departments, shall be directly responsible to the Resident Medical Superintendent, and shall observe habits of cleanliness, order, and subordination, as well as the most unvarying kindness towards the lunatics placed under their charge, or with whom they may come in contact.

lxxix. The attendants shall never absent themselves from their divisions so as to leave the patients unguarded, nor shall they attempt mechanical restraint, seclusion, or the use of the shower or plunge bath, without express directions from either of the Medical Officers. The presence of an attendant or servant, in the case of baths being given, shall be imperative.

lxxxii. They shall be answerable for the safe keeping of the lunatics under their care, and in the event of escape, attributable to any negligence on their part, shall be liable to a fine, or to dismissal.

lxxxviii. No attendant or servant is to be permitted egress from the institution, without the sanction of the Resident Medical Superintendent, or in his absence, if a female, of the Matron, if a male, of the Clerk and Storekeeper, with the sanction of the Consulting and Visiting Physician, by the written pass; and on no account are the children of any domestic to reside in the Asylum.

lxxxix. Attendants or servants are on no account to receive any perquisites, either in money or value, from patients, or from the friends of patients admitted to the Asylum; any infraction of this Rule should be punished by immediate dismissal.

xc. They are to avoid any harsh or intemperate language to patients, and must, by steadiness, kindness, and gentleness, endeavour to contribute to that system of moral government upon which the value of the Asylum depends.

Gatekeeper (extracts only)

cviii. He shall not admit any stranger without entering the name and the object of the visit, neither is he to permit any attendant or servant belonging to the Asylum to go out, except on a pass, with the name of the party inscribed thereon, signed by the Resident Medical Superintendent, or in his absence, by the Matron or Clerk, with the sanction of the Consulting and Visiting Physician.

cix. He shall enter the date of all passes, together with the hours of return in the Gate Porter's Book, which is to be brought up every morning to the office for the examination and signature of the Resident Medical Superintendent, without whose sanction no admittance or exit shall be allowed to any non-resident officer or servant except through the public entrances.

cx. He shall be at all times most cautious in guarding against the unauthorized introduction of spirituous liquors or cordials of any kind, or any other article which may be prohibited by the Board, and shall promptly report to the Resident Medical Superintendent any case of impropriety of conduct which may come under his observation.

Source: 23rd Asylums Report, Appendix H, pp. 262-79, HC 1874 (c. 1004) xxvii. 363.

* * * * *

AMUSEMENTS IN DISTRICT ASYLUMS IN 1873

Omagh District Asylum

Amusements in this Asylum are conducted on a liberal scale, 240 of the inmates being enabled to join in them. They consist of draughts, Chinese billiards, nine pins, steeplechase game, American skittles, dominoes, cards, bagatelle, music and dancing, as well as occasional walking parties outside the grounds. Reading also commands its share of attention, chiefly of periodicals and newspapers, and the latter as a rule, it may be said are much prized in Irish Asylums, as they give rise to discussion and exchange of political opinion, which go a great way in relieving the monotonous life of the more intelligent inmates. There is in this Asylum an excellent band, the services of which are frequently taken advantage of in giving evening entertainments.

Downpatrick District Asylum

Great attention seems to be given to amusements both in and out of doors, such as drafts, music, cards, hand-ball, football, etc; every week dancing parties are held in the large hall, perhaps the finest and most spacious apartment in the kingdom. For those who can read there are cheap periodicals and illustrated papers.

Killarney District Asylum

The amusements both in and out of doors are of the usual kind and variety to be found in District Asylums – books, illustrated papers, drafts, cards, handball, football. There are extensive walks around the grounds on which the patients exercise. We regret there is no approach to a band, or that the monotony of the twelvemonth is not broken by some little festivity at Christmas and Easter.

Source: *23rd Asylums Report*, pp.85, 41, 55, HC 1874 (c. 1004) xxvii. 363.

* * * * *

SOME OBSERVATIONS ON GENERAL PARALYSIS

(Extracts from an article in the *Journal of Mental Science*, Vol. XXII, No. 97, April 1876, pp.82–91.)
By Dr. Isaac Ashe MD, TCD, Resident Medical Superintendent, Londonderry District Asylum.

Although we have, for some time past, begun to emancipate ourselves from the idea that insanity is a disease of the mind, and admit, in theory at least, that it is strictly a disease of the body, as much so as typhus, or any other disease involving body, as much so as typhus, or any other disease involving perturbed mental phenomena, yet we have scarcely hitherto begun to investigate the pathology of insanity from this point of view. Even if we classify the forms of disease involving perturbed mental phenomena, yet we have scarcely hitherto begun to investigate the pathology of insanity from this point of view. Even yet, we classify the forms of the disease by the mental manifestations it presents, and speak of mania, melancholia, dementia &c., when our aim ought to be to differentiate the physical or chemico-vital somatic conditions; we describe the insanity of fear, of pride, exaltation, &c., much as if we should classify ulcers as those of the hand, the arm, the leg, and the trunk, instead of attending to the more important characters of ulcers in general with their true specific differences. For, I venture to think that Professor Ferrier's researches point strongly to the view that the differences in direction, so to speak, taken by the mental phenomena depend to a great extent upon the differences in the portion of brain tissue principally affected. The investigation of the physical causation and conditions of insanity will doubtless be laborious and tedious work, but there can be no doubt that the results to be obtained will more than repay the labour which must be expended in the investigation.

It seems to me that in General Paralysis we have, as it were, a portal to such an investigation – a sort of basis of operations from which our future explorations of unknown territory may with advantage be commenced; in fact that the key of the unknown region lies in a knowledge of this disease, its causes, pathology, and condition.

As regards the causes of this disease, two are usually assigned, and have almost been accepted, name – 1st, Excessive use of alcoholic liquors; and 2nd, Immoderate sexual indulgence.

But as regards the first of these assigned causes, I have to call attention to a very remarkable fact regarding the distribution and statistics of the disease which bears very strongly on this point, and is perhaps very little known. It is this: that General Paralysis is scarcely to be found in Ireland, though so common in England and Scotland. The remarkable absence of the disease in the Irish asylums with which I am acquainted, as contrasted with those of Great Britain, has long since pressed itself on my mind; but I have recently endeavoured to procure as far as I could some exact statistics on this point. As an illustration of the vast differences existing between England and Ireland in this matter, I may direct your attention to one or two particular instances. Thus, in the *Twenty ninth Report of the English Commissioners in Lunacy*, just published, at p. 207, we find the inmates of the West Riding Asylum put down as numbering 1,404; and on the next page, the deaths from General Paralysis during the year are – males, 26; females, 9 – total 35; which will probably give 70, or 5 per cent, as the number of cases at any given date. Per contra, my friend, Dr Merrick, having charge of the Belfast Asylum, containing 400 patients, writes to me – 'We have no case of General Paralysis in the Belfast Asylum at present'. Dr McCabe, of the Central Criminal Asylum, with 163 patients, writes – 'I regret that there are no materials here; I have not had a case of General Paralysis since I took charge, three years ago'. Dr Atkins, the Assistant Physician of Cork, with 700 inmates, writes – 'One spurious case at present in the asylum'. In my own asylum at Londonderry, with 250 inmates, I have at present only one case; but I was fortunate enough to have another well marked case some time ago, and I have also met the disease in private practice.

I cannot but think that such a disproportion in the frequency of the disease in the two countries must be held at once and entire to negative the theory that its development is due to excel in the use of ardent spirits; indeed, I might add that it equally negatives the view that it is due to venereal excesses either; for, certainly, neither in the one direction nor in the other can it be asserted that the Irish peasant is more abstemious than his English neighbour. And, moreover, as regards the use of ardent spirits, any one of us in Ireland could at once count up 10 per cent of our asylum population whose insanity has been caused by the abuse of distilled liquors; but the disease does not take the form of General Paralysis. ....   I think the remarkable absence of the disease in Ireland is quite sufficient to prove further, that even immoderate sexual indulgence is not a vera causa of the disease. Were it so, we should undoubtedly have our share of it here.

Note: Dr Ashe goes on to suggest that the differences in frequency of General Paralysis between Ireland and Great Britain might be explained partially by differences in drinking patterns ('the use of malt liquors rather than to that of spirits') and in diet ('England feeds on a more highly phosphorised diet than Ireland. Where England consumes cereals, a phosphorised diet, Ireland consumes the potato, a non phosphorised'.)

* * * * *

ON THE ALLEGED INCREASE OF INSANITY IN IRELAND

(Extracts from article written in the *Journal of Mental Science*, Vol. XL, No. 171, October 1894, pp.518–47.)
By Dr. Thomas Draper, MB, Resident Medical Superintendent, Enniscorthy District Asylum.

The question of the increase of insanity in Ireland is, of course, but a part of the much larger question, the increase of insanity generally, all the world over. But there is one peculiarity about Ireland which has been repeatedly noticed, of which, as yet, no adequate explanation has been forthcoming, namely, that while in other countries insanity has increased along with, and in a higher ratio than an increasing population, Ireland alone of all civilized countries, so far as I am aware, possesses the unique and unenviable distinction of a contin- uously decreasing population; and, what would appear to be an almost necessary consequence, the proportional rate of increase in Ireland is far beyond what exists elsewhere.

    … The question then remains, are we in a position to explain the increase in the amount of occurring insanity? … Insanity being the expression, the outward and visible sign of defect, derangement, or disease of the supreme nervous centres, it is not unreasonable to suppose that any influences affecting the nervous system generally would be reflected in its highest, most delicate, and most vulnerable part. … From a return kindly supplied to me by the Registrar General, I find that the deaths per million of population from diseases of the nervous system have increased during the last decade, as compared with the previous one, by just 20 per cent. This is exclusive of convulsions and of deaths in asylums, due to diseases of the nervous system, including insanity. It is not an unwarrantable inference that the increase in insanity is to a large extent but part and parcel of a general increase in diseases of the nervous system suggested by the mortality returns. The cause of this general increase is, no doubt, to be found in the influences of 19th century life and civilization, which bear hardly on the nervous system. The stress of modern life is, of course, more operative in large towns and cities, of which there are comparatively few in Ireland: and, the large majority of our insane people coming from rural districts, it may be argued that such an influence can have but little effect on a plodding peasantry. But if the restless ambitions, the thirst for gold, the lust of power or distinction, which characterize the spirit of the age as it affects the dwellers in cities, can exercise but little sway over the minds of the tillers of the soil, still it has its effect upon them, not so direct perhaps, but none the less real. Steam and electricity have revolutionised trade, and all but annihilated distance and, owing to the rapidity of intercourse and swiftness of transport which they have created, every commodity of the remotest region is brought daily to our shores, and distributed throughout the length and breadth of the land. The inevitable result follows - a lessening in value of all home produce. Prices dwindle and profits fine away almost to vanishing point. No one can deny that for many years past, the prevailing tone of agricultural life has been depression, often great depression, and nowadays it is admittedly no easy task to make a living out of this our chief national industry. And so, modern civilization makes itself rudely felt in every Irish farmer's home. Add to this the almost constant political agitation to which our people are subjected, deeply arousing, as it does, the feelings of a naturally emotional race, and we surely have the ingredients for producing a large amount of mental excitement calculated to have prejudicial results.

... Temperament and racial characteristics have, no doubt, much to do with susceptibility to mental derangement; and here the Irish are at a disadvantage. An excitable brain is an easily disturbed brain; and the quick witted, passionate, versatile, and vivacious Celt has, for those qualities which made him so charming, too often to pay the price of instability. Behaviour under the influence of stimulants is, more or less, a rough and ready test of cerebral stability.

... Of other causes which may contribute to the increase of insanity, four are touched upon in the Inspectors' report – heredity, consanguineous marriages, innutritious dietary, and the immoderate use of stimulants.

... While there is hardly any proof that tea drinking, even in excess, is capable of directly causing insanity, there appears to be a well grounded opinion on the part of nearly all the superintendents of Irish asylums that it has to some extent an indirect effect in the production of it. It has a twofold action. By being made a substitute for more nutritious food, the deprivation of the latter leads to general malnutrition. And, secondly, by causing that condition of hyper excitability of the nervous system, so familiar to every practitioner of medicine, it must create a special predisposition to disorders of that system. Even if properly prepared, the excessive use of it would be deleterious, but the mode of decocting it in vogue amongst the Irish peasantry is the one of all others calculated to induce its most pernicious effects. Left stewing, sometimes boiling, for a protracted time, it is frequently taken without milk, and is little better than a strong decoction of tannin.

... We may well ask, the public may well ask, is there no remedy for this increase of insanity? None that can be applied directly. One thing is certain, the old proverb cannot have a more apt application than here – prevention is better than cure.

... There is still a lamentable ignorance of the laws of mental sanitation. ... But, there are some broad principles which even now every medical man, in season and out of season, can and ought to enjoin. The avoidance of injudicious marriages (and this is advice which should be given in time, before the event is inevitable), the pernicious effects of the abuse of narcotics and stimulants, the necessity for control of the passions, for adjusting intellectual labour (especially in the case of children) to the powers of the individual, the careful and constant pruning of every little eccentricity of manner and conduct.

PART THREE
EXPLORING TRENDS

14

A Theoretical Exploration of Institution-based Mental Health Care in Ireland

Damien Brennan

During the past two hundred years, we have witnessed the development of an extensive institution-based mental health-care system in Ireland. This began in the early nineteenth century with the building of a national network of publicly funded asylums and the setting up of an overarching bureaucracy to support this major social intervention. The demand for places in these institutions grew annually, reaching a high point in 1956, when there were 21,720 patients in residence. Ireland, at this time, had the highest rate of psychiatric hospital bed utilisation in the world (see Table 14.1).

Two proposals could be advanced to explain this pattern. The first is that there was an epidemic of insanity in Ireland from the mid-nineteenth to the mid-twentieth century. The second is that social forces, rather than any bio-medical predisposition to insanity, caused the pattern of asylum/mental hospital use in Ireland. In this chapter, the first of these proposals is rejected and the second is explored. Based on empirical data, the degree to which established social theories on psychiatric institutionalisation can be applied to the Irish case is examined. Key theories to be considered include: the influence of the leprosaria model; the impact of colonial oppression; the interaction between industrialisation, capitalism and institutional segregation; the role of private enterprise in asylum provision; the importance of professional power and clinical monopolies; and the role of the Church.

I will argue that these theories do not adequately explain the Irish experience of asylums. Rather, a model highlighting particular points of 'social conjuncture' is proposed. Three points of conjuncture are examined in the development of the asylum/mental hospital system: 1) the early phase of asylum expansion during the mid-nineteenth century; 2) the interruption of this expansion during the late 1950s;

and 3) the closure of psychiatric hospitals in Ireland in the early twenty-first century.

THE POPULATION IN INSTITUTION-BASED MENTAL CARE: EMPIRICAL DATA

The Inspectorate of Lunacy for Ireland, having been established as a separate entity in late 1845, was required to inspect all institutions offering care and treatment for people defined as mentally ill and to publish an annual report detailing the extent and general activities of these institutions with a focus on publicly funded asylums. In 1922, the title of 'Inspector of Lunatic Asylums' was changed to 'Inspector of Mental Hospitals', but the role and function of inspection and annual reporting remained much the same. The following data on bed occupancy are derived mainly from these reports. The numbers referred to in the tables and graphs include everyone designated as a 'lunatic' (nineteenth century) or as a 'mentally ill' person (twentieth century) who was resident in an institution for care or treatment. While the largest numbers of residents were in district asylums/publicly funded mental hospitals, there were also some people in private asylums/mental hospitals, in workhouses/public assistance institutions (up to 1957), and in prisons (1846–99).[1] In some years, there are gaps in the data due to the fact that annual reports from the Inspectorate did not always provide the same data each year. These gaps are filled with data from other official sources, including special reports, hospital census materials, and information from individual hospitals.[2]

Long-Term Trends

A long-term trend in the rate of institutional residency can be established, by recording both the total number of 'mentally ill' persons resident in institutions and the overall population level for the year in question. The dynamic nature of the trajectories of these two variables can be visualised by displaying both trend lines on the same axis. To facilitate this, the total population data-points are divided by a factor of 250. (See Figure 14.1 for the Island of Ireland from 1820 to 1921, and Figure 14.2 for the Republic of Ireland from 1922 to 2000).

As shown in Figure 14.1, there is a strong inverse relationship between the level of institutionalisation of 'mentally ill' people and the overall population of the country. This is significant, as it indicates that asylum expansion occurred at a time when the general

FIGURE 14.1: ISLAND OF IRELAND, 1820–1921: POPULATION TREND AND TOTAL
NUMBER OF 'MENTALLY ILL' PERSONS RESIDENT IN INSTITUTIONS.

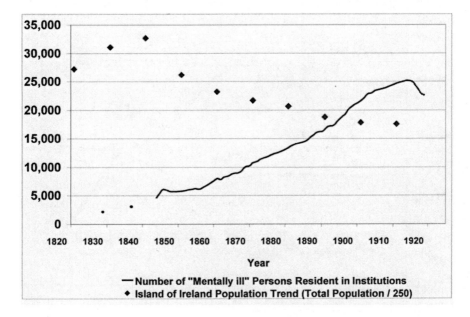

population of Ireland was in rapid decline. This decline resulted in
an acceleration of the actual rate of asylum residency per 100,000 of
the general population. There is one notable spurt and one notable
decline in the asylum population, which are not typical of the overall smooth pattern of continuous asylum expansion (see Figure 14.1).
The first is the sharp increase in the numbers during the late 1840s.
This occurred at the same time as the Great Famine of 1845–7 and
appears to reflect the use of these institutions as a place of refuge
during this time, particularly for older people for whom emigration
was not an option. The second deviation from the overall trend is
the declining level of institutionalisation between 1915 and 1921.
The Inspector of Lunatic Asylums attributed this to an unusually
high death rate rather than a reduction in the admission rates
during this time.

> The decrease in the total number of the insane under care
> which, as pointed out in previous Reports, has been going on
> since 1915 … the reduction in the numbers was not due to any
> lessening of the admission rate in the District Asylums but to a
> heavy death rate … which amounted to 10.5 per cent of the
> average number resident in 1917.[3]

FIGURE 14.2: REPUBLIC OF IRELAND, 1922–2000: POPULATION TREND AND TOTAL NUMBER OF 'MENTALLY ILL' PERSONS RESIDENT IN INSTITUTIONS.

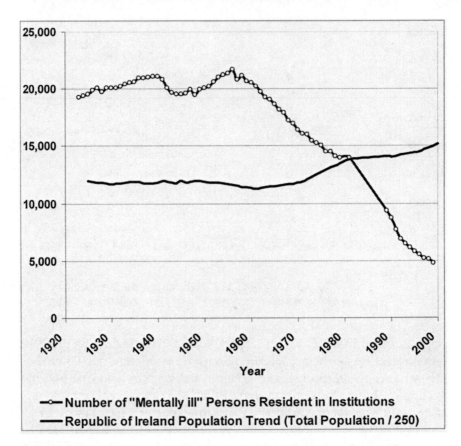

In Figure 14.2, the data shows that the Republic of Ireland experienced an overall pattern of steady growth in the number of 'mentally ill persons' resident in mental hospitals in the first half of the twentieth century – from 19,398 in 1924 to the high point of 21,720 in 1956. The rate of growth was slower than it was in the nineteenth century (as evidenced in Figure 14.1) and there was a period of decline in the patient population between 1939 and 1948. This was paralleled by a similar drop in the number of patients in mental hospitals in Northern Ireland, which may or may not have been linked to increased employment opportunities during World War II.[4] The decline became a trend from 1956 onwards, with numbers falling to 4,522 at the beginning of the twenty-first century. Significantly, the general population of Ireland began a slow and steady upward growth from 1962 onwards. Thus there was an inverse relationship between the institutionalised population of 'mentally ill' people and the general population of Ireland, resulting in a rapid decline in the rate of residency per 100,000 of total population from 1956 onwards. This decline mirrors the trend during the period of rapid growth in asylum use from 1850 to 1910 (see Figure 14.3).

FIGURE 14.3: ISLAND OF IRELAND, 1850–2000: NUMBER OF 'MENTALLY ILL' PERSONS RESIDENT IN INSTITUTIONS PER 100,000 OF POPULATION.

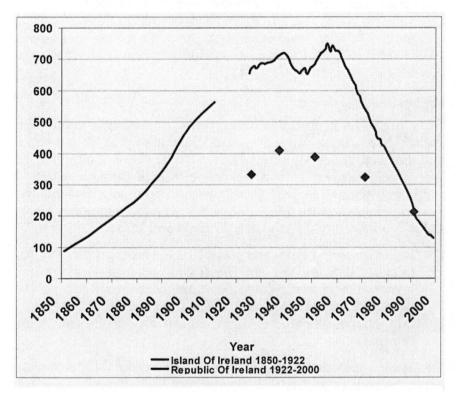

Data points in Figure 14.3 are given for years that have a complete set of verifiable data for all institutions occupied by people defined as 'mentally ill', along with a verifiable total population. As such, this data provides the seminal information required to examine the long-term expansion and decline of institution-based care for 'mentally ill' people in Ireland. The trend line in Figure 14.3 shows an accelerating rate of asylum residency from the mid-nineteenth century, increasing almost six fold, from 88.43 per 100,000 of the population in 1851, to 561.59 per 100,000 in 1911. Increasing rates of institutionalisation for mental illness were characteristic of Irish society both under colonial rule and after independence (from 1922), with rates reaching a high point of 749.35 asylum residents per 100,000 of the population in 1956.

While the focus of this chapter is the island of Ireland before 1922 and on the Republic of Ireland after that date, the trends in Northern Ireland from 1922 are noted in Figure 14.3, so as to provide a point of comparison with the Republic. The data from Northern Ireland are adapted from the work of Prior.[5] As illustrated, Northern Ireland had a similar pattern to that experienced in the Republic of Ireland, but the actual rate of bed occupancy (for mental illness) per 100,000 of the population was significantly lower in Northern Ireland.

International Comparisons

There are several obstacles to providing consistent comparative statistics between countries over time. Difficulties arise from the fact that the actual institutions which provide accommodation for 'mentally ill' people differ between countries, as do the administrative support structures. In 1891, the Inspector of Lunatic Asylums for Ireland referred to his own difficulties when trying to compare statistics on insanity for England, Scotland and Ireland.

> In Ireland the insane poor in District Asylums are not Pauper Lunatics, nor indeed are the insane poor in Workhouses, because the insane in Workhouses are there simply as destitute persons. There are thus no persons in Ireland who are technically Pauper Lunatics. This introduces a difficulty into such comparisons.[6]

The statistics provided by the Inspector in 1891 set out the 'proportion of the Insane Poor per 100,000'. For the year 1889, these numbers are as follows: England, 260 per 100,000; Scotland, 245 per 100,000; and Ireland, 312 per 100,000. The data relating to Ireland was recorded with an explanatory note stating that this figure 'is exclusive of … unregistered Lunatics at Large,' but 'inclusive of Insane in Workhouses'.[7]

While there are serious limitations to any comparative analysis of international data, some general observations may be made. What is important is that the overall trend or trajectory of institutionalisation in Ireland can be understood in the context of trends in other countries, while acknowledging possible differences in institutional provision, types of institutional occupancy and systems of data recording. The rate of institutionalisation for those defined as 'mentally ill' increased in most countries during the late nineteenth and early twentieth centuries. However, it accelerated in Ireland to such an extent that by 1955, it was significantly higher than elsewhere. According to the World Health Organisation's *Annual Epidemiological and Vital Statistics* 1955, which provides statistics including the total population, the number of psychiatric hospitals and the number of psychiatric beds within each country, Ireland ranks first with the highest rate of psychiatric bed provision per 100,000 of the general population. The WHO data was recorded in various years between 1947 and 1952 (see Table 14.1).[8]

TABLE 14.1: WORLD HEALTH ORGANISATION (WHO), TWELVE COUNTRY COMPARISON, 1955: PSYCHIATRIC BEDS PER 100,000 OF POPULATION.

Ranked	Country	Number of psychiatric beds Per 100,000 of population, 1955
1	Ireland	710.34
2	U.S.S.R	617.58
3	United States	511.38
4	Northern Ireland	440.07
5	Scotland	436.09
6	Sweden	422.89
7	Barbados	407.16
8	St. Helena	382.70
9	Hawaii	381.56
10	Switzerland	372.77
11	England and Wales	357.09
12	Australia	332.05

Source: World Health Organisation (1958), *Annual Epidemiological and Vital Statistics 1955*, Geneva: WHO.

There was a decrease in bed occupancy in psychiatric hospitals in most developed countries during the second half of the twentieth century and this decrease was significant, if a bit slow, in Ireland. This is reflected in the comparative data shown in *Irish Psychiatric Hospitals and Units Census 2001*[9] which sets out the rates of in-patients per 100,000 of total population. Scotland came first, with a rate of 179.5 per 100,000, followed by Ireland, with a rate of 119.2 per 100,000; followed by Wales at 74.8 and Northern Ireland at 70.1. The rate for England, 62 inpatients per 100,000 of the population, is the lowest. As can be seen from these statistics, institution-based care for the mentally ill was a significant form of social intervention in Ireland.

THEORIES OF ASYLUM/MENTAL HOSPITAL EXPANSION AND CONTRACTION

As shown in Figure 14.3, mental health care in Ireland was characterised by a rapid expansion in institutionalisation during the second half of the nineteenth century, with continued growth until 1956, followed by a sustained period of decline from 1956 to 2000. Both rates – of expansion and of contraction – were extreme by international standards. I now consider whether or not the Irish case supports any of the established theories used to explain the rise and fall of patient populations in asylums/mental hospitals.

The Leprosaria Model

Foucault[10] argues that the building of large institutions and the practice of asylum confinement had their roots in the classification and segregation of individuals suffering from leprosy. Responses to the spread of leprosy involved the widespread construction of leprosaria. Three dynamics are interesting here. Firstly, the practice of segregation is established, with all its realities of classification, labelling and stigma. Secondly, a physical location selected, as the place of confinement becomes both the site for treating the sick and, paradoxically, the perceived location of the origin of the disease. Thirdly, medical practice is established as the central agent within this process. Essentially, Foucault makes the point that the model for the treatment of leprosy established a physical setting, diagnostic process and form of intervention that was later adopted in the social construction of insanity and the confinement of the insane.

> Leprosy disappeared, the leper vanished, or almost, from memory; these structures remained. Often, in these same places, the formulas of exclusion would be repeated, strangely similar two or three centuries later. Poor vagabonds, criminals, and 'deranged minds' would take the part played by the leper.[11]

However, Ireland did not have a legacy of leprosy or of the construction of leprosaria. Foucault does make a brief reference to Ireland in *Madness and Civilization* – in relation to the opening of a workhouse in Dublin in 1703,[12] but the Irish workhouse system did not provide either the administrative or physical foundation on which the asylum system was later developed. As such, theories that locate leprosaria, or indeed other locations of confinement, as the basis for asylum expansion have limited application to the Irish case.

Colonial Oppression

While some accommodation for 'mentally ill' people was provided in workhouses, there was limited social policy or legislative provision for them prior to the Act of Union 1800 (40 Geo 111 c. 67). At this time, Ireland was under British colonial rule and any major decisions relating to publicly funded social intervention required agreement at parliamentary level in Westminster, prior to its implementation through Dublin Castle. This created a degree of disconnection between the local demand for publicly funded social interventions, the legislative action required to meet social needs, the administration of interventions, and the system of payment for such activities.

A seminal point in the emergence of Irish asylum policy was the initiative by the Chief Secretary for Ireland, Robert Peel, who set up an enquiry in 1814 into the extent of provision for the 'insane' in Ireland. This enquiry found that the public provision was both limited and inadequate. As a result of this enquiry, a select committee on the 'Lunatic Poor in Ireland' was appointed. The report of this committee had a direct and lasting impact on the future of Irish mental health care.[13] The resulting national network of district asylums became the cornerstone of institutional care for the insane from the early nineteenth century until their eventual closure and sale two centuries later, when a politically backed closure policy was proposed in 2006.[14] Drawing on the predominant discourses concerning insanity at the time, classification, segregation, specialisation and moral intervention were endorsed in the 1817 report.

> Your Committee beg leave to call the attention of the House to the detailed Opinion expressed by the Governors of the Richmond Asylum, - that the only mode of effectual relief will be found in the formation of District Asylums, exclusively appointed for the reception of the Insane. They can have no doubt that the successful treatment of Patients depends more on the adoption of a regular system of moral treatment, than upon casual medical prescription.[15]

The development of a national asylum system in Ireland was an exception to the overall policy of minimal social intervention by the state at this time.[16] In essence, the asylum system was an early example of a centrally controlled national bureaucracy of social intervention. It was followed some fifteen years later by a national primary school system which came into being in 1831.[17] Hence, if understood as a system of social assistance, the public asylum system was ground-breaking in the Irish colonial context. Alternatively, if understood as a system of social control, the asylum system was equally remarkable, as it far outpaced the prison system in terms of utilisation during the nineteenth and twentieth centuries.

In 1843, the *Report of Select Committee of the House of Lords Appointed to Consider the State of the Lunatic Poor in Ireland* set out a succinct account of the operational arrangements of these institutions within this colonial context.

> ... the cost of purchasing a Site, building the Asylum, and supporting the Establishment, is advanced from the Consolidation Fund, but repaid by the contributory Counties. All the principal Officers are appointed by the Lord Lieutenant, and the general Superintendence and financial Administration of the Asylums are vested in Boards of Commissioners, also named by the Government, but acting gratuitously. The annual Accounts are required to be examined and passed before the Board of Audit, and the Asylums are brought under the annual Review of the Inspectors General of Prisons.[18]

While the early network of asylums was small, it provided for a centralised bureaucracy that formed an administrative path dependency that shaped the later governance of these institutions. Expansion rather than reform was the primary focus of mid-nineteenth century colonial asylum policy. For example, the *Select Committee* in 1843 noted:

> The Necessity of increasing the Accommodation for Pauper Lunatics in Ireland, and of providing for the Cases of Epilepsy, Idiocy, and chronic Disease, by an increased Number of the District Asylums, by an Enlargement of those Asylums, or by the Erection of Separate Establishments specially appropriated for these Classes of Patients.[19]

An up-beat account of this continued expansion is provided in an early history of Irish Asylums by Kirkpatrick, who asserts that:

> The history of the care of the insane in Ireland during the second half of the nineteenth century need not detain us long. It is the record of the consolidation of positions already won,

rather than of new ground captured; of steady advance along the lines already laid down, and although at the end of the century there remained much to be done, much had already been accomplished, which, we feel sure, will remain a permanent asset to the community.[20]

The continued increase in the rate of asylum residency during the second half of the nineteenth century needs to be contextualised within a wider political dynamic, particularly the increased agitation for Home Rule and the political drive towards Irish independence. While the asylum system was administered centrally, questions relating to its shortcomings were not a priority for the centralised administration or its adversaries. Finnane argues that there was limited political discourse within Ireland on the question of alternatives to asylum care.

> ... while in the early 1900s Britain was stirred by a new discourse on the relation between society and the insane, Ireland remained unmoved: the authority of the state was by this time so seriously compromised that the debate on the 'feeble-minded' passed by without any discernible effect in law or social policy.[21]

Finnane also observes a political dynamic within the boards of individual asylums that centred on competition for representation based on sectarian political interests, essentially party political antagonism along the Catholic/Protestant divide. Sectarian antagonism also existed within the context of the asylum, as reflected in the refusal of some asylum boards to appoint chaplains (for example, the Belfast Asylum). This became a major source of tension between these boards and the central administration at Dublin Castle, as shown in an article entitled 'The Chaplaincy Question at the Belfast Asylum', published in the 1854 edition of the *The Asylum Journal*.[22] An optimistic note on this sectarian tension was made two years later by the editor of this journal, who seemed to suggest that Irish asylums actually provided potential for sectarian reconciliation.

> The real difficulty of the asylum chaplaincy question in Ireland arises, not from any doubt as the propriety and advantage of affording to the insane the means of public worship, but from the fear of introducing into these institutions the elements of religious discord dependent upon the rival faiths which have been so fruitful a source of misery to the country at large. It

may be that the Catholic and the Protestant Priest will, in such an abode of suffering humanity as the hospital for the insane, consent to waive their differences, to suspend their antagonism, and to behave towards each other as they never yet have behaved at any time, or in any place. It may be that on ground so sacred they will act towards each other in perfect charity, or at least in strict neutrality.[23]

At the end of the nineteenth century, while inspection and control of the national asylum system remained with the Inspectorate in Lunacy, responsibility for the direct provision and maintenance of asylums was transferred from the central administration in Dublin to elected local county councils under the Local Government (Ireland) Act 1898 (61 & 62 Vic. c. 37). However, at this stage an extensive publicly funded asylum system was already built and fully operational. As shown by Finnane, there was a period of rapid expansion after 1875 when there was a shift in financing from local taxation to a 'grant in aid of local taxation'.[24] This system now encompassed a large national network of buildings, each with its administration and staffing structure, along with an overarching national bureaucratic and administrative system. Essentially, this created an institutional momentum which made the scaling down or closure of these institutions politically difficult. Between 1870 and 1914, the population of district asylums in Ireland trebled from approximately 7,000 to 21,000.[25] By the close of the nineteenth century, asylums were perceived locally as both a necessary social intervention and an important economic driver in terms of direct employment and the consumption of locally produced goods.

The social policy supporting an institutional approach to the treatment of insanity remained unaltered throughout the struggle for independence, civil war and the setting up of the new state in 1922. The incoming Free State government inherited a large and expensive public asylum system. However, unlike the iconic action of 'Philip Pinel, who took the chains off the lunatics at Bicetre at the time of the French Revolution',[26] the national revolution in Ireland did not usher in the 'liberation' of asylum patients. Instead, these institutions were absorbed silently into the new political environment and continued to expand.

Within the context of the Free State, the Ministers and Secretaries Act 1924 established a Minister and Department of Local Government and Public Health, which consolidated statutory authority for all health-related services, including lunatic asylums.

However, with the exception of the legal changes in procedures for asylum admission in 1945, before the mid-1960s, there was a notable absence of any strategic policy that provided an alternative to the institutional approach to mental illness that had flourished under colonial rule. Independence simply changed the location of government, while the actual physical structures of asylums, the internal administrative bureaucracy and the approaches to care and treatment remained intact. While a colonial administrative structure underpinned the foundation of the Irish asylum system, the continued expansion of these institutions post-partition raises challenges to theories that focus on colonial oppression as a cause of 'mental illness' or of institutionalisation in Ireland. For example, Greenslade asserts that the high level of asylum occupancy, by Irish people, both in Ireland and in the UK, needs to be understood in terms of the structural and psychological impact of colonialism.[27] However, a broad colonial or post-colonial theory that seeks to explain asylum expansion is difficult to sustain, particularly if one examines the international experience. The statistics in Table 14.1 show no clear pattern of association between a legacy of colonial control and psychiatric institutionalisation.

Industrialisation and Capitalism

The macro-economic milieu in Ireland, particularly during the mid-nineteenth and early twentieth century, requires consideration when examining the rise and fall of the population in institutions for the 'mentally ill'. Scull's theory, which locates industrialisation and advanced capitalism as social forces that undermined the capacity of communities to care for the 'mentally ill', argues that:

> ... the main driving force behind the rise of a segregative response to madness (and to other forms of deviance) can much more plausibly be asserted to lie in the effects of the advent of a mature capitalist market economy and the associated ever more thorough-going commercialisation of existence. While the urban conditions produced by industrialization had a direct impact which was originally limited in geographical scope, the market system observed few such restrictions, and had increasingly subversive effects on the whole traditional rural and urban social structure. These changes in turn prompted the abandonment of long-established techniques for coping with the poor and troublesome.[28]

According to this argument, capitalism had an impact on both urban and rural communities in a manner that stimulated the development of asylums as an organisational system that would cater for 'mentally ill' people. Similar institutions also served to separate other unproductive people (children, older people and disabled people) from the able-bodied, the rational and the productive.

However, the limited penetration of both capitalism and industrialisation within Irish economic life is a theme explored in some detail in *Family and Community* in Ireland, first published in 1940, by Conrad M. Arensberg and Solon T. Kimball.[29] This was essentially a comparative ethnographic study of rural and small-town life in the west of Ireland, particularly of County Clare and the town of Ennis. Arensberg and Kimball argued that:

> The result of the first fifty years of the nineteenth century was that Ireland abandoned all pretence of being an industrial country and came to rely on agriculture to a greater extent than any time formerly.[30]

This observation is also made by Scull who notes that 'the market system spread to incorporate all but the Celtic fringe'.[31] During the early nineteenth century, Ireland was rural, colonised and predominantly traditional. With the exception of limited commercial enterprise in urban centres, it did not experience a classic phase of industrialisation and capitalism. In effect, Ireland was what may be described as a 'late moderniser, a latecomer to modernity'.[32] While Arensberg & Kimball's study does not present Ireland as a static and isolated society, it argues that the continuity and centrality of the traditional family as the core social and economic system served to limit the impact of industrialisation and capitalism in Ireland. Commenting on this, Byrne, Edmondson and Varley, observes that,

> For these authors, change wrought by economic or technological demands continually impinged on the ways Irish people lived, but it was absorbed at a pace, allowing it to fit the way of life pursued by the members of the community.[33]

An early comparison of regional variations can be drawn from the statistics provided in the 1843 report of the *Select Committee of the House of Lords Appointed to Consider the State of the Lunatic Poor in Ireland*.[34] This data illustrates a mixed and inconsistent urban/rural divide in rates of occupancy in district asylums (see Table 14.2). Waterford and Cork are reported as having the highest rates of

TABLE 14.2: DISTRICT ASYLUMS IN IRELAND, 1841: OCCUPANCY RATES
PER 100,000 OF POPULATION.

Order of rate of Occupancy	Asylum	1841 Rate of Occupancy Per 100,000 of Population
1	Waterford	58.62
2	Cork	49.52
3	Limerick	38.67
4	Richmond	35.76
5	Belfast	34.47
6	Maryborough	29.95
7	Carlow	27.76
8	Londonderry	25.37
9	Clonmel	23.65
10	Connaught	19.10
11	Armagh	14.66

Source: *Report of Select Committee of the House of Lords Appointed to Consider the State of the Lunatic Poor in Ireland*, pp.iii-iv. HC 1843 (625) x. 439.

asylum occupancy in 1841. While each of these districts contained a city, both districts were predominately rural at this time. Waterford district comprising 23,261 persons living within the city of Waterford compared with 172,971 persons living in County Waterford. Similarly, Cork City had a population of 80,720 persons and County Cork one of 773,398. However, the data shows that there was no consistency in the trends, i.e. rural areas did not always have the highest rates of asylum occupancy. Connaught Asylum (at Ballinasloe), which covered a predominately rural area, is placed tenth in the ranking, whilst the Richmond Asylum, situated in the city of Dublin, a comparatively industrialised area at the time, is placed fourth.

Variations in the rates of urban and rural asylum usage are also shown by Finnane, who noted a comparatively high rate of asylum occupancy in Dublin in 1871, followed by a gradual move to rural overrepresentation by 1911.

> In 1871, and for the following two decades, the admission rates were highest in Dublin and were particularly low in most asylums serving the west: Ballinasloe (Galway and Roscommon), Castlebar (Mayo), Cork, Killarney (Kerry) and Sligo (Sligo and Leitrim). It was these asylums in the west which, by 1911, had doubled or trebled their 1871 admission rates.[35]

In other words, a mixed regional pattern of institutionalisation existed during this period. In the data for 1841, no overall urban/rural pattern is observable (see Table 14.2). During the 1870s, there was a short period during which Dublin showed comparatively high rates of asylum residency. This is followed by a sustained trend of over-representation from rural areas, particularly from the west coast of Ireland. This trend continued right up until the mid-1990s.[36]

Contradicting theories linking industrialisation/advanced capitalism to asylum expansion, the traditional family unit was an enduring economic feature in Ireland as the system grew larger. Conversely, declining asylum populations in Ireland occurred at a time of increased industrialisation and capitalist enterprise. In 1958, a Department of Finance civil servant, T. K. Whittaker proposed a series of economic reforms that initiated a concerted government effort to increase industrial activity in Ireland.[37] While developments were slow, with continued economic depression and enduring emigration up until the late 1980s, the so-called 'Celtic tiger economy' from the early 1990s was a product of this pursuit of industrialisation in Irish economic life.[38] As shown in Figure 14.3, there was a marked decline in the rate of psychiatric institutionalisation during this period of industrial growth. Hence, it cannot be argued that the increase in the institutionalisation of 'mentally ill' people occurred during a period of increased industrialisation or advanced capitalism. Furthermore, the decline in the level and rate of institutionalisation for mental illness coincided with precisely these conditions, i.e. increased industrialisation and capital expansion in Ireland.

International statistics, as presented in Table 14.1, also appear to contradict any association between asylum expansion and the existence of a mature capitalist market economy. In the middle of the twentieth century, Ireland had the highest level of psychiatric bed availability, followed by the USSR and then by the USA – three locations with quite different economies.

Another way of viewing the asylum in relation to the economy is to see it as a site of economic production. An interesting feature of asylums was their capacity to operate as sites of production, where patients engaged in mandatory labour. An insight into how the Irish system operated as a site of economic activity is provided in the Lunacy Inspector's Report of 1845. Section G of the report gives a detailed breakdown of the type of labour, financial outlay, level of production and net profit arising from patient labour. Employment for males included 'Gardening Labour, Agricultural Labour, Weaving and Winding, Tailoring, Shoemaking, Carpentering, Cleaning the House, and Miscellaneous Employment'. For females, employment included, 'Spinning, Needlework, Knitting, Quilting,

Fancy work, Assisting in Laundry, Cleaning the House, and Miscellaneous Employment'.[39] Patient labour for 1845 provided a source of profit of £2,124. 10s.11d. However, as the total cost of running asylums that year came to approximately £40,000, this 'free labour' comes at a high price.[40]

During the twentieth century, the outsourcing of work from private companies to mental hospitals became a feature of what was known as 'Industrial Therapy', recommended for long-term patients in the *Report of the Commission of Inquiry on Mental Illness 1966*.[41] The Commission's views of the benefits of this type of labour were in keeping with those circulating in medical discourse at the time. For example, an article in the *British Journal of Psychiatry* in 1965 notes that:

> If patients are to be rehabilitated and the best use made of their personal resources, their lives within the hospital should be as close as possible to normal life in the community, and it follows that like normal citizens they should be employed at productive, useful and satisfying work for which they should receive proper economic rewards.[42]

'Industrial therapy' in Irish mental hospitals involved the setting up of industrial units on the grounds of asylums, or in public industrial estates. These units, which functioned until the 1990s, took in contract work outsourced from private businesses. These contracts included some for the packaging of black plastic refuse bags for sale in Irish supermarkets; some for the construction of electrical wiring looms for a German car manufacturer; and some for the labelling of plastic security clips for beer and stout barrels for a major Irish drinks company.[43] Patients received a nominal income in return for this labour and, as many did not have permission to leave the hospital grounds, this money was often spent in the hospital shop. In rural areas particularly, agricultural production became a major aspect of mental hospital life, perceived as bringing both economic and therapeutic advantages. For example, in the annual report for 1950, the Inspector of Mental Hospitals wrote:

> In 1950, the area under cultivation in the farms associated with District and Auxiliary Mental Hospitals was 2,190 acres ... Apart from the obvious advantage of having a farm attached to a large institution these farms offer a most valuable opportunity for providing a suitable form of occupational therapy for the patients, particularly in this country where so many are engaged in agricultural pursuits in ordinary life.[44]

Hence, as locations of economic productivity, Irish asylums/mental hospitals reflected a complex set of economic dynamics. While there was ongoing agricultural and industrial employment of the patients in Irish asylums, profits generated were artificial when set against the overall cost of the asylum system. Thus, the expansion and decline of the Irish asylum system does not appear to be linked to their potential as profit-making enterprises.

The Role of Private Enterprise

The extent to which private enterprise in direct asylum provision was a driving force in asylum expansion in Ireland also requires consideration. Commenting on this, Bartlett and Wright wrote:

> Boarding-out was official policy following the 1857 Lunacy (Scotland) Act. Up to one-quarter of registered pauper and private patients were relocated to households where (usually non-related) families were paid to care for a mentally disordered person … Irish authorities, by contrast, apparently resisted attempts to impose a state-sanctioned system of boarding out before World War I.[45]

The use of 'Unlicensed Houses' and 'Private asylums' was limited in Ireland during both the nineteenth and twentieth centuries. While these establishments did exist in parallel to the national asylum system and did receive some government funding, the number of patients resident in these establishments was small when compared to the public system. For example, the peak point in private provision was in 1979, when 1,145 patients were resident in private institutions. In the same year, there were 12,693 patients resident in public mental hospitals.[46] In practice, the Irish asylum system was predominantly a public system, in terms of planning, financing and administration. There was an absence of what Parry-Jones described as a 'trade in lunacy', or the franchising out of responsibility for care of the 'mentally ill' to private enterprise.[47] Hence, there is no evidence to back a theory linking the expansion of the Irish asylum system to capitalist opportunism within a free market in madness.

Professional Power and Clinical Monopolies

The initial wave of Irish asylum construction in the 1820s and 1830s was informed by a philosophy that proposed moral intervention as the most enlightened and effective response to insanity.[48] Psychiatry had not developed as a discipline within medicine at this time and before the 1860s, a medical qualification was not required to secure an appointment as asylum manager. By the mid-nineteenth century, Irish asylums were large scale and complex institutions and as such, their potential as locations of occupational power and security increasingly came to the attention of professional bodies. A number of individuals, most notably Dr. Francis White, moved to secure leadership and management roles for medically qualified persons within this expanding asylum system. In 1835, Dr. Robert Stuart was appointed as resident physician to Belfast Asylum. He was, in effect, the first medically qualified asylum manager in Ireland. In 1841, White was appointed as an Inspector General of Prisons, with special responsibility for 'lunatics'. From this position he was influential in the development of the *Rules for the Regulation of District Asylums 1843*.[49] He also advanced the case for the separation of the inspection of prisons and asylums, which was realised in 1845.

Having successfully argued for an independent inspectorate of lunatic asylums, White was the first to be appointed Inspector of Lunacy for Ireland in early 1846. He was joined one year later by Dr John Nugent.[50] White's professional career pathway is interesting, as it closely resembles the migration of professional practice observed by Foucault in *Birth of the Clinic*.[51] Foucault identified a movement of clinical control and medical practice from the context of identifiable disease within the individuals physical body (White's early speciality was diseases of the eye), to the public social sphere of the epidemic (White was secretary to the Board of Health during the cholera epidemic in 1832), followed by a medical takeover of control of major public institutions (White's appointment as the first Inspector of Lunatic Asylums in Ireland). Supported by the new regulations for district asylums in 1843, White and Nugent used their annual reports strategically to progress the medicalisation of patient care, while also advocating the appointment of medically qualified personnel as asylum managers. This established a hierarchical structure of medical control, supported by a large labour force of attendants/nurses, a structure that endured from the mid-1840s until the late twentieth century and arguably into the twenty first.

The medical press during the 1840s and 1850s suggested that doctors had a higher level of integrity and organisational ability than their lay counterparts in relation to asylums. For example, in 1856, the editor of the *Asylum Journal of Mental Science* discussed two incidents in Irish asylums, one relating to the violent death of a patient at the Ballinasloe asylum and the other relating to corruption in purchasing and provision of supplies for the Londonderry asylum. He noted:

> It is somewhat remarkable that both these unpleasant investigations took place in asylums in which there is no resident medical officer, both of the asylums being under the control of non-medical *managers*.[53]

The replacement of lay managers by medical managers (in district asylums) in the second half of the nineteenth century provided opportunities for the application of medically related scientific principles to the established practice of classification, segregation and selective intervention. However, while asylum expansion served the self-interest of the medical profession by increasing professional employment, this expansion occurred when complete medical control was limited by the involvement of the judiciary in admissions, enshrined in the Dangerous Lunatic Acts 1838 (1 Vic. c. 27) and 1867 (30 & 31 Vic. c. 118), and also by substantial fragmentation between asylum planning at national level and clinical management at local level.

The passing of the Mental Treatment Act 1945 consolidated medical power by shifting patient admission from a judicial to a wholly clinical process. Based on an anti-psychiatry thesis, one would expect increased occupancy rates to be associated with this consolidation of medical dominance, Samson argues that 'because psychiatrists were charged with both defining madness and admitting patients to the asylum, they could effectively create the demand for their own services'.[54] However, as shown in Figure 14.3, this was not the case in Ireland. While an initial increase in numbers did occur after the passing of the new law, a pattern of declining patient numbers was clear from 1956 onwards.

A critique of the biomedical control over mental health and illness that dominated care and treatment in the past two centuries can be found in the writings of Laing, Foucault,[55] Szasz,[56] and Illich, the leading lights in the anti-psychiatry movement of the 1960s. The concept of 'mental illness' is disputed from the outset by these scholars.[57] Rather, it is a dysfunctional form of social control, led by professional psychiatrists in order to justify their occupational security. However, the anti-psychiatry movement, though powerful as a change agent during the 1970s, had little impact in the Irish context.

The Role of the Church

The asylum system in Ireland did not develop in conjunction with established religious bureaucratic administrative frameworks. In fact, the Church (either Catholic or Protestant) had limited power in defining the nature of insanity or in the provision of services for individuals categorised as mentally ill. This is unusual in the Irish context, as church structures became central to other institutional care provision, including hospitals, schools, orphanages and reform schools. While perceived deviance such as homosexuality, alcohol dependence and general non-conformity with social norms were condemned by the Church as immoral, and were often defined by the medical profession as mental illness, the Church had limited involvement in the creation of demand or the supply of services within this particular 'market in deviance'.

This lack of Church involvement in the asylum system in Ireland can be understood by examining the timing of Church–State partnerships in other areas of social intervention, situated as they were within the wider political context of Catholic Emancipation in 1829.[58] While Church authorities were often in conflict with the State during the mid-nineteenth century, both institutions stood to further their strategic interests through cooperation. For example, in the case of primary education in the early 1830s, the State maintained control over the school structure and curriculum but, by co-opting the administrative structures of the Church, it gained both organisational capacity and local compliance. The Church equally benefitted by gaining local control over the delivery of education while receiving direct government funding. This model of cooperation was later adopted for other social interventions, such as orphanages and reform schools.

The lack of involvement of the Church in the management of district asylums may simply be due to the fact that the administrative structures for the Irish asylum system were established early in the nineteenth century, predating Catholic Emancipation. Church personnel did serve on the boards of governors of asylums and, in the late nineteenth century, some auxiliary asylums for chronically ill long-term patients were run by religious orders, with funding from the State. However, the evidence suggests that the asylum system was one of the few areas of Irish social intervention that remained predominantly secular in administration. As public scrutiny today focuses on abuses that occurred in institutions jointly provided by Church and State, the lack of scrutiny of asylums/mental hospitals, which were fully state controlled and by far the largest sites of confinement in Ireland for over two centuries, is astonishing.

TABLE 14.3: CHARACTERISTICS OF POINTS OF SOCIAL CONJUNCTURE IN THE IRISH MENTAL HEALTH CARE SYSTEM.

CONJUNCTURE 1: CREATION OF A TENDENCY TO INSTITUTIONALISE

Centralised social policy planning for asylums expansion/fragmentation of local demand, payment and control

Dangerous Lunatic Acts 1838 & 1867

Fragmentation of judicial/medical control over admission

Medical takeover of asylums/establishing of Inspector of Asylums

All encapsulating diagnostic criteria

1843 Asylum Rules*

Family participation in asylum admissions

Poverty/local economic and social dependency on asylums

CONJUNCTURE 2: INTERRUPTION OF TENDENCY TO INSTITUTIONALISE THE 'MENTALLY ILL'

1945 Mental Treatment Act – Consolidated medical control of admissions

Introduction of psychopharmacology/ECT and psychological interventions

International standardisation of classification systems

European Convention on Human Rights & Fundamental Freedoms (1950)

CONJUNCTURE 3: CLOSURE OF INSTITUTIONS

2001 Mental Health Act

Renewed system of inspection/mandatory legal advocacy

End of local economic dependency on asylums

Celtic Tiger and full employment

Emergence mental health promotion

Sale of asylum buildings

---

*For the 1843 asylum rules, see *Report of the Inspectors-General on District, Local, and Private Lunatic Asylums in Ireland 1843*, Appendix No. 3, pp.43–8, HC 1844 (567) xxx.69.

THE SOCIAL CONJUNCTURE MODEL

There are limitations to the application of any unifying social theory to a phenomenon that covers two centuries, in this case the trajectory of Irish asylum/mental hospital utilisation. However, it would appear that a complex combination of several social factors can be linked to the rise and fall of the size of the population in these institutions. One way of viewing the trends is to apply a theory that examines the impact of particular 'conjunctures' of social forces on asylum occupancy levels. Paige describes a 'conjuncture' as a 'particular combination of structural causes and events, in a particular time and place'.[59] Three points of conjuncture are of particular note: (1) the early phase of asylum expansion during the mid-nineteenth century, (2) the interruption of this expansion during the late 1950s, and (3) the closure of asylum buildings in Ireland in the early twenty first-century. These points reflect the major changes within the trajectory of institutionalisation in Irish asylums/mental hospitals (see Table 14.3 and Figure 14.4).

FIGURE 14.4: A MODEL OF SOCIAL CONJUNCTURE APPLIED TO ASYLUM/MENTAL HOSPITAL RESIDENCY IN IRELAND.

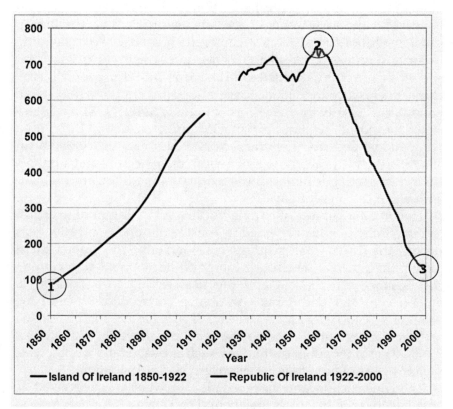

The Creation of a 'tendency' to Institutionalise

The political and administrative dynamic of colonisation is an important feature of nineteenth-century asylum expansion in Ireland, particularly its role in removing the planning and control of localised social interventions for the 'mentally ill' from the local context. The need for asylums was not articulated locally, but by Robert Peel, appointed as Chief Secretary for Ireland in 1812 and by other powerful people, such as Thomas Spring Rice, a member of Parliament, who was also a governor of the Limerick House of Industry, and by other witnesses who appeared before the Select Committee of the Lunatic Poor in Ireland which reported in 1817.[60] The resulting lunacy laws provided for a centrally administered system of district asylums which led to asylum construction throughout Ireland. Once constructed, these buildings were used to full capacity and the development of policy and protocol within these institutions served to further consolidate and embed the administrative structures, which in turn sustained the reproductive momentum of these institutions. While the first wave of asylum building in the early years of the nineteenth century, resulted in small institutions for 100–150 people, the second wave of building (from 1860 onwards) led to an increase not only in the number but also in the size of asylums (with beds for 300–400 people).[61] The career interests of individuals were also a driving force for asylum growth, particularly the Inspectors of Lunatic Asylums, who continuously proposed asylum expansion, thus ensuring their own occupational security. This inspectorate was also instrumental in ensuring the medical takeover of asylum management and administration by the mid-nineteenth century, an administration that endures to the present day.

The broader context of chronic social deprivation in nineteenth-century Ireland, which reached its most acute phase in rural areas during the 1840s, also requires consideration. At various times during the nineteenth century, many in the population, including the unemployed, the old and the sick, existed in a position of vulnerability and uncertainty. An absence of resources within the community, coupled with the existence of an extensive publicly funded asylum system, contributed to the tendency towards institutionalisation. Like other public institutions, such as prisons and workhouses, asylums were often refuges from poverty and degradation.

The construction and categorisation of what was perceived as 'mental illness' in Ireland is time-bound and changes continuously in response to the social, political and medical context at any particular point in time. During the nineteenth century, admission was dominated by the use of the Dangerous Lunacy Acts of 1838 (1 Vic. c. 27) and of 1867 (30 & 31 Vic. c. 118). As shown by Finnane and Prior, while the judicial process of asylum admission allowed for a person to be classified simply as being of 'unsound mind' without any hint of dangerousness, this was used in only a minority of admissions.

There were advantages for the family of the person classified as dangerous – there was an obligation on the authorities to admit the person, and there were no charges levied on the family.[62] The ease of admission, coupled with a lack of structured points of review (or discharge), served to swell the number of long-term residents.

The institutional confinement of people defined as 'mentally ill' in Ireland required the active and willing participation of individuals, families and communities who engaged directly with the committal process. Hence, while the institutions had their own social momentum and while those directly employed in asylums had an interest in ensuring a continuous 'supply of patients', there is no evidence of a programme of active recruitment of patients. In practice, Irish families were willing to commit their kin to asylums during times of crisis or dispute, in addition to the occasions when the individual was in genuine need of care.[63]

The outcome was a national asylum system made up of a network of institutions that were securely embedded within local communities. These institutions served several social functions, including the provision of a location for social intervention, a primary driver of local economic activity and a power base for medical politics. Thus, by the early twentieth century, the reproductive social momentum of these institutions was sufficiently powerful and robust to ensure that they remained intact and largely unchanged during the establishment of the Irish Free State.

The Interruption of Asylum Expansion

No single social force caused the decline in the institutionalisation of 'mentally ill' people in Ireland. Rather, it was the combined impact of interconnected social forces. Core features of this conjuncture were the international standardisation of diagnostic criteria, the rolling out of the provisions contained in the Mental Treatment Act 1945,[64] and the introduction of new psycho-pharmacological inter-ventions in the late 1950s. In particular, the judicial dominance of admission procedures that had characterised asylum expansion was replaced by consolidated medical control. From 1945 onwards, psychiatrists had a narrower set of admission criteria that were applied through a more tightly regulated legal procedure for admissions. The 1945 Mental Treatment Act also provided for routine and regular reviews of patient treatment, and consequently, the possibility of long-term institutionalisation became increasingly problematic. The introduction of new clinical interventions such as electro-convulsive therapy (ECT) and psycho-pharmacology provided forms of intervention that were perceived as medically 'advanced', so there was professional pressure to demonstrate clinical expertise in the application of such interventions as an alternative to long-term institutional care.

The reduced level of institutionalisation that began in 1956 was belatedly endorsed by policy makers, firstly in the *Report of the Commission of Inquiry on Mental Illness* in 1966[65] and, with greater effect, twenty years later, in *Planning for the Future* published in 1984.[66] However, in spite of the decline in the patient population, the actual built environment of mental hospitals continued to function until the 1990s, until their latent functionality and strategic economic usefulness became redundant. This was much later than England and Wales, for example, where buildings were being sold off since the 1980s, but similar to the situation in Northern Ireland, where patient numbers had decreased more rapidly and to a greater degree, but where the buildings remained as part of the mental health care landscape until the early twenty-first century.[67]

The Closure of Mental Hospitals

At the close of the twentieth century, a new point of conjuncture formed, with the confluence of the Mental Health Act 2001, a new social, political and economic context (the Celtic Tiger and near full employment), new systems of mental hospital inspection and, most importantly, new social policies in relation to mental health in *A Vision for Change*.[68] Within this context, the latent functionality and local economic importance of mental hospitals became weakened to such an extent that their closure and sale became politically possible. As a result, both the physical and administrative asylum structures, which had endured as features of Irish social life since the early nineteenth century, are finally becoming extinct.

CONCLUSION

It would appear that the established social theories concerning asylum expansion and contraction have only limited application to the Irish case. However, an analysis of the empirical data suggests that there are identifiable points of social conjuncture that have punctuated the major phases of change in Irish asylum/mental hospital residency pattern. As such, the establishment, expansion and demise of these institutions can be understood as a complex and multi-layered social process, underpinned by a wide range of social forces and enabled through the human action of individuals and groups. It would appear that the physical asylum buildings, the supportive administrative systems and the preferential positioning of institution-based treatment for mental illness became deeply embedded at both the personal and societal level, resulting in extremely high levels of occupancy in asylums/mental hospitals in Ireland for more than two centuries.

NOTES

1. Specific queries on these statistics may be addressed to the author.
2. Order of priority for inclusion of data: Reports of the Inspector of Lunatic Asylums / Inspector of Mental Hospitals; Retrospective data contained in subsequent *Reports of the Inspector of Lunatic Asylums / Inspector of Mental Hospitals*; other Parliamentary Papers and Special Reports; *The Statistical Abstract of Ireland; The Irish Psychiatric Hospital Census 1971, 1981 and 1991;* and Archival material from individual Mental Hospitals.
3. *69th Report on the District, Criminal and Private Lunatic Asylums in Ireland* (Hereafter, *Asylums Report*), p.vi, HC 1921, Cmd. 1127. xv. 165.
4. P.M. Prior, *Mental Health and Politics in Northern Ireland* (Avebury Press: Aldershot, 1993), p.18.
5. Prior, *Mental Health and Politics;* P.M. Prior, 'Where lunatics abound: A history of mental health services in Northern Ireland', in H. Freeman and G.E. Berrios (eds), *150 Years of British Psychiatry. Vol. II: The Aftermath* (London: Athlone Press Ltd, 1996), pp.292–308; Prior, P.M. and B. Hayes, 'Gender trends in occupancy rates in mental health beds in Northern Ireland', *Social Science and Medicine* 52 (2001), pp.537–51.
6. *40th Asylums Report*, HC 1890–1 (c. 6503) xxxvi. 521.
7. *40th Asylums Report*, p.60, HC 1890-1 (c. 6503) xxxvi. 521.
8. World Health Organisation, *Annual Epidemiological and Vital Statistics 1955* (Geneva: WHO, 1958), p.6.
9. D. Walsh and A. Daly, *Irish Psychiatric Hospitals and Units Census* 2001 (Dublin: Health Research Board, 2002), p.22.
10. M. Foucault, *Madness and Civilization: A History of Insanity in the Age of Reason* (Great Britain: Tavistock, 1967).
11. Foucault, *Madness and Civilization*, p.5.
12. Ibid., p.41.
13. *Report of the Select Committee to Consider the State of the Lunatic Poor in Ireland*, p.4, HC 1817 (430) viii.33; For discussion, see A. Williamson,'The beginnings of state care for the mentally ill in Ireland', *Economic and Social Review*, 10.1 (January 1970): pp.281–90.
14. Department of Health and Children, *A Vision for Change: Report of the Expert Group on Mental Health Policy* (Dublin: The Stationery Office, 2006).
15. *Report of the Select Committee to Consider the State of the Lunatic Poor in Ireland*, p.4, HC 1817 (430) viii. 33.
16. M. Reuber, 'Moral Management and the "Unseen Eye": Public Lunatic Asylums in Ireland, 1800–1845', in E. Malcolm and G. Jones (eds), *Medicine, Disease and the State in Ireland, 1650–1940* (Cork: Cork University Press, 1999), p.209.
17. J. Coolahan, *Irish Education: History and Structure* (Dublin: Institute of Public Administration, 1981), p.4.
18. *Report of Select Committee of the House of Lords Appointed to Consider the State of the Lunatic Poor in Ireland*, p.iii, HC 1843 (625) x. 439.
19. *Report of Select Committee of the House of Lords Appointed to Consider the State of the Lunatic Poor in Ireland*, p.xxv, HC 1843 (625) x. 439.
20. T.P.C. Kirkpatrick, *A Note on the History of the Care of the Insane in Ireland: Up to the End of the Nineteenth Century* (Dublin: University Press by Ponsonby and Gibbs, 1931), p.34.
21. M. Finnane, *Insanity and the Insane in Post-Famine Ireland* (London: Croom Helm, 1981), p.15.

22. J.T. Arlidge, 'The Chaplaincy Question at the Belfast Asylum', *The Asylum Journal*. Published by the Authority of the Association of Medical Officers of Asylums and Hospitals of the Insane, vol. 4 March 1 (1854), pp.49–51; For further discussion, see P.M. Prior and D.V. Griffiths, 'The Chaplaincy Question: The Lord Lieutenant of Ireland versus the Belfast Lunatic Asylum', *Eire-Ireland*, 33: 2 & 3 (1997): 137–53, reprinted in this volume.

23. J.C. Bucknill, 'Inspector of Lunatics Ireland Seventh Report', *The Asylum Journal*. Published by the Authority of the Association of Medical Officers of Asylums and Hospitals of the Insane, No. 17, (1856), p.135.

24. Finnane, *Insanity and the Insane*, p.53; Prior, *Mental Health and Politics*, p.17.

25. Finnane, *Insanity and the Insane*, p.53.

26. A.J. Saris, 'The Asylum In Ireland: A Brief Institutional History and Some Local Effects', in A. Cleary and M.P. Treacy (eds), *The Sociology of Health and Illness in Ireland* (Dublin: University College Dublin Press, 1997), p.211.

27. L. Greenslade, 'White Skin, White Masks: Psychological Distress Among the Irish in Britain', in P. O'Sullivan (ed.), *The Irish in the New Communities* (Leicester: Leicester University Press, 1992), pp.202–25; L. Greenslade, 'The Blackbird Calls in Grief: Colonialism, Health and Identity among Irish Immigrants in Britain', in J.M. Laughlin (ed.), *Location and Dislocation in Contemporary Irish Society: Emigration and Irish Identities* (Cork: Cork University Press, 1997), pp.36–60.

28. A. Scull, *Museums of Madness: The Social Organisation of Insanity in Nineteenth-Century England* (London: Penguin Books Ltd., 1979), p.30.

29. C.M. Arensberg and S.T. Kimball, *Family and Community in Ireland*, 3rd edition, (Harvard: Clasp Press, 2001). First published 1940.

30. Arensberg and Kimball, *Family and Community in Ireland*, p.226.

31. A. Scull, *Museums of Madness*, p.30.

32. H. Tovey and P. Share, *A Sociology of Ireland* (Dublin: Gill and Macmillan, 2000), p.41.

33. A. Byrne, R. Edmondson and T. Varley, 'Introduction to Third Edition', in C.M. Arensberg and S.T. Kimball, *Family and Community in Ireland*, p.iii.

34. *Report of Select Committee of the House of Lords Appointed to Consider the State of the Lunatic Poor in Ireland*, pp.iii-iv, HC 1843 (625) x. 439.

35. Finnane, *Insanity and the Insane*, p.136.

36. D. Walsh and A. Daly, *Irish Psychiatric Hospitals and Units Census 2001* (Dublin: Health Research Board, 2002).

37. J.J. Lee, *Ireland 1912–1985: Politics and Society* (Cambridge: Cambridge University Press, 1989); R. Breen, D. Hannan, D. Rottman and C. Whelan (eds), *Understanding Contemporary Ireland: State, Class and Development in the Republic of Ireland* (Dublin: Gill and MacMillan, 1990).

38. P. Kirby, L. Gibbons and M. Cronin (eds), *Reinventing Ireland: Culture, Society and the Global Economy* (London: Pluto Press, 2002).

39. *Asylums Report*, Schedule G, HC 1846 (736) xxii. 409.

40. *Asylums Report*, Schedule K, HC 1846 (736) xxii. 409. (Estimate based on expenditure data for four districts.)

41. S. Butler, 'Mental Health Social Work in Ireland: Missed Opportunities', in N. Kearney and C. Skehill (eds), *Social Work in Ireland Historical Perspectives* (Dublin: Institute of Public Administration, 2005), pp.33–50.

42. H.B. Kidd, 'Industrial Units in Psychiatric Hospitals', *British Journal of Psychiatry III* (1965), p.1250.

43. The author has personal experience of supervising such work when employed as a psychiatric nurse during the 1980s and 1990s.

44. Inspector of Mental Hospitals, *Report of the Inspector of Mental Hospitals for the Year 1950* (Dublin: The Stationery Office, 1950), p.2.

45. P. Bartlett and D. Wright, *Outside the Walls of the Asylum: The History of Care in the Community 1750–2000* (London: The Athlone Press, 1999), p.7.

46. Inspector of Mental Hospitals, *Report of the Inspector of Mental Hospitals for the Years 1977–1979* (Dublin: The Stationery Office, 1977–79).

47. William Parry-Jones, *The Trade in Lunacy* (London: Routledge, 1972).

48. *Report of the Select Committee to Consider the State of the Lunatic Poor in Ireland*, p.4, HC 1817 (430) viii. 33.

49. Inspectors-General, *Report of the Inspectors-General on District, Local, and Private Lunatic Asylums in Ireland 1843*, Appendix No. 3, pp.43–8, HC 1844 (567) xxx. 69.

50. *Asylums Report*, HC 1846 (736) xxii. 409.

51. M. Foucault, *The Birth of the Clinic* (Great Britain: Tavistock, 1973).
52. J.C. Bucknill, 'Inspector of Lunatics Ireland Seventh Report', *The Asylum Journal*. Published by the Authority of the Association of Medical Officers of Asylums and Hospitals of the Insane, No. 17, (1856), p.136.
53. C. Samson, 'Madness and psychiatry' in B.S. Turner (ed.), *Medical Power and Social Knowledge*, 2nd edition, (London: Sage, 1995), p. 59.
54. R.D. Laing, *The Divided Self* (London: Tavistock Publications, 1960); R.D. Laing and A. Esterson, *Sanity, Madness and the Family* (London: Tavistock Publications, 1964).
55. M. Foucault, *Madness and Civilization: A History of Insanity in the Age of Reason* (Great Britain: Tavistock, 1967); Foucault, *The Birth of the Clinic*; M. Foucault, *Discipline and Punish: The Birth of the Prison* (London: Allen Lane, 1977).
56. T. Szasz, *The Myth of Mental Illness* (St Albans: Granada, 1972); I. Illich, *Limits to Medicine, Medical Nemesis: The Expropriation of Health* (London: Marion Boyars Publishers Ltd., 1976); I. Illich, *Disabling Professionals* (London: Marion Boyars Publishers Ltd., 1977).
57. W.C. Cockerham, *Sociology of Mental Disorder*, 3rd edition, (New Jersey: Pearson Education Inc, 2003), p.89.
58. J. Coolahan, *Irish Education: History and Structure* (Dublin: Institute of Public Administration, 1981), p.5.
59. J.M. Paige, 'Conjuncture, Comparison, and Conditional Theory in Macrosocial Inquiry', *American Journal of Sociology*,105: 3 (1999), p.782.
60. Finnane, *Insanity and the Insane*, p.53; A. Williamson, 'The beginnings of state care for the mentally ill in Ireland', *Economic and Social Review*, 10.1 (January 1970): pp.281–90.
61. Finnane, *Insanity and the Insane*.
62. Finnane, *Insanity and the Insane*; P.M. Prior, 'Dangerous Lunacy: The Misuse of Mental Health Law in Nineteenth-Century Ireland', *Journal of Forensic Psychiatry and Psychology*, 14:3 (2003): 525–53.
63. See Elizabeth Malcolm, *Swift's Hospital* (Dublin: Gill and Macmillan, 1989); Finnane, *Insanity and the Insane*.
64. Mental Treatment Act 1945 (Dublin: The Stationery Office, 1945, No. 19).
65. Commission of Inquiry on Mental Illness, *Commission of Inquiry on Mental Illness Report* (Dublin: The Stationery Office, 1966).
66. Department of Health, *Psychiatric Services, Planning For the Future* (Dublin: The Stationery Office, 1984).
67. Prior, *Mental Health and Politics*.
68. Mental Treatment Act 2001 (Dublin: The Stationery Office, 2001, No. 25); Department of Health and Children, *A Vision for Change: Report of the Expert Group on Mental Health Policy* (Dublin: The Stationery Office, 2006).

15

Mental Health Law on the Island of Ireland, 1800–2010

Pauline M. Prior

The underlying assumptions behind the original legal framework that formed the basis for mental health services in Ireland derived from social and political attitudes to vagrants and to the poor. In the nineteenth century, there was little understanding of people caught up in the system, other than the fact that most of them were poor and many were considered to be a danger to themselves or to others. The best approach, it was thought, was separation in a controlled environment. By the twentieth century, these assumptions changed, leading to the integration of mental health services into mainstream health services. This change was due mainly to developments in the medical understanding of mental disorder and of intellectual disability. By the beginning of the twenty-first century, the idea of separating people with mental illnesses in isolated institutions was no longer acceptable, resulting in the concentration of services for mentally ill people in the community, with hospital-based treatment restricted to those regarded as presenting a risk to either themselves or to others. The medical model still prevails as the dominant model underlying modern approaches to mental disorder, but because treatment sometimes involves the deprivation of liberty for some individuals (those who refuse treatment), we need specific laws to protect them from unlawful confinement or treatment. Just as the laws in the nineteenth century were introduced to protect the property and civil rights of the 'insane' person, so now we recognise the need to protect the human rights of mentally ill people.

In this chapter, we will discuss some of the major pieces of legislation that affected the provision of mental health services and the use of these services over the past two centuries on the island of Ireland.[1] As other scholars have already written in more detail on these laws, this is just an overview. Readers who are interested in expanding their knowledge should also read the work of Brendan Kelly, Mark Finnane, Elizabeth Malcolm, Dermot Walsh and Arthur Williamson.[2]

TABLE 15.1: LIST OF SELECTED STATUTES ON MENTAL DISORDER IN IRELAND, 1800–2011.

All Ireland

Criminal Lunatics Act 1800	39 & 40 Geo. 3 c. 94
Lunatic Asylums (Ireland) Act 1817	57 Geo. 3 c. 106
Lunacy (Ireland) Act 1821	1 & 2 Geo. 4 c. 33
Lunacy (Ireland) Act 1825	6 Geo. 4 c. 54
Lunacy (Ireland) Act 1826	7 Geo. 4 c. 14
Richmond Lunatic Asylum Act 1830	11 Geo. 4 & 1 Will. 4 c. 22
Dangerous Lunatics (Ireland) Act 1838	1 & 2 Vic. c. 27
Private Lunatic Asylums (Ireland) Act 1842	5 & 6 Vic. c. 123
Central Criminal Lunatic Asylum (Ireland) Act 1845	8 & 9 Vic. c. 107
Lunatic Asylums (Ireland) Act 1846	9 & 10 Vic. c. 115
Lunatic Asylums Repayment of Advances (Irl.) Act 1855	18 & 19 Vic c. 109
Offences against the Persons Act 1861	24 & 25 Vic. c. 100
Lunacy (Ireland) Act 1867	30 & 31 Vic. c. 118
Lunatic Asylums (Irl.) Accounts Audit Act 1868	31 & 32 Vic. c. 97
Capital Punishment Amendment Act 1868	31 & 32 Vic. c. 24
Lunacy Regulations (Ireland) Act 1871	34 & 35 Vic. c. 22
Private Asylums (Ireland) Act 1874	37 & 38 Vic. c. 74
Lunatic Asylums (Ireland) Act 1875	38 & 39 Vic. c. 67
Trial of Lunatics Act (Ireland) 1883	46 & 47 Vic. c. 38
Local Government (Ireland) Act 1898	61 & 62 Vic. c. 37
Lunacy (Ireland) Act 1901	1 Edw. 7 c. 17
Asylum Officers Superannuation (Irl.) Act 1909	9 Edw. 7 c. 48

cont.

TABLE 15.1: LIST OF SELECTED STATUTES ON MENTAL DISORDER IN IRELAND,
1800–2011 (continued)

Republic of Ireland

Mental Treatment Act 1945	1945, No. 19
Mental Treatment Act 1961	1961, No. 7
Health (Mental Services) Act 1981	1981, No. 17.
Mental Health Act 2001	2001, No. 25
Criminal Law (Insanity) Act 2006	2006, No. 11

Northern Ireland

Criminal Lunatics Act (NI) 1929	20 Geo. 5 c. 19
Mental Treatment Act (NI) 1932	22 & 23 Geo. 5 c. 15
Mental Health Act (NI) 1948	11 & 12 Geo. 6 c. 17
Mental Health Act (NI) 1961	10 Eliz. 2 c. 15
Mental Health (NI) Order 1986	Statutory Instruments 1986 No. 595 (NI 4)

EARLY NINETEENTH CENTURY

The 'lunacy' system in Ireland was part of an overall plan to control vagrancy and to classify and divide the 'deserving' from the 'undeserving poor'. It originated in the report of the select committee on the 'Aged and Infirm Poor' of Ireland in 1804[3] and found expression in the Lunacy Acts of 1817 (57 Geo. 3 c. 106) and 1821 (1 & 2 Geo. 4 c. 33). This was at a time when anti-insurrection laws were being aggressively implemented, so that anyone suspected of revolting against the British colonial administration was in danger of being transported to Australia.[4] The laws governing Irish asylums were different to those in England, due not only to the political situation, but also to different systems of governance and of public administration. Though some publicly funded beds for insane people were opened in the eighteenth century in the houses of industry in Dublin and in Cork, it was not until 1815 that the first publicly funded asylum, the Richmond, opened in Dublin. Following the Acts of 1817 (57 Geo. 3 c. 106) and 1821 (1 & 2 Geo. 4 c. 33), the first of the new district asylums opened at Armagh in 1825, with others following quickly, so that by the middle of the century there were ten district asylums dotted throughout the country, providing over 3,000 beds.

The second wave of asylum building, which began in the middle of the century, was more intensive than the first and by the beginning of the twentieth century, there were twenty-two asylums in Ireland, providing over 16,000 beds.[5]

Lunacy laws in the early years of the century were concerned with laying down the legal basis for the funding and administration of the new network of district asylums. As there was little doubt that this would involve some major public expenditure, there were strict guidelines as to who would qualify for state-funded care and treatment. The regulations for admission to an asylum also offered protection to individuals from the unlawful deprivation of freedom and of the rights that went with it – including the right to vote, to enter into a contract, or to manage money or business.[6] In those early years, admission to the new district asylums was fairly straightforward and simple. People were admitted for being of 'unsound mind' as defined in the Lunacy Acts of 1821 (1 & 2 Geo. 4 c. 33) and 1826 (7 Geo. 4 c. 14). An application was made to the asylum manager by the person's next of kin, who confirmed the poverty of the patient and gave an undertaking to remove him from the asylum when requested. This application was accompanied by a medical certificate of insanity.[7]

This pattern began to change as the demand for asylum places outstripped the supply. A new law, known as the Dangerous Lunatics (Ireland) Act 1838 (1 Vic. c. 27), allowed the direct committal to prison of people designated as dangerous lunatics. These people were then legally transferred to a district asylum, without any further recourse to a local magistrate, whenever a place became available. Though some people continued to be admitted to district asylums as 'ordinary' lunatics (i.e. of unsound mind), the proportion of 'dangerous' lunatic admissions increased as the century progressed. This was due primarily to the fact that the asylums could not refuse admissions from the prison system. However, the numbers awaiting transfer from prison to asylum accumulated as the years went by. In 1864, there were 441 dangerous lunatics in prisons, in 1865 it had risen to 505 and in 1866 it had fallen slightly to 495 – all waiting for places in the district asylum system.[8] There were two major problems with the legislation as it stood. Asylums had no control over the numbers being admitted to prison as dangerous lunatics (though they had an obligation to treat them when places were available) and prisons could not discharge these people home directly even if they showed no sign of insanity, as this could only be done from the asylum to which they were transferred. There were complaints by almost everyone involved in the process, as evidenced in the report of the 1857 *Commission of Inquiry*.[9] For example, James Corry Connellan, Inspector General of Prisons, when asked what amendment to the law he would suggest, answered as follows:

> I see no reason why they [dangerous lunatics] should not be sent direct to asylums. The whole question with regard to the confinement of lunatics in gaols resolves itself into this – first that the greatest injury is done to the discipline of a prison; and secondly, with regard to the lunatics themselves, they are either curable or incurable; if they are curable, it is surely a gross injustice to them to detain them in a place so deficient in the proper means of treatment for their disease as our ordinary gaols; if they are incurable you are perverting the gaol from the object for which it was established.[10]

LATE NINETEENTH CENTURY

As a result of the discussion that took place during the 1857 *Commission of Inquiry*, the law was changed in 1867 (30 & 31 Vic. c. 118). Under Section 10 of this Act, anyone who appeared to be suffering from 'derangement of mind' which might 'lead to him committing a crime', could be committed directly to an asylum by two justices of the peace. As shown by Finnane and Prior, this did not stop the tide of dangerous lunacy admissions, but rather added to it, so that by the end of the century, the majority of admissions to district asylums were on the ground of dangerousness rather than of unsoundness of mind.[11] For example, in 1888, out of a total of 1,821 admissions to all asylums in Ireland, only 10 per cent were ordinary admissions (people of 'unsound mind'). The remainder (90 per cent) were admitted either as dangerous lunatics or as urgent cases.[12]

An examination of patient records shows that most of the patients who were admitted initially as 'dangerous lunatics' became passive and peaceful members of the highly institutionalised population in district asylums, showing very few signs of being dangerous. Policy makers and asylum managers knew that there was a perverse incentive in the existing law, making violent behaviour almost a pre-requisite for admission. The situation had been brought to the attention of the *Poor Law Union and Lunacy Inquiry* (Ireland) 1878–9, which was appointed to look into the need for additional asylum provision.

Under the recent Act 30 and 31 Vic. no less than 979 persons have been committed by magistrates to asylums as dangerous lunatic, fully one half of whom were found harmless, idiotic, or imbecile, and therefore unsuitable cases to be classified or treated under the denomination of 'dangerous lunatic', and who are fixed upon the public rates for support and maintenance.[13]

The main reason for the use of this method of admission was the fact that there were three obvious practical advantages to families who used 'dangerous lunacy' admission procedures rather than 'ordinary' admission procedures. Firstly, the police transported the patient from home to the asylum regardless of the distance, secondly, the asylum could not refuse admission to someone legally deemed dangerous and, thirdly, the family was not responsible for the ongoing maintenance of a patient admitted in this way. Thus, as far as the patient's family was concerned, this was the simplest method of ensuring admission and free treatment at a time when the demand for asylum places far outweighed supply. Numbers of admissions continued to rise, so that by 1900, there were over 20,000 lunatics in publicly funded institutions, representing a rate of forty-seven mentally ill persons per 10,000 of the population.[14]

Though there were changes in the laws governing the administration of asylums at the end of the century, in the form of the Local Government (Ireland) Act 1898 (61 & 62 Vic. c. 37), there were no new lunacy laws. In other words, there was no equivalent in Ireland of the English Lunacy Act 1890 (53 & 54 Vic. c. 5), which rationalised and amended earlier laws. As a result of this, the law on mental disorder in England was reasonably clear (if highly legalistic) at the turn of the century.[15] In Ireland, attempts to amend different aspects of the lunacy law in the late nineteenth century were unsuccessful, due to the constant opposition by local interests to any measure that might increase the financial burden on the Poor Rate.[16] Some minor changes in procedures were contained in the general legislation on local government administration in 1898, when the new local councils were given responsibility for providing and managing accommodation for the lunatic poor. Under Section 9(6) of the 1898 Act, local councils had broad powers

> To make regulations respecting the government and management of every lunatic asylum for their county, and the admission, detention and discharge of lunatics, and the conditions as to payment and accommodation under which private patients

may be admitted into and detained in the asylum.[17]

Patients were admitted to asylums on the basis of a Reception Order based on this section of the 1898 Act. The regulations were very precise. An application for the committal of a person alleged to be of 'unsound mind' was presented by the next of kin to the local resident magistrate or justice of the peace, who sent it (with full details of the person's residence and financial position) to the registrar in lunacy. Having received this application, the registrar sent a medical visitor to the person 'alleged to be of unsound mind', to examine him/her and to inform him/her of the application. The person had four days within which to lodge a written objection with the registrar. The registrar then sent the initial application, the report of the medical visitor and any objections or evidence to the designated representative of the Lord Chancellor, who made the decision 'to make an order' or to ask for a hearing of the case.[18] The law was aimed at protecting the liberty of the individual, but proved to be unpopular due to its cumbersome nature and to the perverse incentives (discussed above) that made admission as a 'dangerous lunatic' more popular. These incentives were taken away by the Lunacy (Ireland) Act 1901 (1 Edw. 7 c. 17), which extended the responsibility for both transportation and maintenance to all patients, regardless of their classification (as dangerous, or of unsound mind) at the point of admission. However, the pattern of defining people as 'dangerous' continued to impact on mental hospital admissions until after the partition of Ireland, when mental health legislation became part of two distinct legal jurisdictions – Northern Ireland (now part of the United Kingdom) and the Republic of Ireland. Since then, there are two distinct systems of mental health law on the island of Ireland, each of which will be examined briefly, starting with Northern Ireland.

MENTAL TREATMENT ACT (NI) 1932

In 1921, the new government of Northern Ireland inherited a mental health system which was underfunded, overcrowded and based on a set of laws that were out of date and complex to administer. Admissions to asylums were subject to one of seven separate laws, depending on the categorisation of the patient – as dangerous, of unsound mind, criminal, private, or from another jurisdiction. Most patients were admitted as 'of unsound mind' under the Local Government Act 1898 (61 & 62 Vic. c. 37) but a substantial number were still being admitted as 'dangerous lunatics' under the Lunacy (Ireland) Act 1867 (30 & 31 Vic. c. 118).[19]

The main catalyst for a change in the law did not come from within Northern Ireland, but from England, where in 1930, a new Mental Treatment Act based on the 1926 report of the Royal Commission on Lunacy and Mental Disorder came into force.[20] By this time, psychiatric opinion in England favoured voluntary treatment of mental illness and emphasised the need for some outpatient or non-residential patient care. In addition, there was public anxiety about the possibility of unnecessary confinement in asylums, following the publication by Dr. Montague Lomax of *The Experiences of an Asylum Doctor*, in which he was very critical of the care being given to patients at Prestwich Hospital, Manchester.[21] All of these opinions were considered by the Royal Commission, which made a number of recommendations, emphasising the need for early treatment of mental disorder, the desirability of admission procedures that allowed treatment without certification, and the need to break the link between the poor law and asylum treatment. At the heart of all of its recommendations was a focus on mental disorder as an illness that could be treated by medical science.

Influenced by what was happening in England, a committee was appointed in Northern Ireland in 1929 to advise the Minister of Home Affairs on necessary changes in the law. The members of the committee were the Chief Medical Officer (Dr. W. R. Dawson) and two resident medical superintendents (Dr. N.J. Nolan, Downshire, and Dr. S.J. Graham, Purdysburn). The task facing them was extremely difficult, as not only was the law in relation to mental disorder out of date, but also that there had been no equivalent in Northern Ireland of the English Mental Deficiency Acts of 1913 and 1927, and no attempt to provide separate accommodation for people with intellectual disabilities. In addition, the ever present problem of severe underfunding continued to dominate decisions on changes to mental health care. Parliamentary debates, in Northern Ireland, on the proposed legislation showed that while there was a general acceptance of the need to bring mental health care and treatment more into line with other areas of health care, there was a reluctance to make changes that would cost more money than the UK Treasury would allow.[22] When the Mental Treatment Act (NI) 1932 was passed, it did indeed leave behind the language and approach of the nineteenth century, but it did not solve the problem of underfunding in mental health services. The most important elements in the Act were:

- The replacement of the language of lunacy and vagrancy by the language of mental illness and disorder.
- The introduction of new procedures for admission to treatment – voluntary admissions (similar to patients requiring treatment for physical illness) and temporary admissions (which were compulsory) for those who had a good chance of recovery. Certification (as being of unsound mind) was also allowed, but was intended for a minority of patients.
- The power to extend treatment for mental disorder outside of the mental hospital (referred to as 'extern' treatment).

There were different views on the impact of this law on mental health services in Northern Ireland. The optimists saw it as a radical shift in policy towards a more enlightened approach to the care and treatment of people with mental disorders, as evidenced in the complete change in language in all aspects of the service. Asylums became hospitals, attendants became nurses, inmates became patients, and there was hope that scientific developments would bring new curative treatments to light. The pessimists saw it as a cosmetic exercise, aimed at convincing the Westminster government that the laws in Northern Ireland were just as humane and as modern as those in Britain. Because there was no change in the method of funding, there was little hope of progress in developing new services attached to the hospital or based in the community. Neither was there any possibility of real change in the daily lives of patients, some of whom would never return home. In other words, because it solved the major legal problems and provided a more acceptable language for the treatment of mental disorder, the Mental Treatment Act (NI) 1932 concealed serious funding shortages and structure deficiencies in the mental health care system.

In the years that followed, there were numerous attempts by the Minister for Home Affairs, Dawson Bates, to get more funding for local councils to run mental health services. He recommended a change in the method of funding mental hospitals, from a block grant to a per-capita payment.[23] These attempts, which included meetings with Prime Minister Sir J. Craig, were unsuccessful. The Minister of Finance, Hugh Pollock, backed by the prime minister and the Cabinet, insisted that there was no money for such a change, as it would mean an increase in public expenditure. Eventually, in 1940 and again in 1945 the block grant was increased slightly, but this did not help many of the hospitals, where the block grant only covered a fraction of their costs. The issue of financing was not resolved until 1948, when the mental hospitals became part of the new nationalised health service in Northern Ireland.

REPUBLIC OF IRELAND: MENTAL TREATMENT ACT 1945

When the Irish Free State came into being in 1922, it inherited the same set of complex lunacy laws as had Northern Ireland before it passed the 1932 Act. Because of the political and economic turmoil of the 1920s and 1930s, the only progress to be made was the introduction of the Hospitals Sweepstakes in 1930, which brought some additional money into the voluntary hospital sector.[24] However, as most of the mental hospitals were in the public sector, this had little impact on the overall standard of services. There was some discussion on the need for reform of mental health law at the *Commission on the Relief of the Sick and Destitute Poor, including the Insane Poor* which reported in 1927.[25] In an effort to stem the tide of overcrowding in district asylums, which were an increasingly intolerable burden on local rates, it recommended the building of auxiliary asylums for incurable patients and the introduction of outpatient clinics and of voluntary admission procedures for hospital treatment. These recommendations reflected the thoughts of psychiatrists at the time. They argued that voluntary admissions would result in earlier and, as a consequence, more successful treatments.[26] However, these recommendations fell on deaf ears, and it was not until the 1940s that the need for radical change in mental health care was discussed. This happened in the context of plans for a complete overhaul of the health care system as proposed by the Departmental Committee on Health Services (which reported in 1945).

The Mental Treatment Act 1945, which completely transformed the legislative basis for mental health services in Ireland, reflected international developments in medicine and law in relation to mental illness. Policy makers did not realise at the time that it would go out of date so quickly or that it would continue to dominate services for the remainder of the twentieth century. It was hoped that this new law would lead to a decrease in patient numbers, which had reached crisis point by 1945, when there were 17,708 patients in asylums in Ireland.[27] Unfortunately, this hope was not realised. Numbers of patients continued to increase until new drugs came on the market and other forms of care became possible in the 1960s. Even then, the Irish reliance on institutional care did not diminish as quickly as in other countries.

The main innovations in the 1945 Act in the Republic of Ireland were very similar to those in the 1932 legislation in Northern Ireland, with a few exceptions. The old discourse of 'lunacy' and 'pauperism' was replaced by medical terminology – asylums became hospitals, attendants became nurses, and inmates became patients. Also, most importantly, recourse to a judicial authority for admissions was abolished completely. In future, admissions could be on a voluntary basis, a temporary basis (compulsory for up to six months) or an indefinite basis (compulsory certification). For a publicly funded or 'chargeable' patient, the application for admission could be made by nearest relative, or an 'assistance officer', with one medical certificate by an 'authorised medical officer'. For a private patient, two medical certificates were required. In all cases, the person had to be examined again by the hospital doctor who retained the right to refuse admission. One of the surprising aspects of the law was the inclusion of addiction (on a par with mental illness) as a criterion for admission as a temporary patient.[28] Also surprising was the retention of some of the language of the past. Patients admitted on a compulsory basis, were 'detained' and the doctor in charge of the hospital was still the 'resident medical superintendent'. Though it did not lead to a decrease in the hospital population, the 1945 Act helped to bring mental health services in Ireland into line with other modern societies. However, it far outlived its usefulness, as it was not changed until the early years of the twenty-first century, when it was finally replaced by the Mental Health Act 2001.[29]

NORTHERN IRELAND LEGISLATION – 1948 AND 1961

Attitudes to mental illness and its treatment kept changing throughout the twentieth century and this was reflected in the legal changes that took place in Northern Ireland, which was now in a different legal jurisdiction to the rest of Ireland. As part of the United Kingdom (UK), it reflected a wider discussion on law and medicine. Although integrated into the general health services structure, the treatment for mental disorder was different (to treatment for physical illness) in that it was possible to deprive some patients of their liberty and treat them on a compulsory basis. This issue did not disappear, though the proportion of patients requiring compulsory treatment decreased throughout the century until it stabilised at its current rate of around 10 per cent of hospital admissions.[30] The legal position was made very clear in the parliamentary debate leading up to the passing of the Mental Health Act (NI) 1948. The Minister of Health and Local Government (NI) put forward the legal case.

> The Government is strenuously opposed to any suggestion that prolonged detention in a mental hospital should be authorised by any method other than by order of a judicial authority. The Lord Chief Justice is also opposed to it. It is submitted that mental illness must be treated differently from physical illness inasmuch as mental illness involves detention against the will of the patient and in some instances against the wishes of his friends or relatives. This means that the liberty of the subject is involved so that the problem is therefore more than a medical one and it is a fundamental principle of British justice that any such prolonged detention must be authorised only by a judicial authority.[31]

When the 1948 law was passed, there was a compromise between those who wished to remove all judicial procedures from mental health treatment and those who regarded them as essential safeguards for those deprived of their freedom. Admission in future would be either voluntary or temporary (compulsory but time limited), based on medical rather than judicial approval. Only when a temporary patient was judged by a resident medical superintendent to have reached a stage where his recovery was 'improbable' was an application made to the judicial authority to have him/her certified (as of unsound mind).[32] This was not a satisfactory situation as far as either the doctors or the lawyers were concerned, but it was seen by many as a step towards the removal of the stigma of certification from the process of receiving mental health treatment.

There were many other positive developments in this law, heralding a radical shift in attitudes to both mental illness and intellectual disability. Most importantly, it established a 'special care' service for people with intellectual disabilities, a service that modernised care for this group of people who had, up to now, been 'warehoused' and forgotten in the back wards of large mental hospitals. Another change that got through vigorous debate into the final legislation (and remains controversial) was the inclusion of addiction as a criterion for temporary admission. This was due to the influence of the discussions that had preceded a similar change in the Mental Health Act 1945 in the Republic of Ireland. This was the last time that mental health legislation in Northern Ireland was influenced by debates in the Republic as the next major changes in the law (in 1961 and 1986) resulted from ideas that came mainly from England.

The first of these, the Mental Health Act (NI) 1961, was passed as a direct result of the work of the Percy Commission (Royal Commission on Mental Illness and Mental Deficiency) 1954–7, the report from which formed the basis for the 1959 Mental Health Act in England. Though no special committee was set up in Northern Ireland, there was widespread consultation between health officials and the newly formed Northern Ireland Association for Mental Health (NIAMH) and professional medical and social work organisations.

The Percy Committee emphasised treatment rather than confinement and the need for less restrictive services outside of the hospital setting.

> We recommend that the law should be altered so that whenever possible, suitable care may be provided for mentally disordered patients with no more restriction of liberty or legal formality than is applied to people who need care because of other types of illness, disability or social difficulty.[33]

This report reflected a new era of optimism in relation to medical treatment of mental illness and also heralded the demise of the large mental institution that had dominated care since the early nineteenth century. In the new legislation, it was clear that treatment could take place in general hospitals as well as specialist mental hospitals, but also in outpatient clinics and community-based facilities. The reaction against legalism, already apparent in the legislation of 1932 and 1948, was even stronger in the new Act. The power of the medical profession was enhanced, not only by new admission procedures, but also by the removal of the judicial authority from decisions about long-term compulsory hospitalisation. In future, under Section 32 of the Act, the hospital management committee could authorise continuing care and/or treatment based on a medical recommendation. In order to protect patients from any possible abuse of medical power, a Mental Health Review Tribunal (NI) was appointed to review the cases of people held in hospital on a compulsory basis. Unlike the English legislation, the Northern Ireland Act gave no extra powers to local authorities to develop community services, though it did state in Section 81 that people suffering from a mental disorder could be included among the recipients of residential accommodation and of domestic help from local councils.

NORTHERN IRELAND: THE MENTAL HEALTH (NI) ORDER 1986 AND
THE BAMFORD REVIEW

The debates in relation to mental health law in the twenty-first century still resonate with those which led to changes in the law over the past two centuries. Now, however, there is a greater emphasis on the protection of the human rights of individuals who might lose their liberty (totally or partially) as a result of refusing what is seen as necessary medical treatment. Northern Ireland is the only part of the UK which has not reformed its mental health law in recent years. However, the process of changing the law is already underway, based largely on the recommendations of the Bamford Review (of mental health and learning disability law and services in NI) which worked from 2002 to 2007 and produced reports on all aspects of mental health services, including detailed recommendations on legal changes.[34]

The Mental Health (NI) Order 1986 was passed as a result of many debates. The initial debates happened in England, where a change in the law occurred in 1983 (Mental Health Act 1983). At the same time in NI, the MacDermott Committee (1978–81) was appointed to make recommendations in the light of legal debates and changes in the law in other parts of the UK.[35] The issues debated most fiercely were – the definition of mental disorder; the grounds for compulsory admission to hospital; and the involvement of justices of the peace (or any representative of the judiciary) in compulsory admissions.[36] When the law came into effect, it was clear that that civil liberties approach taken by the MacDermott Committee had influenced the final procedures for compulsory admission. In summary, admission was for assessment only (Art. 4), not for treatment; an Approved Social Worker (ASW) could apply for admission without any judicial intervention, and overrule the objections of the nearest relative after consultation with a second ASW (Art. 5.4); and the criteria for admission were much narrower than those in the English Act (Art. 4.2). Protection for patients was enhanced by the increased powers given to the Mental Health Review Tribunal (set up under the 1961 Act). For example, the new law authorised an automatic review every two years of patients who had been admitted on a compulsory basis (Art. 73). Further protection was offered by a new Mental Health Commission, which was set up with wide-ranging powers to enquire into any case...

> ... where it appears to the Commission that there may be ill treatment, deficiency in care or treatment, or improper detention in

hospital or reception into guardianship of any patient, or where the property of any patient may, by reasons of his mental disorder be exposed to loss or damage (Art. 86.2).[37]

In many ways, the 1986 Order has many features that continue to be important in mental health care in the twenty-first century. However, as shown in the reports from the Bamford Review, new challenges face both the patient and the professional in the mental health care system, challenges which need new legislative regulation.[38] Developments in medical science have led to new drugs which make it possible for the majority of patients to be treated in their own homes, rather than in hospital, hence the need for compulsory powers that extend to treatment in the community also.

Human rights legislation in Europe and in the UK make it necessary for all other laws to be examined in the light of the issues raised by the need to protect the human rights of all who come in contact with mental health services, especially those who are not willing to receive treatment on a voluntary basis. The rights being emphasised by service users include the right to liberty, the right to privacy, the right to family life and the right to a fair hearing in the event of compulsory treatment. Some of these rights have already been confirmed by the European Court of Human Rights in specific cases brought by patients. Others have become apparent as society becomes more aware of the potential for the abuse or neglect of rights within the health care system.[39]

In addition to these developments in medical science and in the law, mental health professionals have realised that as the population ages, there are increasing numbers of people who may need protection due to the fact that they have lost capacity, either temporarily or permanently, due to dementia. Dementia sufferers and others who have lost capacity for other reasons often do not fit neatly into any of the categories currently covered by the Mental Health (NI) Order 1986 and therefore lack protection, due to the informal nature of some of the arrangements made on their behalf. Other areas of the UK have introduced capacity/incapacity legislation, so Northern Ireland has fallen somewhat behind. This has nothing to do with the mental health lobby, but is rather a result of the difficulties inherent in setting up devolved political structures following years of political conflict. However, the process has begun in both parts of Ireland. In Northern Ireland a consultative document in preparation for a mental capacity bill was published in 2009,[40] and in the Republic of Ireland, a Mental Capacity Bill was published in 2008.

REPUBLIC OF IRELAND: DEVELOPMENTS CULMINATING IN THE
MENTAL HEALTH ACT 2001

Following the passing of the Mental Treatment Act 1945, there were many improvements in the mental health services in Ireland. During the 1950s, the most notable was the expansion of outpatient clinics. By 1959, according to the report of the Inspector for Mental Hospitals, 5,442 patients had made 14,264 attendances.[41] However, the problem of over-institutionalisation of people with mental illnesses continued to be a problem. In 1958, the number of patients receiving hospital care was 20,619 (19,590 in publicly funded beds and 1,029 in private beds), the highest ever recorded in the Republic of Ireland. According to Dr.Dermot Walsh, it was one of the highest rates per head of the population in the world.[42] In the second half of the twentieth century, there were some attempts to change the law and the approach to mental health and illness, but no major changes in procedures for admission or treatment were implemented, due to the financial commitment that would be required. The Mental Treatment Act, 1961 simply amended some of the outdated language and procedures of the 1945 Act. The only changes of note were the introduction of a six-month limit on extensions of temporary hospital admissions for people who were not improving (up to a maximum of eighteen months, when a review was triggered);[43] the authorisation of expenditure on preventive care or aftercare in the community for individual patients;[44] and the renaming of the Central Criminal Asylum as the Central Mental Hospital.[45] In 1966, a special Commission of Enquiry on Mental Illness produced an extensive report with several recommendations on how to improve mental health services but very little happened as a result of this enquiry.[46]

In 1981, there was another attempt to make radical changes to mental health law. The Health (Mental Services) Act 1981 was passed with the purpose of 'making further and better provision for the regulation of the care and treatment of persons suffering from mental disorders'.[47] Like its counterparts in England (1959) and Northern Ireland (1961), it aimed to simplify admission procedures, to abolish certification, to shorten the period for which compulsory treatment was permitted, and establish review boards similar to mental health tribunals in the UK. The law was passed but it was never implemented. Whether or not this was due to the lack of finance to carry it through or to inherent legal problems with the new procedures is not clear. The next attempt did prove successful, though it took a number of years to bring it to the implementation stage. The Green Paper, *Planning for the Future,*[48] with its focus on the need to speed up the process of moving people from hospital to community settings and to integrate psychiatric services more fully into the general health service system, provided the basis for the discussion which led to the publication, in 1995, of a White Paper *A New Mental Health Act.*[49] As discussed by Dr. Dermot Walsh elsewhere in this volume, this now set out in some detail a more formal presentation of the 1992 proposals dealing with the main issues discussed in the Green Paper. It included the following: the criteria for involuntary admission; procedures for voluntary admission; the meaning and duration of detention orders; consent to treatment; and the care and treatment of mentally disordered offenders. This Green Paper formed the basis for both the Mental Health Act 2001 and the Criminal Law (Insanity) Act of 2006.[50] The existing legal framework for the Irish mental health system – the Mental Treatment Act 1945 – even though it had been amended in 1961, no longer met any of the international standards of protection of the rights of people who used the psychiatric services. By then, as in the UK and other European countries, the overly optimistic trust in the medical profession which had characterised mid-century legislation had now been replaced by an awareness of the limitations of medical intervention and of the vulnerability of people who had mental health problems. Following consultation and discussion with interested parties, radical changes in admission and treatment procedures came into being. Mental health tribunals and a mental health commission were introduced with the aim of providing the best level of protection of freedom and of human rights for people who use mental health services. As already discussed, Ireland has also begun the process of introducing capacity legislation, which will give protection to those who have lost capacity and for whom treatment under mental health legislation is not appropriate. As is the case in Northern Ireland, delays in passing this law are being attributed to the difficulties and the cost of setting up the complex legal and medical structures that will have to be put in place to ensure the delivery of a high standard of protection for those involved.

As the twenty-first century progresses, it is likely that mental health law will have to be updated continually, in order to bring it into line with new approaches to the care and treatment of people with mental illnesses. Whether this treatment is carried out in hospital or in the community, it is essential that the law protects the liberty of each individual patient and, at the same time, offers care and treatment that is appropriate for his or her needs. After an era of over-institutionalising people, let us hope that we are not entering an era of neglect.

NOTES

1. For an overview of selected laws throughout the period covered in this chapter, see Table 15.1.
2. Mark Finnane, *Insanity and the Insane in Post-Famine Ireland* (London: Croom Helm, 1981); Brendan Kelly, 'The Mental Treatment Act 1945 in Ireland: an historical enquiry', *History of Psychiatry*, 19:1 (2008): 47–67; Elizabeth Malcolm, *Swift's Hospital* (Dublin: Gill and Macmillan, 1989); Pauline M. Prior, 'Dangerous Lunacy: The Misuse of Mental Health Law in Nineteenth Century Ireland', *Journal of Forensic Psychiatry and Psychology*, 14:3 (2003): 525–53; Dermot Walsh, '200 Years of Irish Psychiatry', *Irish Journal of Psychiatry*, 13 (1992): 3–20; Arthur Williamson, 'The beginnings of state care for the mentally ill in Ireland', *Economic and Social Review*, 10:1 (January 1970): 281–90.
3. *Report of the select committee on the aged and infirm poor of Ireland 1804*, HC 1803–04 (109) v. 771.
4. See Virginia Crossman, *Politics, Law and Order in Nineteenth-Century Ireland* (Dublin: Gill and Macmillan, 1996).
5. Finnane, *Insanity and the Insane*, Table A, p.227.
6. G.W. Abraham, *Law and Practice of Lunacy in Ireland* (Dublin: Ponsonby, 1886); J.M. Colles, *The Lunacy Act and Orders with Forms and County Court Act and Rules*, 2nd edition, (Dublin: William McGee/London: Stevens and Haynes, 1890).
7. Joseph Robins, *Fools and Mad: A History of the Insane in Ireland*, (Dublin: Institute of Public Administration, 1986), p.143.
8. *Asylums Report 1866*, HC (3721) xxxii. 125, p.19.
9. *Report of the Commission of Inquiry into Lunatic Asylums in Ireland 1857*, HC 1857–58 (2436) xxvii.1.
10. Ibid., p.21 (Main report) and p.187 (Evidence of James Corry Connellan).
11. Finnane, *Insanity and the Insane*; Prior, 'Dangerous Lunacy'.
12. *Asylums Report*, HC 1889 (c. 5796) xxxvii. 641, p.8.
13. *Report of the Poor Law Union and Lunacy Inquiry* (Ireland) 1878–9, HC 1878–9 (c. 2239) xxxi.1.
14. *Asylums Report 1901*, p xv. HC (Cd. 760) xxviii. 487.
15. For discussion, see Jones, *A History of Mental Health Services*; Clive Unsworth, *The Politics of Mental Health Legislation* (Oxford: Clarendon Press, 1987).
16. Finnane, *Insanity and the Insane*, p.103.
17. 61 & 62 Vic. c. 37, Section 9(6).
18. *Statutory Rules and Orders*, Revised to December 1903. Vol. 8, pp.44–5. (Dublin: HMSO, 1904).
19. *Report of the Inspectors of Lunatics (NI) for 1921 & 1922*, Cmd. 28, p.20. (Belfast: HMSO, 1924).
20. *Report of the Royal Commission on Lunacy and Mental Disorder 1924–26* (Macmillan Commission), Cmd. 2700. (London: HMSO, 1926).
21. Kathleen Jones, *A History of the Mental Health Services* (London: Routledge, 1972), p.232.
22. For a full discussion on the debates leading up to the passing of the Act, see Chapter 2 of Pauline M. Prior, *Mental Health and Politics in Northern Ireland* (Aldershot: Avebury Press, 1993).
23. For a full discussion on the debates leading up to the passing of the Act, see Chapter 2 of Prior, *Mental Health and Politics*.
24. Kelly, 'The Mental Treatment Act 1945', p.48.
25. *Report of the Commission on the Relief of the Sick and Destitute Poor including the Insane Poor 1927* (Dublin: The Stationery Office).
26. For detailed discussion, see Kelly, 'The Mental Treatment Act 1945'.

27. Dermot Walsh and A. Daly, *Mental Illness in Ireland, 1750–2002: Reflections on the Rise and Fall of Institutional Care* (Dublin: Health Research Board, 2004).
28. Mental Treatment Act 1945, Section 3, (Dublin: The Stationery Office, 1945, No. 19).
29. Mental Treatment Act 2001, (Dublin: The Stationery Office, 2001, No. 25).
30. DHSSPSNI, *NI Hospital Statistics: Mental Health and Learning Disability 2009/10*.
31. PRO(NI) HSS 16/5/70 *Mental Health Bill: Consultations with interested Bodies 1948*.
32. Mental Health Act (NI) 1948, Sect. 9(1).
33. *Report of the Royal Commission on the Law relating to Mental Illness and Mental Deficiency 1954–57*, Cmnd. 169 (London: HMSO), par. 70.
34. *Bamford Review, A comprehensive legal framework*, Report of the Bamford Review of Mental Health and Learning Disability in Northern Ireland (Belfast: DHSSPSNI, 2007). All reports available electronically at http://www.dhsspsni.gov.uk/bamford.htm/.
35. *Report of the Northern Ireland Review committee on Mental Health Legislation* (MacDermott Committee) (Belfast: HMSO, 1981).
36. For a full discussion on the debates leading up to the passing of the Order, see Chapter 6 of Prior, *Mental Health and Politics*.
37. All articles are from the Mental Health (NI) Order 1986.
38. Reports of the Bamford Review of Mental Health and Learning Disability in Northern Ireland 2002–2007 (Belfast: DHSSPSNI, 2007). All reports available electronically on the webpage.
39. Pauline M. Prior, 'Removing children from the care of adults with diagnosed mental illnesses – a clash of human rights?', *European Journal of Social Work*, 6:2 (2003): 179–90; Pauline M. Prior, 'Mentally disordered offenders and the European Court of Human Rights', *International Journal of Law and Psychiatry*, 30: 6(2007): 546–57.
40. DHSSPSNI, *A legislative framework for mental capacity and mental health legislation in NI* (Belfast: DHSSPSNI, 2009).
41. Dermot Walsh, 'Mental Health Services in Ireland 1959-2010', in this volume.
42. Ibid.
43. Mental Treatment Act 1961, Section 18.
44. Ibid., Section 31.
45. Ibid., Section 39.
46. DH, *Report of the Commission of Inquiry on Mental Illness*, (Dublin: The Stationery Office, 1966).
47. Health (Mental Services) Act 1981, No. 17.
48. Department of Health, Green Paper on Mental Health (Dublin: The Stationery Office, 1992).
49. DH, *White Paper: A New Mental Health Act* (Dublin: Department of Health, 1995).
50. Mental Health Act 2001 (2001, No. 25); Criminal Law (insanity) Act 2006 (2006, No. 11).

Bibliography

PRIMARY SOURCES

Parliamentary Papers of the UK Parliament (in chronological order)__

Annual reports on the district, criminal and private lunatic asylums in Ireland, with appendices. (Short title used in text: Asylums Report)

HC 1844 (567) xxx. 69 (Report of the Inspectors General)
HC 1845 (645) xxvi. 269 (Report of the Inspectors General)
HC 1846 (736) xxii. 409 (Hereafter, Report of the Inspectors of Lunacy)
HC 1847 (820) xvii. 355
HC 1849 (1054) xxiii. 53
HC 1851 (1387) xxiv. 231
HC 1852–53 (1653) xli. 353
HC 1854–55 (1981) xvi. 137
HC 1857 Session 2 (2253) xvii. 67
HC 1859 Session 2 (2582) x. 443
HC 1861 (2901) xxvii. 245
HC 1862 (2975) xxiii. 517
HC 1863 (3209) xx. 621
HC 1864 (3369) xxiii. 317
HC 1865 (3556) xxi. 103
HC 1866 (3721) xxxii. 125
HC 1867 (3894) xviii. 453
HC 1867–68 (4053) xxxi. 303
HC 1868–69 (4181) xxvii. 419
HC 1870 (C. 202) xxxiv. 287
HC 1871 (C. 440) xxvi. 427
HC 1872 (C. 647) xxvii. 323
HC 1873 (C. 852) xxx. 327
HC 1874 (C. 1004) xxvii. 363
HC 1875 (C. 1293) xxxiii. 319
HC 1876 (C. 1496) xxxiii. 363
HC 1877 (C. 1750) xli. 449
HC 1878 (C. 2037) xxxix. 395
HC 1878–79 (C. 2346) xxxii. 455
HC 1880 (C. 2621) xxix. 459
HC 1881 (C. 2933) xlviii. 469
HC 1882 (C. 3356) xxxii. 479
HC 1883 (C. 3675) xxx. 427
HC 1884 (C. 4160) xl. 427

HC 1884–85 (C. 4539) xxxvi. 635
HC 1886 (C. 4811) xxxiii. 559
HC 1887 (C. 5121) xxxix. 591
HC 1888 (C. 5459) lii. 595
HC 1889 (C. 5796) xxxvii. 641
HC 1890 (C. 6148) xxxv. 609
HC 1890–1 (C. 6503) xxxvi. 521
HC 1892 (C. 6803) xl. 365
HC 1893–94 (C. 7125) xlvi. 369
HC 1894 (C. 7466) xliii. 401
HC 1895 (C. 7804) liv. 435
HC 1896 (C. 8251) xxxix. Part 2. 1
HC 1897 (C. 8639) xxxviii. 527
HC 1898 (C. 8969) xliii. 491
HC 1899 (C. 9479) xl. 501
HC 1900 (Cd. 312) xxxvii. 513
HC 1901 (Cd. 760) xxviii. 487
HC 1901 (Cd. 760) xxviii. 487
HC 1902 (Cd. 1265) xl. 491
HC 1903 (Cd. 1762) xxvii. 515
HC 1905 (Cd. 2262) xxxv. 549
HC 1906 (Cd. 2771) xxxviii. 565
HC 1906 (Cd. 3164) xxxix. 103 (Supplement: Special report on increase in insanity)
HC 1908 (Cd. 3745) xxiii. 575
HC 1908 (Cd. 4302) xxxiii. 811
HC 1909 (Cd. 4760) xxxii. 1
HC 1910 (Cd. 5280) xli. 593
HC 1911 (Cd. 760) xxxv. 1
HC 1912–13 (Cd. 6386) xxxix. 271
HC 1913 (Cd. 6935) xxxiv. 143
HC 1914 (Cd. 7527) xli. 309
HC 1914–16 (Cd. 7990) xxvi. 675
HC 1917–18 (Cd. 8454) xvi. 547
HC 1917–18 (Cd. 8940) xvi. 639
HC 1919 (Cmd. 32) xxv. 305
HC 1920 (Cmd. 579) xxi. 339
HC 1921 (Cmd. 1127) xv. 165
HC 1924 (Cmd. 28) (Report for NI 1921–22) Belfast: HMSO.

Other Parliamentary Reports and Debates (in chronological order)_

Report of the Select Committee to Consider the State of the Lunatic Poor in Ireland, HC 1817 (430) viii. 33.

Report of Select Committee of the House of Lords Appointed to Consider the State of the Lunatic Poor in Ireland, HC 1843 (625) x. 439.

Report of the Commissioners of Inquiry into the state of the Lunatic Asylums and other Institutions for the Custody and Treatment of the Insane in Ireland (with minutes of evidence and appendices) 1858, HC 1857–8 (2436) xxvii.1.

Report of the Poor Law Union and Lunacy Inquiry (Ireland) 1878–79, HC 1878–9 (C. 2239) xxxi.1.

Report of the commission appointed by the Home Department to enquire into the subject of Criminal Lunacy (England & Wales), HC 1882 (C. 3418) xxxii. 841.

Parliamentary Debates, *Hansard*, Fourth Series, vol. li, 22 July 1897, col. 712.

Parliamentary Debates, *Hansard*, Fourth Series, vol. xlvii, 18 March 1897, col. 943.

Statutory Rules and Orders, Revised to December 1903. Vol. 8, pp.44–5. (Dublin: HMSO, 1904).

Report of the Royal Commission on Lunacy and Mental Disorder 1924–6 (Macmillan Commission), Cmd. 2700. (London: HMSO, 1926).

Report of the Royal Commission on the Law relating to Mental Illness and Mental Deficiency 1954–57, Cmnd. 169 (London: HMSO, 1957).

Northern Ireland and UK Government Reports (in chronological order)

Northern Ireland Hospital Authority (NIHA), *Annual Reports* 1960–1974 (Belfast: NIHA).

NHSSB, 'Centre Voices: A qualitative study of the experiences of people who have been in-patients in Tobernaveen Centre, Holywell Hospital' (Ballymena: Northern Health and Social Services Board, 1998).

DHSSPS (NI) *Mental Health Services in NI*, VFM Review (Belfast: DHSSPS(NI), 2002)

DH, 'Guide on provision of adult acute in-patient care' (London: DH, 2002).

Bamford Review of mental health and learning disability (NI), Reports on different issues published by working groups (Belfast: DHSSPS(NI), 2002–2007).

Republic of Ireland Government Reports (in chronological order)

Report of the Commission on the Relief of the Sick and Destitute Poor including the Insane Poor 1927 (Dublin: The Stationery Office).

Commission of Inquiry on Mental Illness, *Commission of Inquiry on Mental Illness Report* (Dublin: The Stationery Office, 1966).

Reports of the Inspector of Mental Hospitals for the Years 1950, 1956, 1959, 1961–2, 1977–9, 1997 (Dublin: The Stationery Office).

Department of Health, *Psychiatric Services – Planning For the Future* (Dublin: The Stationery Office, 1984).

DHC, *Report of the National Task Force on Medical Staffing* (Dublin: The Stationery Office, 2003). (The Hanly Report.)

DHC, *A Vision for Change: Report of the Expert Group on Mental Health Policy* (Dublin: The Stationery Office, 2006).

DHC, *Guidelines on Good Practice and Quality Assurance in Mental Health Services* (Dublin: The Stationery Office, 1998).

Health Research Board, *Irish Psychiatric Hospitals and Units Census 2001* (Dublin: Health Research Board, 2002).

Mental Health Commission, *Rules Governing the Use of Electro-convulsive Therapy* (Dublin: Mental Health Commission, 2006).

Mental Health Commission, *Annual Report including the report of the Inspector of Mental Health Service* (Dublin: Mental Health Commission, 2007).

ARCHIVES

National Archives
Archives New Zealand, Dunedin Regional Office
Archives New Zealand, Auckland Regional Office

Archives New Zealand, Wellington Regional Office
National Archives of Ireland
Public Record Office Victoria, Australia
Public Record Office of Northern Ireland (PRONI)

Locally Held Archives
Committee of Management of Ballinasloe Mental Hospital. *Minutes of the Proceedings of the Committee of Management of Ballinasloe Mental Hospital*, held in Ballinasloe Psychiatric Hospital.
Annual Reports of the Richmond District Asylum, 1892, 1894, 1895, 1896, in the archive of the hospital, located at St. Brendan's Hospital, Dublin.

Newspapers and Magazines
Belfast Daily Mercury
Evening Mail
Freeman's Journal
Speedwell, Magazine of the staff and patients of Holywell Hospital, Antrim, NI 1959–73.
Northern Whig

SECONDARY SOURCES

Abraham, G.W., *Law and Practice of Lunacy in Ireland*, (Dublin: Ponsonby, 1886).
Ackner, B., A. Harris, A. and A.G. Oldham, *Lancet*. I (1957): 607.
Adams, Annmarie, *Medicine By Design: The Architect And The Modern Hospital, 1893–1943* (Minneapolis: University of Minnesota Press, 2008).
Akenson, Donald Harman, *Half the World from Home: Perspectives on the Irish in New Zealand, 1860–1950* (Wellington: Victoria University Press, 1990).
Ances, B.M., and R. Shelhaus, M.J. Brown, O.V. Rios, S.T. Herman, J.A. French,'Neurosyphilis and Status Epilepticus: Case Report and Literature Review', *Epilepsy Research*, 59 (2004): 67–70.
Anderson, M., 'Mrs Charles Clacy, Lola Montez and Poll the Grogseller: Glimpses of Women on the Early Victorian Goldfields' in I. McCalman, A. Cook and A. Reeves (eds), *Gold: Forgotten Histories and Lost Objects of Australia* (Cambridge: Cambridge University Press, 2001), pp.225–49.
Andrews, Jonathan and Andrew Scull, *Customers and Patrons of the Mad-Trade: the management of lunacy in eighteenth-century London* (London: University of California Press, 2003).
Anonymous, 'Increase in Insanity', *American Journal of Insanity*, 18, (1861): 95.
Anonymous, Obituary of Conolly Norman, M.D., FRCPI, *British Medical Journal*, 29: ii (1908): 541.
Anonymous, Obituary of Conolly Norman, M.D., in the *Journal of Mental Science*, liv: 225, (April 1908): 203-4.
Anonymous, Obituary of John Mallet Purser, M.D., D.Sc., F.R.C.P.I., *The British Medical Journal*, 28 September, 1929, p.600.
Anonymous, Discussion of Conolly Norman's paper, 'Clinical features of Beri-beri', published in *Dublin Journal of Medical Science*, cvii (1899): 309–10.
Arensberg, C.M. and S.T Kimball, *Family and Community in Ireland*, Third Edition: (Harvard: Clasp Press, 2001). First published in 1940.
Arlidge, J.T. 'The Chaplaincy Question at the Belfast Asylum', *The Asylum Journal*,

published by the Authority of the Association of Medical Officers of Asylums and Hospitals of the Insane, Vol. 4 (March 1 1854): 49–51.

Aronson, J.K. *An Account of the Foxglove and Its Medical Uses, 1785–1985: Incorporating a Facsimile of William Withering's 'An Account of the Foxglove and Some of Its Uses'*, published in 1785 (Oxford: Oxford University Press, 1985).

Bartlett, P. and D. Wright, *Outside the Walls of the Asylum: The History of Care in the Community 1750–2000* (London: The Athlone Press, 1999).

Bartlett, P., *The Poor Law of Lunacy: the Administration of Pauper Lunatics in Mid Nineteenth-Century England* (London and New York: Leicester University Press, 1999).

Barton, R., *Institutional Neurosis* (Bristol: John Wright, 1959).

Beckett, Claire, *Thatcher* (London: Haus Publishing, 2006).

BMA (NI) 'Mental Health in Northern Ireland –The Way Forward' (Belfast: British Medical Association NI branch, October 2009).

Berresford-Ellis, Peter, *A History of the Irish Working Class* (London: Pluto Press, 1985).

Bini, L. and U. Cerletti. 'Un nuovo metodo di shockterapia: ' L'electroshock'. *Boll. R. Accad. Med. Roma*, 64 (1938): 136–8.

Bolton, G., 'The Gold Discovery 1851–80 and Ireland' in C. Kiernan (ed.), *Ireland and Australia* (Cork: Mercier Press, 1984), pp.23–33.

Bonwick, R. 'The History of Yarra Bend Lunatic Asylum, Melbourne' (unpublished M. Med. thesis, University of Melbourne, 1996).

Bowden, K.M., *Goldrush Doctors at Ballarat* (Mulgrave, VIC: The Author, 1977).

Boyce, J., *Van Diemen's Land* (Melbourne: Black Inc., 2009).

Breen, R., D. Hannan, D. Rottman and C. Whelan (eds), *Understanding Contemporary Ireland: State, Class and Development in the Republic of Ireland* (Dublin: Gill and MacMillan, 1990).

Brookes, Barbara, 'Women and Madness: A Case-Study of the Seacliff Asylum, 1890–1920', in Barbara Brookes, Charlotte Macdonald, and Margaret Tennant (eds), *Women in History 2* (Wellington: Bridget Williams Books, 1992), pp.129–47.

Brookes, Barbara, 'Men and Madness in New Zealand, 1890–1916', in Linda Bryder and Derek A. Dow (eds), *New Countries and Old Medicine: Proceedings of an International Conference on the History of Medicine and Health, Auckland, New Zealand, 1994* (Auckland: Pyramid Press, 1995), pp.204–10.

Brookes, Barbara and Jane Thomson (eds), *'Unfortunate Folk': Essays on Mental Health Treatment, 1863–1992* (Dunedin: University of Otago Press, 2001).

Brosnahan, Seán G., *Kerrytown Brosnahans* (Timaru: R.J. and H.P. Brosnahan, 1992).

Brown, E.M., 'Why Wagner-Jauregg Won the Nobel Prize for Discovering Malaria Therapy for General Paralysis of the Insane', *History of Psychiatry*, 11 (2000): 371–82.

Browne, I. and D. Walsh, *Mental Health Services in Dublin* (Unpublished document, 1966).

Buckingham, J., *Bitter Nemesis: The Intimate History of Strychnine* (Boca Raton, FL: CRC Press/Taylor and Francis Group, 2008).

Bucknill, J.C., 'Inspector of Lunatics Ireland Seventh Report', *The Asylum Journal*. Published by the Authority of the Association of Medical Officers of Asylums and Hospitals of the Insane, No. 17, (1856): 135–6.

Burdett, H.C., *Hospitals and Asylums of the World: their Origin, History, Construction, Administration, Management, and Legislation*, 4 vols. (London: J. & A. Churchill, 1891).

Butler, S., 'Mental Health Social Work in Ireland: Missed Opportunities', in N.

Kearney and C. Skehill (eds), *Social Work in Ireland Historical Perspectives* (Dublin: Institute of Public Administration, 2005), pp.33–50.

Bynum, W. F., R. Porter and M. Shepherd (eds), *The Anatomy of Madness: Essays in the History of Psychiatry*, Vol. 3 (London: Routledge, 1988).

Byrne, A., R. Edmondson and T. Varley, 'Introduction to Third Edition', in Arensberg and Kimball, *Family and Community in Ireland*, 3rd edition (Harvard: Clasp Press, 2001).

Campling, Penelope, 'Therapeutic Communities,' *Advances in Psychiatric Treatment*, 7 (2001): 365–72.

Carney, William R. Jr., 'Personal accounts: My experiences as a psychiatric patient in the 1960s', *Psychiatric Services*, 56: 12 (December 2005):1499–500.

Carpenter, Kenneth J., *Beriberi, White Rice, and Vitamin B: a disease, a cause and a cure* (London and Los Angeles: University of California Press, 2000).

Carpenter, Mick., 'They still go marching on. A celebration of COHSE's first 75 years.' (London: COHSE, 1985).

Cassel, R.D., *Medical Charities, Medical Politics: the Irish Dispensary System and the Poor Law 1836–72* (Rochester, NY: Boydell Press, 1997).

Clarke, C.R.A., 'Neurological Diseases and Diseases of Voluntary Muscle', in P. Kumar and M. Clark (eds), *Clinical Medicine* (3rd edition) (London: Bailliere Tindall, 1994), pp.871–955.

Clarkson, L. A. and E. Margaret Crawford, *Feast and Famine: A History of Food and Nutrition in Ireland 1500–1920* (Oxford: Oxford University Press, 2001).

Cockerham W. C., *Sociology of Mental Disorder*, 6th edition (New Jersey: Pearson Education Inc, 2003).

Coleborne, C., *Madness in the Family: Insanity and Institutions in the Australasian Colonial World, 1860–1914* (London: Palgrave Macmillan, 2010).

Coleborne, C., 'Passage to the Asylum: the Role of the Police in Committals of the Insane in Victoria, Australia, 1848–1900' in R. Porter and D. Wright (eds), *The Confinement of the Insane: International Perspectives, 1800–1965* (Cambridge: Cambridge University Press, 2003), pp.129–48.

Coleborne, C., *Reading 'Madness': Gender and Difference in the Colonial Asylum in Victoria, Australia, 1848–88* (Perth: Network Books, 2007).

Coleborne, D. and D. MacKinnon (eds), *'Madness' in Australia: Histories, Heritage and the Asylum* (Brisbane: University of Queensland Press, 2003).

Colles, J. M., *The Lunacy Act and Orders with Forms and County Court Act and Rules*, 2nd edition (Dublin: William McGee/London: Stevens and Haynes, 1890).

Conolly-Norman, J., *Richmond Asylum Joint Committee Minutes* (Dublin: Richmond Asylum, 1907).

Conolly-Norman, J., 'A Brief Note on Beri-beri in Asylums', *Journal of Mental Science*, xlv (1899): 503–12.

Conolly-Norman, J., 'The etiology of beri-beri', *British Medical Journal*, 2(2016), 19 August 1899: 487.

Coolahan, J., *Irish Education: History and Structure* (Dublin: Institute of Public Administration, 1981).

Crossman, Virginia, *Politics, Law and Order in Nineteenth-Century Ireland* (Dublin: Gill and Macmillan, 1996).

Daly, A. and D. Walsh, 'An audit of new long-stay inpatients' in *Irish Journal of Psychological Medicine*, 26 (2009): 3.

Daly, A., D. T. Doherty and D. Walsh, 'Reducing the revolving door phenomenon' in *Irish Journal of Psychological Medicine*, 27.1 (2010): 27–34.

Damousi, J., *Freud in the Antipodes: A Cultural History of Psychoanalysis in Australia* (Sydney: UNSW Press, 2005).

Davidson, Andrew (ed.), *Hygiene and Disease in Warm Climates* (Edinburgh & London: Young J. Pentland, 1893).

Davidson, S. and R. Passmore, *Human Nutrition and Dietetics* 7th Edn (Edinburgh: E. & S. Livingstone, 1979).

Delargy, Rosaline, *The History of the Belfast District Lunatic Asylum 1829–1921*. Unpublished Ph.D thesis (Belfast: University of Ulster, 2002).

Digby, Anne, *Making a Medical Living: Doctors and patients in the market for medicine in England 1720–1924* (Cambridge: Cambridge University Press, 1994).

Doroshow, J., 'Performing a cure for schizophrenia: insulin coma therapy on the wards', *Hist of Med. Allied Sci.* 62 (2007): 213–43.

Dörries, A., Beddies, T., 'The Wittenauer Heilstätten in Berlin: a Case Record Study of Psychiatric Patients in Germany, 1919–60', in R. Porter and D. Wright (eds), *The Confinement of the Insane: International Perspectives, 1800–1965* (Cambridge: Cambridge University Press, 2003), pp.149–72.

Duffy, C. G., *My Life in Two Hemispheres*, 2 vols. (London: T. Fisher Unwin, 1898).

Egan, B., 'Springthorpe, John William (1855–1933)' in J. Ritchie (ed.), *Australian Dictionary of Biography*, Vol. 12 (Melbourne: Melbourne University Press, 1990), pp.38–9.

Fairburn, Miles, *The Ideal Society and its Enemies: The Foundations of Modern New Zealand Society, 1850–1900* (Auckland: Auckland University Press, 1989).

Farmer, P., 'Ethnography, Social Analysis, and the Prevention of Sexually Transmitted HIV Infections among Poor Women in Haiti', in: M.C. Inhorn and P. J. Brown (eds), *An Anthropology of Infectious Disease* (Amsterdam: Gordon and Breach 1997), pp.413–18.

Farmer, P., 'Pathologies of Power: Rethinking Health and Human Rights', *American Journal of Public Health*, 89 (1999): 1486–96.

Farmer, P., *Pathologies of Power* (Berkeley: University of California Press, 2003).

Farthing, M.J.G., D.J. Jeffries, J.M. Parkin, 'Infectious Diseases, Tropical Medicine and Sexually Transmitted Diseases', in P. Kumar and M. Clark (eds) *Clinical Medicine*, 3rd edition (London: Bailliere Tindall, 1994), pp.1–105.

Finnane, M., *Insanity and the Insane in Post-Famine Ireland* (London: Croom Helm, 1981).

Finnane, M., 'Asylums, Families and the State', *History Workshop*, 20 (1985): 134–48.

Finnane, M., 'The Irish and Crime in the Late Nineteenth Century: a Statistical Inquiry', pp.77–98 in O. MacDonagh and W.F. Mandle (eds), *Irish-Australian Studies: Papers Delivered at the Fifth Irish-Australian Conference* (Canberra: Australian National University, 1989).

Fitzpatrick, David, *Irish Emigration, 1801–1921* (Dundalk: Irish Economic and Social History Society, 1984).

Fitzpatrick, D., *Oceans of Consolation: Personal Accounts of Irish Migration to Australia* (Ithaca, NY and London: Cornell University Press, 1994).

Fleetwood, J.F., *The History of Medicine in Ireland*, 2nd edition (Dublin: Skellig Press, 1983).

Foucault, M., *Discipline and Punish: The Birth of the Prison* (London: Allen Lane 1977 and New York: Vintage Books, 1995).

Foucault, M., *Madness and Civilization: A History of Insanity in the Age of Reason* (London: Tavistock, 1967).

Foucault, M., *The Birth of the Clinic* (London: Tavistock, 1973).

Fox, John W., 'Irish Immigrants, Pauperism, and Insanity in 1854 Massachusetts', *Social Science History*, 15:3 (1991): 315–36.

Fraser, Lyndon, *To Tara Via Holyhead: Irish Catholic Immigrants in Nineteenth-Century Christchurch* (Auckland: Auckland University Press, 1997).

Fraser, Lyndon, *Castles of Gold: A History of New Zealand's West Coast Irish* (Dunedin: Otago University Press, 2007).

Friedman, Lester D. (ed.), *Cultural Sutures: Medicine and Media* (Durham, US: Duke University Press, 2004).

Gandevia, B., 'Cussen, Patrick Edward (1792–1849)' in D. Pike (ed.), *Australian Dictionary of Biography*, Vol. 1 (Melbourne: Melbourne University Press, 1966), pp.272–3.

Garton, S., *Medicine and Madness: a Social History of Insanity in NSW, 1880–1940* (Sydney: UNSW Press, 1988).

Gavigan, Arthur C., The mental hospital magazine, *Psychiatric Quarterly*, 17(1963): 243–8.

Geary, L., *Medicine and Charity in Ireland, 1718–1851* (Dublin: University College Press, 2004).

Geary, L. and O. Walsh (eds), *Philanthropy and Nineteenth-Century Ireland* (Dublin: Four Courts Press, forthcoming 2012).

Goffman, Erving, *Asylums: Essays on the Social Situation of Mental Patients and Other Inmates* (Chicago: Doubleday, 1961).

Goodman, D., *Gold Seeking: Victoria and California in the 1850s* (Sydney: Allen & Unwin, 1994).

Greaves, C. Desmond, *The Irish Transport and General Workers' Union: The Formative Years* (Dublin: Laurence and Wishart, 1988).

Greeley, H., *Bird's Nest Soup* (Dublin: Figgis and Co., 1987).

Greenslade, L., 'The Blackbird Calls in Grief: Colonialism, Health and Identity among Irish Immigrants in Britain', pp.36–60 in J. M. Laughlin (ed.), *Location and Dislocation in Contemporary Irish Society: Emigration and Irish Identities* (Cork: Cork University Press, 1997).

Greenslade, L., 'White Skin, White Masks: Psychological Distress Among the Irish in Britain', pp.202–25 in P. O'Sullivan (ed.), *The Irish in the New Communities* (Leicester: Leicester University Press, 1992).

Gürses, C., M. Kürtüncü, J. Jirsch, N. Yeşilot, H. Hanağasi, N. Bebek, B. Baykan, M. Emre, A. Gökyiğit, F. Andermann. 'Neurosyphilis Presenting with Status Epilepticus', *Epileptic Disorders*, 9 (2007): 51–6.

Guthrie, D.A., *History of Medicine* (London: Nelson, 1945).

Haigh, Rex, 'Acute wards: problems and solutions modern milieux: therapeutic community solutions to acute ward problems', *Psychiatric Bulletin*, 26 (2002): 380–2.

Haldane, R., *The People's Force: A History of the Victoria Police* (Melbourne: Melbourne University Press, 1986).

Hallaran, W.S., *An Enquiry into the Causes producing the Extraordinary Addition to the Number of Insane together with Extended Observations on the Cure of Insanity with hints as to the Better Management of Public Asylums for Insane Persons* (Cork: Edwards and Savage, 1810).

Handler, Richard, 'Erving Goffman and the Gestural Dynamics of Modern Selfhood', *Past & Present*, 203: Supplement 4 (2009): 280–300.

Henderson, D.K. and I.R.C. Batchelor, *Henderson's and Gillespie's Textbook of Psychiatry*, 9th edition (London: Oxford University Press, 1962).

Hinshelwood, R.D., *Suffering Insanity: Psychoanalytic Essays on Psychosis* (Hove, England/New York: Brunner-Routledge, 2004).

Hogan, J.F., *The Irish in Australia* (London: Ward & Downey, 1887).

Hoult, Adrienne, 'Institutional Responses to Mental Deficiency in New Zealand, 1911 1935: Tokanui Mental Hospital' (MA, University of Waikato, 2007).

Illich, I., *Limits to Medicine, Medical Nemesis: The Expropriation of Health* (London: Marion Boyars Publishers Ltd., 1976).

Illich, I., *Disabling Professionals* (London: Marion Boyars Publishers Ltd., 1977).

Jones, G., 'The Campaign Against Tuberculosis in Ireland, 1899–1914', pp.158–76. in E. Malcolm and G. Jones (eds), *Medicine, Disease and the State in Ireland, 1650–1940* (Cork: Cork University Press, 1999).

Jones, Kathleen, *A History of the Mental Health Services* (London: Routledge, 1972).

Jones, Kathleen, *Asylums and After: A Revised History of the Mental Health Services: From the Early Eighteenth Century to the 1990s* (London: Athlone Press, 1993).

Kaplan, H.I. and B.J. Saddock, *Concise Textbook of Clinical Psychiatry* (Baltimore: Williams & Wilkins, 1996).

Kelly, B.D., 'Structural Violence and Schizophrenia', *Social Science and Medicine*, 61 (2005): pp.721–30.

Kelly, B.D., 'The Power Gap: Freedom, Power and Mental Illness', *Social Science and Medicine*, 63 (2006): 2118–28.

Kelly, B.D., 'Murder, Mercury and Mental Illness: Infanticide in Nineteenth-Century Ireland,' *Irish Journal of Medical Science*, 176 (2007): 149–52.

Kelly, B.D., 'One Hundred Years Ago: the Richmond Asylum, Dublin in 1907', *Irish Journal of Psychological Medicine*, 24 (2007): 108–14.

Kelly, B.D., 'Mental Health Law in Ireland, 1821–1902: dealing with the 'increase of insanity in Ireland', *Medico-Legal Journal*, 76 (2008): 26–33.

Kelly, B.D., 'The Mental Treatment Act 1945 in Ireland: An Historical Enquiry', *History of Psychiatry*, 19: 1(2008): 47–67.

Kelly, B.D., 'Syphilis, Psychiatry and Offending Behaviour: Clinical Cases from Nineteenth-Century Ireland', *Irish Journal of Medical Science*, 178 (2009): 73–7.

Kelly, W., *Life in Victoria, or Victoria in 1853 and Victoria in 1858*, (1859), reprint, 2 vols. (Kilmore, VIC: Lowden Publishing, 1977).

Kelly, W., *A Stroll through the Diggings of California* (London: Simms and McIntyre, 1852).

Keshavjee, S., and M. C. Becerra, 'Disintegrating Health Services and Resurgent Tuberculosis in Post-Soviet Tajikistan: An Example of Structural Violence', *Journal of the American Medical Association*, 283 (2000): 1201.

Kidd, H.B., 'Industrial Units in Psychiatric Hospitals', *British Journal of Psychiatry*, III (1965): 1250.

Kirby, P., L. Gibbons and M. Cronin (eds), *Reinventing Ireland: Culture, Society and the Global Economy* (London: Pluto Press, 2002).

Kirkpatrick, T.P.C., *A Note on the History of the Care of the Insane in Ireland: Up to the End of the Nineteenth Century* (Dublin: University Press by Ponsonby and Gibbs, 1931).

Labrum, Bronwyn, 'Looking Beyond the Asylum: Gender and the Process of Committal in Auckland, 1870–1910', *New Zealand Journal of History*, 26 (1992): 125–44.

Laing, R.D., *The Divided Self* (London: Tavistock Publications, 1960).

Laing, R.D. and A. Esterson, *Sanity, Madness and the Family* (London: Tavistock Publications, 1964).

Lee, J.J., *Ireland 1912–1985: Politics and Society* (Cambridge: Cambridge University Press, 1989).

Lerner, Arthur, 'A look at poetry therapy', *The Arts in Psychotherapy*, 24:1 (1997): 81–9.

Lewis, M., *Managing Madness: Psychiatry and Society in Australia, 1788–1980* (Canberra: Australian Government Publishing Service, 1988).

Malcolm, E.L., *Swift's Hospital* (Dublin: Gill and Macmillan, 1989).

Malcolm, E.L., 'Australian Asylum Architecture through German Eyes: Kew, Melbourne, 1867', *Health and History*, 11: 1 (2009): 46–64.

Malcolm, E.L., '"A most miserable looking object" – the Irish in English Asylums, 1851–1901: Migration, Poverty and Prejudice', pp.121–32 in J. Belchem and K. Tenfelde (eds), *Irish and Polish Migration in Comparative Perspective* (Essen: Klartext Verlag, 2003).

Malcolm, E.L., '"What would people say if I became a policeman?" The Irish Policeman Abroad', pp.95–107 in O. Walsh (ed.), *Ireland Abroad: Politics and Professions in the Nineteenth Century* (Dublin: Four Courts Press, 2003).

Manning, F.N., 'President's Address: Psychology Section', pp.816–33 in *Intercolonial Medical Congress of Australasia: Transactions of Second Session Held in Melbourne, Victoria, January 1889* (Melbourne: Stillwell & Co, 1889).

Manning, N., *The Therapeutic Community Movement: Charisma and Routinisation* (London: Routledge, 1989).

Manson, Patrick, 'The Prophylaxis and Treatment of Beri-beri', *British Medical Journal*, 20 September 1902, p.834.

Manson, Patrick. *Tropical Diseases: A Manual of Diseases of Warm Climates* (London: Cassell, 1898).

McCabe, Anton, 'The Stormy Petrel of the Transport Workers', 1994, *Saothar* No. 19: 41–52.

McCalman, J., *Sex and Suffering: Women's Health and a Women's Hospital. The Royal Women's Hospital, Melbourne, 1856–1996* (Melbourne: Melbourne University Press, 1998).

McCance, R.A. & E.M. Widdowson, *The Composition of Foods*, Medical Research Council, Special Report Series, no. 297 (London: HMSO, 1960). Fourth revised edition by A.A. Paul & D.A.T. Southgate (London: HMSO, 1978).

McCandless, P., 'Curative asylum, custodial hospital: the South Carolina Lunatic Asylum and State Hospital, 1828–1920', pp.173–92 in R. Porter and D. Wright (eds), *The Confinement of the Insane: International Perspectives, 1800–1965* (Cambridge: Cambridge University Press, 2003).

McCarthy, Angela, *Irish Migrants in New Zealand, 1840–1937: 'The Desired Haven'* (Woodbridge: The Boydell Press, 2005).

McCarthy, Angela, 'Ethnicity, Migration, and the Lunatic Asylum in Early Twentieth Century Auckland, New Zealand', *Social History of Medicine*, 21:1 (2008): pp.47–65.

McClaughlin, T., *Barefoot and Pregnant: Irish Famine Orphans in Australia* (Melbourne: Genealogical Society of Victoria, 1991).

McClaughlin, T., '"I was nowhere else": Casualties of Colonisation in Eastern Australia during the Second Half of the Nineteenth Century', pp.142–62 in T. McClaughlin (ed.), *Irish Women in Colonial Australia* (Sydney: Allen & Unwin, 1998).

McClelland, Roy, 'The Madhouses and Mad Doctors of Ulster', *Ulster Medical Journal*, 57:2 (1988): 101–20.

MacDonagh, O., 'The Irish in Victoria, 1851–91: a Demographic Essay', pp.67–92 in T.D. Williams (ed.), *Historical Studies VIII* (Dublin: Gill and Macmillan, 1971).

McDonald, D. and I. Campbell, 'Francis Rawdon Hastings (1798–1877)', pp.345–6. in D. Pike (ed.), *Australian Dictionary of Biography*, Vol. 3 (Melbourne: Melbourne University Press, 1969).

McDonald, D. I., 'Gladesville Hospital: The Formative Years, 1838–50', *Journal of the Royal Australian Historical Society*, 41: 4 (1965): 273–95.

McDonald, D.I. 'Manning, Frederic Norton (1839–1903)', pp.204–5 in D. Pike (ed.), *Australian Dictionary of Biography*, Vol. 5 (Melbourne: Melbourne University Press, 1974).

Merrit, H.H., R. Adams and H.C. Solomon, *Neurosyphilis* (Oxford: Oxford University Press, 1946).

Mills, Alden Brewster, *Hospital Public Relations Today* (Chicago: Physicians Record Co, 1965).

Mocellin, George, 'Occupational therapy and psychiatry', *International Journal of Social Psychiatry*, 25: 29 (1979): 29–37.

Moncrieff, Joanna, 'An investigation into the precedents of modern drug treatment in psychiatry', *History of Psychiatry*, 10: 40 (October 1999): 475–90.

Monk, L.A, *Attending Madness: At Work in the Australian Colonial Asylum* (Amsterdam and New York: Rodopi, 2008).

Mulholland, Marc, *To Care Always: 100 Years of Holywell Hospital, Antrim, 1898–1998* (Antrim: Holywell Hospital, 1999).

Murphy, Donal A. (ed.), *Tumbling Walls: The Evolution of a Community Institution. St. Fintan's Hospital Portlaoise, 1833–1983* (Ireland: Midland Health Board, 1983).

Murphy, D.A., *Unpublished manuscript on union organisation in Cork Asylum, 1906–1960's* (Cork: Our Lady's Hospital Cork Historical Society, 1973).

Murphy, M., 'The Irish in Australian Mining History', pp.81–90 in S. Grimes and G. Ó Tuathaigh (eds), *The Irish-Australian Connection* (Galway: University College Galway, 1989).

Nevin, Donal, *Trade Union Century* (Cork: Mercier Press, 1993).

Ni Nuallain, N., A. O'Hare and D. Walsh, 'Incidence of Schizophrenia in Ireland', *Psychological Medicine*. 17: 943–8.

Nolan, Peter, *A History of Mental Health Nursing* (London: Chapman and Hall, 1993).

O'Connor, Emmet, *Syndicalism in Ireland 1917–1923* (Cork: Cork University Press, 1988).

O'Donnell, Peadar, *There Will Be Another Day* (Dublin: Dolmen Press, 1963).

O'Donnell, Peadar, *Monkeys in the Superstructure* (Galway, Ireland. 1986).

O'Farrell, P.J., *The Irish in Australia, 1788 to the Present*, 3rd edition (Sydney: UNSW Press, 2000).

O'Farrell, P.J. (ed.), *Letters from Irish Australia, 1825–1929* (Sydney and Belfast: NSW University Press and the Ulster Historical Foundation, 1984).

O'Keane, V., D. Walsh and S. Barry, *The Irish Psychiatric Association Report on the Funding Allocated to Adult Mental Health Services: where is it actually going?* (Dublin: Irish Psychiatric Association, 2005).

O'Reilly, D. and M. Stevenson, 'Mental health in Northern Ireland: Have "The Troubles" made it worse?' *Journal of Epidemiology and Community Health*, 57: 7 (2003): 488–92.

O'Shea, Brian and Jane Falvey, 'A History of the Richmond Asylum (St. Brendan's Hospital)', Dublin, pp.407–33 in Hugh Freeman & German E. Berrios (eds), *150 Years of British Psychiatry, Volume II, The Aftermath* (London: Athlone Press, 1996).

O'Sullivan, D.M, 'William McCrea' (1814–99), p.138 in D. Pike (ed.), *Australian Dictionary of Biography*, Vol. 5 (Melbourne: Melbourne University Press, 1974).

Paige, J.M., 'Conjuncture, Comparison, and Conditional Theory in Macrosocial Inquiry', *American Journal of Sociology*, 105: 3 (1999): 781–800.

Parry-Jones, William, *The Trade in Lunacy* (London: Routledge, 1972).

Pickelharing, C.A. & C. Winkler, *Beri-beri: Researches concerning its nature and cause and the means of Arrest, made by order of the Netherlands Government*, translated by Dr. James Cantile (Edinburgh and London: Young J. Pentland, 1893).

Porter, Roy, *A Social History of Madness: Stories of the Insane* (London: Phoenix, 1996).

Porter, Roy, *The Greatest Benefit to Mankind: A Medical History of Humanity from Antiquity to the Present* (London: Fontana Press, 1999).

Powell, Enoch, Speech given at annual conference of the NAMH (London) in 1961. Available at http://www.nhshistory.net/water tower.html.

Preston, M. and M. Ó hÓgartaigh (eds), *Gender and Medicine in Ireland, 1700–1950*, (New York: Syracuse University Press, 2012).

Prestwich, P.E., 'Family Strategies and Medical Power: "Voluntary" Committal in a Parisian Asylum, 1876–1914', pp.79–99 in R. Porter and D. Wright (eds), *The Confinement of the Insane: International Perspectives, 1800–1965* (Cambridge: Cambridge University Press, 2003).

Prior, P.M., *Mental Health and Politics in Northern Ireland: A History of Service Development* (Aldershot: Avebury, 1993).

Prior, P.M., 'Mental health policy in Northern Ireland', *Social Policy and Administration*, 27: 4 (1993): 323–34.

Prior, P.M., 'Where lunatics abound: A history of mental health services in Northern Ireland', pp.292–308 in H. Freeman and G.E. Berrios (eds), *150 years of British Psychiatry. Vol. II: The Aftermath* (London: Athlone Press Ltd, 1996).

Prior, P.M., 'Dangerous Lunacy: The Misuse of Mental Health Law in Nineteenth-Century Ireland', *Journal of Forensic Psychiatry and Psychology*, 14:3 (2003): 525–53.

Prior, P.M. and B. Hayes, 'Gender trends in occupancy rates in mental health beds in Northern Ireland', *Social Science and Medicine*, 52 (2001): 537–45.

Prior, P.M., *Madness and Murder: Gender, Crime and Mental Disorder in Nineteenth-Century Ireland* (Dublin and Portland, Oregon: Irish Academic Press, 2008).

Prior, P.M., 'Psychiatry and the fate of women who killed infants and young children 1850–1900', pp.92–112, in C. Cox and M. Luddy (eds), *Cultures of care in Irish medical history 1750–1970* (Basingstoke: Palgrave-Macmillan, 2010).

Prior, P.M., 'Emigrants or Exiles? Female Ex-Prisoners Leaving Ireland, 1850–1900', *Australasian Journal of Irish Studies*, 8 (2008/9): 30–47.

Prior, P.M. and D.V. Griffiths, 'The Chaplaincy Question: The Lord Lieutenant of Ireland versus the Belfast Lunatic Asylum', *Eire-Ireland*, 33: 2 & 3 (1997): 137–53.

Psychiatrist, 'Insanity in Ireland', *The Bell*, 7 (1944): 303–10.

Reuber, M., 'Moral Management and the "Unseen Eye": Public Lunatic Asylums in Ireland, 1800–1845', pp.208–233 in E. Malcolm and G. Jones (eds), *Medicine, Disease and the State in Ireland, 1650–1940* (Cork: Cork University Press, 1999).

Reynolds, J., *Grangegorman: Psychiatric Care in Dublin since 1815* (Dublin: Institute of Public Administration, in association with Eastern Health Board, 1992).

Reznick, J., *Healing the Nation: Soldiers and the Culture of Care-giving in Britain during the Great War 1914–1918* (Manchester: Manchester University Press, 2004).

Riese, W., 'The Structure of Galen's Diagnostic Reasoning' in *Bulletin of the New York Academy of Medicine* 44: 7 (1968): 778–91.

Robins, Joseph, *Fools and Mad. A History of the Insane in Ireland* (Dublin: Institute of Public Administration, 1986).

Sadlier, J., *Recollections of a Victorian Police Officer* (Harmondsworth: Penguin Books, 1973). (Reprint of 1913 publication.)

Salize, H.J. and H.E. Dressing, 'Epidemiology of involuntary placement of mentally ill people across the European Union', *British Journal of Psychiatry* 184 (2004): 163–86.

Samson, C., 'Madness and psychiatry', pp.55–83 in B.S. Turner (ed.), *Medical Power and Social Knowledge*, 2nd edition (London: Sage, 1995).

Saris A.J., 'The Asylum in Ireland: A Brief Institutional History and Some Local Effects', pp.208–20 in A. Cleary and M.P. Treacy (eds), *The Sociology of Health and Illness in Ireland* (Dublin: University College Dublin Press, 1997).

Scheper Hughes, Nancy, *Saints, Scholars and Schizophrenic* (Berkeley: University of California Press, 2001).

Scull, Andrew, *Museums of Madness: The Social Organisation of Insanity in Nineteenth-Century England* (London: Penguin Books Ltd., 1979).

Scull, Andrew (ed.), *The Asylum as Utopia: W.A.F. Browne and the mid nineteenth century consolidation of psychiatry* (London: Tavistock/Routledge, 1991).

Serle, G., *The Golden Age: a History of the Colony of Victoria, 1851–61* (Melbourne: Melbourne University Press, 1963).

Serle, G., *The Rush to be Rich: a History of the Colony of Victoria, 1883–9* (Melbourne: Melbourne University Press, 1971).

Sherer, J., *The Gold-Finder in Australia: How He Went, How He Fared, How He Made his Fortune*, reprint of 1853 publication (Harmondsworth: Penguin Books, 1973).

Shorter, Edward., *A History of Psychiatry: From the Era of the Asylum to the Age of Prozac* (New York: John Wiley and Sons, 1997).

Showalter, Elaine, *The Female Malady: Women, Madness and English Culture 1830–1880* (London: Virago Press, 1987).

Smith, C., 'The Central Mental Hospital, Dundrum, Dublin', pp.1351–3 in R. Bluglass and P. Bowden (eds), *Principles and Practice of Forensic Psychiatry* (Edinburgh: Churchill Livingstone, 1990).

Smith, D.A. and M.A. Woodruff, 'Deficiency diseases in Japanese prison camps', *Medical Research Council Special Report Series*, no. 274 (London: HMSO, 1951).

Smith, Walter, Discussion of Conolly Norman's, paper 'The clinical features of Beri-beri', read to the Royal Academy of Medicine in Ireland and published in *Dublin Journal of Medical Science*, cvii (1899): 309.

Stein, George and Greg Wilkinson (eds), *Seminars in General Adult Psychiatry*, 2nd edition (London: Royal College of Psychiatrists, 2007).

Sturma, M., *Vice in a Vicious Society: Crime and Convicts in Mid Nineteenth-Century New South Wales* (Brisbane: University of Queensland Press, 1983).

Szasz, T., *The Myth of Mental Illness* (St Albans: Granada, 1972). (First published 1961.)

Tooth, G.C. and E. Brooke, 'Trends in the mental hospital population and their effects on future planning', *Lancet*, 1 (1961): 710–3.

Torrey, E.F. and J. Miller, *The Invisible Plague: The Rise of Mental Illness from 1750 to the Present* (New Jersey: Rutgers University Press, 2001).

Tovey, H. and P. Share, *A Sociology of Ireland* (Dublin: Gill and Macmillan, 2000).

Tuke, D.H., 'Increase of Insanity in Ireland', *Journal of Mental Science*, 40: 171 (1894): 549–61.

Unsworth, Clive, *The Politics of Mental Health Legislation* (Oxford: Clarendon Press, 1987).

Vamplew, W. (ed.), *Australians: Historical Statistics* (Sydney: Fairfax, Syme & Weldon Associates, 1987).

Vander Stoep, A. and B. Link, 'Social Class, Ethnicity and Mental Illness: the Importance of Being More than Earnest,' *American Journal of Public Health*, 88 (1998): 1396–402.

Vanja, Christina, 'Madhouses, Children's Wards, and Clinics: The Development of Insane Asylums in Germany' in N. Finzsch & R. Jütte (eds), *Institutions of Confinement: Hospitals, Asylums, and Prisons in Western Europe and North America, 1500–1950* (Cambridge: Cambridge University Press, 1996).

Verschuur, A.F. and G. van Ijsselsteyn, Report translated by Daniel F. Rambaut, as 'The Epidemic Disease in the Richmond District Lunatic Asylum in Dublin', *Dublin Quarterly Journal of Medical Science*, 109: 5 (1900): 369–81; and 109: 6 (1900): 446–54.

Walsh, Dermot, '200 Years of Irish Psychiatry', *Irish Journal of Psychiatry*, 13 (1992): 3–20.

Walsh, D. and A. Daly, *Irish Psychiatric Hospitals and Units Census* 2001 (Dublin: Health Research Board, 2002).

Walsh, D. and A. Daly, *Mental Illness in Ireland 1750–2002: Reflections on the Rise and Fall of Institutional Care* (Dublin: Health Research Board, 2004).

Walsh, Oonagh, 'Lunatic and Criminal Alliances in Nineteenth-Century Ireland' in P. Bartlett & D. Wright (eds), *Outside the Walls of the Asylum: Historical Perspectives on Care in the Community in Modern Britain and Ireland* (London: Athlone Press, 1999).

Walsh, Oonagh, 'The Designs of Providence: Race, religion and Irish insanity', in J. Melling and B. Forsyth (eds), *Insanity and Society: The Asylum in its Social Context* (London: Routledge, 1999).

Walsh, Oonagh, '"Danger and Delight": conceptualising the insane in nineteenth-century Ireland' in M. Preston and M. Ó hÓgartaigh (eds), *Gender and Medicine in Ireland, 1700–1950* (New York: Syracuse University Press, 2012).

Wandsworth, N. and A. Miles, 'Industrial Therapy in Psychiatric Hospitals, A King's Fund Report' (London: Ministry of Health, 1969).

Ward-Perkins, Sarah (ed.), *Select Guide to Trade Union Records in Dublin* (Dublin: Irish Labour History Society and Irish Manuscripts Commission, 1996).

Webb, M., R. McClelland and G. Mock, 'Psychiatric services in Ireland: North and South', *Irish Journal of Psychiatric Medicine*, 19:1(2002): 21–6.

WHO, *Expert Committee on Mental Health: 3rd Report* (Geneva: WHO, 1953).

WHO, *Annual Epidemiological and Vital Statistics 1955* (Geneva: WHO, 1958).

WHO, *Mental Health Services in Pilot Study Areas* (WHO: Regional Office for Europe, Copenhagen, Denmark, 1987).

Williamson, Arthur, 'The beginnings of state care for the mentally ill in Ireland', *Economic and Social Review*, 10:1 (January 1970): 281–90.

Wilson, D., *The Beat: Policing a Victorian City* (Melbourne: Circa, 2006).

Wright, David, 'Getting out of the Asylum: Understanding the Confinement of the Insane in the Nineteenth Century', *Social History of Medicine*, 10:1 (1997): 137–55.

Index